RURAL-URBAN FRINGE

PERSPECTIVES IN URBAN GEOGRAPHY
Volume Nine

Concept's International Series in Geography

No. 1 Perspectives in Agricultural Geography
(In Five Volumes) Edited by Noor Mohammad

No. 2 Perspectives in Geomorphology (In Four Volumes)
Edited by S.H. Sharma

No. 3 Perspectives in Urban Geography
Edited by C.S. Yadav

1. New Directions in Urban Geography
2. Comparative Urban Research
3. Comparative Urbanization: City Growth and Change
4A. Models in Urban Geography (Theoretical)
4B. Models in Urban Geography (Mathematical)
5. Urban Research Methods: Central Place, Hierarchical and City Size Models
6. Contemporary City Ecology
7. Slums, Urban Decline and Revitalization
8. Contemporary Urban (Issues)
9. Rural-Urban Fringe
10. Morphology of Towns
11. Cities and Housing
12. Perceptual and Cognative Image of the City
13. Urban Economics
14. City Planning: Problems and Prospects
15. City Planning: Administration and Participation
16A. Urban Planning and Policies: Reorientation of Policy Norms
16B. Urban Planning and Policies: Cross-Cultural Urban Policies

Concept's International Series in Geography No. 3

Perspectives in Urban Geography

Volume Nine

RURAL-URBAN FRINGE

Edited by

C.S. YADAV

CONCEPT PUBLISHING COMPANY, NEW DELHI-110 059

ISBN: 81-7022-080-7 (Set)
ISBN: 81-7022-032-7 (Vol. IX)

First Published 1987
Reprinted 2007

Published and Printed by
Ashok Kumar Mittal
Concept Publishing Company
A/15-16, Commercial Block, Mohan Garden
New Delhi-110059 (INDIA)
Phones : 25351460, 25351794 *Fax* : 091-11-25357103
Email : publishing@conceptpub.com

Dedicated
In the cherished memory of
my mother-in-law
Smt. Kalawati
who left for her heavenly abode
on 19th March, 1987.

Preface

NATURE OF URBAN GEOGRAPHY

There are several studies on urban geography which reveal that, as a major sub-discipline, it has a long tail but a short body. However, the spectrum is so vast and broad that researchers are able to make general statements in defence of its conception, philosophy, nature and orientation. Urban geography today encompasses and interfaces with various disciplines which are interested in urban studies. As an introduction to this series, our task here is to make an attempt to briefly review the development of geographical interest in various aspects of cities.

There are several reviews of the early development of urban geography which have been dealt with by Berry and Harton (1970)[1] and Carter (1974).[2] Berry and Harton in their book, **Geographical Perspective on Urban System**, have made an attempt to introduce readers to its present-day status. They have clearly resolved that "the formative years of the social science in the late nineteenth century and early twentieth century were also the years in which urban studies first developed,"[3] thus providing the context for geography's emerging interest in cities. However, the emergence of urban studies dates back to the writings of Greek scholars, but as a sub-discipline, it has reached its present-day status only in the past 30 years.

In their historical perspective the works on urban geography show that the pre-20th century studies primarily concerned themselves with themes of location, size and shape of the cities. The initial findings were strongly subjective, descriptive and dependent more on observation such as the works of Hassert (1907)[4] and Blanchard (1911).[5] In the succeeding years the conceptual framework of site and situation was criticized by Aurousseau (1924)[6] and Crowe (1938)[7], their conception being that cities were not inanimate objects in landscape. but also organic elements which involved people and their movements. The morphologist, later in 1960, truly brought the indigenous line of evolution in the sphere of urban geography and studies on the build-up fabric of cities (Conzone, 1960).[8] Smails (1955)[9] constituted the prime base of urban geography, which remained articulated without any major conceptual change till early 1960s. The studies on the morphological aspects of the urban system were influenced by external forces, consequently the methodological frameworks got impetus within the discipline. At this juncture the evolution of concepts was not based on environment but took shelter under the umbrella of economics of location, and incorporated analysis of land values and rents, and the concept of nodality and accessibility. These concepts were derived from the economic theories of Cooley (1894)[10], Weber (1899),[11] and Hurd (1903).[12]

The Chicago School of Urban Ecology hastened the evolution of urban geography. In his monumental work Park (1925)[13] developed the idea of order and analysis of towns. Further, a powerful thrust and much of the rationale was provided to the studies of urban geography by the Central Place Theory of Christallar (1933).[14]

The impact of the statistical method was powerful and it brought rapid and enormous changes in the field of urban geography. It also brought new insights into the development and application of urban geography towards increased quantification. Brian J. Berry, a pioneer in the field, analysed the spatial order, size and location of towns and cities. There was widespread use of innovative techniques to explore the nature of urban problems, hypotheses were tested, new theories propounded and old theories remodelled. The statistical methods were put to a variety of uses. Smith (1965)[15] evaluated the classification of settlements; Berry and Garrison (1956)[16] examined the utility of the rank-size rule for urban populations. The models of Park and Burgess (1925),[17] Harris and Ullman (1945)[18] and Homar Hoyt (1939)[19] were tested and re-examined by various geographers.

A new impetus to urban geography came from social area analysis which was initially propounded by Shevky and Bell (1955)[20] and later on this provided a basis for factorial ecology. The collaboration of this stream in urban geography was offered by Berry (1971)[21], Herbert (1972)[22] and Johnston (1971).[23] As a consequence of these thrusts in geography after 1960, the techniques of investigation were sharpened and this has provided the basis for a scientific explanation of cities. Attempts were made to introduce new theories and frame laws to make the explanation of events more rational and logical. Sophisticated models were propounded as urban geography entered a new era of rationalizing the subject matter of urban studies on the basis of new philosophies, new concepts, new theories, new methodologies and applications.

However, the status of contemporary urban geography has been elevated only recently by the behavioural approach. The studies of perception and cognition which have a long tradition in physiology were first introduced into the field of geography by Lynch (1960)[24] Dowson and Stea (1973)[25], Gould and White (1974).[26] At present there is a sudden spurt in the studies on the subject with a new paradigm. But the full impact of behavioural approaches upon urban geography has yet to be realized.

The aim of this series is to seek reorientation of the discipline strengthened by new philosophies, methodologies, subject matters or application. The series has been arranged in such a way that all contemporary viewpoints are covered comprehensively. Hopefully, this series will inspire researchers to appreciate the work already done by geographers in studying cities. Geography by nature seems to be a synthesizing field of inquiry. As such we have made an endeavour to combine some of the otherwise disparate facts garnered by other disciplines in such a manner that we can gain a better understanding of the urban system. The study of urban geography is essential if we are to analyse the human consequences of the settlements in which we live. It is useful to planners, decision makers in government and corporations and also to each one of us as citizens. Finally, it gives us a perspective on what may be happening to our cities and to the nature.

To achieve the above goal only those contributions with originality and contrasting viewpoints were selected for inclusion in this series. In doing so the editor does not wish to compete with the journals in the field in which innovative research and methodological aspects are presented. But he does wish to convey, and convey with conviction, that significant researches are being undertaken in the different branches of urban geography and in other allied disciplines. The present series is an attempt to provide a selective reappraisal and rigorous examination of the assumptions and the urge to disseminate new knowledge created by the mutual interaction. Emphasis is also placed on the conceptualization and theorization of the subject matter so that general laws may emerge. A conscious effort has been made to organize the series in such a way that it reflects the philosophical approach parallel to that of the behavioural school. Finally, a vigorous attempt has been made to demonstrate throughout the series how geographers are basically involved in solving the urban problems.

C. S. YADAV

REFERENCES

1. Berry and Harton, **Geographic Perspectives on Urban Systems: with Integrated Readings**, New Jersey, Prentice Hall, Inc, Englewood Cliffs, 1970.
2. Carter, **The Study of Urban Geography**, Edward Arnold, London, 1974.
3. Berry and Harton, 1970.
4. Hassert, K., **Die Stadte Geographisch Betrachect**, Leipzig, 1907.
5. Blanchard, R., **Grenoble: Etude de Geographic Urbanine**, Paris, 1911.
6. Aurousseau, M., "Recent Contributions to Geography: A Review," **Geographical Review**, 1924, 14, p.444.
7. Crowe, P.R., "On Progress in Geography," **Scottish Geographical Magazine**, 1938, 54, 1-19.
8. Conzone, M.R.G., "The Plan Analysis of an English City Centre," In Norkorg (Ed), **Proceedings of I.G.U. Symposium on Urban Geography**, C.W.K. Gleerup, Lund, 1962.
9. Smails, A.E., "The Urban Mess of England and Wales," **Transactions and Papers**, Institute of British Geographers, 1946, 11, 85, p.101.
10. Cooley, C.H., "The Theory of Transportation," **Publications of the American Economic Association**, 1894, 9, p.5-7.
11. Weber, A.F., **The Growth of Cities in the Nineteenth Century: A Study in Statistics**, New York, 1899.
12. Hurd, R., **Principles of City Land Values: New York Record and Guide**, 1903, p. 19-21.
13. Park, R.E., "Suggestions for the Investigation of Human Behaviour in an Urban Environment," in R.E. Park, E.W. Burgess, R.D. Mackenzie (eds), **The City**, University of Chicago Press, 1925.
14. Christallar, W., **Central Place in Southern Germany**, Gustar Fischer, Teno, 1933.
15. Smith, R.M.T., "Method and Purpose in Functional Town Classification," **Annals of the Association of American**

Geographers, 1965, 55, pp.539-548.
16. Garrison, W.L., "Applicability of Statistical Inference to Geographical Research," **Geographical Review**, 1956, 46, p. 427, 429.
17. Burgess, E.W., "The Growth of City," in R.E. Park, E.W. Burgess and R.D. Màckenzie (eds), **The City**, University of Chicago Press, 1925.
18. Ullman, E.L., "The Nature of Cities," **Annals, American Academy of Political and Social Science**, 1945, 242, 7-17.
19. Hoyt, H., **The Structure and Growth of Residential Neighbourhoods in American Cities**, Washington, Federal Housing Administration, 1939.
20. Shevky, E. and Bell, W., **Social Area Analysis**, Stanford University Press, Stanford, 1955.
21. Berry, B.J.L. (ed), "Comparative Factorial Ecology," **Economic Geographic (Supplement)**, 1971, 47.
22. Herbert, D.T., **Urban Geography: A Social Perspective**, David and Charles, Newton Abbot, 1972.
23. Johnston, **Urban Residential Pattern**, Bell, London, 1971.
24. Lynch, **Image of the City**, Massachusetts, Cambridge, 1960.
25. Dowson and Stea, **Image and Environment**, Chicago and London, 1973.
26. Gould and White, R., **Mental Maps**, London, 1974.

Acknowledgements

We are highly thankful to Prof. David G. Dickason, Western Michigan University Kalamazoo (U.S.A.) who guided us whole heartedly during the initial stage of the the Project. We regret that his name was not acknowledged in earlier volumes.

We also thank Editors Gerd-Michael Hellstern, Frithjof Spreer Hellmut Wollmann, **Heft 2, Vol. II** and **Vol. III** for their permission to use material from "Applied Urban Research", Proceedings of the European Meeting on Applied Urban Research, Essen, 2-4, Oct. 1981.

Contents

List of Contributors

Yoram Bar-Gal: Haifa University, Mount Carnel, Haifa, Israel

Diana DeAre: Population Division, United States Department of Commerce Bureau of Census, Washington D.C - 20233

Anjana Desai: Head, Department of Geography, Gujarat University, Ahmedabad (India)

Ram Swaroop Dixit: Head, Department of Geography, Isabella Thoburn College, Lucknow University, Lucknow, (India)

Jean Frinwis Langumier : Charge de Missiong a Cooperation et Amenagement, Universite Toulouse-le-Mirail, 109 bis, rue vauquelin, 31058 Toulouse Cedex

Pierre S. Guertin: Architect and Urbanist, Doctor in Urban Studies, Quebec, Universite Laval, Quebec, P.Q. (Canada)

Smita Sen Gupta: Department of Geography, Gujarat University, Ahmedabad - 380009 (India)

George F. Hepner: Assistant Professor, Department of Geography, College of Arts and Sciences, University of Kentucky, Lexington, Kentucky 40506-0027

George M. Johnston: Eastern Oregon State College, La Grande, Oregon

Jean-Paul Laborie: Professeur a l 'Institut Geographie, Universite Tulouse-le-Mirail, 109 bis, rue Vauquelin, 31058 Toulouse Cedex, (France)

Larry Long: Population Division, United States Department of Commerce Bureau of the Census, Washington - D.C. 20233

Dashrath S. Pal: Lecturer, Department of Geography, T.D. College, Auraiya, Etawah (U.P.) (India)

Lorne H. Russwurm: Department of Geography, University of Waterloo, Waterloo, Ontario, Canada N21 3G1

A. Allan Schmid: Michigan State University, Michigan

D.S. Shrivastava: Reader, University of Saugar, Sagar (M.P.) (India)

M.L. Soni: D.N. College, 28-A Bazara, Fatehgarh (U.P.) 209601 (India)

Frank L. Sweetser: Professor Emeritus, Boston University, Boston (U.S.A.)

Rudiger Voigt: Professor, Department of Political Science, University of Siegen, Siegen
C.S. Yadav: Head, Department of Geography, Bhagat Singh College, Delhi University, New Delhi

ONE

C.S.Yadav

Introduction

The research orientation of urban geographers in the past has been strongly influenced by the idea of a unicentred city. They have assessed the relationship of various urban landuses and their associated human activities in terms of distance from the city centre. For all purposes their interpretations have often used the city centre as a reference point from which locational patterns could be discerned. Nevertheless, current research has deviated from this standpoint, because city is expanding beyond its limits, at a considerable distance from the city centre, so there is a change occurring on the outer periphery of the built-up area which is day by day becoming a hub of activities. As a matter of fact change at the edge of the city is occurring as a reaction to congestion, crowding and environmental deterioration of the city core, so people move to the periphery of the city where the lure of open air and spaciousness of the countryside with sanitary improvements and comforts attract the city dwellers to move towards the periphery. Thus it is concluded that cities are expanding beyond their built-up limits into the countryside. This expresses what is in many ways a dominant theme for researchers, because at present changes on the edge of the city involve day-to-day lives of more people. In addition many geographical changes at the urban periphery are associated with the transfer of land from rural to urban purposes, which may be a more fundamental alteration than many other landuse changes which take place in urban areas (Johnson, 1974).[1] Another reason why geographers are interested in exploring the nature of suburbs is that here the life and landscape are in much closer adjustment because there is transformation of the landscape demographically and organizationally. Scholars have observed various forms of urban development taking shape on the "green field" area which is within the commuting range of the city. More obviously than likely it gives a direct expression of the behaviour of contemporary urban society and perhaps provides a more accurate clue to the nature of the future (Johnson, 1970).[2] Another important factor which has aroused the curiosity of the scholars and attracted their attention to the city suburbs is that the land to which the city will find its extension and on which it will find its expansion has previously acquired a particular planning status, because its future use has been specified in development plans, although planning control is less strict or operates less comprehensively, which has encouraged leap-frogging peripheral growth which in turn has generated different types of urban communities.

Problems of Definition

Clearly, in the modern era of urban expansion, the rural-urban interaction is at its maximum, and so the term rural urban fringe has assumed an important significance. There is a vast scholarly literature available on the urban fringe. However, no precise definition has yet emerged, there is a lack of clarity about different facets of life and landscape of the rural-urban fringe. There is no dearth of subjective definitions propounded by various scholars which are not adequate and universally applicable to a particular situation. However, the term fringe denotes a transition between rural and urban way of living. It then connotes that it actually lies on the periphery of urban areas, surrounding it and distinguishing it from the rural areas. A historical perspective of the term rural-urban fringe, since its inception, provides better clues about the term. Pryor (1968)[3] attributes the first use of the urban fringe to T. L. Smith who employed it to signify the "built-up area just outside the corporate limits of the city". After his contribution there was a sudden spurt of literature mainly by Americans who had pronounced upon the subject in a systematic way, and thus the term had acquired more or less the meaning it carries at present. Broadly, Carter[4] has recently attempted a review of the attitude to the urban fringe, and has propagated that two aspects of the problem have attracted the attention of most of the scholars. First, there is a notion of the fringe as a distinctive area, which is neither urban nor rural in character, and which is primarily designated by mixed landuse patterns. Second, there is a notion that the social characteristics of the population of the fringe are transitional between those of the urban and those of the rural.

Another problem arises simply from the meanings given to

the term which is based upon American experience which created confusion in terminology derived from various case studies. The diversity of terminology further created confusion. Kurtze and Eicher (1958)[5] have illustrated the problem while attempting to differentiate between "fringe" and suburbs. Wissink (1962)[6] in a comprehensive survey of the fringe areas of American cities evolved "fringe" suburbs, "pseudo-suburbs, "satellites" and pseudo-satellites". It is an interesting fact that while some observers grapple with complexities of defining different types of terms and make an attempt to distinguish between these terms, a few other researchers have attempted comparative assessments of "rurban" land or of "suburb" (Thomas).[7]

Pryor (1968),[8] while attempting to resolve the various issues pertaining to areal differentiation of the urban-fringe, came across another problem. For example, Andrews (1942)[9] had distinguished urban-fringe from rural-urban fringe, and McKain and Burnight (1953)[10] had evolved the terms "limited fringe" and "extended fringe". Reinemann (1960)[11] had analysed a "suburban fringe zone" and an "outlying adjacent zone". Duncan and Reiss (1956)[12] had provided altogether a different version when they distinguished between "rural non-farm" and "rural farm" subdivisions of the fringe, while Myers and Beegle (1947)[13] made a distinction between "true fringe" and "partial fringe".

Thus, it is clear that there is a great diversity in the use of the term rural-urban fringe. Pryor (1968)[14] rose to the occasion and tried to eliminate all the ambiguities of the previous definitions which he propounded in the following manner: "The rural-urban fringe is the zone of transition in landuse and social and demographic characteristics, lying between (a) the continuously built-up urban and suburban areas of the central city and (b) the rural hinterland, characterized by the almost complete absence of non-farm dwelling occupations and land use; and of urban and rural social orientation; and incomplete range and penetration of urban utility services; unconditioned zoning or planning regulation; areal extension beyond although contiguous with the political boundary of the central city and an actual and potential increase in population density, with the current density above that of surrounding rural districts, but lower than the central city." Thus, in its essence, rural-urban fringe is really an extension of the city itself, actually and potentially.

Some distinctive features of the fringe

The suburban growth of the city particularly in America stimulated geographers and other social scientists to explore the land use composition and the function of the fringe developments. Much of our knowledge about the characteristics of the urban fringe stems from the works of Wehrwein (1942)[15] whose investigations are regarded as the formative framework in the field of study. The author postulated that railways have played a crucial role for decentralization of urban population and urban landuses. Nevertheless the automotive means of transportation later on greatly enhanced the initial effect which modified the agricultural zone around the city. It will not be wrong to assert that wherever highways and railways entered the city through this zone, residences, commercial establishments and industrial plants spread out along these corridors. Due to the radial pattern of these routes, the urban fringe occupied rural landscape pierced by fingerlike projections of the urbanized land uses. Wehrwein has identified the following important characteristics. The first is nature of residential growth, which is stimulated by the flexibility of transportation between city edge and city centre. As a matter of fact real estate speculators persuaded the people employed in suburban offices and factories to build houses in the fringe area.

From past studies, one can infer that city does not expand outward in an orderly manner, rather it extends haphazardly, thus an incoherent land use pattern represents the fringe area. The mixed landuse pattern is a representative character of the fringes which range from the old, untouched rural villages to modern residential estates; from a variety of commercial establishments, including out-of-town shopping centres to the city services and industries which produce perishable and non-perishable goods (Carter, 1970),[16] Wehrwein (1942)[17] characterizes the fringe of the USA as an "institutional desert because of uncontrolled, sporadic location of unpleasant and noxious establishments, such as slaughter-houses, junk yards and wholesale oil storages, sewage plants and cemeteries. Wissink (1962)[18] more appropriately analysed the nature of rural-urban fringe in contemporary context and evaluated that various landusers, older villages, newer residential extensions, commerce, industry, city services and the prevalent farming are not systematically organized into a homogeneous area but are mixed in a random fashion, and it is this which distinguishes rural-urban fringe from city centre. Gollege (1960),[19] another pioneer in the field, proposed seven aspects of the rural-urban fringe: (i) there is a constantly changing pattern of land occupance, (ii) farms are small, (iii) crop production is intensive, (iv) population is mobile and of low or moderate density, (v) residential expansion is rapid, (vi) the provision of services and public utilities is incomplete, and (vii) speculative building is common. R. E. Pahl (1965)[20] has also attempted to summarize the characteristic features of the fringe. According to him, it is a zone of segregation. Also the major residential tracts of the fringe old villages, private housing, council estates and miners' estate are all distinctly segregated with the private estates usually located closest to the old village cores. Large planned areas are occupied by commercial, educational and institutional users. The second aspect which he highlighted is that it is a zone of selective immigration, because it attracts primarily mobile middle-class commuters which tend to live and work in district, separate social and economic worlds from the established populations. According to Pahl (1965),[21] the rural-urban fringe is a zone where "a new population is invading local communities, bringing in national values and class consciousness at the same time that a new type of community, associated with dispersed living, is emerging".

Changing nature of the urban fringe

It is an obvious fact that the nature of the urban fringe has changed considerably over time. There is a reason to believe that the fringes of the pre-industrial cities were inhabited by less advantaged groups, some perhaps employed in the more noxious occupations, Sjoberg (1960).[22] In this zone these workers were remotely located from the city centre, where social, political and economic influences were all manipulated. Nevertheless, due to improvement in the means of transportation, in the late 19th century, the fringe was still used for residential uses, and there was rapid conversion of rural land for urban purposes, but the dominant contrast was witnessed in the fact that this zone was predominantly housed by those people who could afford a long journey to the workplace. In the long process, the fringe was also occupied by large noxious establishments of various kinds which did not require immediate access to the whole city. The 20th century city, on the other hand, has witnessed new suburban employment, new shopping centres and new forms of recreation, which have created more complex journey patterns on the periphery of the city. These changing patterns of urban activities have greatly expanded the transition zone between urban and rural landuses during the 20th century.

Problems associated with rural-urban fringe

Perhaps the most significant problem associated with the urban fringe is in the realm of inefficiency of landuse. It is a truism that uncommon procedures have been followed in the areal expansion in the form of residential subdivisions, new commercial and industrial districts and other types of developments in the urban fringe. As a matter of fact these developments, beyond the existing margins of the city, occupy those areas which are physically suitable for development, are accessible and are such that development on them may be made at a minimum cost. The spread of fringe may extend from five to 15 miles away from the built-up urban area with which the development is functionally linked, with the intervening area being used for farming operations. Although the resident inhabitants may enjoy the "country atmosphere" of these developments, objections to uses made of the adjacent tracts of land may be raised, which may lead to perceived conflicts among landusers. Further, development of the urban fringe creates problems for agriculturists who find themselves in the doldrums because they are sandwiched between two advancing fronts of urban development, in that the value of farm land may increase instantly and the tax load may become excessive. The leap-frog growth pattern of the rural-urban fringe creates a problem for the behaviour pattern, activities and life-style of those on each side of the fringe.

Another problem which arises due to the development of the rural-urban fringe is the progressive loss of farm lands, especially those of highest quality.

ABOUT THE VOLUME

The research orientation of the urban geographers in the past has been strongly influenced by the idea of a unicentred city. They have assessed the relationship of various urban landuses and their associated human activities in terms of distance from the city centre. For all purposes their interpretations have often used the city centre as a reference point from which locational patterns could be discerned. Nevertheless, contemporary research orientation has deviated from this stand-point, because a large majority of scholars are now devoting their attention to exploring the nature of that zone which lies on the outer periphery of the city where considerable changes are occurring in the landuse patterns and activities. This zone in common usage is referred to as rural-urban fringe where there is areal expansion of urban concentrations beyond city limits. The sprawling of the urban activities into the rural landscape involves conversion of land peripheral to urban centres that have previously been used for non-urban purposes into one for more urban uses. In essence, the land absorbed by the urban activities becomes a functional part of the urban agglomerations and is occupied by people who in attitude, behaviour and activity are integrated into an urban society. The zone into which town expansion takes place as the process of dispersion operates has created the concept of a rural-urban fringe. This volume in that context concentrates largely but not exclusively on the rural-urban fringe. However, the volume is intended to provide an outline of the rural-urban fringe. The articles included in the present volume provide us the cultural heritage and the beauty of contemporary life existing in the rural-urban fringe. The first section of this volume deals with the clarification of the term "the evolution of the urban fringe". It provides a comparative outlook of different characteristics of the rural-urban fringe in various cultural regions. The second section of the volume is concerned with the rural-urban continuum. This section includes those articles which provide a coverage of the rural-urban effect in the present-day context. The third section deals with the delineation of umland in India and provides an insight into the concept of umland and city umland relation. It also explains the services rendered by umland.

The contemporary urban research scholars have actively demonstrated the rural urban interaction through flow of people and goods to and fro. Most researchers have concluded that integration of cities and their immediate hinterland is a response to rising incomes, increased mobility and increased leisure time associated with population and employment growth in urban areas. There is no doubt that technological innovations, improved transportation and communication along with personal perception have made possible the dispersal of population and economic activities into the open countryside, which have resulted in the evolution of a regional city, consisting of concentrated built-up urban areas and a dispersed part consisting of hamlets, villages and towns embedded amidst farm land and other open land. Lorne H. Russwarm in his article, "Comparative Land Management in Rural-Urban Fringe of New World Cities", first defines the two key terms of land management and rural urban fringe. Two broad sections constitute the paper. First, the regional city concept is developed as the over arching settlement form of which the rural-urban fringe is a part. Second, a framework is presented for dealing comparatively with the landuse management in the rural-urban fringe. The author is of the view that since the advent of the automobiles, the regional city has been the emerging urban-form organizing human activities and settlement patterns in the Anglo New World countries. Today instead of city and country, a more appropriate term is regional city as city and region are increasingly integrated. Generally people living within the hinterland of a city no longer think of the city as a strange world occasionally visited but as a world that is part of their regular lives. City and region are today but part of a single system. Numerous flows of people, goods, money and information integrate the populations and activities of the regional city. Thus two broad sections constitute the paper. First, the regional concept is developed as the over arching settlement form of which the rural-urban fringe is a part. Second, a framework is presented for dealing comparatively with land use management in the rural-urban fringe. The assumption prevails throughout the paper and comparative study is a prime means of developing a sounder theoretical basis than that which currently exists in the rather disparate existing rural fringe studies. A further assumption is that regional cities as subsystems organise the socio-economic structure of new world countries.

In the urbanization process accepted the world over, the rural settlements are transformed into urban settlements when these are located in the metropolitan fringe. The uses of non-agricultural land, in a limited size such as industry and commerce, have started to appear in the urban fringe villages but this appearance is still in its embryo. The infiltration of urban functions into the rural areas is limited by the internal laws of the settlements as well as by the restrictions existing as in Israel regarding the transformation of agricultural land into urban land. Dr. Yoram Bar-Gal in his paper, "Social Pluralism and the Urban Fringe - The Israel Case," emphasizes that there are four processes which may transform a rural settlement into an urban settlement: emigration from the city to the village, commuting, recreational village and a second home. According to the author, settlements which are under the influence of such processes are under continuous urban pressure. The field in which the urban pressure is especially strong is described in literature as the urban fringe. In areas of this type we come across the "metropolitan villages". The urban fringe consists of two different populations: the urban population which infiltrates into the villages and the traditional rural population of the settlement. Due to population shift in this belt, there is a rise in the price of land, change in the use of land, changes in the demographical cultural field, and changes are apt to take place in the composition of the population and its occupation.

In Israel, as in other countries in the world, urbanization of villages is not a new phenomenon, and it has already existed for many decades. The main objective of the author in this paper is to compare the processes which the various Jewish communities are undergoing with those of the Arab communities in Israel. The author reveals that there exists a cultural pluralism in Israel which will influence the types of urban processes taking place in the urban fringe. According to him, the findings of this analysis show that the Arab villages will be those where the strong influence of the urbanization processes exists. They are apt to become, within a period of one generation, a part of the metropolitan alignment, whereas the Jewish villages, due to their cooperative character, do not allow urbanization to penetrate them and thus leaves them untouched in that scenery as rural settlements. Only those Jewish settlements where the land is private tend to change into urban areas.

Because of the inter-dependance between the elements which make up the city, it is difficult in practice to isolate any one of these elements in order to analyse and evaluate its behaviour or evolution. If one accepts the preceding remark, it appears necessary to study the present problematic over the re-development and re-vitalization of the central city area in close relation to the situation of the peripheral districts and suburbs, since they also form an integral part of the larger system. Guertin in his article, "The Future of the Urban System: Compared Situation between the Centre and the Suburbs of Quebec City", demonstrates that a system represents a particular way of perceiving or conceiving the world, and as such he advocates that the city could be considered as a system composed of three integrated constituents each of which has its own dynamism. These are: infrastructures, superstructures and inhabitation. After referring briefly to these three basic sub-systems of which the city is constituted the author describes the three integrated phases of the urbanization cycle in order to make explicit the framework of analysis which will be used to study the present situation of the central and sub-urban areas in terms of their redevelopment. The author feels that this procedure will allow in the final stage of the study to better comprehend the nature of the dynamic relations which exist between the central area and the suburbs and to bring out the prospects for improving the quality of living in both areas. In his concluding remarks the author has rightly asserted that his analysis shows that there is an urgent need not to renovate the city centre, but rather to give priority to the development of the suburbs. He reminds the planners that the suburbs of Quebec City run the risk of becoming even more marginal in the near future. He does not deny the fact that they are over-equipped with infrastructures of all kinds, but at the same time he also states that they are suffering from a deplorable lack of super-structures. He goes further and says that several services and facilities which were dearly acquired are now deteriorating and even are completely disappearing. The author further illustrates that due to the widespread slow-down in the construction industry and the presence of heavy infrastructures, which are draining the revenue, the suburbs find themselves in a situation where they have increased financial commitments which they must try to meet with revenues that are not increasing any faster than the rate of inflation. The author also comments that suburbs are in great need of architectural unification and urban tissue consolidation. The author warns that neither present nor future looks too bright for them in comparison to the city centre. He suggests that to save the suburbs from an uncertain future, one would have to consciously and voluntarily formulate and implement an urban revitalization policy based on the following four vectors: polarizing suburban space around existing superstructures; consolidating and complementing the architectural formations within existing infrastructure network; communitizing social activities and relations which are either too collective or too "individualistic"; and developing a local urban life-style of a spatialized nature.

In the USA there had been unexpected demographic developments during the 1970s involving population redistribution. This has changed the nation's settlement patterns towards one of significantly less concentration. Population deconcentration seems to be occurring at a variety of spatial levels that include an interregional shift of population from the more densely settled States of heavy industrialization to the less densely settled States of the sun belt and rocky mountain region, an inter-metropolitan shift of population from central cities to the outer fringes of their suburban rings. This shift of population towards suburbs which was set in the 1970s has been underway throughout much of the 20th century as advances in transportation, like the trolleys and street-cars and the more widespread ownership of automobiles, allowed people to live farther from their places of work. Nevertheless the pace of suburbanization quickened after World War II as cheap mortgages, the baby boom and other factors increased the attractiveness and availability of housing beyond the city boundaries. Larry Long and Diana De Are in their article, "Population Distribution: An Overview of City, Suburban and Non-metropolitan Population in the 1960s and 1970s", focus their attention on some major unanswered questions. First, whether the existing pattern would persist through the decade and be confirmed by the 1980s census. Second, whether the rate of population shift to non-metropolitan areas would slow down if the attractiveness of low-density settlements were to be diminished by rising prices of gasoline and nagging doubts about its future availability. The authors, in their efforts, have rigorously compared the censuses of the 1960s and 1970s and tried to offer some answers to the questions posed above, also taking into consideration the 1980 census results presently available. In doing so the purpose of the authors has been to highlight some significant features of the realignment of city, suburb and non-metropolitan populations of the 1960s and 1970s. The authors in their discussion have paid more attention to population changes in the metropolitan and non-metropolitan cities of the USA covering a period of 20 years, 1960 to 1980. They have also made generalizations about the regional patterns by metropolitan size besides documenting comprehensively the growth of population in the suburbs. Nevertheless, they conclude that the pace and amount of suburbanization are difficult to measure precisely over a long period of time because of annexation. When central cities annex suburban territory, the typical result is transfer growth from the suburban to the central category. The authors have identified a new word, which seems to be creeping into the vocabulary of population distribution. There are growing references to "exurbia" or "exurbs" to designate areas of population growth that lie on the margins of suburban territory. The authors also classify the suburbs into inner suburbs and outer suburbs.

The economic rent and profit largely affect the land conversion process in a given area. The implication of economic rent is that, unlike profits, rent cannot be competed away. At the edge of cities, the proxy measures to be used for economic rent and profit are land value appreciation and land site price. Site price includes development costs (clearing land, road, services, etc.), agricultural opportunity costs and some variations in site size. Ideally, the price paid for land to be converted for urban uses should be taken as the basis for calculating land value appreciation. George M. Johnson and A. Allen Schmid in their article, "The Impact of Government Policies on Suburb and Land Conversion", reveal that Governments try to influence the location and quality of urban landuse by controlling the conversion of land from rural to urban use at the growing edge of the cities. The authors have a firm belief that among the methods used are landuse controls such as zoning, provision of infrastructure and tax policy. In this paper the authors explore the interaction of some of these Local Government policies and the land conversion market and present some empirical results from a model of that interaction.

The Phoenix Arizona rural-urban fringe is experiencing many of the problems inherent in undirected urban expansion. Annexation conflicts, flooding, soil subsistence, escalating costs of remote service purveyance and loss of prime farmland and natural areas are among these problems. Many of the problems and the lack of appropriate institutional response is due to a lack of understanding of the complex nature of the rural-to-residential landuse conversion process. George Hepner in his article, "Magnitude and Implications of Rapid Residential Development in the Phoenix Arizona Rural-Urban Fringe", provides a descriptive analysis of the location and rate of residential landuse conversion. He concludes that the urban expansion of Phoenix and adjacent suburbs is occurring at a very rapid and largely undirected pace. He uses aerial photographic analysis to document this expansion for the period 1970-78. He further finds that factors of amenities, prestige, variable costs of agricultural and desert land and availability of services are indicated by the analysis as the primary influence on the rate and location of this growth, and confirms that the management of these factors could ensure that the patterns of future expansion of the Pheonix urban area would be more environmentally, socially and economically acceptable than in the past.

In France, the 1970s have been marked by a slowdown in the high urban growth which had started 20 years earlier and by a re-moulding of urban features. Post-war urbanization has greatly affected the capital and the largest towns in the country in a spectacular way. From the 1970s onwards, towns people, living in provincial suburbs have become more numerous than those of the Parisian suburbs. Jean Paul Laborie in his article, "Peripheric Industrialization: An Extension to the Ground Division of Work and to the Social Split", says that the aspects of agglomerations which have modified in a new way during the past 10 years are the growth through weaker, has become more extensive and more diffuse around large and average towns in the country. The peripheric areas, sometimes 50 or 80 km away from downtown, have been the privileged places of the new phase. The author in the first section discusses peripheric urbanization and economic crisis. In the second section he deals primarily with a new process of industrialization in the suburban areas. It includes sub-sections on increased economic and social divisions in the suburban areas, the loosing; a growth process loosing and socio-economic marking or urban peripheries.

Until recently, the Indian cities were very compact in landuse pattern due to socio-economic reasons. But during the past 10 to 15 years or so, the city limit has started to progress externally. Unlike Western cities, where a fall in the population of a city centre leads to a growth of the suburbs by outmigration, the growth of residential suburbs in the Indian cities is rather different. It is an outcome of both the outward migration of residents from the city centre and immigration of residents from other nearby villages or towns. In this spatial process, among the new settlers, the relatively younger and richer form their own suburbs, whereas relatively poorer migrants settle in a crowded corner in the city centre where early settlers continue to live as well. As a result, both the city centres and the suburbs have grown simultaneously in the Indian cities. According to Anjana Desai and Smitha Sen Gupta, Ahmedabad is going through the same process as stated above from the point of view of landuse. They feel that agricultural land in the fringe is changing fast into residential with spacious bungalows'and modern flats. According to them it is interesting that the original village core in the fringe is also existing side by side. The changing landuse pattern has posed many problems for suburban planning. They clearly indicate that, firstly, the loss of agricultural land has increased the cost of vegetables due to shortage of supply. Secondly, the earmarked non-agricultural land may not be used even up to 15 years. Thirdly, the density of population of the suburbs has increased without the development of civic and basic amenities. Lastly, they visualize that the suburbs of Ahmedabad city have developed a dual character. The core village has a rural type of housing without many facilities and other residents are engaged in low-skilled or caste-based traditional occupations, while in the new suburbs, residents have housing with facilities and have a higher socio-economic background. Lastly, she suggests that a comprehensive suburban planning is required for managing the unused land, developing the infrastructure and the environmental quality of life so that the spatial inequality can be reduced.

The development of suburbs around cities is not a new phenomenon. However, studies of the suburbs have not been made in India on a significant scale. Dr. Shrivastava in his article, "Suburban Development in Central India: A Model for Cities of Madhya Pradesh", has undertaken a study of the suburb in respect of cities in the regional urban geography. He finds that suburbs have developed around all the large urban centres of the State. The Census of India data on urban "outgrowth" relates strictly to centres outside the statutory urban limits, and identification of suburbs on this basis alone is likely to overstate the phenomena. A suburb as understood by this study is any urban development away from the densely settled parts of the city. It may be both within and outside the civic boundary. The author distinguishes them as "nearer suburbs" and "distant suburbs". The nearer suburbs are characterized by the residents or the employees of the State Government and of well-to-do people. The author finds that the distant suburbs lie at some distance from the city and have been developed either by the Madhya Pradesh Housing Board, or private colonizers or have grown around a formerly rural nucleus.

The author demonstrates that suburbs play a vital rôle in the development of cities in the State. It is important that a thorough investigation of the processes of this development is made. The author suggests that looking at the chaotic conditions of the suburbs in some cities of Madhya Pradesh, it is essential that a strict regulatory control is exercised on all the developments in the peripheral areas.

Rudiger Voight in his article, "Social Economic Change in Rural-Urban Continuum", analyses the problems of suburbs from the point of view of political organization. He makes an attempt to explain the structural discrimination. He feels that in the rural areas considerable supply deficit still exists in the technical infrastructure, vocational training competition and enlargement of universities, public transport, spare time infrastructures, etc. The author also analyses the Regional Cumulations. He finds that the gap between rural and central densely populated areas is increased by lesser availability of services in the rural areas. He highlights the criterion of quality, concentration at the expense of rural area strategies to achieve consensus and problem of enforcing regional development.

It has only recently been fashionable among social scientists interested in residential areas to consider the effects of city size neighbourhood and community characteristics. Frank L. Sweetser in his article, "Community Size and the Urban-Rural Continuum: Australia and the United States", has concluded that urban neighbourhood communities could be divided into four urban community size classes—from very large to large, medium sized and small cities—and found that a majority of the indicators varied non-technically, with regular and sometimes large increases and decreases from size class to size class. This finding raised the question as to whether such continuous variation extends also in the rural areas; in short to the problem of the validity of the concept of an urban-rural continuum. According to Sweetser, the rural urban contrasts tend to be stronger than inter-city size differences. Accordingly, a general theoretical conclusion was formulated. "The hypothesis of a unitary urban-rural continuum of neighbourhood variation in urban industrial societies must be rejected in favour of the view that the city size and urban-rural contrast differential linear affects the neighbourhood characteristics. It is the purpose of this paper to report an initial test of the proposition that the two modes of differentialization are indeed similar in separate urban industrial societies when a comparison is made between the available data for Australia for 1971 and for the USA for 1950. The author demonstrates for the USA and Australia generally very close similarities in the patterning of differences of a dozen social indicators along the continuum from very large to large, medium sized and small cities to rural communities. The author predicts that both urban-rural and city size effects are clearly evident in the data and they are manifested in almost identical ways for most variables in both nations. The author feels that the proposition that two modes of linear differentiation, one relating to city size and the other to the urban-rural contrast, explain many of the differing characteristics of neighbourhoods and communities in urban industrial societies is strongly supported by these findings.

The term "umland" is no longer a new jargon in the field of urban geography. In fact, whatever the definition of the term, Dr. Ram Swaroop Dixit in his article, "Glimpses of the Umland of a Metropolis: The Case of Kanpur", clearly means that the "umland" is a tributary area immediately around the city and functionally, economically, socio-culturally and politically integrated with it. In terms of regional taxonomy, it is a functional model region. The umland serves the city and the city serves the umland in a myriad ways. They weave a closely knit matrix of centripetal and centrifugal forces, in-bound and out-bound flows of goods, services and ideas. Thus between city and umland is an intrinsic relationship. The author in this paper has vigorously attempted those criterion which are responsible for delimiting the umland of Kanpur. He analyses the delimitation typology and hierarchy of umlands. He describes the salient geographical features of umland in terms of physical landscape and climate.

Dr. Dasarath S. Pal in his paper, "Functional Classification of the Service Centres of the Umland of Kanpur Metropolis", has adopted the methodology of Nelson. According to Dr. Pal most of the service centres are found to be specialized in more than one function. The analysis reveals that there are seven centres specialized in one function in primary activities, ten centres in two functions, 13 in three functions, 11 in four functions and 13 in five functions and two centres carry on six functions. It has been highlighted that not a single centre is having specialized functions. Thus the author has arrived at the conclusion that the umland of Kanpur metropolis like the greater part of the country has a predominantly traditional agrarian economy and is functionally unbalanced.

The analysis of the functions of service centres is undoubtedly a very important aspect of regional central places studies. In his paper, "Functional Classification of Service Centres in the Umland of Lucknow", M. L. Soni has classified the service centres based on H. J. Nelson's method. The occupational data obtained from the 1971 Census have been analysed to highlight the functional structure of the selected service centres.

According to M. L. Soni the umland of Lucknow consists of partially or wholly 11 districts (Lucknow, Barabanki, Faizabad, Gonda, Bahraich, Kheri, Sitapur, Hardoi, Unnao, Rae Bareli and Sultanpur). He recognizes 86 service centres with 1,000 or more population and dominantly non-agricultural, which are grouped into 67 towns and town groups. The application of Nelson's method and the resultant functional categories show that out of the 67 service centres, 16 are monofunctional, 23 are bifunctional, 23 are trifunctional and five are multifunctional.

REFERENCES

1. James H. Johnson, "Geographical Processes at the Edge of the City" in Johnson (Ed.), **Suburban Growth**, John Wiley and Sons, London 1974.
2. J.H. Johnson, "Urbanization and its Implications, Some general comments" **Geoform**, 1970, 14-15.
3. R.J. Pryor, "Defining the Rural Urban Fringe" **Social Forces** 1968, 47, 202-15
4. Carter, **The study of Urban Geography** Edward Arnold Publisher, 1976.
5. H.A. Kurtze and J.B. Eicher, "Fringe and Suburbs: A confusion of concepts", **Social forces**, 1958, 32-7.
6. G.A. Wissink, American Cities in Perspective with Special Reference to the Development of their Fringe Areas, Assen 1962.
7. David, Thomas, "The Urban Fringe: Approaches and Attitudes" in Johnson (Ed), **Suburban Growth**, John Wiley & Sons, London.
8. Pryor, op. cit.
9. R.B. Andrews, "Elements in the Urban Fringe pattern" **Journal of Land and Public Utility Economics**, 1942, 169-83.
10. W.C. McKain and R.G. Burnight, "The Sociological Significance of the Rural-Urban Fringe from the Rural Point of View" **Rural Sociology** 18, 1953, 109-16.
11. M.W. Reinemann, "The Pattern and Distribution of Manufacturing in the Chicago Area", **Economic Geography**, 36, 1960, 139-44.
12. O.D. Duncan and A.J. Reiss, "Suburbs and Urban Fringe", in **Social Characteristics of Urban and Rural Communities**, New York, 1956.
13. R.B. Myers and J.A. Beegle, "Delineation and Analysis of the Rural Urban Fringe", **Applied Anthropology**, 6, 1947, 14-22.
14. Pryor, op.cit.
15. G.S. Wehrwein, "The Rural Urban Fringe", **Economic Geography**, 18, 1942, 217-28.
16. Carter, op. cit.
17. Wehrwein, op. cit.
18. Wissink, op. cit.

19. R.G. Gollege, "Sydney's metropolitan Fringes: A Study in Urban-Rural relations," **Australian Geographer, 7,** 1960, 243-55.
20. R.E.Pahl, Urbs in Rure. The Metropolitan Fringe in Hertfordshire. London School of Economics and Political Science, Geography Paper No. 2. 1965.
21. R.E. Pahl op. cit.
22. G. Sjoberg, **The pre-industrial City.past and Present,** New York 1960, 80-107.

SECTION ONE

THE EVOLUTION OF THE URBAN FRINGE

TWO

Lorne H. Russwurm

Comparative Land Management in the Rural-Urban Fringe of New World Cities

After More than 15 years of studying rural-urban fringe developments in Canada (Russwurm, 1961, 1967, 1970, 1976, 1977 and 1980), my research was expanded to the predominantly English-speaking countries of the United States, Australia and New Zealand. These countries have a similar historical link to Great Britain from whence came their initial attitudes towards land. They are also similar in the way their space economy is organized by cities, in a strong emphasis on private property rights and in the post-World War II resettlement of their city's surroundings by exurbanites.

Related to these similarities and a number of differences to be discussed later, is the topic of comparative land use management in the rural-urban fringe (Russwurm, 1982).

Rather than presenting a detailed review of existing research (this is being undertaken for a book scheduled for completion in 1983), the paper represents an attempt to assess some of the main threads of land use management as personally perceived from lengthy field and literature experience added to during a sabbatical year 1981-82 in the United States, Australia and New Zealand.

The two key terms of 'land use management' and 'rural-urban fringe' need clarification. Management rather than planning is deliberately used to encompass both any and all effects of private and public actors manipulating and using land. Rural-urban fringe sometimes called just urban fringe also has broad connotations (Russwurm, 1977b). Spatially, it covers the approximately 50 kilometre zone around cities. A distinction should be made between an inner fringe of about 10 to 15 kilometres into which the city is physically expanding and an outer fringe extending another 25 to 50 kilometres ending in an urban shadow zone which faces much lesser urban influence. Combined the urban shadow and rural-urban fringe equates with the external part of the urban field (Friedmann and Miller, 1965). Elsewhere the terms urban surroundings, city's countryside, urban regions and metropolitan regions are used for this extensive zone which comprises the domain of the regional city (Bryant, Russwurm and McLellan, 1982; Simmons, 1974; Blumenfeld 1982).

Two broad sections constitute the paper. First, the regional city concept is developed as the overarching settlement form of which the rural-urban fringe is a part. Second, a framework is presented for dealing comparatively with land use management in the rural-urban fringe. The assumption prevails throughout the paper that comparative study is a prime means of developing a sounder theoretical basis than that which currently exists in the rather disparate existing rural-urban fringe studies. A further assumption is that regional cities as subsystems organize the socio-economic structure of New World countries.

THE REGIONAL CITY

Since the advent of the automobile, the regional city has been the emerging urban form organizing human activities and settlement patterns in the Anglo New World countries. Today instead of city and country, a more appropriate term is regional city as city and region are increasingly integrated (Blumenfeld, 1980, 1982). Generally people living within the hinterland of a city no longer think of the city as a strange world occasionally visited but as a world that is part of their regular lives. City and region are today but part of a single system. Numerous flows of people, goods, money and information integrate the population and activities of the regional city.

Integration of cities and their immediate hinterlands is a response to rising incomes, increased mobility and increased leisure time associated with population and employment growth in urban areas. Technological accessibility in transportation and communications along with personal choice has made easily possible the dispersal of population and economic activities into surrounding settlement nodes and the open countryside (Russwurm, 1982). Consequently a regional city form has evolved consisting of a concentrated built-up urban part and a dispersed part consisting of hamlets, villages and towns embedded amidst farm land and other open land. Since World War II, scattered new non-farm residences gradually exceeded in number the scattered farmsteads. In the analytical research done in Canada using census data 1941 to 1976 the dispersed population of the regional city could be divided into scattered farm, scattered urban and nodal (Bryant, Russwurm and McLellan, 1982). A threshold level of 10,000 is used to define concentrated urban areas; this minimum size is seen as a reasonable lower limit defining a city (Canadian Rural Development Council, 1979; Russwurm 1980).

Of main concern for land management at a national scale is the notion that the space economy of a country is best assessed as an urban system made up of regional cities encompassing most of the nation's space (Simmons, 1974). Where settlement is fairly dense as in the St. Lawrence Lowlands in Canada or the Northeastern United States, regional cities based on the lower limit of 10,000 concentrated population usually overlap within 50 kilometre radii. In such areas, land management in the rural-urban fringe is particularly important. Wherever a considerable extent of good, well-watered, agricultural land occurred, many cities also developed; hence, there can be serious national concern about urban encroachment on agricultural land. For instance, New Zealand (New Zealand Land Use Advisory Council, 1980) has strictly protected good agricultural land around cities partly on the basis of the need to maintain its agricultural export levels. Two Canadian provinces, British Columbia and Quebec, and two American states, Hawaii and Oregon, have agricultural protection policies at the provincial and state scale (Bryant, Russwurm and McLellan, 1982). Even the United States, most blessed among world nations in its abundance of good agricultural land, recently saw the need for a major study of urban influences on agricultural land (NALS, 1981).

At the scale of individual regional cities a surrogate measure based on rural and urban population components was developed to categorize the rural-urban intermixture in the urban surroundings. Rural and urban as population, spatial, or lifestyle descriptors are still distinguishable at the extremes of the rural-urban continuum. But it is their overlap in the dispersed part of the regional city that characterizes the processes and form of the regional city and has given rise to many land management concerns. Basic societal processes in Anglo New World countries involving common educational, shopping, and media access for populations, regardless of location in or out of the built-up city, have greatly helped the integration of urban and rural. Moreover, the exurbanite resettlement uniformly witnessed in the New World countries has locationally intermixed farm and non-farm populations thereby promoting integration while increasing land management needs.

The measure used to characterize the rural-urban integration is based on the ratio of non-farm to farm population (Russwurm, 1970). Based on the rural-urban continuum concept, four categories are defined. They are: rural, less than or equal to 0.2; semi-rural, 0.3 to 1.0; semi-urban, 1.1 to 5.0; and urbanizing, greater than 5.0. Expressed another way, rural means there are five farm households to every non-farm household in the spatial unit used for analysis. The measure has been successfully applied at differing urban scales from census sub-divisions (tens of square miles) to one quarter square mile sections (Yeates, 1975; Krueger, 1978; Maguire, 1979).

Underlying this typology is the important assumption that the level of interaction and potential conflicts over land varies directly with the relative magnitude of the scattered non-farm population. It is argued that once non-farm households exceed farm households in a rural municipality, political control is in jeopardy for the farming community. For this reason and because of likely increasing land management concerns as non-farm population increases, the semi-urban category is considered a crucial one. Krueger (1978) has made this point for the Niagara Fruitlands in Southern Ontario and is currently involved with further similar research in the Okanagan Valley fruitlands of British Columbia. Moreover, other production functions, such as water and mineral resource use, and place functions, such as utility lines and waste disposal sites, face increasing conflict as population density in the dispersed part of the regional city increases.

An important land management dilemma exists about the resettlement of the city's countryside. It is generally accepted that agricultural land should be protected where feasible but it is also strongly accepted that people should be as free as possible to live where they desire and do what they want with their land. In the Anglo New World countries, many people wish to live in the city's countryside amidst the farming community. One planning approach is to prohibit further exurbanite settlement in good agricultural areas on the ground that it is detrimental to agriculture (Ontario Ministry of Housing and County of Huron, 1976; Rodd and Van-Vuuren, 1975). Such an approach, however, ignores the threshold question about how many non-farm residences can co-exist with farmsteads before adverse effects occur. An excellent recent study on the Montreal-Ottawa urban surroundings concluded that benefits of exurbanite resettlement generally outweighed adverse impacts (McRae, 1982).

Application of the rural-urban typology could lessen this dilemma, if indeed the semi-urban category is the crucial one. Thus, exurbanite resettlement could be safely allowed in a farming municipality or part of one up to some threshold where non-farm population considerably exceeds farm population. Possibly this threshold may be as high as the lower limits of the urbanizing category, i.e., five non-farm households to each farm household per unit area. Comparative study between New World regional cities should shed further light on exurbanite resettlement and land management needs.

Exurbanite resettlement is certainly a key element in regional city evolution (Walker, 1976, McQuinn, 1978, New Zealand Land Use Advisory Council, 1980). Only for Canada has its magnitude been empirically and consistently determined for individual regional cities (Russwurm and Bryant, 1982; Bryant, Russwurm and McLellan, 1982). For the 52 regional cities in Canada which had over 40,000 people in the built-up part, 1976, data were compiled 1941 to 1976 by census year for a 50 kilometre radius. These 52 regional cities accounted for 65 per cent of Canada's population, 1941, and 76 per cent, 1976. In aggregate for these regional cities, farm population in 1941 exceeded scattered urban population by five to one; by 1976 a reversal had occurred and the scattered urban population outnumbered farm population by three to one. Over the 35-year period farm population had declined by 1976 to less than half of the 1941 number while the scattered urban population increased about six-fold. In aggregate, the scattered urban population first exceeded the farm population by 1966. As expected, considerable variation existed between the regional cities but by 1976 only the dispersed part of Regina and Saskatoon, Saskatchewan, showed population ratios close to rural values (five farm households to one scattered urban household). Efforts are being made to compile similar data for 22 selected regional cities in the United States, Australia and New Zealand.

Clearly then, if the Canadian data should be similar to those of the other Anglo New World countries significant redistribution has occurred amongst the population components in the rural-urban fringe as the regional city form evolved. In the next section, a general land management framework is developed for comparative study and is related to broad types of planning approaches.

A COMPARATIVE LAND MANAGEMENT FRAMEWORK FOR RURAL-URBAN FRINGE STUDY

A goal of comparative empirical study in geography is to develop better theoretical constructs for explanation of whichever form or process is of research concern. Towards fulfilling this goal for rural-urban fringe research, elements considered important in Anglo New World countries are selected using the traditional geographical approach of similarities and differences (Russwurm, 1982). These elements are then related to a three-fold typology of planning approaches to land management problems in the rural-urban fringe.

The Selected Comparative Elements

Similarities

Four elements are considered to be essentially similar amongst the four New World countries. First is the regional city concept already discussed. Second is the critical importance to the countries concerned of their rural-urban fringe lands. Direct conflict between the production, protection, place and play functions of land characterize the rural-urban fringe (Russwurm, 1977b). In Anglo-America, only in the Interior Plains of Canada and the United States with their extensive settlement patterns do large areas of valuable land occur that face minimal conflicts over the four main functions of land. In Australia, vast areas of grazing land are far removed from city influence but most of the population lives in coastal cities where the dispersed part contains building material deposits and the more specialized agricultural lands, e.g., sugar cane, Brisbane; market garden and fruitlands, Melbourne, Adelaide, Sydney. Land values and land value gradients are also an important aspect of the critical nature of land around cities (Bryant, 1982), as is land speculation which is inherent wherever private property rights are sacrosanct.

Pervasiveness of technological accessibility and firmly

held rights in private property are two other elements of similarity among Anglo New World countries. It is the technological accessibility of automobile, telephone, and communication media which has made rural-urban fringes comfortable places for exurbanites to live in by allowing a level of services approaching that of the built-up city. While some people would readily live in the city's countryside with minimal services, most people expect services to be reasonably comparable to those found in the city from whence most came. The option to live in the city's countryside is part of the accepted private property rights; (closely associated are firmly held beliefs about the value of private space to households). Private property rights and private territory are two of four strongly accepted individual rights linked closely to land in the Anglo New World countries (Russwurm, 1977a). The other two are the rights to life style preferences and accessibility to services.

Differences

Eight elements reflecting a reasonable degree of difference between regional cities and sometimes countries form an important part of the analytical comparative framework. They concern the natural environment, private land tenure, division of land between municipalities, land use and settlement patterns, development of land on the city's edge (inner fringe), public regulation of land, attitudes to accepting regulations over land and population density.

Already discussed are population density, and the ratio of its rural and urban components. It is seen as a composite surrogate measure reflecting total pressures on land in the rural-urban fringe. It also is closely linked to differences in the natural environment which relate directly to the resource base available for production function. In turn production functions are reflected in land use patterns and settlement forms. Compare the landscapes patched by irrigated agriculture surrounding Phoenix and Tucson with the continuous high quality agricultural landscapes surrounding U.S. Midwest or Southern Ontario cities. Or the complex physical landscapes surrounding parts of Auckland, Adelaide and Melbourne with the simpler physical landscapes surrounding Winnipeg or Canberra.

The remaining five elements concern the division of land and its regulation. Considerable variety exists in both how land was subdivided initially for both private and public purposes. The division into square mile sections in most of interior Anglo America is well-known and contributes to more rectangular city forms. Other regional cities have varying mixes of larger and smaller parcels. Unusual is the pattern east of Melbourne, Victoria state, Australia where a single large property may contain within it several smaller parcels all of which can legally be separated under existing property rights. Irregular metes and bounds subdivision of land is the mode in eastern North America. Adding to the complexity of the initial land subdivision are the differing patterns of further subdivision (or consolidation) that occurred over time. For land management, given the strength of private property rights, different patterns and sizes of land parcels pose different possibilities for inner fringe development and availability of suitable lots for county residential locations. For instance around some regional cities (in whole or part) large parcels for planned unit developments may be hard to obtain.

Just as many differences occurred in the private subdivision of land so many differences occurred in how land was organized into the public territory of municipalities. And just as private territory once defined became sacrosanct so did public territory. As emphasized in the regional city discussion earlier, socio-economic integration has occurred over a large area. But this larger unity of the regional city is in most cases still divided into many municipal territories ranging from under 10 to over 100 for individual regional cities. In the United States 30 to 50 separate municipalities are a common number for regional cities though in Texas and Louisiana fewer than 10 may occur, e.g., San Antonio, Baton Rouge. In much of Southern Ontario 10 to 15 is a more common number. However, in the neighbouring province of Quebec regional cities may contain 50 to 75 municipalities e.g., Montreal and Quebec City.

Adding to the complexity of the public territory division is the differing distribution of rights among municipalities. For instance, in Texas and Louisiana, cities have much more power than do counties or parishes. Territorial reorganization of municipalities over time to better meet the needs of people adds further complexity. Examples are annexations, amalgamations and regional governments (eg. Ontario). The study of public territory, its relation to land management and its role in shaping settlement form is seriously under-researched.

Somewhat better studied is development on the city edge in the inner rural-urban fringe (Chapter 4, Bryant, Russwurm and McLellan, 1982). Again considerable differences exist between regional cities. Canada is characterized by fewer, larger development firms which may be national in operating scale (Lorimer, 1978; Spurr, 1976). In contrast the United States, Australia and New Zealand are more characterized by many smaller development firms. One can hypothesize that the more firms operating, the more diverse should be the pattern of development especially if the public territory context is also one of many municipalities.

Another aspect needing consideration is the place of public agencies in the urban land development process. Public land banking for residential purposes has also had prominence around some cities, eg. Saskatoon, Regina and Red Deer in the Canadian Prairie Provinces (Ravis, 1973; Spurr, 1976) and around Sydney, Australia (New South Wales Land Commission, 1981).

New towns (communities) in the inner fringe or elsewhere in the regional city are also part of the inconsistent public role in urban land development in Anglo New World countries. In one case an almost parallel development occurred in regional cities thousands of miles apart, namely, Hamilton, the steel city of Southern Ontario and Adelaide, the metropolis of the State of South Australia. In the early 1970s land for a new town was purchased by province and state about 50 kilometres from the city edge. Hundreds of thousands of dollars were spent in preparing detailed plans but as growth pressures lessened in the late 1970s both proposals foundered and the land is to be resold.

The main role of public land management endeavours, however, relates to regulations developed to control private land activities that are considered to be undesirable for the community at large. While there are many similarities between the Anglo New World countries in subdivision development procedures, significant differences exist between countries and regional cities within countries in the implementation of regulations. Of the four countries investigated only non-federated New Zealand has the possibility of centralized control and thus a direct means of developing consistent nationwide regulations. To some degree New Zealand has done so especially in relation to maintaining agricultural land on the city edge. But even in New Zealand, significant differences exist in the development pattern between Christchurch which is surrounded by few municipalities and larger land parcels and Auckland which has many more municipalities, smaller land parcels and a more lacerated city edge in its regional city form. For Canada, the United States and Australia, land regulations are provincial and state matters with consequent differences resulting in regulations. More detailed discussion of the variety of regulatory tools used is outside the scope of this paper (but see Hagman and Misczynski, 1978).

An eighth element reflecting differences is the complex one of readiness to accept regulatory controls on the private use of land. Field experience in the four countries suggests that differences do exist both between countries and sometimes to an equal degree within countries. My judgment is that in general people in Australia and the United States are least willing to accept firm controls over what can be done with privately owned land, Canada is in between and New Zealand is most amenable. However, people in states like Texas and Oregon are about as far apart in accepting controls as are Australia and New Zealand. And in Canada, Ontarions accept a bureaucratic planning machinery more readily than people in Quebec or the Atlantic Provinces.

Perceptions about the importance of various aspects of the land resource also differ. Oregon is considered to be the heart of Ecotopia in a recent book on North America (Garreau, 1981) reflecting a greater recognition of land as a resource rather than a commodity, a more prevalent view in a state like Texas or Arizona.

The four elements of similarity and the eight elements of difference comprise a comprehensive framework for general comparative studies of rural-urban fringes of different cities. Each of the identified elements, of course, contains a wide range of complexities that meaningful land management of both the public and private sector must recognize. In the next section, an attempt is made to categorize planning approaches to land management in the rural-urban fringe keeping in mind the context of the elements just discussed.

PLANNING APPROACHES TO LAND MANAGEMENT IN THE RURAL-URBAN FRINGE

Land management methods propagated through governmental planning agencies can be categorized broadly as negative-regulatory, persuasive-regulatory or positive-regulatory (Bryant, Russwurm and McLellan, 1982). Until some time after World War II, a negative-regulatory approach based primarily on relatively rigid zoning techniques predominated. Regulations over land were kept to an absolute minimum and were primarily aimed at protecting individual property values and public welfare and safety. Acceptance of zoning was contested strongly in the United States until a 1926 court decision legally established it. Thus, the key aspect of negative-regulatory approaches is the least possible interference with private property rights.

As rapid urban growth took place in the 1950s, in all four countries the potential sprawl-creating effects of the large numbers of municipalities in any given regional city became reality. Each municipality wanted its share of growth and on the individual side the existing negative-regulatory controls were applied as little as possible. Gradually both public and private sectors became more critical of the haphazard development patterns occurring. Higher levels of government had to do something.

The "something" was a move towards persuasive-regulatory approaches, which generally developed about ten years earlier in Canada than in the United States. Such approaches evolved based on voluntary associations of adjoining municipalities usually partly supported by federal, state, or provincial funds. Still implicit in such approaches was the acceptance that both private property rights and local municipal rights should be curtailed as little as possible. Examples in Canada were joint planning boards between municipalities, and regional planning commissions in Alberta consisting of voluntary members; elsewhere, examples are the Councils of Government such as the Association of Bay Area Governments (San Francisco) or the Greater Sydney plan in Australia. Many excellent planning documents were developed with an occasional implementation. While co-ordination improved, the emphasis remained on local municipal rights and by extension individual rights. Not uncommonly, a bureaucratic planning process developed (eg. Ontario, California) as persuasion was exercised for specific purposes pushed by different agencies. Nevertheless, the discussion and effort that went into the persuasive strategies gradually focussed the notion that development rights are not inherent in a parcel of land but are created by societal demand (Reilly, 1973). In consequence, an equity dilemma surfaced as rights of individual land owners conflicted with community rights expressed by land regulations expected to lead to improved land use patterns.

Resolution of this dilemma could be called a positive-regulatory planning approach involving a more actively consistent enforcing role by higher levels of government while still retaining most local municipal land management powers (Bryant, Russwurm and McLellan, 1982). Three key assumptions exist; (1) that most individual and collective rights can be accommodated; (2) that a more efficient use of land is possible; and (3) that a more active role of higher level governments will contribute to more efficient land use patterns. These assumptions have been challenged by economists using the argument that market failure in land allocation has not been demonstrated (Gardner, 1977). In the Ontario context, Frankena and Scheffman (1980) also provide reasonable evidence to this effect.

In Ontario the provincially dictated amalgamation of municipalities into two tier regional municipalities during the 1970s are an example of a positive-regulatory approach (Bryant, Russwurm, and McLellan, 1982). Existing county territories were usually maintained but municipalities contained therein were amalgamated to reduce numbers. The regional municipalities were usually in territorial extent of a regional city nature, e.g., Ottawa-Carleton, Hamilton Wentworth, with land use management being both a regional and local function. Local plans had to fit into the regional plan. The main reason for moving towards regional municipalities were hopes of solving existing land use problems associated with the criticality of rural-urban fringe land.

Ontario, however, stopped short of applying this approach over the entire province but Oregon did not in its positive-regulatory approach to land management. In Oregon, the main reason was concern over agricultural land. Again this was dominantly a rural-urban fringe problem because most of its best agricultural land is in the Willamette Valley where most of Oregon's population lives in cities. The approach involved development of state-wide land management goals by 1973, and their merger with local municipal plans by 1980 with the legal system as the moderator (Oregon Land Conservation and Development Commission, 1978; 1000 Friends of Oregon, 1980). First evaluations of the agricultural land preservation aspects have been done by Furuseth (1980, 1981) and were basically favourable.

Other examples of positive-regulatory planning approaches arising out of agricultural land and urban sprawl concerns are those of the Hawaiian State Land Use Law (Myers, 1976, Lowrey, 1980), British Columbia Agricultural Land Commission (Pierce, 1981, Manning and Eddy, 1978) and a similar commission in Quebec (Quebec, Government of, 1979).

Farmland protection strategies in North America arose out of concern over possible damage to the production function of agricultural land in the urban surroundings. Often a positive-regulatory approach is deemed essential for such strategies whose success, however, is difficult to evaluate properly (Bryant and Russwurm, 1982).

In summary, planning approaches to land management in the rural-urban fringes of Anglo New World countries have been outlined in a stage model based on acceptance of individual rights in land by individuals and municipalities. On Table 2.1, a highly generalized outline of these stages in relation to the three main groups of actors is presented.

TABLE 2.1
Land Management, Planning Regulatory Stages and Main Groups of Actors

Regulatory Stage	Main Groups Of Actors		
	Property owners and developers	Local Municipalities	Higher levels of Government
Negative	Maximum rights in land	Inconsistent univariate regulations	Inactive
Persuasive	Rights in land being questioned	Multivariate regulations being considered	Becoming active
Positive	Rights in land protected but modified	Consistent multivariate regulations developing	Active

The main implications of this stage model of planning approaches for land management are the recognition that land is both a commodity and a resource, that as more competition arises for the four main functions of land (production, protection, place and play), more comprehensive regulatory approaches are necessary, and that collective rights in land though still not dominant, have become more important relative to individual rights. In the Anglo New World countries, private rights continue to be strongly protected by legal systems. Stage models, however, should be testable using empirical data. Partly towards this end, a comparative research agenda aimed at achieving better understanding of land management in the rural-urban fringe concludes this paper.

A COMPARATIVE RESEARCH AGENDA

A comparative research agenda for land management in the rural-urban fringe is developed from the similarities and differences framework presented earlier. Briefly recapitulated, rural-urban fringe research needs to be set in the context of the regional city form of which the rural-urban fringe is a part. Permeated by a strong private property rights land ethic, socio-economic integration of the regional city settlement form became a reality because of the high degree of technological accessibility which exists in Anglo New World countries. This integration, however, has been accompanied by increasing competition for the production, protection, place and play functions of land. Planning approaches to land management were gradually forced to recognize these similarities in all Anglo New World countries. One instance was the collapse of the Sydney metropolitan plan based on British premises about stronger acceptance of regulatory controls over land (South Wales Planning and Environment Commission, 1968).

Differentiating elements of the territorial division of land into various types and sizes of private property holdings and municipalities, sometimes congruent, sometimes not, with the natural environment resource base and its related land use and settlement characteristics pose different land management problems. A variety of planning regulations were developed tempered by inner fringe land conversion processes on the edge of cities and by concern for agricultural and other resources in the outer fringe. Willingness to implement regulations varies between and within Anglo New World countries. In an attempt to develop one simple measure that could act as a useful surrogate for the complex socio-economic integration of the regional city settlement form, categories of rural to urban dispersed populations were devised and used in the Canadian context to place the dispersed area of regional cities in whole and in part along the rural-urban continuum.

Emphasis in the research agenda which follows is on empirical means of providing comparative information on the similarity and differentiating elements. Once the comparative data is compiled, it hopefully can be placed in the context of land economics, diffusion theory and a stage model of regional city evolution already sketched out in the Canadian context (Russwurm and Bryant, 1984). The set of observations used is 30 regional cities (12 in the U.S.A., eight in Canada, six in Australia, four in New Zealand).

These cities were selected largely on three criteria: location of a major university and thus expected local research, different population sizes, and different regional environments. Population sizes range from Sydney (3 million) to Charlotte town, P.E.I. Canada (30,000). Only part of the extended urban regions (Bourne and Simmons, 1982) to which the entire space of the country is allocated were used. Instead a 50 to 60 kilometre radius reflecting approximately a one-hour travel time from the city centre was used; the focus is thus on the nearer urban surroundings where the competition for the production, protection, place and play functions is greatest. A specific definition of the rural-urban fringe is not considered to be important; rather what is considered important is the level of competition for land which decreases outward from the city edge in fairly predictable ways.

The comparative static measure of the ratio of scattered urban to rural population is used to represent the stage of integration of the dispersed part of the regional city. It is hypothesized that once an area is categorized on the rural-urban typology (rural, semi-rural, semi-urban, urbanizing) as semi-urban it is well integrated as part of the regional city. This measure based on the scattered urban population living outside the settlement nodes thus embodies the notion that the colonization of the open countryside by exurbanites is a key element in the evolving regional city form (Walker, 1976). Two data demands exist for application of the urban to rural population ratios: reasonably small spatial units (ideally less than about 100 square kilometres) and census data which allows identification of farm population and scattered rural non-farm population by the spatial units.

A second comparative research thrust is the outlining of the settlement form and its development pattern including the concentrated urban core. Empirical information on the number, size, location, function and growth rates of settlement nodes is desired along with general land use patterns associated with the settlements and the resource base provided by the natural environment. In addition, original land survey patterns, the municipal territorial division and its relation to land use and the resource base should be assessed. Such data can then be related to theories of economic rent, central place, diffusion and urban growth.

A third comparative research thrust is on assessing the importance of the land resource base of the selected regional cities at regional, state/provincial and national scales. This involves assessing the quantity and quality of land related to the four land functions. Function and use can be two quite different things (Bryant, Russwurm and McLellan, 1982).

For the production functions data are needed on the quantity, quality and location of agricultural, mineral, forest and water resources and their use. Water supplies for instance are under competition for municipal, industrial, agricultural and recreational uses. For the place function, data are needed on the location of residential, commercial, manufacturing, and institutional developments and their associated transportation, communications and utilities infrastructure.

Much is still unknown about the rapidly changing patterns associated with the place functions in the urban surroundings and the same is true about the play functions. For instance is the outdoor recreation and leisure behaviour of exurbanites in the dispersed part of the regional city similar to that of inhabitants of the built-up part? For the play function data are needed on both the public and the private sector recreation facilities. For instance, in Canada, the United States and Australia, numerous trailer parks have arisen over the past 20 years which provide a second-home recreation function in rural-urban fringe locations. Are such developments a poor man's substitute for a lake or seashore cottage?

Finally, for the protection function data are needed on how important ecological functions are maintained through the planning approaches used. Of selective interest here are stream and lake quality maintenance, water source protection, and policies and methods for the maintenance of natural ecosystems.

These three research thrusts on population, land use - settlement, and land function components combined with the fourth research thrust on planning approaches and regulations and their implementation could provide a comprehensive systems perspective on land management in the rural-urban fringe. The underlying framework is a systems approach (Bryant, Russwurm and McLellan, 1982), set in the context of the regional city concept. Most geographers reading this will readily recognize the regional geography overtones which permeate the comparative research agenda. Regional cities and their permanent rural-urban fringes provide fascinating examples of our landscapes where we can apply the geographer's "highest art" (Hart, 1982).

REFERENCES

Blumenfeld, H. **Metropolis and Beyond**, New York, J. Wiley, 1980.

Blumenfeld, H. **Where Did all the Metropolitanites Go**? Paper No. 32, Toronto: Urban and Regional Planning, University of Toronto, 1982.

Bryant, C.R. **The Rural Real Estate Market**, Publication Series No. 18, Waterloo: Department of Geography, University of Waterloo, 1982.

Bryant, C.R. and Russwurm, L.H. "North American farmland protection strategies in retrospect" **Geojournal**, 1982, 66: 1-12.

Bryant, C.R., Russwurm, L.H. and McLellan, A.G. **The City's Countryside**, London: Longman's 1982.

Bourne, L.S. and Simmons, J.W. "Defining the area of interest: definitions of the city metropolitan areas and extended urban regions" in L.S. Bourne, ed. **Internal Structure of the City.** Second ed., Oxford and New York: Oxford University Press, 1982, pp.57-72.

CRDC (Council on Rural Development, Canada) **A Rural Information System for Canada**, Hull; Council on Rural Development, Canada, 1979.

Friedmann, J. and Miller, J. "The Urban Field", **Journal of the Institute of American Planners**, 31(4): 1965, pp.312-20.

Furuseth, O.J. "The Oregon agricultural protection program: a review and assessment", **Natural Resources Journal**, 20, 1980, pp. 603-14.

Furuseth, O.J. "Update on Oregon's protection program: a land use perspective", **Natural Resources Journal**, 21, 1981, pp. 57-70.

Gardner, B.D. "The economics of agricultural land preservation," **American Journal of Agricultural Economics**, 59(5), 1977, pp. 1027-36.

Garreau, J. **The Nine Nations of North America**, Boston: Houghton-Mifflin, 1981.

Hagman, D. and Misczynski, D. eds., **Windfalls or Wipeouts**, Chicago: American Society of Planning Officials, 1978.

Hart, J.F. "The highest form of the geographer's art" **Annals, Association of American Geographers**, 72, 1982, pp. 1-19.

Hodge, G. and Gadeer, M.A. **Towns and Villages in Canada**, Report to the Ministry of State For Urban Affairs; Kingston: School of Urban and Regional Planning, Queen's

University, 1977.

Krueger, R.R. "Urbanization of the Niagara Fruit Belt" **The Canadian Geographer**, 22, 1978, pp. 179-94.

Lorimer, J. **The Developers**, Toronto: James Lorimer, 1979.

Maguire, G. "The urban fringe: perspectives on land use in the North Okanagan" in **The Urban Fringe in the Western Provinces**, ICURR Occasional Paper, Toronto: Intergovernmental Committee on Urban and Regional Research, 1979, pp. 11-20.

McQuinn, P. **Rural Retreating : A Review and an Australian Case Study**, Armidale, N.S.W.: Department of Geography, University of New England, 1978.

McRae, J.D. **The Impact of Exurbanite Settlement in Rural Areas: a Case Study in the Ottawa-Montreal Axis**, Working Paper No. 22, Ottawa: The Lands Directorate, Environment Canada, 1981.

New South Wales Planning and Environment Commission, **Sydney Region Outline Plan 1970-2000**, Sydney: New South Wales Planning and Environment Commission, 1968.

New South Wales, Land Commission, **Annual Report, 1980**, Sydney: Land Commission of New South Wales, 1981.

New Zealand Land Use Advisory Council (1981) W.J.F. Bishop, ed., **Proceedings of the Seminar on Peri-Urban Land Use**, University of Waikato, Hamilton, Dec. 1979, Wellington: Department of Lands and Survey.

1000 Friends of Oregon, **Four Year Report 1975-1979**, Portland: 1000 Friends of Oregon 1980.

Oregon Land Conservation and Development Commission, **Statewide Planning Goals and Guidelines**, Salem: Land Conservation and Development Commission, 1978..

Quebec, Government of, **Loi sur la protection du territoire agricole: renseignements generaux**, Quebec: Commission de Protection du Territoire Agricole du Quebec, 1978.

Ravis, D. **Advance Land Acquisition of Local Government: the Saskatoon Experience**, Ottawa: Community Planning Association of Canada, 1973.

Reilly, W. ed. **The Use of Land: A Citizen's Guide to Urban Growth**, New York: Crowell for the Rockefeller Fund, 1973.

Rodd, R.S. and Van Vuuren W. "A new methodology for countryside planning", **Canadian Journal of Agricultural Economics**, Workshop Proceedings, 1975 pp. 109-140.

Russwurm, L.H. **The Rural-Urban Fringe: a Comparative Study of London, Kitchener-Waterloo and Sarnia**, M.A. Thesis, London: Department of Geography, University of Western Ontario, 1961.

--------- "Expanding urbanization and selected agricultural elements: a case study: Southwestern Ontario 1941-1961"

Land Economics 43, 1967, pp. 101-7.

Russwurm, L.H. **Development of an Urban Corridor System, Toronto to Stratford Area, 1941-1966**, Regional Development Branch Research Paper 3, 1970 Toronto: Queen's Printer.

-----, "Country residential development and the regional city form in Canada", **Ontario Geography** 10, 1976 pp. 79-96.

-----, **The Surroundings of Our Cities**, Ottawa: Community Planning Press, 1977a.

-----, "The urban fringe as a regional environment" in L.H. Russwurm, R.E. Preston, and L. R. G. Martin, **Essays on Canadian Urban Process and Form I**, Publication Series 10, Waterloo: Department of Geography, University of Waterloo: 1977b pp. 181-180.

-----, "Land in the urban fringe: conflicts and their policy implications", in R.E. Preston and L.H. Russwurm, eds. **Essays on Canadian Urban Process and From II**, Publication Series 15, Waterloo: Department of Geography, University of Waterloo, 1980, pp.457-505.

-----, "A comparative approach to rural-urban fringe studies: Anglo New World experience", in K.B. Beesley and C. Cocklin, eds., **Perspectives on the Rural-Urban Fringe**, Occasional Paper No. 2, Guelph: Department of Geography, University of Guelph, 1982, pp. 46-56.

-----, and Bryant, C.R. 1981 **Regional Differences on the Evolution of the Regional City Form in Canada 1941 to 1976**, paper presented at the Annual Meeting, Canadian Association of Geographers, Corner Brook, Nfld., Aug. 1981, Waterloo: Department of Geography, University of Waterloo, Mimeo.

-----, and Bryant, C.R., (Forthcoming, 1983, "Changing) Population components and regional city evolution, Canada 1941 to 1976" in Y. Brunet, ed. **Proceedings, Symposium on the Urban Exodus**, Montreal: Universite de Montreal Press.

Simmons, J.W. **Canada as an Urban System: A Conceptual Framework**, Research Paper No. 62, 1974, Toronto: centre for Urban and Community Studies, University of Toronto.

Spurr, P. **Land and Urban Development**, Toronto: James Lorimer, 1976.

United States National Agricultural Lands Study, **Final Report**, Washington: U.S. Government Printing Office, 1981.

Upper Yarra Valley and Dandenong Ranges Authority, **Regional Strategy Plan**, Melbourne; Upper Yarra Valley and Dandenong Ranges Authority, 1980.

Walker, G. "Social perspectives on the countryside: reflec-

tions on territorial form north of Toronto" **Ontario Geography** 10, 1976, pp. 54-63.
Yeates, M. **Main Street: Windsor to Quebec City**, Toronto: Macmillan, 1975.

THREE

Yoram Bar-Gal

Social Pluralism and the Urban Fringe

The Israeli Case

INTRODUCTION

According to Clout, four processes may transform a rural settlement into an urban settlement (Clout 1972): Emigration from the city to the village, commuting, recreation villages and a second home.

Settlements which are under the influence of such processes are under continuous urban pressure. This urban pressure is expressed by various characteristics, such as - a rise in the price of land, changes in the use of land - all these are physical changes (Lassey, 1977, Johnson 1974). In the demographic-cultural field, changes are apt to take place in the composition of the population and its occupation, whereas in the field of values-ideology, the points of view, the approaches, aims and ways of life, change (Berler, 1973).

The field, in which area the urban pressure is especially strong, is described in literature as "the urban fringe" (Pryor, 1968). In areas of this type, we come across the "metropolitan villages" (Masser et al., 1965). In these villages two different populations are generally found—the urban population which is infiltrating to the villages (or the population that has already undergone an urbanization process) as well as the traditional rural population of the settlement. The services network in such settlements is apt to changes—it is usually conquered by the nearest neighbouring city (Pahl, 1970).

THE PROBLEM OF THE RESEARCH

In Israel, as in other places in the world, urbanization of villages is not a new phenomenon, and it already exists since many decades. This phenomenon has been studied in Israel, especially from the point of view of the Jewish population and in certain types of agricultural villages, which were transformed into cities (Moshavot) (Efrat, 1976, Gonen, 1972). A similar research has been conducted also among the Arab population and modernization processes have been analyzed in such settlements (Bar-Gal and Soffer, 1981, 1976).

Our aim in this present article is to compare between the processes which the various Jewish communities are undergoing with those of the Arab communities in Israel. This refers to such settlements which are under great urban pressure, such settlements as are found in the urban fringe (see Fig. 3.1).

There exists a cultural pluralism in Israel (the different Jewish communities and the Arab community), and we assume that this pluralism will influence the types of urban processes taking place in the "urban fringe". This pluralism will determine the urbanization process in a stronger form than other factors, such as the distance between the city and the village, and the emplacement of the village within the metropolitan framework. The cultural pluralism will divert the process of transforming the villages into urban settlements with the assistance of the legal systems, the attitudes and the approaches of the various groups to the urban pressures.

JEWISH VILLAGES IN THE URBAN FRINGE

Characteristics of the population and the uses of land

Out of the 700 Jewish settlements in Israel, there exist about 20 village settlements which are in close contact with the urban area. They can be described by the aid of three area denominators: They keep their self-definition as settlements, they are close to the urban area, and the way of approach to them is through the city. These settlements belong to three cultural sub-sectors in accordance with the rate of cooperation in them: i.e., private settlements—with little cooperation; Moshavim—cooperative settlements, Kibbutzim-collective settlements.

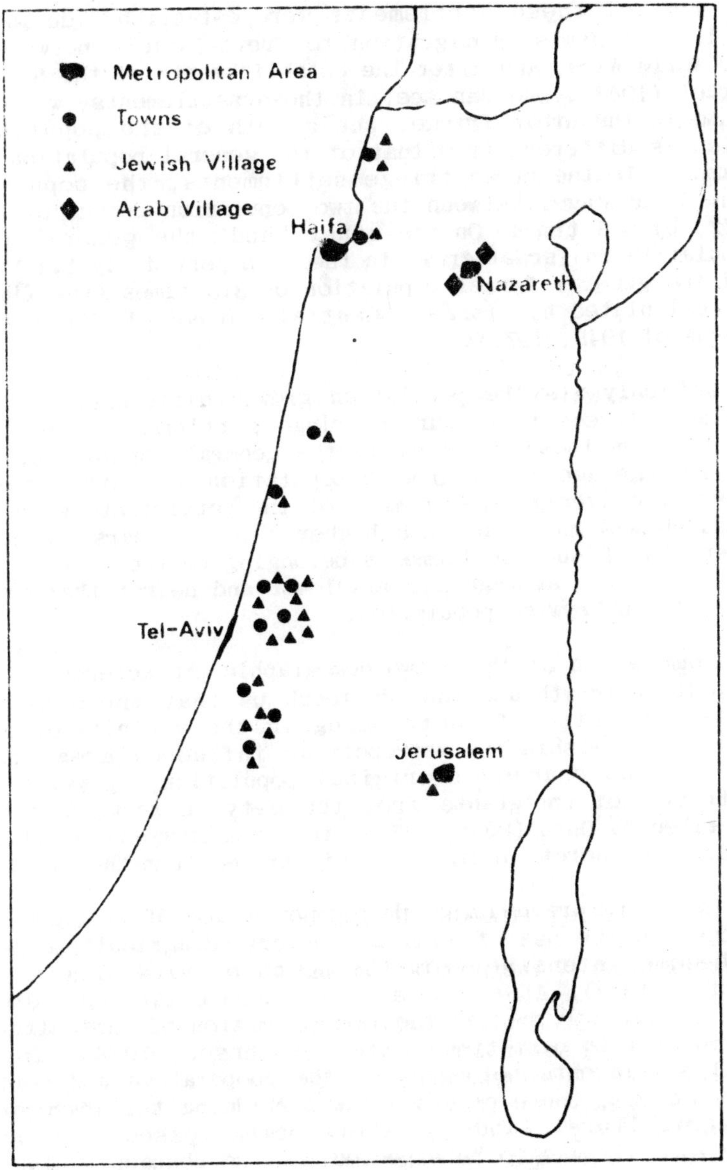

FIG.3.1 The distribution of villages in the urban fringe.

Most of these settlements were established during the periods of Jewish immigration to Eretz-Israel, between the two World Wars, and after the establishments of the State of Israel (1948). One can see, in these settlements, which are found in the urban fringe, the growth of the population, which is different from that of the general population. For example: In the urban fringe settlements, the population grew in average, between the two population census of 1948-1972, by 0.3 times. On the other hand, the general rural population in Israel grew, in the same period, by 1.4 times, and the general Israel population by 3.0 times (the figures are calculated by: Israel, Central Bureau of Statistics-Census of 1948, 1972).

Not only was the population growth different, but also the age classes in the urban fringe settlements were different from those existing in the general population, when the average age of the Jewish population in Israel was 25 years, the average age in most of the settlements where the research was made was much higher : 35-54 years, with the exception of such settlements belonging to the kibbutz sector, where the average age was lower and nearer that of the general countrywise population.

Examination of these two demographic characteristics_the periodical growth and the age teach us that these settlements, in spite of their being in the vicinity of large cities, and within the metropolitan influence area, there has been no change of original population, by way of infiltration of immigrants from the city, a process nicely described by Dunn (Dunn, 1976), in the metropolitan villages in Britain whereto immigrants infiltrated from the city.

In literature dealing with urbanization of villages, the changes in the use of land are described_agriculture turns to become intensive from the point of view of area unit (Munton, 1974). At the same time, there exists an abandonment of agriculture and the transformation of agriculturers (farmers) into part-time farmers (Johnson, 1974). In the rural settlements belonging to the cooperative and collective sectors, there exists a law forbidding the abandonment of agricultural lands or their being leased to others. Therefore, it was to be expected that no changes would have taken place in the agricultural occupations or in the uses of the land. However, the contrary has happened. The kibbutzim in Israel (collective settlements) have undergone a strong industrialization process (Bar-Gal, 1976), whereas in the Moshavim (cooperative settlements) in Israel, about 45 per cent of their total members found their means of living outside agriculture (farming) or as part-time farmers (The Agricultural Census 1971, p.34). Similar processes took place in the urban fringe settlements—increase of non-agricultural labour in the rural settlement. As a classical example, one can see the Kfar Bialik settlement (in the north of Israel, a suburb of Haifa). When it was established in 1934, 6 per cent of its total inhabitants were not farmers (doctors, teachers, accountants), whereas today, two-thirds of the total families in the settlement derive their main income not from agriculture. Therefore, the situation of occupational labour in the urban fringe Jewish settlements is not different from that of the general rural settlement in Israel. On the other hand, there is an outstanding difference in the standard of services existing in these settlements. In the Moshavim and the private villages, there is practically no development in the internal services and these are supplied by the nearest neighbouring city. Whereas the Kibbutz..., the collective sub-sector is inclined to develop an independent system of services in the settlement in spite of the nearness of the city.

The uses of non-agricultural lands, in a limited size, such as industry and commerce, have started to appear in the urban fringe villages, but this appearance is still in its embryo. The infiltration of urban functions into the rural areas is limited by the internal laws of the settlements as well as by the restriction existing in Israel regarding the transforming of agricultural land into urban land.

In conclusion it can be stressed that the Jewish settlements in the urban fringe keep their rural scenery, but their population, which is the original rural population, is inclined to find work outside agriculture (see Fig. 3.2).

The Urbanization Process as Compared to the Cultural Pluralism in the Jewish Settlement

In the urbanization process accepted the world over, the rural settlements are transformed into urban settlements when these are found in the metropolitan fringe. In the study carried out by Gavish (Gavish, 1976) in the metropolitan fringe of Tel-Aviv, he discerned a differential process of village urbanization. Villages which were defined as private settlements were those mainly affected by the urbanization process, and turned into cities. On the other hand, villages belonging to the cooperative or collective sectors were but little influenced by the urbanization process and kept their rural character. (For discussion on this subject - see Wientraub et al., 1969). The Kibbutzim and the Moshavim are forms of villages where a strong ideological influence exists on all phases of life. These settlements have an internal law which restricts the possibilities of the individual and at the same time assists and protects him. The plots of land and the farm's units do not belong to the individual—and he is not free in his decisions towards his agricultural farm.

Furthermore, strong countrywide organizations exist in the Kibbutzim and the Moshavim, which supply them with manpower and financial means. These organizations assist in complementing young populations to the settlements—a feature which explains the presence of young populations in the Kibbutzim which are found in the urban fringe, as compared to the grown-up populations in the private villages.

There exists a strong influence in the political network in the countrywide organizations of the Moshavim and the Kibbutzim, a thing which enabled them to increase the quantity of lands and other means of production (water and finance), in their settlements (Eisenstandt, 1973). Therefore, the Kibbutzim and the Moshavim in the urban fringe were in a position to continue and exist as independent, economic units. As compared to the private villages which were obliged to accept the idea of earning their living in the cities, because of lack of sufficient production means.

This analysis leads to the conclusion that the social-ideological pluralism in the rural Jewish community represents a central factor in its standing before the urbanization factor. The more the cooperation and its organizational involvement, the more the villages are strong to stand against the process of demographic degeneration and keep their rural character. The cultural factor appears against space factors: such as distance from the city or its place in the urban-scale of Israel. This conclusion shows the difference existing between the Jewish villages and the villages in other parts of the world, where the space-urban factor is the important one, as it transpires from the work of Dunn (Dunn 1976).

ARAB VILLAGES IN THE URBAN FRINGE

Most of the Arab villages in Israel (in the frontiers of 1967) are centred in the north. Out of about hundred Arab settlements, only three are situated in the urban fringe

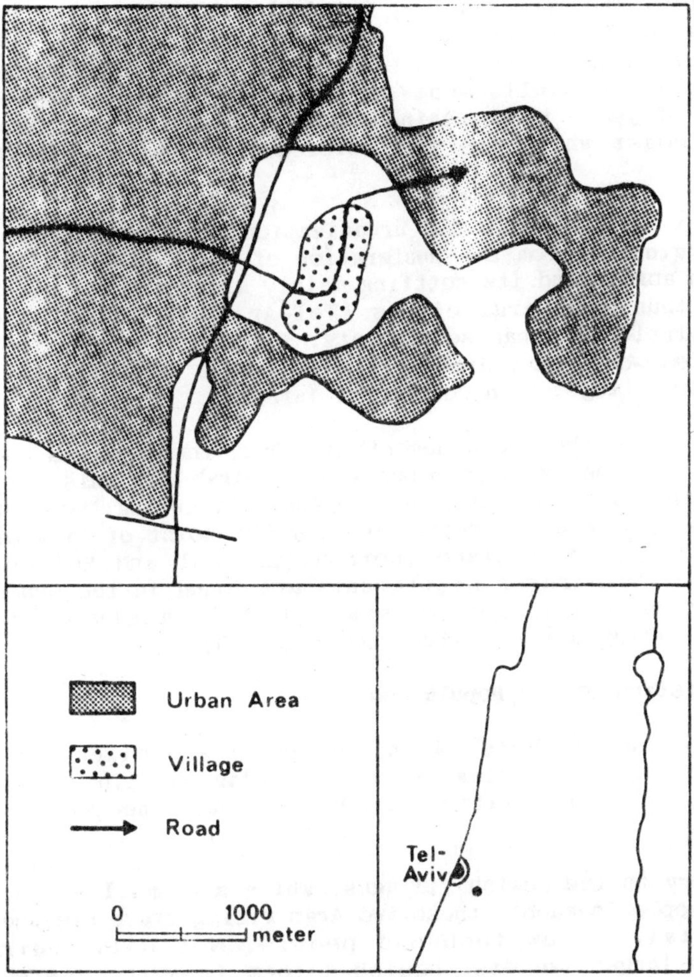

FIG.3.2 Jewish village (Moshav) under "urban seige".

close to urban settlements, and are defined as independent settlements. The appearance of few Arab villages in the urban fringe can be explained by two main factors_both of them historical factors: the first factor is connected with the settling and establishment of these settlements before hundreds of years in mountainous areas, being far-off from the sea coast which was then covered with swamps (Karmon, 1973).

The second factor is the urbanization process in Israel which originated from the immigration of the Jewish population from abroad and its settling mainly along the sea coast creating thus two large cities (Tel-Aviv and Haifa) and other additional urban settlements. Therefore, a situation was created where many Arab settlements were geographically far from the large urban centres of Israel.

In spite of the facts described above, there exists one city in Israel whose main population is Arab and this city is Nazareth. Nazareth has grown considerably during the last generation and became a metropole from the point of view of the process that took place therein (Bar-Gal and Soffer, 1981). Two Arab rural settlements are found in the urban fringe of Nazareth, and we shall try to analyze the processes taking place in them (see Fig. 3.3).

Characteristics of the Population

The two settlements YAF'A and RENAH are mixed Arab settlements from the point of view of religion, i.e., two-thirds of their population are Moslems and one-third is Christian.

Contrary to the Jewish villages, which are small (a few hundred people in each), these two Arab villages are big and each contain a few thousand people. Not only their definitely large size distinguishes them from the Jewish villages, but mainly the rate of population growth - as per details of the Population Census of 1948-1971, these settlements have grown 5.0 times and more. This growth derives mainly from the high birth rate in the Arab population of Israel, which is among the highest in the world_ about 4.0 per cent per annum! (Israel, Yearly Statistics 1979). Since this population is not inclined to migrate to urban centres, they cause a rapid growth of the villages. The population growth in these two villages brought about an increase in the pressure exercised on agricultural lands. The growing population in these settlements, which are situated in mountainous areas poor in fertile agricultural lands, started to look for sources of livelihood, not specially agricultural. The available manpower of these villages met the demands of manpower of the urban centres, mainly in the industrial areas of Haifa, 40 kms away from the Nazareth area. So, the commuter movement developed, a thing which brought about the restriction of agricultural labour in the villages. From a field study conducted in 1980, it transpires that 7 per cent only are engaged in agriculture in these two Arab villages, and about another 10 per cent do part-time farming for domestic uses. In total, more than 80 per cent of the available manpower turn to non-agricultural occupations. As the income from industry and services is higher than that from agriculture, the standard of living has gone up very quickly in these two villages and they underwent a modernization process, expressed in massive construction, acquisition of cars and other goods such as electrical refrigerators, TVs, etc. These processes influenced the space alignment of the population in the villages. There existed in the past a strong social segregation on the basis of family and religion. The modernization process and the money at the disposal of the village settlers assisted in reducing this segregation and in increasing the social mixing inside the village. This brought about significant changes in the physical formation of the settlement.

Urbanization Process and Changes in the Scenery of the Arab villages

Contrary to the Jewish villages, the ownership of the land in the Arab villages is private and no internal legal network exists as in the Jewish cooperatives. In other words, private enterprise and a free market allow for a "display" of the metropolitan forces in the Arab villages in the urban fringe. This theory has been examined both in Yafia and in Reine villages, and it shows that both these villages have been transformed into urban suburbs, as regards physical scenery as well as in the sense of mental urbanism.

The physical transformation in these villages took place as from the mid-fifties and especially during the sixties and seventies. These settlements which were set out as a dense nucleus were transformed into open settlements. Building expanded in all directions and mainly along the axis of the main road connecting the villages with the city of Nazareth. The road was a central factor not only in its influence on the building alignment but also in the character

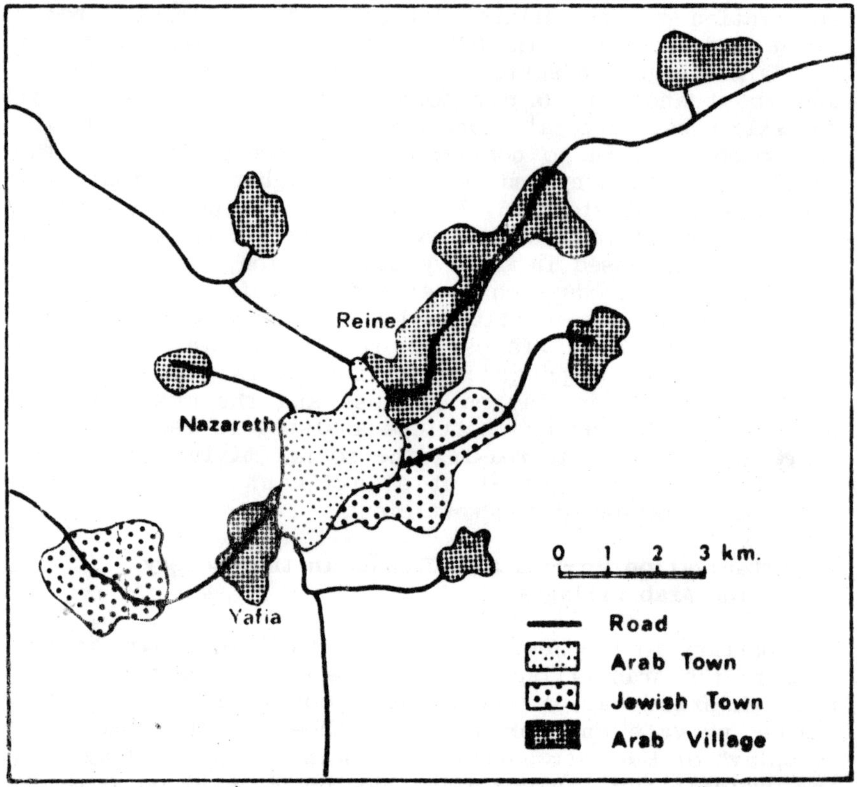

FIG.3.3 Nazareth conurbation and surrounding area.

the land was used. The population of the villages understood the importance of their emplacement and built houses of two-three storeys, destining the lower floor for business purposes, such as shops, garages, various workshops, etc. Expansion of the villages in the built-up area brought about the physical meeting with the urban area of Nazareth which had expanded towards various similar directions and the result was creation of a suburbs alignment which included these two villages.

The difficulties experienced in connection with housing and the price of dwellings in the city of Nazareth, about ten years ago, brought about a new feature in the Arab villages—migration of the city population and its settling in these villages. This fact would not have occurred if no mental changes had taken place in the two villages. These mental changes were not only modernization of the community but also a change in the attitude of the village settlers towards their settlement.

About three—fourths of the total village settlers see in their village an urban settlement and not a rural settlement. This attitude is that of the young population and the middle aged one. However, the older population, those over 50 years of age, tend still to see in the settlement, a village. A similar disruption caused questions connected with the readiness of absorbing foreigners in the village in general, and near the house of the interviewed one in particular. This preparedness to absorb foreigners as settlers in the village is part of the general inclination of the settlers to introduce innovations to the villages. These innovations—in the fields of building style, dress style, ways of life, etc.— were brought about to the villages by the commuters who found their livelihood in the Jewish urban areas.

During the last generation, Yafia and Reine were transformed into urban quarters inside the Nazareth suburbs area. This characteristic is especially outstanding as regards YAF'A but is also strongly felt in the second village, which will become very shortly an integral part of the city of Nazareth.

CONCLUSION

In this work, the processes taking place in the urban fringe villages in Israel have been studied. As said, there exists a cultural pluralism in Israel between the Arab and the Jewish communities.

It was assumed that this pluralism will influence the size of urbanization of the villages in the urban fringe. This, under the general assumption that urban pressure may transform village settlements into urban settlements.

The findings teach us that the Arab villages will be those where the strong influence of the urbanization processes exists. They are apt to become within the period of one generation, a part of the metropolitan alignment, whereas the Jewish villages, due to their cooperative character, do not allow urbanization to penetrate them, and thus leaves them untouched in their scenery as rural settlements. Only such Jewish settlements where the land is private tend to change into urban areas. Their urbanization occurred already in the fifties, and only in rare cases, private Jewish villages turned into urban settlements during the sixties and seventies. The cultural-ideological factor is a barrier in the space urbanization process in Israel.

REFERENCES

Bar-Gal, Y. and Soffer, A., (1981), **Geographical Changes in the Traditional Arab Villages in North Israel,** Centre for Middle Eastern and Islamic Studies, University of Durham.

Bar-Gal, Y., (1976), "Diffusion of Industry among Collective villages in Israel," in F.E.I. Hamilton (ed.), **The Organization of Spatial Industrial System,** I.G.U. Novosibirsk, pp. 195-197.

Berler, A., (1973), "Communication and its impact on cultural urbanization," **City and Region,** Vol. I., pp. 35-48. (Hebrew)

Clout, H.D., (1972), **Rural Geography,** Pergamon Press, London.

Dunn, M.C., (1976), "Population change and the settlement pattern," in G.E. Charry (ed.), **Rural Planning Problems,** Barnes and Noble, New York, pp. 13-40.

Efrat, E., (1976), **Towns and Urbanization in Israel,** Achiasf, Tel-Aviv. (Hebrew).

Eisenstandt, S.N., (1973), **Israeli Society, Background, Development, Problems,** the Magness Press, the Hebrew University, Jerusalem. (Hebrew)

Gavish, D., (1976), "Changes in rural land-use on the urban fringe of Tel-Aviv," in D.H.K. Amiran and Y.Ben-Arieh (eds.), **Geography in Israel,** the Israeli National Committee, Jerusalem, pp. 218-238.

Gonen, A., (1976), "The Suburban mosaic in Israel" in D.H.K. Amiran and Y. Ben-Arieh (eds.), **Geography in Israel,** the Israeli National Committee, Jerusalem, pp. 163-180.

Israel, Central Bureau of Statistics, (1972), **Census of Population and Housing-1972, Demographic Characteristics of the Population**, Part III, Jerusalem.

Johnson, J.H. (ed.), (1974), **Suburban Growth, Geographical Processes of the Edge of Western City,** John Wiley, New York.

Karmon, Y., (1978), **Israel - A Regional Geography,** John Wiley, Chichester.

Lassey, W.R., (1977), **Planning in Rural Environment,** McGraw-Hill, New York.

Masser, F.I. and D.C. Strand (1965), "The Metropolitan Village," **Town Planning Review,** Vol. 36, pp. 111-124.

Munton, R.J.C., (1971), "Farming on the urban fringe," in J.H. Johnson (ed.), **Suburban Growth,** John Wiley, New York, p. 201.

Pahl, R.E., (1970), **Urbs in Rure, The Metropolitan Fringe in Hertfordshire,** London.

Weintraub, E. et al., (1970), **Moshava, Kibbutz, Moshav,** Cornell University Press, Ithaca.

FOUR

Pierre S. Guertin

The Future of the Urban System

Compared Situation Between the Centre and the Suburbs of Quebec City

INTRODUCTION

Because of the interdependance between the elements which make up the city, it is difficult in practice to isolate any one of these elements in order to analyze and evaluate its behaviour or evolution. This is particularly true in the case of studies dealing with the future and such studies cannot be realized without referring to the whole urban system. If one accepts the preceding remark, it appears necessary to study the present problematique over the redevelopment and revitalization of the central city area in close relation to the situation of the peripheral districts and suburbs, since they also form an integral part of the larger system. After referring briefly to the three basic sub-systems of which the city is constituted, we will describe the three integrated phases of the urbanization cycle in order to make explicit the framework of analysis which will be used to study the present situation of the central and suburban areas in terms of their redevelopment. This description and analysis will allow us, in the final stage of our study, to better comprehend the nature of the dynamic relations which exist between the central area and the suburbs and to bring out the prospects for improving the quality of living in both areas.

Special reference will be made to the metropolitan area of Quebec City where one observes an apparent tendency towards the concentration of redevelopment projects involving the construction of new facilities and amenities in the central area.

REFERENCE MODEL: THE URBAN SUB-SYSTEMS

If one admits that a system represents no more than a particular way of perceiving or conceiving the world, it follows as a starting-point that a city could be considered as a system composed of three integrated constituents, each of which having its own dynamism, inasmuch as each supposedly represents one vital aspect of the "balanced" functioning of the whole urban system. These three integrated constituents are infrastructures, superstructures and inhabitation.[1]

Infrastructures

The infrastructural sub-system consists of two kinds of urban facilities accompanied by the appropriate supporting elements. It includes first of all industrial illustrations of all types designed for the production of perishable or non-perishable goods. This sub-system also encompasses all facilities, services and right-of-ways required for the transportation of people, material resources and energy. These facilities supply industry and insure the marketing of its products.

In general, an infrastructure has the effect of rendering the area it occupies subservient to itself and of controlling the resources which it transforms. At the same time, this sub-system draws inhabitants and their dwellings towards itself due to an attraction which originates in the population's desire for survival or for prosperity. In this respect, transportation facilities and networks afford access to surrounding regions and the resources they contain, while industry most often causes the sedentarization of the population. Similarly both the creation of transportation links and the implantation of industries encourage the concentration of the population proportionally to the size of the resulting networks and facilities. Both are therefore important factors in the process of urbanization.

Thus, the dynamism of the infrastructures, originating from a quest to control space, resources and resource transformation and distribution, is characterized mainly by a growth or expansion process which organizes the environment to an initial degree and thereby polarizes inhabitant and inhabitation.

Superstructures

Superstructures control in a more subtle way than the urban environment from which they appear to stem. Superstructures comprise two types of services, each of which corresponds to facilities installed in the environment in the form of buildings or in the form of surface developments. Thus, this urban sub-system includes first of all facilities required for commercial exchange as well as for other associated types of exchange of goods and services: banking, brokerage, personal care, maintenance... Analogously, superstructures are also represented by management and public service facilities generally managed and dispensed by the various levels of government and the so-called social institutions. Note that the latter generally take the form of a traditional prolongation of housing: education, hospitalization, recreational activities...

In contrast to infrastructures, superstructures - almost by definition - emerge in an endogenic manner from the city and even spring up inside the pre-existing urban fabric itself. Since they most often lack sufficient space in the urban area into which they could settle in order to "serve" the population which they, at least partially, supplant, superstructures paradoxically "displace" certain constituents of the inhabited milieu: the urban area is divested of its dwellings, while its inhabitants are "displaced" or even deported to the outer parts of the urban region.

In this way, superstructures gradually but relentlessly, and often radically, modify built-up areas. Hence, unlike infrastructures, superstructures have a depolarizing effect on inhabitation, the constituents of which are later to be found, scattered and disorganized, on the outskirts of the city. There exists thus an insoluble paradox: the inhabited milieu is partially displaced in order to be better served, superseded in order to complement its activities, pushed out to the outskirts in order to revamp the central urban area. Superstructures are without a doubt motivated by a force directed towards the control of man and his activities.

In summary, then, superstructures, transforming as they do an already structured environment, are strictly speaking, a cause of development in a city, unlike infrastructures which represent the very source of city growth.

Inhabitation

Inhabitation is the third urban sub-system and is composed of inhabitants, their dwellings and the immediate extension in the urban zone of the activities generated by the combination inhabitant-inhabitation. Inhabitation almost by definition, constitutes the very foundation of a city and thus represents its raison d'etre insofar as the latter would be inconceivable without inhabitants. The latter constitute the localization points for, and play a predominant role in, infrastructures implantation in the contemporary urban context, if only insofar as production and, more particularly, consumer activities are concerned. Furthermore, history shows that inhabitation is associated with the city temporal continuity even in the absence of adequate goods and services. One could even say that inhabitation insures urban continuity and the continued presence of infrastructures and superstructures.

This ability to persist in time gives inhabitation an inertia which both encourages the development of a community (unified from the point of view of social and spatial forms) and restrains the forces of radical transformation coming either from within itself or from the outside. This can be seen in the survival of a great number of old or historical areas which modern society, with its recently-formed concept of symbolic value, is now bringing to public attention. Thus the inhabitation sub-systems tends to resist metamorphosis: it is, from this point of view, characterized by the slowness of its evolution.

Needless to say, inhabitation cannot exist without the presence and support of the two types of structure identified and defined above, and even in areas of spontaneous habitat such as shanty-towns, informal infrastructures and superstructures grow up and often operate very efficiently, in spite of the absence of easily identifiable concrete forms. In practice, therefore, inhabitation remains difficult to dissociate from structures. The two are inextricably linked together in an urban area - be it a highly "structured" city or a "looser" or more "spontaneous" type of agglomeration.

Some of the systemic characteristics of the three constituents described above deserve mention. A first characteristic of urban infrastructures and superstructures is that they produce, exchange and manage a group of goods and services consumed by the inhabited milieu, which in return provides for the correct functioning of the two types of structures. By virtue of this characteristic, inhabitation situates itself at the centre of a system in which it plays the role of both producer and consumer: it thus both sustains the forces surrounding it and derives sustenance from them, if only in order to insure its own survival. Lastly, the dynamic relations which are instituted between inhabitation, on the one hand, and infrastructures and superstructures, on the other, correspond to a balance between competition and cooperation which is often freely agreed to by both parties, in a way which reminds one of the behaviour of species and individuals within living systems regulated by the laws of natural ecology. In fact, this parallel is not a mere analogy with natural ecosystems, but a characteristic common to all living systems.

PHASES OF A CYCLICAL URBANIZATION MOVEMENT

Reposing as it does on the forces which motivate each of the three sub-systems identified above, urbanization evolves in a cycle which is punctuated by successive phases. Thus, the three sub-systems come into contact and link up with one another in different ways in time and space so as to produce three phases of variable duration within the relatively discontinuous but predictable movement of the cycle. It should be noted that the temporal dimension of each of these phases and the extent of their influence on the urban landscape are closely linked to contingent events which are most of the time exogenic with respect to the urban system itself, the latter being considered closed for the purpose of the present analysis.

A first phase which polarizes inhabitation

The first phase of urbanization is characterized by the polarization of inhabitation. If one were to analyse the 20th century period of the North American urban system, the end of the "first" phase of this period could be situated around 1930 when the urban system showed a relative "balance" between its three basic components - infrastructures, superstructures and inhabitation. This applies not only to North American cities but also particularly well to those of the province of Quebec.[2] Needless to say, on the world scene several complete cycles preceded this "first" phase and the choice of the 20th century is simply a convenient starting-point in the continuous cyclical movement. From this first point of view, this first phase of urbanization resulted in the present urban network which has structured and polarized most regions. At the end of the above expansion movement, city space took on a spatial and functional organization which was to have a determining effect on the future. Thus, by around 1930, the basic quebecois cities existed already, cities of the type which is now designated by the terms "traditional city" or "historical city". In the case of Quebec City, the relevant urbanized territory is situated more or less to the east of Salaberry Avenue and Langelier Boulevard and extends down to the St. Charles River, as shown on Fig. 4.1 on the following page.[3]

How exactly did this basic structure become implanted? Starting with infrastructures, large production and transportation facilities moved in along and prolonged the lines of force of the urban region or of the existing small town. The construction of bridges, harbours, train-stations and industries was complemented by the appearance of industrial centres, and even of new cities based primarily on resources. As for superstructures, their role was to consolidate the emerging central area, already in its inception phase, by moving in and creating favourable conditions for its densification and growth, while at the same time attracting part of the population out towards the circumference (the growing worker's neighbourhoods). Thus the district of the banks, of the city hall and of the business which are now situated in the city centre were already implanted by the end of the 1930s.

As they progressed in space, both infrastructures and, to a lesser extent, the superstructures acted like magnets, attracting inhabitation which moved closer to them for reasons of employment and proximity. For analogous reasons, to which tradition should perhaps be added, inhabitants have settled in dense and continuous areas forming characterized districts which tended to become more and more specialized: the harbour area, the area around the train station, the business and warehouse districts, and the industrial zone (often containing only one or two plants). The populations of such districts were not very mobile, being restricted in their choice of jobs, place of work, housing and means of travel. As a consequence of the processes described above, this first relatively balanced phase of Quebec and Canadian urbanization, while having a polarizing effect on inhabitation, did encourage the development of a form of community life well anchored in space, with the neighbourhood or district forming a small community into itself.

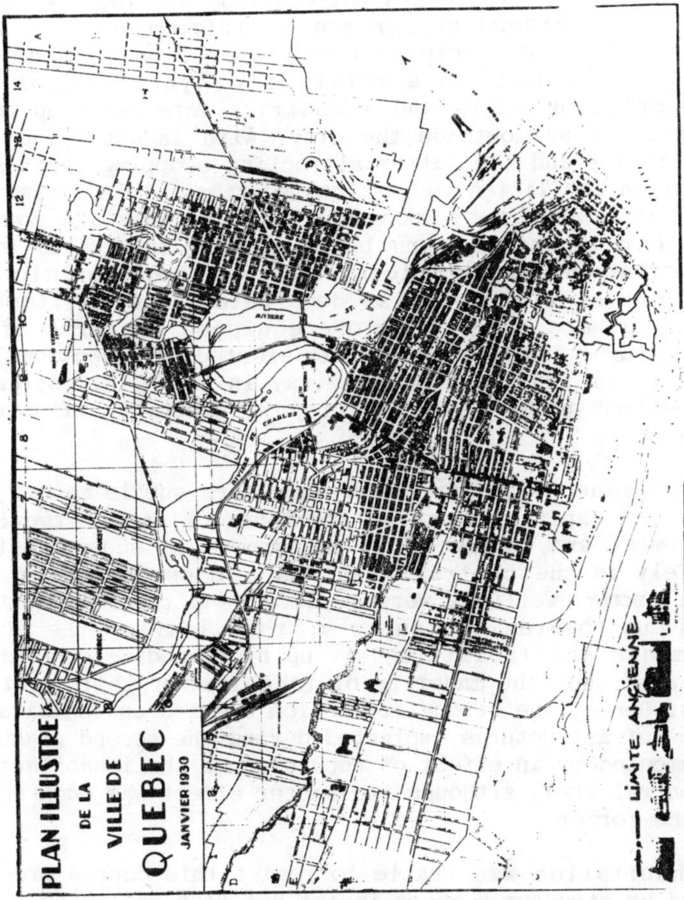

Fig. 4.1 PLAN OF QUEBEC CITY IN 1930. CITY BLOCKS AS THEY APPEAR IN THE NORTH AND NORTH-WEST WERE NOT BUILT UPON AT THAT TIME.
SOURCE: QUEBEC CITY ARCHIEVES.

A second phase of dissemination

The second phase of urbanization is characterized by the dissemination of inhabitation. This phase, which corresponds approximately to the period between 1930 and 1973, witnessed a rapid and disorderly growth of infrastructures which resulted in vast peripheral and inter-city zones becoming urbanizable. Thus, in a relatively synchronized way, transportation links and industries were built up on the outskirts of and outside the city, with industries calling for highways and the latter attracting shopping centres and production facilities to its intersections. This disseminating action caused many secondary poles of work and commerce to appear, these in turn being solidly integrated into a transportation and communication network open to individual use. This spatial dynamism demarcated vast territories - vast containers which were overequipped in terms of infrastructures and because of this exerted an exceptional attraction on inhabitation. The way in which this spreading process took place in Quebec City is partially illustrated on Fig. 4.2.

Simultaneously, but in a much more subtle manner, the effects of Capital (commerce and finance) and of the State (management and services) on the growth of superstructures were felt in the central area. As a consequence of this growth, some dwellings were replaced and their inhabitants pushed out towards the suburbs, thus leaving the social equipments and facilities set up by preceding generations under-used; but the majority of inhabitants left by themselves. Hence, the strong attraction exerted on inhabitation by the infrastructures implanted during the second phase was complemented by an effect of repulsion on the inhabitants of the central area, although the latter effect was much weaker than the former.

Inhabitation was unable to resist this double pressure exerted by structures whose impact has been reflected in the urban landscape. Thus the architectural formations already present in the central area underwent a partial disintegration, while individual dwellings were scattered throughout the territory surrounding the city. This scattering took the form of a veritable multidirectional dissemination which even left its mark on the landscape situated beyond the infrastructures which had initially acted on it as a pole of attraction. The low settlement density which resulted from this spreading out was accompanied by considerable architectural uniformity, due mainly to the utilization of a single

FIG.4.2 PLAN OF QUEBEC CITY AROUND 1975. ALL CITY BLOCKS AS THEY APPEAR WERE THEN BUILT UPON.
SOURCE: QUEBEC CITY PLANNING SERVICE.

type of technology, in contrast to the diversified character of housing in the preceding period. It should be mentioned, lastly, that by the end of the second phase of urbanization, new residential areas and the infrastructures which had defined and demarcated them had fallen into a state of considerable under-utilization. These areas were conceived and utilized rather as tools for territorial planning than as basis for organizing city life, since they grew up in a context of great physical mobility in space and great job mobility. For this reason, community life resulting from the dissemination of dwellings throughout the area surrounding the city was itself spread thin, diluted and very often dissociated from the place of residence.

A third phase of consolidation

The third phase of urbanization is characterized by a consolidation of inhabitation within the delimitated urban space. It began around 1970, moved into full force by 1973, and has continued ever since. It coincided with the present economic crisis. This period has witnessed a sharp decline, followed by an almost complete cessation, of the implantation of new production and transportation structures. The discounting of construction programs for buildings and highways, the drop in industrial production and the closure of many factories illustrate clearly the present stagnation of infrastructure growth and the declining use of existing infrastructures. Conversely, the city centre is presently enjoying a sharp increase in the development of superstructures for commerce and exchange as well as for management and services. This can be seen not only from the city's plans to make central city services and facilities into profit-making enterprises but also from the creation of new building programs to develop vacant areas or lots situated within that part of the basic city zone which as been assimilated to the centre of the city.

How does inhabitation behave and evolve in the face of this new spatio-economic situation on which it is necessarily itself dependent? As far as can be seen, the city is presently witnessing a new form of polarization, directly encouraged by financial incentives from public authorities; a case in point is the sale at a reduced price of certain central area lots by the Quebec City municipal council for residential or other purposes. This polarization first began in the area immediately surrounding the facilities and services of the city centre. In all probability it will continue in the business and service centres situated within the urban agglomeration, as well as in secondary centres of employment, as occurred during the first phase of industrial development. The reasons behind this centripetal movement are not exclusively ones of convenience and proximity: the constraints of the economic situation and the uncertainty of the future leads people to want to be close to neighbours, to be within easy reach of facilities which are extensions of the basic home activities, and to situate themselves with respect to a square, a public space or a community centre. Other factors have reinforced the tendancy described above, as is the case for the recent reduction in mobility: restrictions on the choice of jobs, housing, places to shop, means of transportation, as well as restrictions on the number of trips within and outside the city. All this is the consequence of an unemployment rate which affects almost one out of every eight workers (June 1982) and of automobile operating costs which have gone up roughly 20% in the last year (May 1982).

Insofar as the impact on city landscape of the recent polarization is concerned, the "filling up" of vacant lots in the central part of Quebec City seems to point to a new tendancy towards densification which will probably produce a city which is more continuous on the horizontal plane and even perhaps more well-proportioned when looked at in cross-section. The conditions summarized above thus favour a consolidation of the urban fabric and constitute, furthermore, an integral part of the process, as is the case for all living systems. Moreover, these conditions foster the consolidation and development of a localized community life-style, in contrast to a "metropolitan" one, as was the case in the second phase of urbanization which was characterized by the dissemination of inhabitation throughout the urban region.

PRESENT SITUATION OF THE CONSTITUENTS OF THE URBAN SYSTEM

In the preceding sections were described, albeit succinctly, the nature and content of each of the three main phases of the urban cycle of Canadian and Quebec cities, as well as the effects on the organization of urban space and life which infrastructures and superstructures produce as they act upon inhabitation. In the sections which follow will be done a critical analysis of the spatial constituents of the contemporary city in the way they tend to react to the present tendencies of urban development. It will be concluded from this analysis that Quebec City today has beyond all doubt embarked upon the third phase of urbanization.

The situation of the central area

In the present context, given the very nature of urban infrastructures, the central area is relatively well-equipped with basic infrastructures. Its water, sewage and power systems were rationalized quite recently and were even completely replaced in some sectors during the second phase of urbanization, which required the installation of extensions connected to existing networks in order to insure the growth of the suburbs. The construction of transportation and communication facilities has increased the central area s capacity and efficiency, particularly since these facilities have been tied in to the new networks in the suburbs. The case of Quebec City comes to mind, with its comparatively over-developed urban highway network with respect to the other cities of the province.

But what is most striking is not so much the presence of new infrastructures in the central area (this presence being often difficult to perceive) as the level and speed at which superstructures are developing, regardless of whether they result from private or state investment. Thus, after a period of regression corresponding to the exceptional growth of the suburb, investment in the downtown area has been on the upswing since the mid-1960's and has taken almost phenomenal proportions in the last ten years. This development has been caused mainly by the growth of the civil service and of large State institutions which manage resources and human activities. Another factor has been the transformation and expansion of the banking, administration and commerce institutions situated in the central area.

A look at the redevelopment projects and new buildings in the centre of Quebec City gives an idea not only of how the past decade has brought about a "renewal" of the central part of the city but also of the rapidity with which superstructural facilities have been built in this area and the resulting concentration of such facilities in the city centre. Fig. 4.3 shows, firstly, Parliament Hill, a vast area which was almost completely demolished, rebuilt and "enriched" with the Grand Theatre]1[, the "G" Block]2[and the "H" Block]3[, to which a group of three major hotels was recently added]4[, the second building of the Laurentian Insurance Company]5[, the St-Amable Condominium]6[, the apartments installed in the former Good Shepherd Monastery]7[and the senior citizen's dwellings installed in the

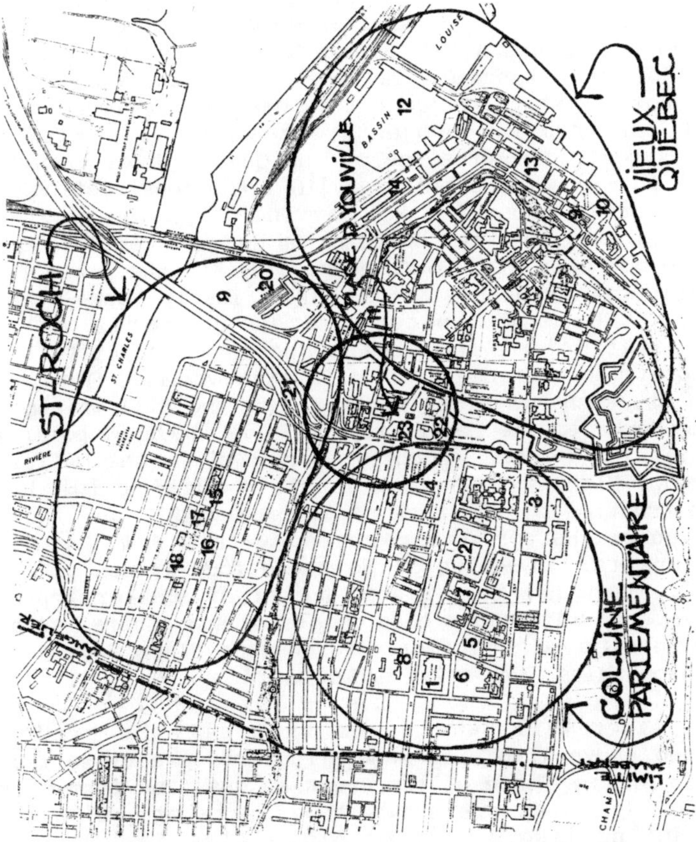

FIG.4.3 PLAN OF QUEBEC CITY IN 1980 ILLUSTRATING ITS FOUR CENTRAL AREAS (PARLIAMENT HILL, OLD QUEBEC, ST-ROCH AND D'YOUVILLE SQUARE) AND THEIR RECENTLY REALIZED AND PLANNED PROJECTS.
DRAWING BY: ROGER CHOUINARD.

Jeffrey Hale Hospital]8[. Next, one finds Old Quebec where Place Royale]9[has recently been restored, along with the Royal Battery]10[, the Arsenal Block]11[and the Old Harbour, where a Marina]12[, a Museum of Civilization]13[, and a block of luxury dwellings]14[will be constructed shortly. Besides all of this, there is a large area of the city which is undergoing major transformations: it is called St. Roch Neighbourhood, an area whose very name only fifteen years ago evoked unsanitory living conditions, physical and social deterioration and falling real estate values. This area is now beginning to project an ever better image due to several construction projects: the Mall]15[with its covered street, the presence of the Quebec Urban Community (Q.U.C.) in a renovated building]16[, the construction of a new building to house the Holiday Inn]17[, the moving of the City Library to a new building on Jacques Cartier Square]18[, the now completed Court-house]19[and the plans for a new intermodal transit station]20[. Finally there remains probably the most strategic area in terms of the "rehabilitation" of the central part of the city. It is situated at the meeting-point of Parliament Hill, Old Quebec and the St. Roch District, halfway down the hill which runs from the Upper to the Lower City. This is the area polarized by d'Youville Square recently "serviced" by the Dufferin-Montmorency Highway]21[the d'Youville parking lot]22[, the construction of the Bank of Montreal]23[, and the implantation of the services required by this new tower and its occupants. In addition to these four groups of large projects, there has been a good number of smaller improvements, some of which have been completed and others, such as the conversion of a former warehouse on Place Royale into condominium units, are still under way.[4]

The reader will have noted that all the projects enumerated above involving superstructures are closely connected in space. Three of the areas in question form a triangle inside which one finds the fourth one, d'Youville Square acting like a sort of hinge with its banking, brokerage and management activities, as well as a transfer point between bus lines resulting from its central location. This spatial organization cannot be the product of mere chance. Fig.4.3 shows not only the location of the recently-installed superstructures in the central area of Quebec City but also the marked tendency of the three components of the city centre to cluster around a central core which combines financial and traffic functions.

To produce a complete picture, one must also briefly

describe the overall impact on the urban landscape of the implantation of these new superstructures in central Quebec City. In almost all cases the appearance of each new superstructure occasioned an architectural novelty with respect to the milieu, that is, a building having dimensional or technological characteristics which completely differ from those of the surrounding formal environment. In addition, most of the new buildings have adjoining parking lots which required the demolition of existing dwellings and the evacuation of the occupants. The cumulative effect of these constructions and evacuations has been to metamorphose city landscape. Metamorphic transformation applies to new radical architecture, dissociated from its spatial context, whereas morphogenic transformation refers to the creation of vacuums, through demolition, capable of receiving new architectural forms. Their cumulative effect on the horizontal plane is illustrated on Fig. 4.4 which represents the areas affected by morphogenic (demolition and the creation of vacuums) and metamorphic (radical forms) changes, respectively, within the circumference of Quebec City's Parliament Hill. A high, quasi-punctual concentration of radical architectural changes can be observed, this new architecture being composed of skyscrapers having nothing in common with the existing form system. This radical architecture is surrounded by areas where dwellings have been demolished (vacuum) in order to "free" space for the construction of parking lots for the benefit of skyscrapers. These vacuums thus constitute subversive transformations since they disrupt the established spatial order by eliminating several of its components. Moreover, one can also observe a spreading effect of radical and subversive changes from the core of this central area which will eventually bring about a complete metamorphosis of size, technology and form if it is not checked now, when it has affected only one-third of the threatened area. In conclusion, then, the effect of the construction of public or private superstructures on the city landscape is one of disruption with the past (represented by the existing milieu) and results in the creation of a new, if not more unified, urban landscape.

The most important fact to remember from the above discussion is that at the present time, central Quebec City is highly structured and consolidated in terms of facilities and services and will become more so in the near future if all the projects now on the drawing-board are carried out as planned. Moreover, the central area is unquestionably overdeveloped in terms of facilities and services as compared with the suburbs. In this respect, not only are almost all

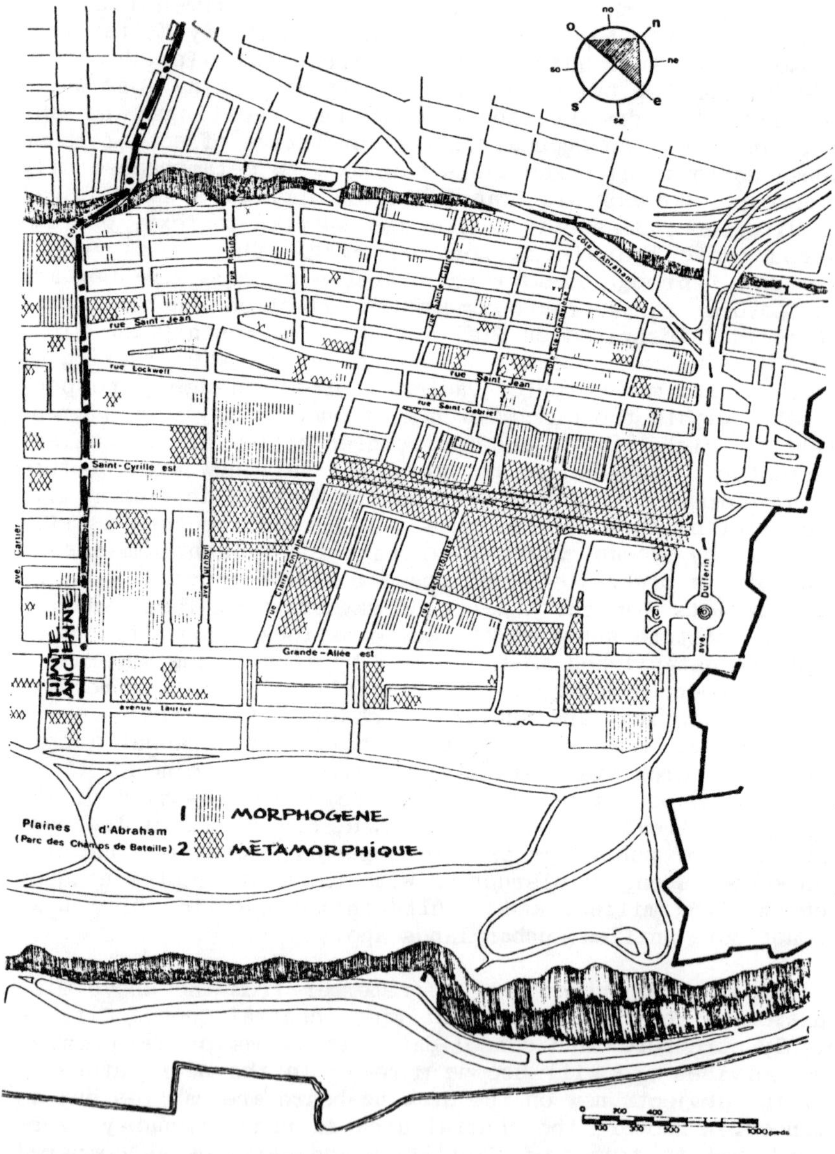

FIG.4.4 MORPHOGENIC (DEMOLITIONS) AND METAMORPHIC (LARGE SCALE) CHANGES WITH THE BOUNDARIES OF PARLIAMENT HILL.
SERVEYED BY: PIERRE S. GUERTIN. DRAWING BY: ROGER CHOUINARD.

of the large urban development projects located in the central area but, what is more important to point out, private and public investors are able to come up with financial resources to carry them out during a period when financial resources are strictly limited. In this economic context, such a concentration of investment and such a scale of expenditures for facilities and services in the central area cannot but have an adverse effect on the suburbs, assuming that the latter urgently require vital services in order to develop an urban life-style of comparable quality to that of the central part of the city.

The state of the suburbs

What is the plight of the suburbs in the present phase of urbanization, characterized as it is by a tendency towards consolidation? Recall that by around 1973, the suburbs were highly structured and well-served due to the installation of numerous infrastructures during the preceding phase. Even today the suburbs contain almost all of the industries and industrial parks. Transportation and communication networks insuring the circulation of energy, resources, goods, persons and information link these industries adequately to supply and consumer centres. But these networks are under-utilized, having often been planned according to standards which were much higher than present demand. Such is also the case of certain water and sewer facilities: pipes were put into the ground and even portions of street networks put up for dwellings that were never built. Similarly, one observes that a great many factories are presently operating at part-capacity, when they have not closed down completely. These are all cases of human and capital investments which are not contributing as much as forecast to the vitality of the suburbs and to municipal resources. On the contrary, they act often as maintenance burdens on the municipality and as fiscal ones to its inhabitants.

In spite of their being over-equipped in infrastructures, the suburbs are nonetheless under-equipped as far as management, exchange and service superstructures are concerned. And when this type of facility exists, it is often shared between more than one suburban municipality, as in the case of schools, fire-fighting equipment recreation facilities, etc. In addition, these facilities are often so far away or hard to get to for users because of distance, lack of direct access route, or inefficiency of the public transit system serving the suburbs, that people are obliged to drive them in private vehicles. The case of shopping centres comes to mind. They are at first sight the only facilities which appear to serve the suburbs satisfactorily: their number, floor space and variety in terms of merchandise have given the suburbs the image of a "consumers' paradise". But the concentration of a large number of businesses in locations chosen solely for their proximity to the intersections of main traffic arteries leaves them vulnerable to the danger of becoming increasingly inaccessible if the cost of individual transportation were to go up at the same rate as during the last five years.[5] In fact, over the past twelve months, several shopping centres have been partially closed or have been "barely keeping their noses above water". The simultaneous springing up of all sorts of neighbourhood shops and "corner stores" both in the city and in the suburbs is not foreign to the phenomenon evoked above.

Which suburbs have been placed at a disadvantage by the present form of urban organization and are, for the moment, prisoners of a transformed urban environment which there is little they can do to change? For the Quebec City area, the following municipalities and parts of municipalities, all members of the Quebec Urban Community (Q.U.C), are under-equipped: Saint-Augustin, Ancienne-Lorette, Val Belair, Neufchatel, Les Saules, Duberger, Loretteville, Lake St. Charles, St. Emile, Orsainville, Charlesbourg, Ste-Therese-de-Lisieux and part of Beauport (Couville, Boischatel). Fig. 4.5 shows the location of these suburbs and their position with respect to the centre the Quebec agglomeration.

One notes, first of all, that the suburban cities and the suburban parts of Quebec City are quite numerous. Together they contain about one half of the population of the metropolitan area covered by the Quebec City census. Geographically they describe a continuous, almost regular semicircle around the central part of the agglomeration. This makes one think that the phenomenon appears systematically with respect to the centre and that its form and location result from structural forces and not from chance or accident. But what strikes one above all is that most of these peripheral areas are generally considered as the poorer or more modest suburbs of the Quebec urban region.

What situation prevails in these areas as regards city facilities and services ? At the risk of simplifying things, we will point the following "robot portrait" of the typical suburb in this under-developed urban belt, insofar as super-

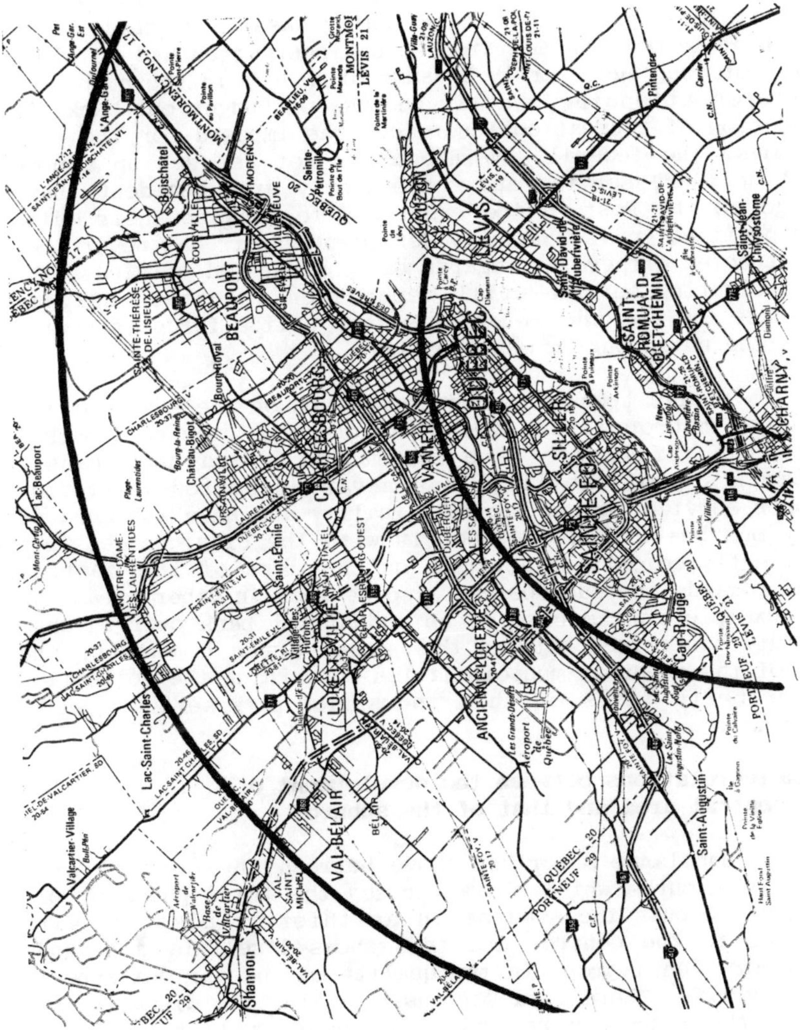

FIG.4.5 LOCATION OF THE SUBURBS WITH RESPECT TO THE CENTRAL AREA OF QUEBEC CITY.
SOURCE: MINISTRY OF TRANSPORT, QUEBEC GOVERNMENT, 1981.

structures are concerned. Firstly, the typical suburb obviously doesn't have a hospital on its territory and is still waiting for a school to be built which would put an end, at least partially, to the daily bussing of students to and from school. In addition, the kindergarten had to close down not long ago, partly because of a drop in the number of children attending, partly because of budget cut-backs. A reduction of recreational services was imposed for the same reasons. The federal Government has not yet set up a home mail delivery service and consequently area residents have to go to the Post Office every day to pick up their mail. The promised Local Community Services Center[6] has never been constructed either. As regards basic municipal services, the fire-fighting service still depends on volunteer help to operate, while the recently set up police force is shared with the neighbouring municipality.

The public transit system, conceived on the scale of the greater metropolitan area by an organism concerned mainly with the vitality of the central area and the transit network's profitability, has never attempted to provide proper service inside the municipality and have assigned it only one bus line to connect it with the city centre. This indirectly colonizing attitude on the part of the central area towards the suburbs can also be seen in other areas, as for example in the case of an industrial park over which a dispute has arisen between the Quebec Urban Community and one of the suburban municipalities concerning the collection of property taxes of this industrial park set up a short time ago.

Dynamic relations between the development of the central area and that of the suburbs

The unbalance described above between the central area and the suburbs which characterizes the third phase of urbanization puts the suburbs in an inferior position with respect to the centre, and this shows itself by a stagnation, or even a drop, in the quality of the various aspects of city life. There is a serious risk that the disparity between the city centre and the suburbs will become even wider, to the detriment of the suburbs, especially if the city elite maintains, spreads and materializes three ideas which do not bear critical examination, namely:

> that there is a movement back to the traditional style city, that is, a movement back to the central area,

- that the latter is under-equipped in terms of superstructures;
- that its present state of neglect requires a revamping operation possible only through massive injections of investments.

These positions need to be reviewed and analyzed. The concept of a move back to the central or traditional city implies a mass movement affecting a large number of people from different socio-professional classes dwelling in a wide variety of types of housing. However, this is not the case at all, and nothing justifies the optimism shown by town-concillors.[7]. From the quantitative point of view alone, the distribution of new dwellings within the Metropolitan Quebec City Census Area in 1981 indicates the relatively weak power of attraction of the central area in this respect, as can be seen from the following table 4.1:

This table shows that the number of new dwellings in the central area represents only 30% of the dwellings built in Quebec City, 10% of those built on the territory of the Q.U.C., taking into account only the North Shore suburbs, and 8% of the total of all dwellings constructed inside the metropolitan census area, which takes in all the suburbs surrounding Quebec City. The relatively small number of dwellings built in the central area becomes even more obvious when one compares the figures for the last five years, as shown in the table 4.2:

Thus, despite a sharp rise in 1979 (from 0.6 to 4.0%), the percentage of dwellings built in the city centre has shown a tendency to become stable over the past three years. Furthermore, considering the fact that the new federal and provincial budgets contain direct incentives for the building of individual houses located specifically in the suburb - reduced interest rates, direct buyer subsidies - everything suggests that the much hoped for "move back to the city" has not yet come about, nor will it do so as soon or as spectacularly as previously thought, in spite of certain favourable conditions. Moreover, the housing statistics published by the City and quoted above neither identify those "new" dwellings which result from the partitioning of existing dwellings, nor do they give the number of demolitions of existing dwellings. This information can be found in table 4.3.

Conversions, or "additional" dwellings, to use the expression one finds in the annual report of the Quebec City Building Permit Bureau, are the results of the subdivision

TABLE 4.1

Distribution of new dwellings within the Quebec City Metropolitan Census Area - 1981[8]

Administrative areas	Dwellings Number	Dwellings Percentage
Central city wards or districts	308	8.1
Remainder of Quebec City (defined according to new boundaries)	721	19.2
Sum-total of city (308 + 721)	1,029	27.4
Remainder of Quebec Urban Community (12 municipalities)	1,971	52.6
Total of Q.U.C. (13 municipalities) (1,029 + 1,971)	3,000	80.8
Outside Q.U.C.(remainder of Metropolitan Census Area)	746	19.3
Total, Metropolitan Census Area (3,000 + 746)	3,746	100.0

TABLE 4.2

Comparison between the evolution of the construction of new dwellings in the central area and in the Metropolitan Quebec City Census Area from 1977 to 1981

Administrative area / Year	Central area (Champlain, St.Roch, St.Jean-Baptiste Wards)	Quebec City Metropolitan Census Area (Urban area)	%
1977	32	8,456	0.4
1978	43	7,004	0.6
1979	209	5,186	4.0
1980	320	3,545	9.0
1981	308	3,746	8.2
Total	912	27,937	
Yearly average	182	5,587	3.3

of large dwellings into smaller units and of the conversion of schools, monasteries and convents into residential dwellings. No schools have been converted into dwellings to the east of Salaberry Street during the past five years. All that remains therefore under the heading of "conversion" is the subdivision of existing large dwellings, which adds nothing to the amount of available housing space, and the conversion of residences belonging to religious orders, which to all intents and purposes affects only the typology of the dwellings in question. For example, between 1980 and 1981 the Good Shepherd Monastery "produced" through conversion about 200 dwellings, as it was transformed into a housing cooperative.[10] It should also be pointed out that the great majority of "additional" dwellings are the product of direct government intervention and even of projects financed entirely by state funds. In the case of housing conversion, government intervention is involved in approximatively 4/5 of all projects. Consequently, the thesis of a spontaneous movement of the people towards the central area cannot be maintained.

TABLE 4.3

Housing construction, conversion and demolition in the Central area of Quebec city, from 1977 to 1981[11-12]

Dwellings Year	Construction	Conversion[13]	Total	Demolition	Balance
1977	0	32	32	29	3
1978	31	12	43	12	31
1979	119	90	209	17	192
1980	214	106	320	33	287
1981	88	220	308	52	256
Total	452	460	912	143	769
Yearly average	90	92	182	29	153
Yearly average excluding Conversions					61

The preceding table also takes into account the demolitions, which are not mentioned at all in the annual reports of the Quebec City Permanent Housing Committee.[14] The number of demolitions occurring every year in the central area reduces considerably the numerical significance of new constructions, and, consequently, their relative importance in the over-all picture of the metropolitan area. Thus, if one removes from table 4.2 the yearly figures for dwelling demolitions and conversions, the ratio of dwellings built in the central area to those built in the greater metropolitan area is sharply reduced. In the following pairs, the figure on the left represents this new percentage and the one in brackets, the original percentage from table 4.2:

0.3% (0.4%); 0.3% (0.6%); 1.9% (4.0%); 5.1% (9.0%); 0.9% (8.2%).

Thus, except in 1980, when the percentage of dwellings built in the central area was 5.1%, the latter's contribution during the last four years has been negligible, even in 1981. Thus a so-called "move back to the city" is out of the question. The yearly average of 61 new housing starts in the central area, as shown in Table 4.3, is insignificant compared to the total of 156,000 existing dwellings in the Quebec Urban Community, formed by the 13 amalgamated municipalities of the North Shore (Q.U.C., 1981), and to the 195,000 dwellings of the metropolitan census area (Quebec Bureau of Statistics 1981), which house about 576,000 inhabitants. In any case, the last vacant lots in the central area are about to be built upon and further demolitions will be necessary if any appreciable number of new dwellings is to be constructed.

One can also analyse the "move back to the city" from the qualitative point of view. In this respect, one observes that the new dwellings are intended for a category of inhabitants with special needs or on whom such needs are imposed: studios or small apartments are the rule, while three and more bedroom apartments are the exception - so much so that the new Quebec City zoning by-law contains a provision setting the minimum percentage of two and three bedroom apartments in new buildings.[15] Needless to say, what are now called "large" apartments are in a position of numerical inferiority with respect to single bedroom and one-room dwellings. This tendency is reinforced by the various "conversion" operations, which doubtless result in a higher number of dwellings but which adversely affect dwelling size and especially dwelling variety. Consequently, conversion produces "reductionism" and uniformity.

As regards the market for which these new city centre dwellings are intended, both their construction costs and rental rates indicate that they are aimed at a socially and numerically "marginal" group. Thus, a new two bedroom apartment of standard quality located in a condominium block costs around $64,000. Promoters offer interest rates of approximately 15% per annum, to which individual and collective expenses of about $2,500 must be added (property tax, electricity, heating, miscellaneous). It therefore costs $12,000 a year to reside in an apartment like this.[16] Thus, from whatever point of view one analyzes the situation, the characteristics of the move back to the city show it to be a "move" which is purely marginal.

Who then is going back to the city centre? What characterizes these new inhabitants? Part of the answer to these questions was given above when the yearly rent for new city centre apartments was analyzed. It stands to reason, furthermore, that the rent of existing apartments cannot remain indifferent to the presence of such "ambitious" neighbours: thus, during the past ten years, due to the construction of new dwellings, to numerous transactions involving older buildings and to the mass conversion of the latter into condominiums, rents have gone up considerably in the central part of the city. As a consequence, a much richer socio-professional class gradually replaced the lower income inhabitants who traditionally lived in the centre. Thus the number of new inhabitants in the central area who belong to the class of the well-off or even rich is on the increase, and everything indicates that this tendency will become more and more pronounced.

This new class of inhabitants brings with itself a certain number of things which are likely to transform the physico-spatial characteristics of the city centre. First of all, they bring private capital which is used to rehabilitate newly-occupied dwellings. The State also participates in these operations through its various subsidy programs for home purchase, renovation, heating or insulation. In addition, new inhabitants arrive at the gates of the city with a whole series of new ideas on how to build or rebuild the city and on the "contemporary" concept of city living: "town-house", "agora", "mall" and "pedestrian street" are now expressions which are no longer limited to the jargon of architects and town planners. More importantly, behind these concepts lie the desire and financial means to realize them. On the one hand, this desire to fulfill their dream of how the city should be is mainly the consequence of their recent gesture of appropriation which, in order to manifest itself calls for the complementary gesture of transforming the environment. On the other hand, the means which they have at their disposal for fulfilling this dream of a better city life-style can be situated at two levels: the new inhabitants influence the people who make the city revitalization decisions (they belong themselves to this group); in addition, they orient institutional and state capital, which they themselves also manage. These new inhabitants would obviously never have decided to move back to the city to find themselves in a ugly and depreciated environment and would never have invested in the renovation of a dwelling without being sure beforehand that other public investments would be made at the same time to consolidate and even make their assets gain in value. And this is exactly what has happened, as the above description of the many private and state projects in central Quebec City shows.

The time has come to summarize the mechanism of this phenomenon in order to better bring out its structural aspect: when the higher income socio-professional classes moved out of the downtown in order to build up the suburbs from 1945 on, investment followed them (and even preceded them) in the form of the installation of all kinds of infrastructures designed to act as a framework and basis for urbanization (right-of-ways, highways, industries). When this same class of people decided to move back to the centre from about 1973 on, investment followed them on again, and often even preceded them, in the form of superstructures which had the initial effect of creating jobs in the area and consolidating the city fabric. The role of superstructures was thus to reinforce and accelerate the rehabilitation of the city centre which was initiated by the new inhabitants' arrival. Consequently, these phenomena show a cyclical movement in time and space in which one can discern a continual beginning and beginning again. They are also characterized by a convergence and coincidence - or more properly, a simultaneity - between the movement of the elite and that of investment in structures. This coincidence between the relocation of the classes, investment and the deterioration-rehabilitation of the central area through the action of superstructures cannot be due to mere chance and points to the existence of rules which regulate these phenomena, especially in view of their cyclical nature.

Thus, two processes which are both part of the same spatial dynamism succeed one another in both space and time. The first process, fairly well known, is that of "filtering down" and is characteristic of the period from 1940 to 1973: the downtown area is gradually deserted as the suburbs swell in size, and, consequently, dwellings previously occupied by the middle class are "freed" for occupancy by the poor and lower middle classes. This phenomenon was followed, from 1973 on, by a "filtering up" process, which is diametrically opposed to the first one. Its result is undeniably to rehabilitate the central area, but for the sole benefit of the socio-professional group which displaces the inhabitants who had previously taken possession of it.

CONCLUSION

The conclusions of the preceding analysis are self-evident, especially considering the desire of the public authorities to further consolidate the central area in the near future. What our analysis and the various urban problems which it has brought to light show is that there is an urgent need, not to renovate the city centre, but rather to give priority to the development of the suburbs. Of course, it is necessary to repair the ravages on the central area caused by the evacuations and the architectural radicalism of the previous period; but on the whole, the city centre is in good shape, and if present trends continue, it will be in even better shape in the near future. In spite of the present economic crisis, investments have been flowing in over the past decade in quantities which are completely out of proportion with those presently made in the suburbs. Moreover, a new generation of city-dwellers - young, educated, well-to-do and equipped with vision and determination - are moving in and replacing a population of more limited means. Finally, facilities and services of all kinds are appearing in all sectors of the central area as if it were a pioneer territory for experiments in urban development and urban living. A new style of city living is being developed, new standards for the quality of community life are gaining acceptance and a new street landscape is beginning to take shape. All things being equal, the future of the centre of Quebec City is neither uncertain nor in danger.

One cannot say as much for the suburbs, as they run the risk of becoming even more marginal in the near future. Although they are over-equipped with infrastructures of all kinds, they suffer a deplorable lack of superstructures. On the one hand, several services and facilities which were dearly acquired during the preceding phase are now deteriorating and even completely disappearing. On the other hand, due to the wide-spread slowdown in the construction industry and to the presence of infrastructures which are draining revenue, the suburbs find themselves in a situation where they have increased financial commitments which they must try to meet with revenues that are not increasing any faster than the rate of inflation. In addition, this precarious financial situation is reinforced, if not provoked, by the "colonizing" influence of the central area on the suburbs. The centre fosters the creation of consumer service jobs within its limits, organizes specialized recreational and cultural activities, attracts tourists, and rebuilds or restores its historical buildings... Moreover, considering the well-known and often deplored fact that the suburbs are in great need of architectural unification and urban tissue consolidation, neither the present nor the future looks too bright for them in comparison to the city centre.

Can the suburbs escape from this fateful situation caused by exogenic factors and outside agents ? To save the suburbs from an uncertain future, one would have to consciously and voluntarily implement an urban revitalization policy based on the following four vectors: polarizing suburban space around existing superstructures (local centres); consolidating and complementing the architectural formations within existing infrastructure networks (architectural unity and continuity); communitizing social activities and relations which are either too collective or too individualistic; and lastly, developing a local urban lifestyle of a spatialized nature (anchored in space).

NOTES

1. This model was utilized in the following research project: Guertin, Pierre S., **La dynamique spatiale du changement de forme architecturale. Etude de la morphologie urbaine de la haute ville de Quebec.** Quebec, Universite Laval, Centre de recherche en amenagement et en developpement, juillet 1982, 453 pages.
2. This "first" phase was followed by a period of relative urban stagnation between 1930 and 1940 which itself was even accompanied by a partial return to the country (ruralization).
3. This definition of the limits of the central area is that given by the city of Quebec itself: Ville de Quebec, Service d'urbanisme, Centre-ville de Quebec, Quebec, 1977. Dossiers I et II.
4. The 23 projects mentioned on page 51 represent major investments. For example, the wharves for the new harbour will cost about 15 million dollars, the Museum, 25 million, the intermodal transit station, 40 million and the Old Harbour, 60 million dollars (1982).
5. The Federal Government does not forecast but "guarantees" that the cost of energy will increase between now and 1986, based on the recently signed fiscal agreements with oil-producing provinces.
6. Centre local de services communautaires: neighbourhood centre dispensing health and general social services.

7. Duchesne, Vianney. Optimism in Quebec City. The trend back to the city is now well under way. Le Soleil, Quebec City, April 13, 1982, p.A-9.
8. Data obtained from the Quebec Bureau of Statistics.
9. Includes the Champlain, St.Roch and St.Jean Baptiste Wards.
10. The inappropriate term "recycling" is often used to refer to the conversion of buildings into dwellings.
11. The central city area includes the Champlain (Old Harbour and Old Quebec), St.Jean.Baptiste (including Parliament Hill) and St-Roch districts or wards.
12. Table based on unpublished statistics of the Quebec City Building Permit Bureau.
13. Dwelling conversion corresponds to the operational concept of "additional dwellings" used by the Building Permit Bureau. According to Bureau officials, this category takes in mostly new dwellings resulting from subdivisions of existing dwellings, in addition to dwellings created by the conversion of institutional buildings ("recycled" schools or monasteries, for example).
14. Quebec City Permanent Housing Committee. Housing Prospects (yearly). Quebec City 1978-82.
15. Cf. especially the 1978 zoning by-law for the Montcalm district.
16. These figures are based on calculations made by a real estate agent in April 1982 for an average apartment located in the Upper City just outside the central area.

FIVE

Larry Long and Diana DeAre

Population Redistribution

An Overview of City, Suburban, and Non-metropolitan Populations in the 1960s and 1970s

Perhaps the most unexpected demographic developments during the 1970s involved population redistribution, especially the changes that appear to be altering the nation's settlement pattern toward one of significantly less concentration. For the first decade in the nation's history, population deconcentration seemed to be occurring at a variety of spatial levels that include an interregional shift of population from the more densely settled states of heavy industrialization to the less densely settled states of the sunbelt and rocky mountain region, an intra-metropolitan shift of population from central cities to the outer fringes of their suburban rings, and a new shift of population growth to many small towns and rural areas that lie outside of metropolitan territory(see J. Long, 1981).

The first two of these types of redistribution have been underway for quite some time, although the pace of change in the 1970s was somewhat greater than during the 1950s and 1960s. Early in the 1970-80 decade population estimates indicated that growth in many southern and rocky mountain states was far greater than had been suggested by earlier trends. Moreover, partly because of coverage improvements, the 1980 census counted nearly five million more Americans than estimated. Most of these, it now appears, live in the south and west. The overall result is that in the 1970s population continued to grow more rapidly in many of the less densely settled states, as was expected; the redistribution of population to such areas was greater than indicated by early projections, however.

A continued shift of population from central cities to

suburbs was observed throughout the 1970s in various surveys and intercensal population estimates. Such a trend has been underway throughout much of the twentieth century as advances in transportation, like the building of trolleys and streetcars and the more widespread ownership of automobiles, allowed persons to live farther from their place of work. The pace of suburbanization quickened after World War II as cheap mortgages, the baby boom, and other factors increased the attractiveness and availability of housing beyond city boundaries. That trend became so pronounced that one of the milestones recorded by the 1970 census was that for the first time the suburban population exceeded the central city population.

There was evidence in the 1970s and earlier that population growth was slowing or even beginning to decline in some of the older "inner" suburbs that lie along city boundaries (Sternlieb and Lake, 1975; Guest, 1979; Fava, 1979; Long and Dahmann, 1980). If so, then the area of population loss might be spreading outward from some of the larger cities known to be experiencing population decline, suggesting an image of metropolitan areas in the form of a doughnut whose hole, the area of population decrease, was expanding. This type of pattern can be more clearly examined with census data than the intercensal surveys or local estimates.

The most surprising aspect of population deconcentration was that early in the 1970s nonmetropolitan territory collectively was observed to have a faster rate of population growth than metropolitan territory (cities and their suburbs). Historically the opposite pattern prevailed, with metropolitan areas having net immigration from and growing more rapidly in population than the small towns and rural areas that comprise nonmetropolitan territory. This reversal of relative growth rates of metropolitan and nonmetropolitan territory was evident in surveys taken in the 1970s and in the intercensal country population estimates prepared and published by the Census Bureau from the early 1970s through 1979 (see Long, 1980; Brown and Wardwell, 1980). With the possible exception of the onset of the baby boom in the late 1940s, this reversal of relative growth rates of metropolitan and nonmetropolitan territory may be the most surprising large-scale demographic development in the United States in the last 50 years.

The reversal and some possible reasons for it were noted in a number of analyses which received widespread media coverage (Beale, 1975; Morrison 1976; Tucker, 1976; Berry and Dahmann, 1977) and prompted considerable discussion of a possible back-to-the-countryside movement. A major unanswered question was whether the pattern would persist through the decade and be confirmed by the 1980 census. Another question was whether the rate of population shift to nonmetropolitan areas might be slowed if the attractiveness of low-density settlements were to be diminished by rising prices of gasoline and nagging doubts about its future availability.

These are some of the types of questions that can be asked of the 1980 census population counts for counties, cities, and other localities. A more dynamic view and a more complete analysis of the types of population redistribution discussed above must await preparation of migration statistics and other data from the 1980 census, but analysis and monitoring of intercensal population developments suggest some issues that need verification with 1980 census data.

* Was the shift of population from metropolitan to nonmetropolitan areas as great as had been indicated by the intercensal estimates?
* Can the metropolitan-to-nonmetrpolitan shift of population be called pervasive, implying a wide regional extent?
* Did nonmetropolitan growth extend beyond what might reasonably be considered the "exurban" fringe where metropolitan areas spill over into nonmetropolitan territory?
* Has the nation become less metropolitan as a result of rapid population growth in rural areas and small towns?
* Did the slowdown in metropolitan population growth in the 1970s apply to small as well as large metropolitan areas?
* Is population decline spreading outward from central cities into the "inner" suburbs?
* Was the shift of population growth to nonmetropolitan territory-first observed before the 1973-74 oil embargo-slowed by the rising price and occasional uncertainty of supply of gasoline in the latter part of the decade?

A historical perspective on deconcentration trends of the 1970s was provided in an earlier Census Bureau study (J. Long, 1981). The analysis in the following pages compares the 1960s and 1970s and offer some answers to the questions stated above, based on 1980 census results presently available. The purpose is to highlight some significant features of the realignment of city, suburban, and nonmetropolitan populations of the 1960s and 1970s. We would like to identify the development and possible course of some major changes in population geography. A subsequent study is intended to identify some employment changes that have accompanied the shift of population growth toward nonmetropolitan settings.

THE NONMETROPOLITAN TURNAROUND

Prior to the early 1970s, American metropolitan areas steadily grew more rapidly in population than nonmetropolitan territory. Successive censuses in the 20th century showed an increased proportion of Americans living in metropolitan areas. The 1970 census confirmed this historical pattern, as the Census Bureau noted (U.S. Bureau of the Census, 1971). For nearly every year since the early 1970s, however, the Bureau has published survey statistics or county population estimates showing the nonmetropolitan territory to have surpassed the population growth rate of metropolitan territory. The reversal of nonmetropolitan territory from growing less rapidly to growing more rapidly than the national average has come to be known as the nonmetropolitan "turnaround."

Some unanswered questions from more than one and half decade's research on this phenomenon have included whether the intercensal data were accurately reflecting the degree of difference between metropolitan and nonmetropolitan growth rates and whether the 1980 census would confirm the pattern. Of equal interest was whether the pattern would be sustained when the metropolitan area boundaries were updated to 1980. The answer to the latter question has become especially problematic because since 1970 a large number of counties have been added to metropolitan areas and many new metropolitan areas have been designated. These numerous changes in metropolitan-area boundaries also make interdecade comparisons very difficult.

In simplified terms, a metropolitan area (i.e., a standard metropolitan statistical area, or SMSA) consists of a city of 50,000 or more population or a group of cities whose combined population is at least 50,000, along with the balance of the county in which the city or cities is located. Contiguous counties may be included in an SMSA if commuting data and other characteristics show them to be metropolitan in character and socially and economically integrated with the central county. SMSAs thus are built up from counties, except in New England, where towns and cities—areas smaller than counties—are used. For New England however, there is also a classification scheme based on whole counties, and the resulting metropolitan areas are called New England County Metropolitan Areas, or NECMAs. Except as noted, subsequent metropolitan figures in this study are for all counties that were included in NECMAs in New England, and in SMSAs elsewhere, as of January 1, 1980. All other counties are considered nonmetropolitan. Working with whole counties will enable us to later subdivide nonmetropolitan counties into those adjacent and nonadjacent to a metropolitan area in order to examine the spillover question.

Since the nonmetropolitan category is a residual, it is steadily diminished as metropolitan-area boundaries are updated. Territorial reclassifications occur as some metropolitan areas expand outward and encompass counties that were formerly nonmetropolitan; reclassification also occurs when nonmetropolitan cities grow to exceed 50,000 population and thereby automatically qualify for designation as a new metropolitan area. Metropolitan counties are almost never reclassified as nonmetropolitan. Responsibility for making these classifications rests with the Office of Management and Budget.

Acquiring the metropolitan designation can be advantageous for an area because it can then qualify for a number of federal grant and aid programs that are limited to metropolitan areas (U.S. Department of Commerce, 1978). Cities nearing 50,000 population often welcome the opportunity to be reclassified as independent metropolitan areas, and already established metropolitan areas tend to welcome the addition of new counties because many advertisers and market analysts use an area's population-size ranking as an indicator of marketing potential (Shryock, 1957; Allis, 1980; Carlson, 1981).

In the 1970s a series of additions of counties were made to the metropolitan category for various reasons. As the 1970 census results became available, a few cities were found to have passed the 50,000 threshold. The criteria themselves were changes in 1971 so that if a nonmetropolitan city did not have 50,000 population it could still become a metropolitan area if its population combined with that of nearby cities passed the 50,000 mark. The commuting data from the 1970 census indicated that many nonmetropolitan counties on the fringes of metropolitan areas had sufficient commuting to the central county of a metropolitan area to be incorporated into that area. Finally, throughout the decade the intercensal population estimates and special censuses successively indicated that through growth and annexations a number of nonmetropolitan cities qualified for designation as new metropolitan areas. As 1980 census data become available, this process is being repeated.

At some point the reclassification of counties from the nonmetropolitan to the metropolitan category will probably choke off the higher rate of growth observed in the nonmetropolitan counties in the early 1970s. But this point has not yet been reached, at least according to the SMSA/NECMA boundaries in effect as of January 1, 1980. Table 5.1 shows 1960-70 and 1970-80 population change in metropolitan and nonmetropolitan territory according to this constant set of boundaries. The 1980 counts correspond to those published in the Advance Report series, PHC80-V-1 through 52.

The nonmetropolitan "turnaround" is dramatically evident. As is marked in the table, metropolitan counties in the 1960-70 decade grew by 17.1 per cent in population—a far greater rate of increase than the 3.9 per cent registered by nonmetropolitan counties. But in the 1970-80 decade a reversal occurred: metropolitan counties grew by only 10.0 per cent, compared with a growth rate of 15.4 per cent in the nonmetropolitan counties. The 1980 census data thus strongly confirm a new pattern that appears to have existed for about 10 years.

Still, most Americans live in metropolitan areas. Out of the 226.5 million persons counted in the 1980 census nearly 166 million lived in one of the SMSAs/NECMAs recognized on January 1, 1980; only about 60.5 million persons were in the nonmetropolitan sector. Reflecting the larger metropolitan base, most of the national population increase went to metropolitan areas. Between 1970 and 1980 the nation's population grew by about 23 million persons, and most of this increase—65 per cent—went to metropolitan areas. But the proportion going to the metropolitan sector was far below that of the previous decade, when nearly 92 per cent of the nation's population increase went to metropolitan areas (as defined on January 1, 1980).

What is surprising, however, is that for the first time the per cent of the total population living in metropolitan areas decreased, at least if a constant set of boundaries is employed. As is evident from the table, the per cent of the U.S. population living within the January 1, 1980 boundaries of metropolitan areas fell from 74.2 in 1970 to 73.3 in 1980. Historically, the use of constant, end-of-period boundaries in this fashion has shown a growing proportion of the nation's population to be living in metropolitan territory (U.S. Bureau of the Census, 1971,; Taeuber, 1972). Albeit small, this decline in the proportion of the population living in metropolitan areas is an important milestone that is one indicator of the hypothesis that the 1970s represented a "clean break" with past patterns of population redistribution (Vining and Strauss, 1977).

TABLE 5.1

Population change in metropolitan and nonmetropolitan counties of the United States: 1960 to 1980

(SMSA/NECMA boundaries as of January 1, 1980 are used)

	United States	Metropolitan counties	Nonmetropolitan counties
Total Population (000's)	3.20	450	5.50
1960	179,311	128,841	50,470
1970	203,302	150,883	52,419
1980	226,505	165,993	60,511
Per cent of Total U.S. Population			
1960	100	71.9	28.1
1970	100	74.2	25.8
1980	100.0	73.3	26.7
Per cent Change in Population			
1960-70	13.4	17.1*	3.9*
1970-80	11.4	10.0*	15.4*
Per Cent of National Population Growth			
1960-70	100.0	91.9	8.1
1970-80	100.0	65.1	34.9

* The nonmetropolitan "turn around"

These figures do not mean that we are reverting to a rural nation. There is no basis for inferring a massive back-to-the-land movement or a large scale return to agricultural pursuits (see Brown and Wardwell, 1980). Much of the migration away from large cities and their suburbs is to smaller cities and towns and the suburbs of such places, some of which will develop into new metropolitan areas.

The small decline in the per cent of population living in metropolitan areas is subject to qualification. The 73.3 per cent of the U.S. population shown in table 5.1 to be living in metropolitan areas is a slight understatement because it excludes some counties which will be shown to be functionally a part of a metropolitan area when population and commuting data from the 1980 census are taken into account. Inclusion of such counties will raise the per cent of population classified as metropolitan. But the key point is that past censuses still showed an increase in the per cent of population living in metropolitan areas without this type of updating. Moreover, the metropolitan designations in effect on January 1, 1980 probably represent a generous concept of what is metropolitan. Included in this definition (and therefore in Table 5.1) are a number of recently-designated standard metropolitan statistical areas that reflect the relaxed central city size criteria. The average size of the largest central city in each of the 44 post-1970 SMSAs was just 46,000 in 1980, hardly bringing to mind the image of a metropolis. More dramatic than the modest decline in the per cent of population living in metropolitan areas is the decline in the per cent living in large metropolitan areas, as will be shown later.

REGIONAL CONTEXTS OF THE TURNAROUND

The nonmetropolitan turnaround began in the Northeast in the 1960s. Of course, in all regions of the United States in the 1950s and 1960s there were some rural localities that went against the trend and grew faster than metropolitan territory. But, as shown in table 5.2 within metropolitan-area boundaries in effect in 1970, the Northeast was the only region to have a faster rate of population growth outside than inside metropolitan areas in the 1960s. The United States as a whole and the north central, south, and west regions continued in the 1960s to experience the long-standing trend for population to grow more rapidly inside than outside metropolitan areas. A map of the major regions is shown as figure 5.1.

The nonmetropolitan turnaround has, in a manner of speaking, proceeded further in the northeast than in the other regions, for in the 1970-80 decade the northeast was the only region to experience an absolute decrease in its metropolitan population. For the United States as a whole and the north, central, south, and west regions, metropolitan populations increased between 1970 and 1980.

TABLE 5.2

Rates of population change in metropolitan and nonmetropolitan territory, by region, according to successively changing boundaries of metropolitan areas: 1960 to 1970 and 1970 to 1980

Decade and type of residence	United States	North-east	North Central	South	West
1960-70 POPULATION CHANGE					
1970 boundaries					
Metropolitan growth rate	16.7	9.0	13.0	22.0	28.5
Nonmetropolitan growth rate	6.7	13.4	3.6	5.8	10.6
1974 boundaries					
Metropolitan growth rate	17.1	10.0	13.0	22.2	28.4
Nonmetropolitan growth rate	4.4	8.4	2.8	3.1	9.7
January 1, 1980 boundaries					
Metropolitan growth rate	17.1	10.0	13.1	22.2	28.4
Nonmetropolitan growth rate	3.9	8.4	2.0	2.6	9.0
1970-80 POPULATION CHANGE					
1970 boundaries					
Metropolitan growth rate	8.8	-2.5	1.7	19.3	21.4
Nonmetropolitan growth rate	17.3	11.8	8.6	20.8	33.0
1974 boundaries					
Metropolitan growth rate	9.8	-1.8	2.4	21.2	21.9
Nonmetropolitan growth rate	15.8	12.8	7.7	17.8	32.2
January 1, 1980 boundaries					
Metropolitan growth rate	10.0	-1.8	2.6	21.5	22.1
Nonmetropolitan growth rate	15.4	12.8	7.4	17.3	31.6

The effect of changing boundaries is quite important in assessing the degree of difference in growth rates of metropolitan and nonmetropolitan territory. Within the 1970 census boundaries, the nonmetropolitan population of the U.S. grew at a rate nearly twice as fast as the metropolitan population in the 1970-80 decade (17.3 per cent for non-metropolitan territory vs. 8.8 per cent for metropolitan territory). Within the 1974 and 1980 boundaries, the non-metropolitan population growth rate was only one and one-half times as fast as that for the metropolitan population. The January 1, 1974 boundaries are also shown to reflect the large number of nonmetropolitan counties that had been reclassified as parts of existing metropolitan areas, based on commuting data from the 1970 census. If population continues to disperse to nonmetropolitan territory at the present rate, at some point in the future territorial

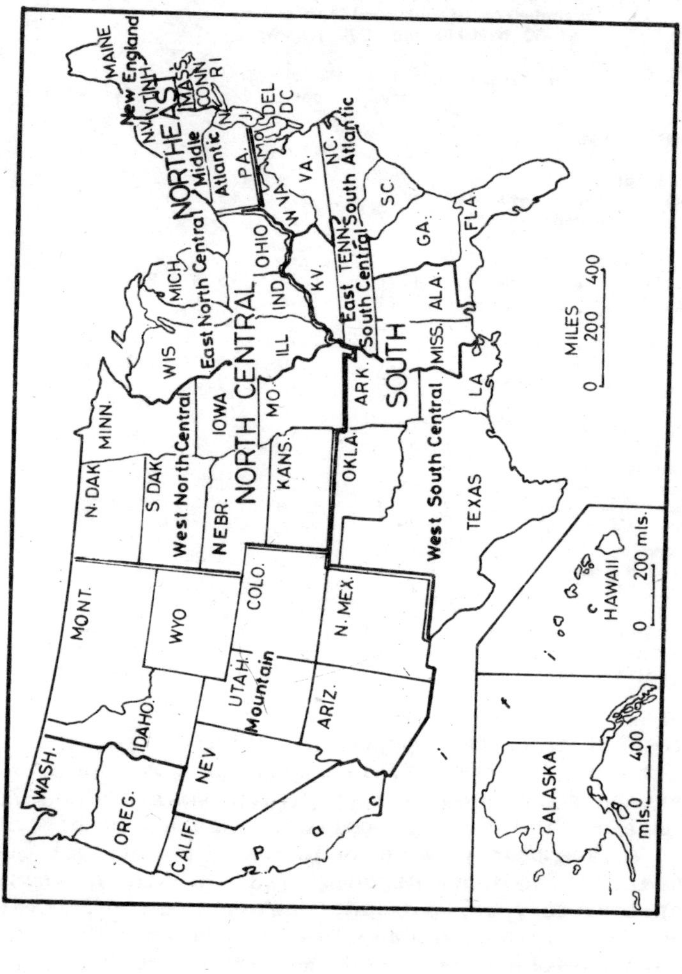

FIG.5.1 REGIONS AND GEOGRAPHIC DIVISIONS OF THE UNITED STATES

reclassifications may become great enough to choke off the faster rate of growth in nonmetropolitan territory.

For the south this point may already have been reached. Observe in table 5.2 that within the 1970 boundaries, nonmetropolitan population growth in the South between 1970 and 1980 exceeded that in metropolitan areas. This is a "turnaround" from the previous decade. But as new metropolitan areas were designated out of growing nonmetropolitan counties and as other nonmetropolitan counties were added to the fringe of Southern metropolitan areas, the "turnaround" was reversed. That is, according to the 1970 boundaries the Southern nonmetropolitan population grew more rapidly than the metropolitan population, but with the 1974 or 1980 boundaries the opposite was true and the "traditional" pattern once again prevailed. A vivid illustration of the accretion of metropolitan areas is the Atlanta Standard Metropolitan Statistical Area, which grew from five counties in 1970 to 15 in 1980.

One of the ironies of population growth in nonmetropolitan locations is that it can cause them to be reclassified as metropolitan. Very often the long-run result of rapid population growth in nonmetropolitan settings is to add to the metropolitan population. Because of this irony, the nonmetropolitan turnaround cannot continue indefinitely, although an end to it brought about by territorial reclassification alone will not put an end to the underlying process of population dispersal to areas of lower density.

THE SPILLOVER HYPOTHESIS

Of course, by using the boundaries in effect on January 1, 1980 some metropolitan areas are being "underbounded," meaning that their boundaries understate their true territorial extent. The simple metropolitan/nonmetropolitan dichotomy is inadequate if many metropolitan areas are rapidly growing on their fringes and spilling over into nonmetropolitan territory. Metropolitan-area definitions lag behind such changes because county-level commuting data, the primary basis for adding new (nonmetropolitan) counties to existing metropolitan areas, are available only from the decennial censuses, and the necessary 1980 data are not now available.

The spillover hypothesis states that the faster rate of population growth in nonmetropolitan than in metropolitan areas can be explained by rapidly growing fringe counties adjacent to but not officially a part of existing metropolitan areas because of data lags. One way of testing this hypothesis is simply to separate the nonmetropolitan counties into those that are adjacent and not adjacent to a metropolitan area, as is done in table 5.3. If the hypothesis is correct, then we ought to find that the residual group of counties—the nonmetropolitan counties not adjacent to a metropolitan area—are growing less rapidly than metropolitan counties.

TABLE 5.3

Per cent change in population in nonmetropolitan counties adjacent and not adjacent to metropolitan areas, by region: 1970 to 1980

(SMSA/NECMA boundaries as of January 1, 1980 are used)

Type of area	United States	North-east	North Central	South	West
Metropolitan areas	10.0	-1.8	2.6	21.5	22.1
Nonmetropolitan counties adjacent to metropolitan areas	16.7	13.1	8.6	19.6	34.4
Nonmetropolitan counties not adjacent to a metropolitan area	13.8	11.8	6.0	14.7	28.8

The hypothesis is not supported, at least for the United States as a whole. Even the nonmetropolitan counties not adjacent to a metropolitan area grew more rapidly (13.8 per cent) than metropolitan areas (10.0 per cent) between 1970 and 1980. This pattern holds for each region except the South.

As a further test, a category to encompass all counties designated metropolitan as of January 1, 1980 <u>and</u> all nonmetropolitan counties adjacent to them can be created. This hybrid category includes virtually all counties that are even remotely likely to be picking up population directly as a result of metropolitan-area spillover. Between 1970 and 1980 this hybrid category of SMSAs and their surrounding counties grew 11.1 per cent, <u>less rapidly</u> than the 13.8 per cent for the nonmetropolitan counties not adjacent to a metropolitan area. Rather clearly, the 1980 census results confirm that the nonmetropolitan turnaround extends into fairly remote territory and is a more complex phenomenon than simply an overflow of population from metropolitan areas into adjacent nonmetropolitan territory.

One should not conclude that rapidly suburbanizing nonmetropolitan counties failed to grow rapidly. As a group, they are rapidly growing, as will be shown in more detail shortly. The point for now is simply that the nonmetropolitan turnaround is not explained solely by population growth in counties adjacent to metropolitan areas. While the nation's population growth rate was slowing during the 1970s, growth in the nonmetropolitan counties not adjacent to a metropolitan area was nearly 14 times what it was in the 1960-70 decade and above the national growth rate.

ARE THESE RESULTS SURPRISING?

Statistics like those quoted above show a dramatic change between the 1960s and 1970s in relative growth rates of metropolitan and nonmetropolitan populations. But was change of the magnitude recorded by the 1980 census entirely unexpected? In terms of the types of broad population patterns being examined, censuses should provide relatively few complete surprises, assuming that demographers make full use of intercensal surveys and other data sources and can develop procedures for making reasonably accurate intercensal population estimates for local areas. On this basis, one of the initial analytical uses of census data might be to confirm the existence of population trends measured from non-census sources and assess more precisely the magnitude of the intercensal trends. The 1980 census data clearly confirm a nonmetropolitan population turnaround as it was defined above and as it was initially identified from noncensus sources of data. But was the degree of change greater or less than what would have been expected on the basis of intercensal data?

To answer this question, we constructed table 5.4, which shows the growth rates that were observed and expected in metropolitan counties, in nonmetropolitan counties adjacent to metropolitan counties, and in all other nonmetropolitan counties. The observed values are based on the 1970 and 1980 census results. The expected values were from the county population estimates prepared by the Bureau to show population change from 1970 to 1978 (U.S. Bureau of the Census, 1980); a similar set of estimates was prepared by the Bureau annually from 1971 through 1978. We used the 1978 county population estimates in an earlier study of population change in metropolitan and nonmetropolitan territory, and the expected rates of population change are taken from that study (Long and DeAre, 1980).

TABLE 5.4

Observed and expected population change in metropolitan areas and in nonmetropolitan counties adjacent and not adjacent to metropolitan areas: 1970 to 1980

(SMSA/NECMA boundaries as of January 1, 1980 are used)

Type of area	Average annual rate of population growth			
	Observed (1970 and 1980 census figures)	Expected (intercensal county population estimates through 1978)	Ratio of expected to observed rate of growth	Ratio of expected to observed population
Metropolitan counties	0.96	0.73	0.77	0.98
Nonmetropolitan counties	1.44	1.18	0.82	0.97
Adjacent to a metropolitan area	1.55	1.25	0.81	0.97
Not adjacent to a metropolitan area	1.29	1.09	0.84	0.98

For each of the categories of counties the observed rate of growth was higher than had been indicated by the intercensal county population estimates through 1978. This result reflects the fact that in the nation as a whole the population count in the 1980 census included nearly five million more persons than had been anticipated on the basis of the 1970 count and vital statistics data. For metropolitan areas as a whole the expected average annual growth rate was about 77 per cent of what was observed; for nonmetropolitan counties adjacent to a metropolitan area the expected growth rate was about 81 per cent of what was observed; and for nonmetropolitan counties not adjacent to a metropolitan area the expected growth rate was 84 per cent of what was observed between 1970 and 1980. These results tell us that the degree of understatement of intercensal population growth rates was greatest in metropolitan areas, somewhat less for nonmetropolitan counties adjacent to a metropolitan area, and least for nonmetropolitan counties not adjacent to a metropolitan area.

These differences were not large enough to appreciably bias analyses of the direction and approximate extent of the metropolitan-to-nonmetropolitan population redistribution based on the Census Bureau's county population estimates of the 1970s. Indeed the expected metropolitan population (based on the intercensal estimates through 1978 and projected to 1980) was 98 per cent of what was counted in the 1980 census; on this basis the population expected to be living in nonmetropolitan counties adjacent to a metropolitan area was 97 per cent of what was counted in the census; and the population expected to be living in nonmetropolitan counties not adjacent to a metropolitan area was about 98 per cent of what the census found. From these findings, we conclude that the 1980 census results are basically in agreement with the intercensal county population estimates in confirming not only the existence of a nonmetropolitan turnaround, but also in confirming the approximate degree of population shift to nonmetropolitan settings both adjacent and not adjacent to metropolitan areas. Thus, the direction and magnitude of the 1980 census results on the nonmetropolitan turnaround should not come as a surprise to analysts and officials who monitored the pace of change indicated by the Census Bureau's intercensal county population estimates.

NEW AND OLD METROPOLITAN TERRITORY

Between 1970 and 1980 the metropolitan population of the United States increased, but at a rate slower than that of the nonmetropolitan population. Some of the metropolitan population growth occurred in territory that was defined as metropolitan at the time of the 1970 census, and some occurred in territory that was reclassified from nonmetropolitan to metropolitan since then. Typically, such reclassifications are of two types: (1) suburbanizing rural counties on the periphery of metropolitan areas and (2) the birth of new metropolitan areas as nonmetropolitan cities grow large enough to qualify for metropolitan status. In trying to assess past and future sources of growth of metropolitan territory, a perennial question seems to be whether the geographical expansion of existing metropolitan areas is more rapid and adds more people to the metropolitan category than the growth of nonmetropolitan cities into metropolitan status (for estimates for decades from 1900 to 1970, see Berry and Kasarda, 1977, pp. 161-178).

To these two sources of growth in metropolitan population, we have to add a third for the 1970s: a change in the criteria for defining metropolitan areas. In 1971 a change in the rules allowed more nonmetropolitan cities to qualify as new, independent metropolitan areas. The requirement that a city (or twin cities) must have a minimum population of 50,000 in order to qualify was changed so that a single city of as little as 25,000 population could qualify if its inclusion with neighbouring cities and towns produced a population of 50,000 or more, for a total metropolitan area population of 75,000 or more. To our knowledge, the importance of this change in criteria has not been assessed relative to the two traditional sources of expansion of metropolitan territory. Figure 5.2 was constructed to show the 1980 population and 1970-80 rates of growth in the three categories of "new" metropolitan territory in addition to population change in counties classified as metropolitan in 1970.

Of the three types of new metropolitan territory, the one representing growth on the fringes of metropolitan areas was the most important in adding to the metropolitan population. In 1980 about 5.6 million persons lived in counties added to metropolitan areas after 1970 census data on commuting showed these "exurban" areas to have become functionally a part of an already existing metropolitan area as a result of substantial commuting into the central city. Most of these counties were added in 1973 when the 1970 census commuting data became available, but of course some of these counties acquired the qualifying levels of commuting many years before 1970. The population of these counties as a group grew by 33.8 per cent between 1970 and 1980—faster than either of the two other types of new metropolitan territory.

The change in criteria added 5.3 million persons to the 1980 metropolitan population—only slightly less than that added by the "exurban" fringe counties. Virtually all of these counties were added as new metropolitan areas when the revised criteria were announced in 1971; their 1970 census populations allowed them to qualify under the new rules. As a group, these counties grew in population less rapidly than the exurban counties between 1970 and 1980.

The third category of new metropolitan territory consist of counties added fairly regularly throughout the 1970s. These counties which represented new metropolitan areas were able to qualify as a result of an updating of their city populations in a special census or the revenue-sharing estimates prepared by the Bureau at successive intervals in the 1970s. Some of these new metropolitan areas were able to qualify only because of the revised criteria that were introduced in 1971. This group of counties added about 2.4 million persons to the total 1980 metropolitan population. Like the "new criteria" counties added around 1971, they

FIG.5.2:Population Change in "Old" and "New" Metropolitan Territory: 1970 to 1980

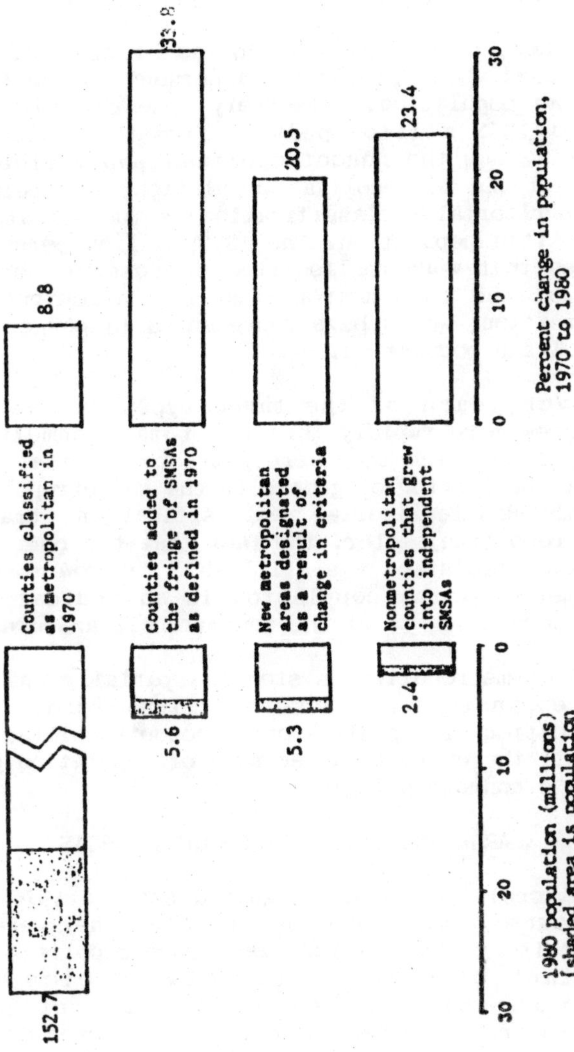

grew somewhat less rapidly than the exurban counties that were added to the fringes of metropolitan areas.

Altogether, these three categories of new metropolitan counties added about 13.3 million persons to the total 1980 metropolitan population. Conversely, one can say that they subtracted 13.3 million persons from the nonmetropolitan population. Since the nonmetropolitan population is much smaller than the metropolitan population, the relative effect of territorial reclassification is much greater on the nonmetropolitan population. The 13.3 million persons living in counties that were reclassified represented only eight per cent of the 1980 metropolitan population but, without reclassification, would have represented 18 per cent of the nonmetropolitan population.

Moreover, each of the three types of reclassified counties grew more rapidly than the total nonmetropolitan population from which they were extracted. Quite clearly, a substantial proportion of growth in the nonmetropolitan sector was, through territorial reclassification, transferred to the metropolitan sector. The fact that the remaining nonmetropolitan population was still able to grow more rapidly than the metropolitan population is an indicator of the force and pervasiveness of the nonmetropolitan turnaround.

The total metropolitan system is spatially and demographically expanding into a more diffuse form. Continued reclassification of rapidly growing nonmetropolitan counties will curtail the current faster rate of population growth in the nation's nonmetropolitan sector.

LARGE AND SMALL METROPOLITAN AREAS

The metropolitan areas designated between 1970 and 1980 were, of course, small, and the fact that they were created out of territory that in 1970 was nonmetropolitan suggests an important blurring of the distinction between metropolitan and nonmetropolitan. Most of these new metropolitan areas had central cities with fewer than 50,000 residents—a population size far below what some people might consider as metropolitan. The metropolitan/nonmetropolitan contrast appears to have become somewhat artificial and suggests a sharper distinction than in fact may exist. For analytic purposes, it may be more appropriate to examine population patterns by size of metropolitan area, for what appear to be "metropolitan" population patterns may be limited to only certain size groups. Just as the nonmetropolitan counties were earlier divided into those that were adjacent to a metropolitan area and those that were not, the metropolitan areas can be disaggregated by size as is done in Figure 5.3.

In the 1960s the national pattern was for every metropolitan-area size category to grow much more rapidly in population than the nonmetropolitan sector. In the 1970s the largest metropolitan areas (those with three million or more inhabitants) recorded absolute declines, and growth rates in metropolitan areas in size categories between 250,000 and three million slowed relative to their 1960-70 rates. In contrast, small metropolitan areas—those with 100,000 to 250,000 population and those under 100,000 population—and nonmetropolitan territory grew more rapidly in the 1970s than in the 1960s.

Thus, the nation's slower population growth in the 1970s was most pronounced in the larger metropolitan areas, particularly those with over 500,000 population. For the nation as a whole, the "turnaround" observed during the 1970s for the nonmetropolitan sector also encompassed metropolitan areas of under 250,000.

Of course, not every metropolitan area of over 250,000 population experienced a slowdown of population growth in the 1970s, nor did every place smaller than this record a speeding up of population growth. However, the figures do mean that for the nation as a whole, above-average rates of population growth shifted toward the lower end of the size-of-place distribution shown in figure 5.3. Note that of the seven size-of-place categories, the highest growth rate in the 1960s was in the next-to-largest metropolitan size class (those with one to three million persons), but in the 1970s the fastest growing category consisted of the smallest metropolitan areas—those with under 100,000 population, some of which were created out of territory that in 1970 was nonmetropolitan.

An issue in examining the relationship between size and growth in the metropolitan context is whether to use the SMSAs/NECMAs, as has been done in this paper, or to use a combination of SMSAs/NECMAs and groupings of SMSAs known as Standard Consolidated Statistical Areas (SCSAs), or some ndividual metropolitan areas into

FIG.5.3 PERCENT CHANGE IN POPULATION FROM 1960 TO 1970 AND 1970 TO 1980, BY SIZE OF METROPOLITAN AREA

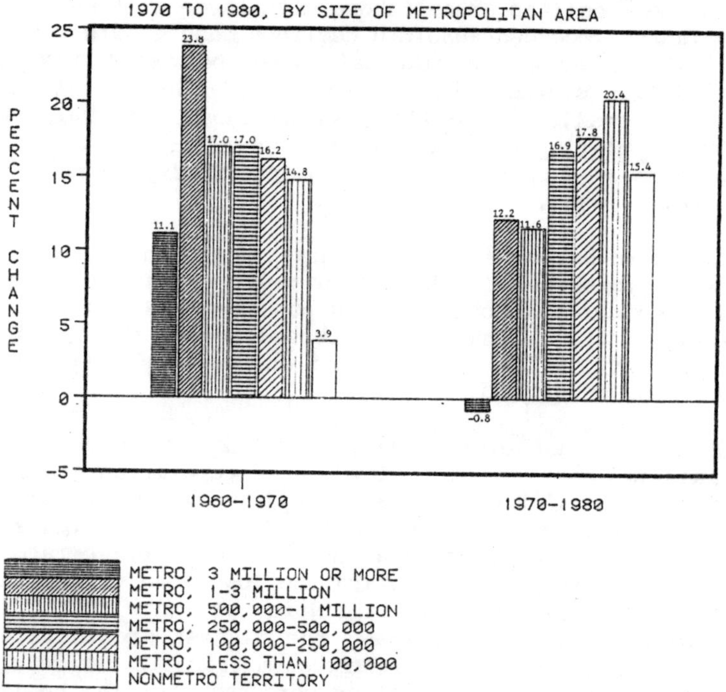

NOTE: SMSA/NECMA BOUNDARIES ARE AS OF JANUARY 1, 1980, METROPOLITAN AREA SIZE IS AS OF 1970

million (the population of the New York-Newark-Jersey City, N.Y.-N.J.-Conn. SCSA), or an area of 42 million, the population of Jean Gottmann's megalopolis, the urbanized northeastern seaboard extending from Boston to Washington, D.C.? Should a resident of Kenosha, Wisconsin, be classified as living in an area of 123,000 people (the Kenosha SMSA)? For the size categories used in this paper, the summary characterizations of growth rates by metropolitan size are not much affected. Compare the growth rates below:

	1960–70		1970–80	
	SCSAs	SMSAs/ NECMAs	SCSAs	SMSAs/ NECHAs
3,000,000 or more	13.8	11.1	1.6	-0.8
1,000,000 to 2,999,999	25.2	23.8	13.9	12.2
500,000 to 999,999	16.1	17.0	12.0	12.0
250,000 to 499,999	15.4	17.0	17.8	16.9
100,000 to 249,999	15.7	16.2	17.9	17.8
Under 100,000	14.7	14.8	20.4	20.4

Regardless of which of the two schemes is used, changing relationships can be observed: (1) the size category of maximum growth shifted from the one to three million interval in the 1960s to the smallest category (under 100,000) in the 1970s and (2) except for the largest size category, the generally positive association between size and growth rates in the 1960s shifted to a negative association in the 1970s.

REGIONAL PATTERNS BY METROPOLITAN SIZE

Generalizations about the nation as a whole tend to mask the variety of regional contexts in which population growth and decline occur. As shown in figure 5.4, the transition of very large metropolitan areas from growth to outright decline occurred only in the Northeast. There, metropolitan areas of 3,000,000 or more population went from growth of 7.5 per cent in the 1960s to decline of 5.1 per cent in the 1970s, and areas of one to three million population collectively shifted to decline of 2.9 per cent in the 1970s from an increase of 12.4 per cent in the 1960s. By contrast, the smallest metropolitan areas (under 100,000 population) and the nonmetropolitan territory of the Northeast region grew more rapidly in the 1970s than in the 1960s.

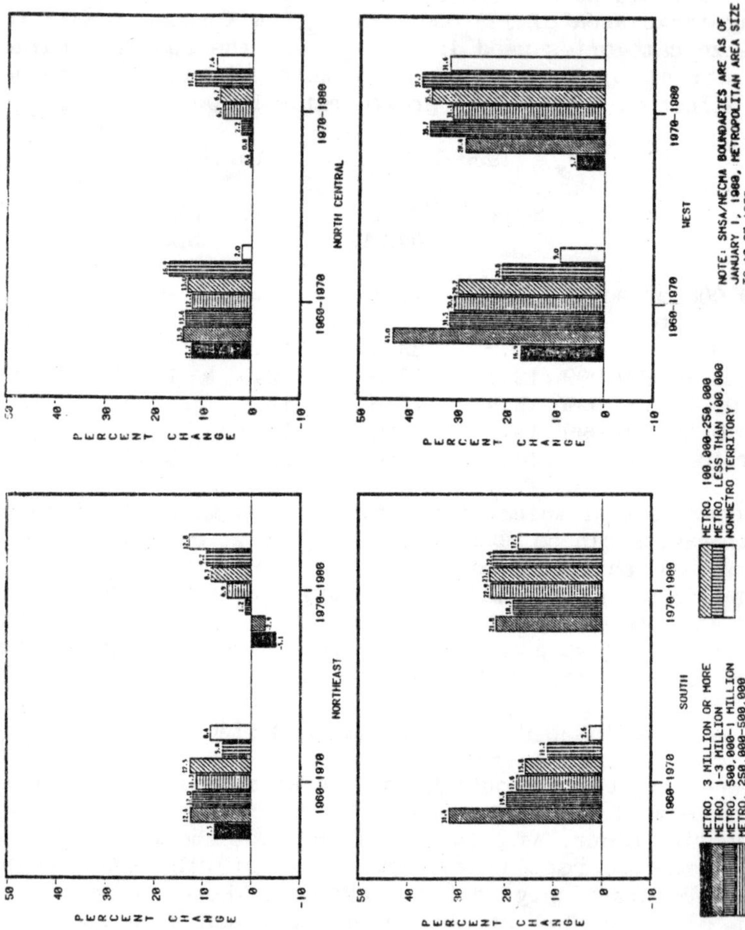

FIG.5.4 PERCENT CHANGE IN POPULATION FROM 1960 TO 1970 AND 1970 TO 1980, BY SIZE OF METROPOLITAN AREA, FOR REGIONS

In each of the four major regions population growth rates in nonmetropolitan territory increased between the 1960s and 1970s. Except for the North Central region, an increase in growth rates also occurred in smaller metropolitan areas (those under 100,000 population). These data attest to the pervasiveness of a population turnaround in nonmetropolitan territory and small metropolitan areas.

Like the two northern regions, the South and West experienced a relative shift of population growth from the larger to smaller metropolitan areas. Excluding metropolitan areas of over three million residents (of which there were none in the South in 1970), one finds a striking positive association between size of metropolitan area and rate of population change during the 1960s. That is, in the South and West during the 1960s the larger the metropolitan area, the faster it grew. During the 1970s, however, there was little association between size of metropolitan area (again excluding the very largest category) and rate of population growth: metropolitan areas of small and moderate size all grew at rates that were not strikingly dissimilar. This leveling out of population growth rates within the metropolitan and nonmetropolitan sectors at rates far above the national average is an indicator of the pervasiveness of the shift of population growth to the South and West.

CITIES AND SUBURBS

Although evident for the Northeast and in a few scattered locations in the 1960s (Brown and Wardwell, 1980), the shift of population growth to the nonmetropolitan sector was first evident for the nation as a whole in the 1970s. A form of population deconcentration that is of much longer duration is the shift of population growth from cities to their suburban rings. Suburbanization has entailed a faster rate of population growth in the suburbs than in central cities and a growing proportion of the nation's population living in suburbs, which are often defined to include the total population living in metropolitan areas outside of central cities. Suburbanization has been occurring in most metropolitan areas of the United States throughout the 20th century (Berry and Kasarda, 1977).

Suburbanization accelerated after World War II as the parents of the baby boom generation looked for spacious homes and large backyards and as the nation's housing policies and industry accommodated those preferences. During the 1970s the intrametropolitan shift in favour of suburbs continued to increase, as measured by the ratio of suburb to central city growth rates. There are some reasons for expecting a slowdown in the absolute pace of suburban growth, however. For one thing, the baby boom is over, and even though fertility rates may rise somewhat, they are unlikely to return to the high levels that persisted through the 1950s and into the 1960s. Also, the increase in population growth rates in nonmetropolitan counties may be draining population growth from suburban territory as more persons move to or choose to remain in exurban locations or the small towns and rural areas that lie farther beyond the suburban fringe. Hence, we would expect the 1980 census to show the beginning of a slowdown in rates of population growth in suburban territory.

The pace and the amount of suburbanization are difficult to measure precisely over long periods of time because of annexations. When central cities annex suburban territory, the typical result is to transfer growth from the suburban to the central city category. Taking such annexations into account over several decades has been impossible because of the lack of population counts for the annexed parcels in successive censuses. Some of the problems have been overcome in recent censuses, but carrying such adjustments back for a number of decades with a high degree of accuracy is not possible.

Ideally, one might compare 1960-70 and 1970-80 rates of population change in central cities and the suburban balances of metropolitan areas using constant 1970 city boundaries, but it is not now possible to do so. It is, however, possible to compare 1960-70 population change in 1960 city boundaries and 1970-80 population change in 1980 city boundaries, as is done in figure 5.5. In figure 5.5 "suburban territory" refers to the entire portion of metropolitan areas outside of the respective city boundaries. For metropolitan areas constant boundaries as of January 1, 1980 were used.

One of the important results shown in figure 5.5 is the demonstration that central cities in the aggregate made a historic transition from growth to decline. Central cities collectively grew by 0.7 per cent between 1960 and 1970 but registered a 1.5 per cent decrease in population between 1970 and 1980. In all previous intercensal decades of the 20th century central cities collectively experienced population increases (Berry and Kasarda, 1977). Even in recent decades as individual large cities were decreasing in population, there was offsetting growth in smaller cities. But in the 1970-80 decade for the first time population growth in growing cities was no longer great enough to offset losses in declining ones.

The 1970-80 population loss in central cities occurred in spite of annexations. If "current" city boundaries were used (those in effect in 1970 and then in 1980) rather than constant boundaries (as of 1980), central cities still would have lost population. The decrease would have involved only 96,000 persons, for a rate of decline of only 0.1 per cent—but a decline nevertheless. These figures come from records maintained by the Census Bureau indicating that the 1970 population in areas annexed by central cities during the 1970s was about 895,000.

Population growth rates in suburban territory slowed between the 1960-70 and 1970-80 decades. For the United States as a whole, population growth rates in the portion of metropolitan areas outside the central cities declined from 32.5 per cent in the 1960-70 decade to 19.4 per cent in the 1970-80 decade. Suburban population was still growing more rapidly than the national average in the 1970s, but the degree to which it exceeded the national growth rate was somewhat less. In the 1960s the suburban growth rate was nearly 2.5 times the nation's growth rate, and in the 1970s it was 1.7 times the national average. In each of the four regions suburban population grew more rapidly in the 1960s than in the 1970s.

Figure 5.5 is also useful in illustrating that population decline in central cities in the 1970s was for the most part a phenomenon of the Northeast and North Central regions. Central city population in the Northeast fell by 11 per cent in the 1970s, and in the North Central region the decline was nearly as great— 10 per cent. In the South and West, central cities collectively continued to grow and at higher rates than in the 1960s. These figures mean that in the 1970s the amount of population gain registered by central cities in the South and West was less than the loss experienced by central cities in the Northeast and North Central regions. The result was that for the first intercensal decade in the nation's history central-city population declined.

FIG.5.5 PERCENT CHANGE IN POPULATION IN CENTRAL CITIES AND SUBURBAN TERRITORY, BY REGION: 1960 TO 1970 AND 1970 TO 1980

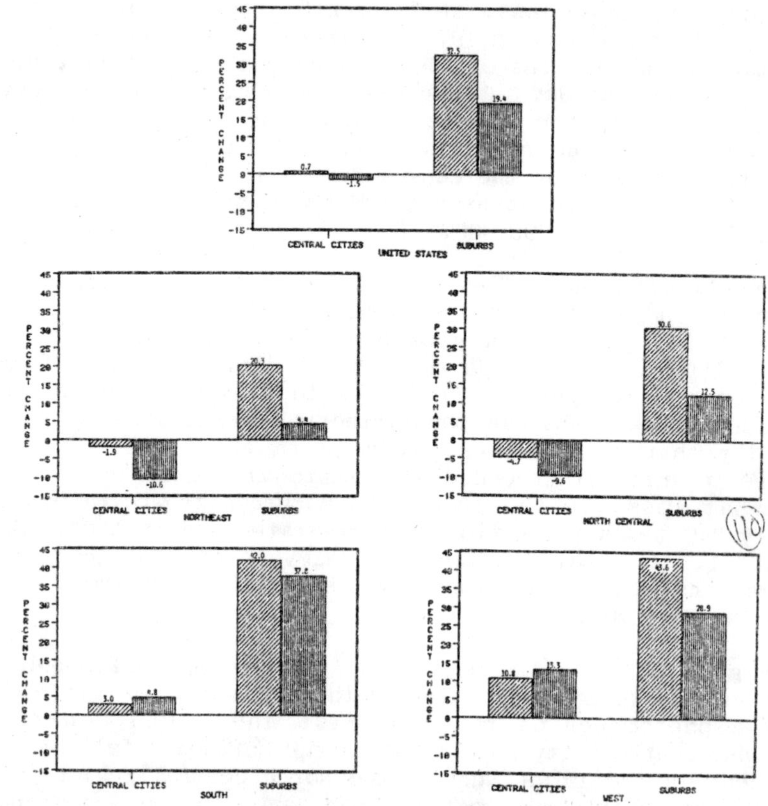

1960-70
1970-80

NOTE: SMSA/NECMA BOUNDARIES ARE AS OF JANUARY 1, 1980

SUBURBIA AND EXURBIA

A new word seems to be creeping into the vocabulary of population distribution. There are a growing number of references to "exurbia" or the "exurbs" to designate areas of population growth that lie on the margins of suburban territory and represent the presumed limits from which one reasonably might be able to commute into the central city. Such concepts have no official definition, but it is useful to compare relative rates of population growth in suburban territory as it is often defined (the entire part of metropolitan areas outside the central cities) and locations slightly farther out.

One approach is to compare suburban rates of growth with rates of growth in the nonmetropolitan counties that were identified earlier as being adjacent to a metropolitan area. These counties share borders with metropolitan areas and on occasion have been labelled exurban (Roseman, 1980). Figure 5.6 presents a comparison of relative growth rates for four categories of residence—central cities, suburban territory, the nonmetropolitan counties adjacent to metropolitan areas, and the remaining nonmetropolitan counties—for the United States and each of the four major regions.

The growth rate in the counties adjacent to metropolitan areas did not quite catch up with that of suburban territory, but it is not far behind. In the 1970s the population of the adjacent nonmetropolitan counties grew by 16.7 per cent, compared with a growth rate of 19.4 per cent for suburban territory. These figures represent a substantial narrowing of growth-rate differentials between the suburbs and the adjacent nonmetropolitan counties. In the 1960s, however, suburban territory grew more than five times as rapidly as the adjacent nonmetropolitan counties, whereas in the 1970-80 decade the suburban territory grew only about 16 per cent more rapidly than the adjacent (exurban) counties.

Even the nonmetropolitan counties not adjacent to metropolitan areas grew more rapidly than the nation as a whole. In the 1960s the growth rate for this group of counties was less than one-tenth of that of the United States as a whole, but in the 1970s nonadjacent counties experienced a growth rate more than one fifth above the national average. Therefore, all three categories of noncentral-city residence grew more rapidly than the nation as a whole.

FIG.5.6 PERCENT CHANGE IN POPULATION IN CENTRAL CITIES, THE SUBURBAN BALANCE OF METROPOLITAN AREAS, AND IN NONMETROPOLITAN COUNTIES ADJACENT AND NOT ADJACENT TO METROPOLITAN AREAS, BY REGION: 1970 TO 1980

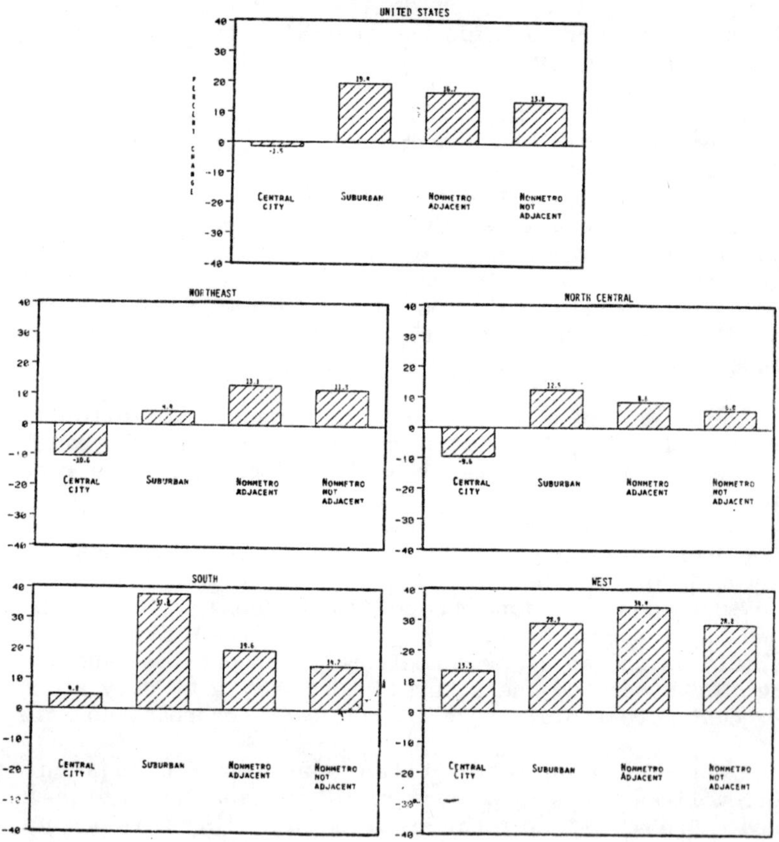

NOTE: SMSA/NECMA BOUNDARIES ARE AS OF JANUARY 1, 1980

There has been a substantial spreading out of population growth away from the urban cores of metropolitan areas. Growth rate differences among the suburban territory, adjacent nonmetropolitan counties, and nonadjacent counties were considerably reduced as growth slowed in the suburbs and rose in each of the two nonmetropolitan categories between the 1960s and the 1970s. The suburbs have now lost some of their distinctiveness as a locus of rapid population growth. Population growth appears to be moving beyond what has traditionally been defined as suburban territory.

These processes have progressed further in the Northeast than in the other regions. In a striking change from the 1960s, suburban growth rates in the Northeast in the 1970s fell behind that of each of the two nonmetropolitan categories by a substantial margin. In fact, suburban territory in the North-east in the 1970s grew only about one-third as rapidly as nonmetropolitan counties adjacent to metropolitan areas. Even the more remote group of nonmetropolitan counties that were not adjacent to metropolitan areas grew much more rapidly in population than suburban territory. These changes resulted from a rather sharp decline in population growth rates in suburbs of the Northeast and increases in growth rates in nonmetropolitan counties adjacent as well as those not adjacent to metropolitan areas. More clearly than in the other three regions, the locus of population growth in the Northeast has shifted beyond the suburbs.

The West, like the Northeast, experienced a higher rate of population growth in the adjacent nonmetropolitan counties than in suburban territory. But unlike the Northeast, the West's central cities grew in population. In the West all four residential categories—central cities, suburban territory, counties adjacent, and counties not adjacent to metropolitan areas—grew more rapidly in population than the nation. There was, however, a narrowing in the 1970s of growth-rate differences among the four residential categories in the West.

In the other two regions—the North Central and the South—suburban territory continued to outpace growth in each of the nonmetropolitan categories of residence. For each of the four regions population growth rates in sub-urban territory declined between the 1960s and 1970s. In all four regions, therefore, there was convergence of population growth rates in suburban territory and the adjacent and more remote nonmetropolitan residential categories.

The general picture that emerges is one of the diffusion of population growth beyond the suburban rings of cities of metropolitan status. This spreading out of population growth occurred as growth rates slowed in suburban territory and rose in every major region in nonmetropolitan counties adjacent as well as not adjacent to metropolitan areas. In this sense, population growth appears to be moving farther from central cities, to "exurban" and other areas beyond the suburban fringe of metropolitan territory.

THE INNER SUBURBS

If population growth is moving to and beyond the fringes of suburbia, is population decline spreading outward from central cities? There are several reasons for supposing that population decline might be moving from central cities to encompass suburban territory that is near city boundaries. One reason for expecting such a pattern to emerge is that like the central cities they surround, many of the incorporated suburban municipalities adjacent to city boundaries are surrounded by other jurisdictions which inhibit the annexation of growth in unincorporated territory. Hence, the opportunity to grow through annexation is being closed for many suburbs that lie along city boundaries. Also, many of these suburban areas were built around the time of World War II and were initially populated by parents of the baby-boom generation, but as the baby-boom children left home, many of the suburbs they left behind have come to be inhabited by empty-nest households. This declining household size in many instances may have become great enough to produce declines in total population. Finally, many older suburbs adjacent to large cities may be increasingly subject to a spillover of crime, congestion, pollution, and other disamenities that have been associated with recent population declines in large cities.

Like the "exurbs" referred to earlier, there is no official or standard definition of what constitutes an "inner suburb". Indeed, many cities, especially those in the South and West, do not have a ring of inner suburbs, but for cities that are almost entirely surrounded by incorporated places, we can examine population trends in the suburban municipalities that lie along city boundaries. Most of the large cities that experienced substantial population decline in the 1970s decade are almost completely encircled in this fashion. Figures from the 1960, 1970, and 1980 censuses on population change in the central city, the ring of inner suburbs and in the balance of the metropolitan area (that is, beyond the ring of inner suburbs) are presented in table 5.5 for 11 metropolitan areas whose central cities would probably be included in almost any list of cities in America that are large, old and declining in population. A few cities that would also likely be included in such a list were excluded (e.g., Baltimore) because they are not surrounded by enough incorporated municipalities to clearly establish an inner ring of suburbs. Data for unincorporated places (now termed census defined places—CDP's) from the 1980 census were not available at the time of this analysis.

All of the 11 cities decreased in population by at least 10 per cent between 1970 and 1980, and all but two (Kansas City and New York City) also lost population in the 1960s. Moreover, for the nine that lost population in both decades, the rate of decline was higher in the 1970s than in the 1960s, indicating an acceleration of a pattern of population loss that began in a number of older, larger urban areas around 1950.

In some cases, the rate of loss is quite large. St. Louis, Cleveland and Detroit each lost at least 20 per cent of its population in the ten years following 1970. St. Louis has lost nearly one-half of the peak population it reached in 1950, and it now has shrunk to its 1890 population. Cleveland has lost 37 per cent of its population since 1950 and has shrunk to what its population was around the time of World War I. Detroit has lost 35 per cent of its population peak reached in 1950 and now has about as many residents as it did in the 1920s.

Up to the present each of the above three cities has tended to have growing suburbs whose population increases were great enough to offset declines in the central city, and in this way their metropolitan areas continued to register population growth. In the 1970-80 decade, however, a change occurred. For the metropolitan areas of St. Louis, Cleveland, Detroit, and a number of other cities, population growth in the suburbs was no longer great enough to offset decline in the central city. The result was that entire metropolitan areas shifted to population decline. As can be seen, the population of the St. Louis metropolitan area declined by 2.3 per cent between 1970 and 1980, after growing by 12.4 per cent in the 1960-70 decade. The Cleveland metropolitan area population declined by eight per cent in the 1970s, after growing by eight per cent in the 1960s. The

TABLE 5.5

Population change in the central city and the inner and outer suburban jurisdictions of 11 Metropolitan Areas: 1960 to 1970 and 1970 to 1980
(SMSA boundaries as of January 1, 1980 are used)

Metropolitan area	Population			Percent distribution of population			Percent change in population	
	1960	1970	1980	1960	1970	1980	1960-70	1970-80
St. Louis metropolitan area	2,144,205	2,410,884	2,355,276	100.0	100.0	100.0	12.4	-2.3
St. Louis city	750,026	622,236	453,085	35.0	25.8	19.2	-17.0	-27.2
Inner suburbs	269,011	256,840	217,733	12.5	10.7	9.2	-4.5	-15.2
Remainder of metro area	1,125,168	1,531,808	1,684,458	52.5	63.5	71.5	36.1	10.0
Cleveland metropolitan area	1,909,483	2,063,729	1,898,720	100.0	100.0	100.0	8.1	-8.0
Cleveland city	876,050	750,879	573,822	45.9	36.4	30.2	-14.3	-23.6
Inner suburbs	520,757	599,404	531,878	27.3	29.0	28.0	15.1	-11.3
Remainder of metro area	512,676	713,446	793,020	26.8	34.6	41.8	39.2	11.2
Detroit metropolitan area	3,949,720	4,435,051	4,352,762	100.0	100.0	100.0	12.3	-1.9
Detroit city	1,670,144	1,514,063	1,203,339	42.3	34.1	27.6	-9.3	-20.5
Inner suburbs	794,796	904,896	792,528	20.1	20.4	18.2	13.9	-12.4
Remainder of metro area	1,484,780	2,016,092	2,356,895	37.6	45.5	54.1	35.8	16.9
Pittsburgh metropolitan area	2,405,435	2,401,362	2,263,894	100.0	100.0	100.0	-0.2	-5.7
Pittsburgh city	604,332	520,089	423,938	25.1	21.7	18.7	-13.9	-18.5
Inner suburbs	410,913	434,994	395,834	17.1	18.1	17.5	5.9	-9.0
Remainder of metro area	1,390,190	1,446,279	1,444,122	57.8	60.2	63.8	4.0	-0.1
Washington, D.C. metropolitan area	2,096,662	2,910,111	3,060,240	100.0	100.0	100.0	38.8	5.2
Washington city	763,956	756,668	637,651	36.4	26.0	20.8	-1.0	-15.7
Inner suburbs	438,859	514,427	448,373	20.9	17.7	14.7	17.2	-12.8
Remainder of metro area	893,847	1,639,016	1,974,216	42.6	56.3	64.5	83.4	20.5

Continued 5.5

Philadelphia metropolitian area	4,342,897	4,824,110	4,716,818	100.0	100.0	100.0	11.1	-2.2
Philadelphia city	2,002,512	1,949,996	1,688,210	46.1	40.4	35.8	-2.6	-13.4
Inner suburbs	642,430	698,061	665,263	14.8	14.5	14.1	8.7	-4.7
Remainder of metro area	1,697,955	2,176,053	2,363,345	39.1	45.1	50.1	28.2	8.6
Boston metropolitan area	2,688,083	2,899,101	2,763,357	100.0	100.0	100.0	7.9	-4.7
Boston city	697,197	641,071	562,994	25.9	22.1	20.4	-8.1	-12.2
Inner suburbs	663,262	657,097	606,006	24.7	22.7	21.9	-0.9	-7.8
Remainder of metro area	1,327,624	1,600,933	1,594,357	49.4	55.2	57.7	20.6	-0.4
Kansas City metropolitan area	1,108,620	1,273,926	1,327,020	100.0	100.0	100.0	14.9	4.2
Kansas City	475,539	507,330	448,159	42.9	39.8	33.8	6.7	-11.7
Inner suburbs	164,105	268,362	286,504	14.8	21.1	21.6	63.5	6.8
Remainder of metro area	468,976	498,234	592,357	42.3	39.1	44.6	6.2	18.9
Milwaukee metropolitan area	1,278,850	1,403,884	1,397,143	100.0	100.0	100.0	9.8	-0.5
Milwaukee city	741,324	717,372	636,212	58.0	51.1	45.5	-3.2	-11.3
Inner suburbs	252,328	294,902	285,706	19.7	21.0	20.4	16.9	-3.1
Remainder of metro area	285,198	391,610	475,225	22.3	27.9	34.0	37.3	21.4
Chicago metropolitan area	6,220,913	6,974,755	7,102,328	100.0	100.0	100.0	12.1	1.8
Chicago city	3,550,404	3,369,357	3,005,072	57.1	48.3	42.3	-5.1	-10.8
Inner suburbs	736,425	882,621	824,156	11.8	12.7	11.6	19.9	-6.6
Remainder of metro area	1,934,084	2,722,777	3,273,100	31.1	39.0	46.1	40.8	20.2
New York City metropolitan area	9,539,655	9,973,716	9,119,737	100.0	100.0	100.0	4.6	-8.6
New York City	7,781,984	7,895,563	7,071,030	81.6	79.2	77.5	1.5	-10.4
Inner suburbs (N.Y. State only)	431,771	447,376	416,131	4.5	4.5	4.6	3.6	-7.0
Remainder of metro area	1,325,900	1,630,777	1,632,576	13.9	16.4	17.9	23.0	0.1

metropolitan areas of Detroit, Philadelphia, Boston, Milwaukee, and New York City each declined in population in the 1970s after having grown in the 1960s. Clearly, population decline has come to encompass a number of entire metropolitan areas.

One of the reasons why suburban population growth is not always great enough to offset central city decline is that in a growing number of cases a ring of inner suburbs has shifted from growth to decline. Ten of the 11 cities shown in table 5.5 have a ring of suburbs which collectively declined in population between 1970 and 1980; in the 1960s only two of these cities had inner suburban rings that declined in population.

In some cases the transition of the inner suburbs from growth to decline is quite pronounced. Cleveland's inner suburbs went from 15.1 per cent growth in the 1960s to 11.3 per cent decline in the 1970s. Detroit's inner suburbs shifted from growth of 13.9 per cent in the 1960s to 12.4 per cent decline in the 1970s. An abrupt transition from growth to decline in close-in suburban areas is not limited to these two metropolitan areas.

Moreover, the transition from growth to decline of population in inner suburbs was frequently more abrupt than the similar transition made by central cities. A typical pattern of many industrial cities of the Northeast and Midwest was to experience a slowdown in growth during the 1930s, followed by a modest revival of growth in the 1940s and a change to moderate population decline after 1950 or 1960. Many of the rings of inner suburbs, however, were largely built in the years following World War II and experienced very rapid rates of population growth through the 1950s and sometimes even the 1960s. Hence, they have gone from rapid growth to rather substantial population decline in a shorter period of time than did cities, and by implication, this more rapid alteration in population growth patterns could put even greater strain on public facilities and management than was faced by cities. After housing and educating a substantial proportion of the baby boom generation of the 1950s and 1960s, many inner suburbs were suddenly confronted by empty classrooms in the 1970s and now face the need to re-cycle school buildings and accommodate an aging population. Other implications will become somewhat clearer through analysis of the changing socioeconomic characteristics of persons living in suburban areas that are now undergoing population loss.

There are several points to emphasize from currently available data from the 1980 census. The overall decline in the growth rates in suburban territory of the nation as a whole reflects more than just a gradual slowing of population growth as a result of falling fertility levels; the growth rate reduction is partly the product of a rapid shift to population decline among a growing number of suburban municipalities adjacent to large central cities. Not only is the area of population decrease spreading outward to encompass the inner suburbs of many older, larger central cities, but the locus of vigorous growth is shifting beyond what is traditionally defined as suburbia. These data provide a basis for looking upon a growing number of metropolitan areas as doughnuts whose centres (the area of population decline) are expanding. These trends imply a lessened distinctiveness of the suburbs as places of rapid population growth, for clearly there is a growing heterogeneity of patterns of population change in individual suburban locations.

The relatively rapid transition from growth to decline in the inner suburbs of the cities examined in this section comes as something of a surprise. Certainly there were abundant reasons for expecting a slowing of growth in such areas, but this type of change is one that is not easily analyzed with the data sources available between the decennial censuses. The commonly used surveys are not large enough to capture such a change, and since the inner suburbs are subcounty units, their transition from growth to decline was not reflected in the intercensal county population estimates which revealed the "turnaround" in population growth in nonmetropolitan areas. Hence the diffusion of population decline beyond the boundaries of many of the older and larger cities is a somewhat unexpected accompaniment to the diffusion of growth beyond the boundaries of metropolitan areas.

CONCLUSION: THE DURATION OF DECONCENTRATION

The last question posed at the beginning of this study was whether the shift of population growth to nonmetropolitan areas was slowed by rapid rises in the price of gasoline and occasional uncertainties regarding its supply in the years following the 1973-74 oil embargo. Such developments might severely affect low-density nonmetropolitan locations where public transportation is almost nonexistent and residents are highly dependent on private automobiles. Because of high fuel costs, industry, too, might be reluctant to relocate to low-density settings, and the overall result might be to slow the faster rate of population growth in nonmetropolitan settings.

Obviously these are questions that the decennial census data alone cannot answer with certainty. One way to deal with these issues, however, is to utilize the Census Bureau's intercensal county population estimates that were prepared and published annually from 1970 through 1978. We earlier concluded that when extrapolated to 1980, these estimates came fairly close to representing the degree of difference in metropolitan and nonmetropolitan population growth rates as shown by the 1970 and 1980 census results. Hence, the intercensal estimates probably are useful in providing clues as to whether the higher population growth rate in nonmetropolitan areas was slowed relative to that of metropolitan areas in the latter part of the decade.

An earlier study did, in fact, make these comparisons and concluded that the difference in population growth rates between metropolitan and nonmetropolitan territory was greater in 1974-78 than in 1970-74 (see Long and DeAre, 1980). In 1970-74 the growth rate of population in nonmetropolitan territory exceeded that of metropolitan territory by 48 per cent. In 1974-78 the differential was greater: the nonmetropolitan growth rate exceeded that of metropolitan territory by 64 per cent.

These figures suggest that the shift of population growth to nonmetropolitan settings had not slowed by 1978, in spite of rising fuel costs that might be detrimental to rural and low-density settings. Of course, the faster rate of total population increase in nonmetropolitan settings is a complex interplay of several factors, including more persons deciding to remain rather than leave such areas, more persons leaving metropolitan areas, and differences in family size of migrants between the two residential categories (Tucker, 1976; 1981). Even if the number of persons moving to nonmetropolitan areas were to fall, a momentum to total population growth in the nonmetropolitan sector appears to have been established through the current childbearing of previous migrants to nonmetropolitan territory.

For these reasons, a faster rate of growth in total population in non-metropolitan than in metropolitan areas is likely to continue and be a distinguishing feature of demographic patterns of the 1980s. But as new equilibria are reached and as some growing rural counties are reclassified as suburban parts of metropolitan agglomerations and as new metropolitan areas are carved out of nonmetropolitan territory, the differences in population growth rates between the nonmetropolitan and metropolitan residential categories will narrow. At the moment, one can anticipate this eventuality without knowing exactly when it will occur.

These considerations suggest the continued spatial expansion of the American metropolitan system. The 1980 geographical boundaries of metropolitan territory encompassed more land, more people, and a larger share of the American population than did the 1970 boundaries (Forstall, 1981). Without doubt, the 1990 census will find still more land, more people, and a larger share of the total population living in what at that time is classified as metropolitan. What was different about the 1970s was that without territorial expansion the proportion of Americans living in metropolitan territory would have fallen—a reversal of a historical pattern. The duration of this new aspect of American metropolitanization is uncertain.

REFERENCES

Allis, Sam. December 16, 1980. "Localities Aim for Lucrative Rank of Standard Metropolitan Areas." **The Wall Street Journal.**

Beale, Calvin L. 1975. **The Revival of Population Growth in Nonmetropolitan America.** Washington, D.C.: Economic Research Service, U.S. Department of Agriculture.

Berry, Brian J.L. and Donald C. Dahmann. 1977. **Population Redistribution in the United States in the 1970s.** Washington, D.C.: National Academy of

Berry, Brian J. L. and Jonn D. Kasarda. 1977. **Contemporary Urban Ecology.** New York: The Macmillan Company.

Brown, David L. and John M. Wardwell (eds.). 1980. **New Directions in Urban-Rural Migration: The Population Turnaround in Rural America.** New York: Academic Press, Inc.

Carlson, Eugene. November 17, 1981. "Small Cities Have a Big Stake in Being Defined as SMSAs." **The Wall Street Journal.**

Fava, Sylvia. 1979. "Changing Suburban Images: Is the Bloom Off the Rose?" **New York Affairs,** 5, pp.6-14.

Forstall, Richard L. 1981. "Is America Becoming More Metropolitan?" **American Demographics.** December, pp. 18-22.

Guest, Avery M. 1979. "Patterns of Suburban Population

Growth, 1970-75." **Demography.** 16, pp.401-415.

Long, John F. 1981. **Population Deconcentration in the United States,** 1981. Special Demographic Analyses, CDS-81-5. Washington, D.C.: U.S. Government Printing Office.

Long, Larry H. 1980. "Back to the Countryside and Back to the City in the Same Decade." pp. 61-76 in Shirley Laska and Daphne Spain (eds.), **Back to the City: Issues in Neighborhood Renovation.** Elmsford, New York: Pergamon Press.

Long, Larry H. and Donald C. Dahmann. 1980.**The City-Suburb Income Gap: Is It being Narrowed by a Back-to-the-City Movement?** Special Demographic Analyses, CDS-80-1, U.S. Bureau of the Census. Washington, D.C.: U.S. Government Printing Office.

Long, Larry H. and Diana DeAre. 1980. **Migration to Nonmetropolitan Areas: Appraising the Trend and Reasons for Moving.** Special Demographic Analyses CDS-80-2, U.S. Bureau of the Census. Washington, D.C.: U.S. Government Printing Office.

Morrison, Peter A. 1976. **Rural Renaissance in America? The Revival of Population Growth in Remote Areas.** Washington, D.C.: Population Reference Bureau.

Roseman, Curtis C. 1980. "Exurban Areas and Exurban Migration." pp. 51-53 in Stanley D. Brunn and James O. Wheeler (eds.), **The American Metropolitan System: Present and Future.** New York: V. H. Winston and Sons.

Shryock, Henry S., Jr. 1957. "The Natural History of Standard Metropolitan Areas." **American Journal of Sociology.** 63(September): pp.163-170.

Sternlieb, George and Robert W. Lake. 1975. "Aging Suburbs and Black Homeownership." **Annals of the Academy of Political and Social Science**, 422, pp.105-117.

Taeuber, Irene. 1972. "The Changing Distribution of th Population of the United States in the Twentieth Century." pp.29-107 in U.S. Commission on Population Growth and the American Future, **Population, Distribution, and Policy**, edited by Sara Mills Mazie. Washington, D.C.: U.S. Government Printing Office.

Tucker, C. Jack. 1976. "Changing Patterns of Migration between Metropolitan and Nonmetropolitan Areas in the United States: Recent Evidence." **Demography.** 13(November): pp.435-443.

Tucker, C. Jack 1981. "Age and Educational Dimensions of Recent U.S. Migration Reversal." **Growth and Change.** 12(April): pp.31-36.

U.S. Bureau of the Census. 1971. **General Demographic Trends for Metropolitan Areas, 1960 to 1970.** Final Report PHC(2)-1, 1970 Census of Population and Housing.

Washington, D.C.: U.S. Government Printing Office.

_______. 1980. "Estimates of the Population of Counties and Metropolitan Areas: July 1, 1977 and 1978." **Current Population Reports,** Series P-25, No. 873. Washington, D.C.: U.S. Government Printing Office.

U.S. Department of Commerce. October 24, 1978. Office of Federal Statistical Policy and Standards, "Report on the Uses of Standard Metropolitan Statistical Areas in Federal Programs—1978." Washington, D.C.: U.S. Government Printing Office.

Vining, D. R. and A. Strauss. 1977. "A Demonstration that the Current Deconcentration of Population in the United States is a Clean Break with the Past." **Environment and Planning.** 9(July), pp.751-758

A1 2P

TABLE 5.A1.

Population change from 1960 to 1970 and from 1970 to 1980 in metropolitan areas and in nonmetropolitan counties adjacent and not adjacent to metropolitan areas, by region, for metropolitan areas as defined in 1970.

Region and type of residence	1980	1970	1960	Change Number	1970-80 Percent	Change, Number	1960-70 Percent
UNITED STATES							
Total population	226504825	203302031	179310672	23202794	11.41	23991359	13.38
Metropolitan counties	152656498	140324312	120263586	12332186	8.79	20060726	16.68
Nonmetropolitan counties	73848327	62977719	59047086	10870608	17.26	3930633	6.66
Adjacent to a metropolitan area	38905304	32638812	29519645	6266492	19.20	3119167	10.57
Not adjacent to a metropolitan area	34943023	30338907	29527441	4604116	15.18	811466	2.75
NORTHEAST							
Total population	49136667	49060514	44677819	76153	.16	4382695	9.81
Metropolitan counties	39053773	40045383	36725060	-991610	-2.47	3320323	9.04
Nenmetrpolitan counties	10082894	9015131	7952759	1067763	11.84	1062372	13.36
Adjacent to a metropolitan area	7575348	6765865	5851197	809483	11.96	914668	15.63
Not adjacent to a metropolitan area	2507546	2249266	2101562	258280	11.48	147704	7.03
NORTH CENTRAL							
Total population	58853804	56590294	51619139	2263510	4.00	4971155	9.63
Metropolitan counties	38315469	37672375	33350785	643094	1.71	4321590	12.96
Nonmetropolitan counties	20538335	18917919	18268354	1620416	8.57	649565	3.56
Adjacent to a metropolitan area	10690051	9716590	9078432	973461	10.02	638158	7.03
Not adjacent to a metropolitan area	9848284	9201329	9189922	646955	7.03	11407	.12

Continued 5.A1

SOUTH							
Total population	75349155	62812980	54960610	12536175	19.96	7852370	14.29
Metropolitan counties	42016056	35208212	28860020	6807844	19.34	6348192	22.00
Nonmetropolitan counties	33333099	27604768	26100590	5728331	20.75	1504178	5.76
Adjacent to a metropolitan area	15967747	12752212	11672293	3215535	25.22	1079919	9.25
Not adjacent to a metropolitan area	17365352	14852556	14428297	2512796	16.92	424259	2.94
WEST							
Total population	43165199	34838243	28053104	8326956	23.90	6785139	24.19
Metropolitan counties	33271200	27398342	21327721	5872858	21.44	6070621	28.46
Nonmetropolitan counties	9893999	7439901	6725383	2454098	32.99	714518	10.62
Adjacent to a metropolitan area	4672158	3404145	2917723	1268013	37.25	486422	16.67
Not adjacent to a metropolitan area	5221841	4035756	3807660	1186085	29.39	228096	5.99

Note: Metropolitan refers to Standard Metropolitan Statistical Areas (SMSA's), except for New England where New England County Metropolitan Areas (NECMA's) are used.
Nonmetropolitan refers to outside SMSA's (NECMA's in New England).

TABLE 5.A2.

Population change from 1960 to 1970 and from 1970 to 1980 in metropolitan areas and in nonmetropolitan counties adjacent and not adjacent to metropolitan areas, by region, for metropolitan areas as defined in 1974.

Region and type of residence	1980	1970	1960	Change, Number	1970-80 Percent	Change, Number	1960-70 Percent
UNITED STATES							
Total population	226504825	203302031	179310672	23202794	11.41	23991359	13.38
Metropolitan counties	163502644	148879913	127178541	14622731	9.82	21701372	17.06
Nonmetropolitan counties	63002181	54422118	52132131	8580063	15.77	2289987	4.39
Adjacent to a metropolitan area	35341392	30121253	28117396	5220139	17.33	2003857	7.13
Not adjacent to a metropolitan area	27660789	24300865	24014735	3359924	13.83	286130	1.19
NORTHEAST							
Total population	49136667	49060514	44677819	76153	.16	4382695	9.81
Metropolitan counties	41715627	42480535	38609277	-764908	-1.79	3871258	10.03
Nonmetrpolitan counties	7421040	6579979	6068542	841061	12.78	511437	8.43
Adjacent to a metropolitan area	5750853	5085817	4625363	665036	13.08	460454	9.95
Not adjacent to a metropolitan area	1670187	1494162	1443179	176025	11.78	50983	3.53
NORTH CENTRAL							
Total population	58853804	56590294	51619139	2263510	4.00	4971155	9.63
Metropolitan counties	40032676	39107479	34604593	925197	2.37	4502886	13.01
Nonmetropolitan counties	18821128	17482815	17014546	1338313	7.66	468269	2.75
Adjacent to a metropolitan area	10015015	9214693	8712608	800322	8.69	502085	5.76
Not adjacent to a metropolitan area	8806113	8268122	8301938	537991	6.51	-33816	-.40

Continued 5.A2

SOUTH							
Total population	75349155	62812980	54960610	12536175	19.96	7852370	14.29
Metropolitan counties	47708546	39352782	32199408	8355764	21.23	7153374	22.22
Nonmetropolitan counties	27640609	23460198	22761202	4180411	17.82	698996	3.07
Adjacent to a metropolitan area	14911794	12393641	11803071	2518153	20.32	590570	5.00
Not adjacent to a metropolitan area	12728815	11066557	10958131	1662258	15.02	108426	.99
WEST							
Total population	43165199	34838243	28053104	8326956	23.90	6785139	24.19
Metropolitan counties	34045795	27939117	21765263	6106678	21.86	6173854	28.37
Nonmetropolitan counties	9119404	6899126	6287841	2220278	32.18	611285	9.72
Adjacent to a metropolitan area	4663730	3427102	2976354	1236628	36.08	450748	15.14
Not adjacent to a metropolitan area	4455674	3472024	3311487	983650	28.33	160537	4.85

Note: Metropolitan refers to Standard Metropolitan Statistical Areas (SMSA's), except for New England where New England County Metropolitan Areas (NECMA's) are used.

Nonmetropolitan refers to outside SMSA's (NECMA's in New England).

TABLE 5.A3.

Population change from 1960 to 1970 and from 1970 to 1980 in metropolitan areas and in nonmetropolitan counties adjacent and not adjacent to metropolitan areas, by region, for metropolitan areas defined as of January 1, 1980.

Region and type of residence	1980	1970	1960	Change, 1970-80 Number	Change, 1970-80 Percent	Change, 1960-70 Number	Change, 1960-70 Percent
UNITED STATES							
Total population	226504825	203302031	179310672	23202794	11.41	23991359	13.38
Metropolitan counties	165993492	150882700	128840848	15110792	10.01	22041852	17.11
Nonmetropolitan counties	60511333	52419331	50469824	8092002	15.44	1949507	3.86
Adjacent to a metropolitan area	34470044	29536194	27811313	4933850	16.70	1724881	6.20
Not adjacent to a metropolitan area	26041289	22883137	22658511	3158152	13.80	224626	.99
NORTHEAST							
Total population	49136667	49060514	44677819	76153	.16	4382695	9.81
Metropolitan counties	41715627	42480535	38609277	-764908	-1.79	3871258	10.03
Nonmetrpolitan counties	7421040	6579979	6068542	841061	12.78	511437	8.43
Adjacent to a metropolitan area	5750853	5085817	4625363	665036	13.08	460454	9.95
Not adjacent to a metropolitan area	1670187	1494162	1443179	176025	11.78	50983	3.53
NORTH CENTRAL							
Total population	58853804	56590294	51619139	2263510	4.00	4971155	9.63
Metropolitan counties	41166100	40126222	35472834	1039878	2.59	4653388	13.12
Nonmetropolitan counties	17687704	16464072	16146305	1223632	7.43	317767	1.97
Adjacent to a metropolitan area	9966404	9179886	8792744	786518	8.57	387142	4.40
Not adjacent to a metropolitan area	7721300	7284186	7353561	437114	6.00	-69375	-.93

Continued 5.A3

SOUTH							
Total population	75349155	62812980	54960610	12536175	19.96	7852370	14.29
Metropolitan counties	48697008	40087856	32807839	8609152	21.48	7280017	22.19
Nonmetropolitan counties	26652147	22725124	22152771	3927023	17.28	572353	2.58
Adjacent to a metropolitan area	14307500	11963703	11474811	2343797	19.59	488892	4.26
Not adjacent to a metropolitan area	12344647	10761421	10677960	1583226	14.71	83461	.78
WEST							
Total population	43165199	34838243	28053104	8326956	23.90	6785139	24.19
Metropolitan counties	34414757	28188087	21950898	6226670	22.09	6237189	28.41
Nonmetropolitan counties	8750442	6650156	6102206	2100286	31.58	547950	8.98
Adjacent to a metropolitan area	4445287	3306788	2913395	1138499	34.43	388393	13.31
Not adjacent to a metropolitan area	4305155	3343368	3183811	961787	28.77	159557	5.01

Note: Metropolitan refers to Standard Metropolitan Statistical Areas (SMSA's), except for New England where New England County Metropolitan Areas (NECMA's) are used. Nonmetropolitan refers to outside SMSA's (NECMA's in New England).

TABLE 5.A4.

Metropolitan population change from 1960 to 1970 and from 1970 to 1980, by size and region, for metropolitan areas as defined in 1970

Region and size	1980	1970	1960	Change, 1970-80 Number	Change, 1970-80 Percent	Change, 1960-70 Number	Change, 1960-70 Percent
UNITED STATES							
All metrpololitan areas	152656498	140324312	120263586	12332186	8.79	20060726	16.68
Metropolitan areas of:							
3 million or more population	41058961	41439919	37065943	-380958	-.91	4373976	11.80
1 to 3 million	44906182	40202369	32754121	4703813	11.70	7448248	22.74
500,000 to 1 million	26766998	24190354	20562086	2576644	10.65	3628268	17.65
250,000 to 500,000	22289758	19126367	16404738	3163391	16.54	2721629	16.59
100,000 to 250,000	15697236	13697717	11970507	1999519	14.60	1727210	14.43
Under 100,000	1937363	1667586	1506191	269777	16.18	161395	10.72
NORTHEAST							
All metropolitan areas	39053773	40045383	36725060	-991610	-2.47	3320323	9.04
Metropolitan areas of:							
3 million or more population	19182622	20109492	18395137	-926870	-4.60	1714355	9.32
1 to 3 million	6561612	6967599	6588685	-405987	-5.82	378914	5.75
500,000 to 1 million	7784209	7737361	6894586	46848	.61	842775	12.22
250,000 to 500,000	3858243	3676850	3432017	181393	4.93	244833	7.13
100,000 to 250,000	1567430	1462802	1328323	104628	7.15	134479	10.12
under 100,000	99657	91279	86312	8378	9.18	4967	5.75
NORTH CENTRAL							
All metropolitan areas	38315469	37672375	33350785	643094	1.71	4321590	12.96
Metropolitan areas of:							
3 million or more population	11145961	11179198	9983273	-33237	-.29	1195925	11.98
1 to 3 million	11111037	11149139	9851088	-38102	-.33	1298051	13.18
500,000 to 1 million	5666998	5524346	4834545	142652	2.58	689801	14.27
250,000 to 500,000	4855181	4607294	4073224	247887	5.38	534070	13.11
100,000 to 250,000	4961821	4694158	4158252	267663	5.70	535906	12.89
Under 100,000	574471	518240	450403	56231	10.85	67837	15.06

Continued 5.A4

SOUTH							
All metropolitan areas	42016056	35208212	28860020	6807844	19.34	6348192	22.00
Metropolitan areas of:							
3 million or more population	0	0	0	0	0	0	0
1 to 3 million	16146687	13440481	10266822	2706206	20.13	3173659	30.91
500,000 to 1 million	9265279	7965463	6595738	1299816	16.32	1369725	20.77
250,000 to 500,000	8907672	7273077	6168194	1634595	22.47	1104883	17.91
100,000 to 250,000	6621914	5640295	5012224	981619	17.40	628071	12.53
Under 100,000	1074504	888896	817042	185608	20.88	71854	8.79
WEST							
All metropolitan areas	33271200	27398342	21327721	5872858	21.44	6070621	28.46
Metropolitan areas of:							
3 million or more population	10730378	10151229	8687533	579149	5.71	1463696	16.85
1 to 3 million	11086846	8645150	6047526	2441696	28.24	2597624	42.95
500,000 to 1 million	4050512	2963184	2237217	1087328	36.69	725967	32.45
250,000 to 500,000	4668662	3569146	2731303	1099516	30.81	837843	30.68
100,000 to 250,000	2546071	1900462	1471708	645609	33.97	428754	29.13
Under 100,000	188731	169171	152434	19560	11.56	16737	10.98

Note: Metropolitan refers to Standard Metropolitan Statistical Areas (SMSA's), except for New England where New England County Metropolitan Areas (NECMA's) are used.
Nonmetropolitan refers to outside SMSA's (NECMA's in New England). Size refers to SMSA/NECMA population in 1970.

TABLE 5.A5.

Metropolitan population change from 1960 to 1970 and from 1970 to 1980, by size and region, for metropolitan areas as defined in 1974

Region and size	1980	1970	1960	Change, 1970-80 Number	Percent	Change, 1960-70 Number	Percent
UNITED STATES							
All metrpololitan areas	163502644	148879913	127178541	14622731	9.82	21701372	17.06
Metropolitan areas of:							
3 million or more population	39875200	40207454	36197354	-332254	-.82	4010100	11.08
1 to 3 million	50523975	45044547	36399297	5479428	12.16	8645250	23.75
500,000 to 1 million	28640172	25672133	21943511	2968039	11.56	3728622	16.99
250,000 to 500,000	24650687	21117685	18042599	3533002	16.73	3075086	17.04
100,000 to 250,000	17605978	14961693	12901237	2644285	17.67	2060456	15.97
Under 100,000	2206632	1876401	1694543	330231	17.60	181858	10.73
NORTHEAST							
All metropolitan areas	41715627	42480535	38609277	-764908	-1.79	3871258	10.03
Metropolitan areas of:							
3 million or more population	17689732	18646419	17339188	-956687	-5.12	1307231	7.54
1 to 3 million	9129190	9399104	8359837	-269914	-2.86	1039267	12.43
500,000 to 1 million	8501682	8397330	7497210	104352	1.24	900120	12.01
250,000 to 500,000	4465922	4257525	3826064	208397	4.89	431461	11.28
100,000 to 250,000	1829444	1688878	1500666	140566	8.32	188212	12.54
under 100,000	99657	91279	86312	8378	9.18	4967	5.75
NORTH CENTRAL							
All metropolitan areas	40032676	39107479	34604593	925197	2.37	4502886	13.01
Metropolitan areas of:							
3 million or more population	11455090	11409806	10170633	45284	.40	1239173	12.18
1 to 3 million	12487823	12383264	10867774	104559	.84	1515490	13.94
500,000 to 1 million	5299803	5186952	4572043	112851	2.18	614909	13.45
250,000 to 500,000	5083362	4792383	4272578	290979	6.07	519805	12.17
100,000 to 250,000	5118147	4804921	4260100	313226	6.52	544821	12.79
Under 100,000	588451	530153	461465	58298	11.00	68688	14.88

Continued 5.A5

SOUTH							
All metropolitan areas	47708546	59352782	32199408	8355764	21.23	7153374	22.22
Metropolitan areas of:							
3 million or more population	0	0	0	0	.0	0	.0
1 to 3 million	17792522	14607350	11118659	3185172	21.81	3488691	31.38
500,000 to 1 million	10617526	8976844	7508429	1640682	18.28	1468415	19.56
250,000 to 500,000	10397942	8481139	7198453	1916803	22.60	1282686	17.82
100,000 to 250,000	7715232	6295007	5464947	1420225	22.56	830060	15.19
Under 100,000	1185324	992442	908920	192882	19.44	83522	9.19
WEST							
All metropolitan areas	34045795	27939117	21763265	6106678	21.86	6173854	28.37
Metropolitan areas of:							
3 million or more population	10730378	10151229	8687533	579149	5.71	1463696	16.85
1 to 3 million	11114440	8654829	6053027	2459611	28.42	2601802	42.98
500,000 to 1 million	4221161	3111007	2365827	1110154	35.68	745178	31.50
250,000 to 500,000	4703461	3586638	2745504	1116823	31.14	841134	30.64
100,000 to 250,000	2943155	2172887	1675524	770268	35.45	497363	29.68
Under 100,000	333200	262527	237846	70673	26.92	24681	10.38

Note: Metropolitan refers to Standard Metropolitan Statistical Areas (SMSA's), except for New England where New England County Metropolitan Areas (NECMA's) are used.
Nonmetropolitan refers to outside SMSA's (NECMA's in New England). Size refers to SMSA/NECMA population in 1970.

TABLE 5.A6

Metropolitan population change from 1960 to 1970 and from 1970 to 1980, by size and region, for metropolitan areas as defined as of January 1, 1980

Region and size	1980	1970	1960	Change, 1970-80 Number	Change, 1970-80 Percent	Change, 1960-70 Number	Change, 1960-70 Percent
UNITED STATES							
All metrpololitan areas	165993492	150882700	128840848	15110792	10.01	22041852	17.11
Metropolitan areas of:							
3 million or more population	39875200	40207454	36197354	-332254	-.82	4010100	11.08
1 to 3 million	50523975	45044547	36399297	5479428	12.16	8645250	23.75
500,000 to 1 million	28640172	25672133	21943511	2968039	11.56	3728622	16.99
250,000 to 500,000	24882530	21287427	18199135	3595103	16.89	3088292	16.97
100,000 to 250,000	18460852	15671719	13487957	2789133	17.80	2183762	16.19
Under 100,000	3610763	2999420	2613594	611343	20.38	385826	14.76
NORTHEAST							
All metropolitan areas	41715627	42480535	38609277	-764908	-1.79	3871258	10.03
Metropolitan areas of:							
3 million or more population	17689732	18646419	17339188	-956687	-5.12	1307231	7.54
1 to 3 million	9129190	9399104	8359837	-269914	-2.86	1039267	12.43
500,000 to 1 million	8501682	8397330	7497210	104352	1.24	900120	12.01
250,000 to 500,000	4465922	4257525	3826064	208397	4.89	431461	11.28
100,000 to 250,000	1829444	1688878	1500666	140566	8.32	188212	12.54
under 100,000	99657	91279	86312	8378	9.18	4967	5.75

Continued 5.A6

NORTH CENTRAL							
All metropolitan areas	41166100	40126222	35472834	1039878	2.59	4653388	13.12
Metropolitan areas of:							
3 million or more population	11455090	11409806	10170633	45284	.40	1239173	12.18
1 to 3 million	12487823	12383264	10867774	104559	.84	1515490	13.94
500,000 to 1 million	5299803	5186952	4572043	112851	2.18	614909	13.45
250,000 to 500,000	5083362	4792383	4272578	290979	6.07	519805	12.17
100,000 to 250,000	5525404	5178356	4584199	347048	6.70	594157	12.96
Under 100,000	1314618	1175461	1005607	139157	11.84	169854	16.89
SOUTH							
All metropolitan areas	48697008	40087856	32807839	8609152	21.48	7280017	22.19
Metropolitan areas of:							
3 million or more population	0	0	0	0	0	0	0
1 to 3 million	17792522	14607350	11118659	3185172	21.81	3488691	31.38
500,000 to 1 million	10617526	8976844	7508429	1640682	18.28	1468415	19.56
250,000 to 500,000	10629785	8650881	7354989	1978904	22.88	1295892	17.62
100,000 to 250,000	8162849	6631598	5727568	1531251	23.09	904030	13.78
Under 100,000	1494326	1221183	1098194	273143	22.37	122989	15.20
WEST							
All metropolitan areas	34414757	28188087	21950898	6226670	22.09	6237189	28.41
Metropolitan areas of:							
3 million or more population	10730378	10151229	8687533	579149	5.71	1463696	16.85
1 to 3 million	11114440	8654829	6053027	2459611	28.42	2601802	42.98
500,000 to 1 million	4221161	3111007	2365829	1110154	35.68	745178	31.50
250,000 to 500,000	4703461	3586638	2745504	1116823	31.14	841134	30.64
100,000 to 250,000	2943155	2172887	1675524	770268	35.45	497363	29.68
Under 100,000	702162	511497	423481	190665	37.28	88016	20.78

Note: Metropolitan refers to Standard Metropolitan Statistical Areas (SMSA's), except for New England where New England CountyMetropolitan Areas (NECMA's) are used.

Nonmetropolitan refers to outside SMSA's (NECMA's in New England). Size refers to SMSA/NECMA population in 1970.

TABLE 5.A7.

Central city population change from 1960 to 1970 and from 1970 to 1980, by size of metropolitan area and region, for metropolitan areas as defined in 1970

Region and size	1980 city boundaries		1960 city boundaries		Change, 70-80 (In 1980 city boundaries)		Change, 1960-70 (In 1960 city boundaries)	
	1980	1970	1970	1960	Number	Percent	Number	Percent
UNITED STATES								
All metrpololitan areas	63135969	64586556	60012730	59947129	-1450587	-2.24	65601	.11
Metropolitan areas of:								
3 million or more population	18174634	19916827	19889757	19915487	-1742193	-8.74	-25730	-.12
1 to 3 million	14819797	15307149	14504353	14376887	-487352	-3.17	127466	.89
500,000 to 1 million	11719597	11981556	10474024	10579547	-261959	-2.18	-105523-	.99
250,000 to 500,000	9252631	8743485	7767243	7713010	509146	5.82	54233	.70
100,000 to 250,000	7829541	7395368	6271644	6261371	434173	5.87	10273	.16
Under 100,000	1339769	1242171	1105709	1100827	97598	7.86	4882	.44
NORTHEAST								
All metropolitan areas	15407023	17260568	17230510	17575505	-1853545	-10.73	-344895	-1.95
Metropolitan areas of:								
3 million or more population	9619864	10782944	10782944	10763892	-1163080	-10.78	19052	.18
1 to 3 million	1375877	1647172	1647172	1822021	-271295	-16.46	-174849	-9.59
500,000 to 1 million	2802377	3088716	3059931	3149675	-286339	-9.26	-89744	-2.84
250,000 to 500,000	923276	1033857	1032971	1126012	-110581	-10.69	-93041	-3.25
100,000 to 250,000	622020	641949	641562	648652	-19929	-3.09	-6990	-1.07
Under 100,000	63609	65930	65930	65253	-2321	-3.51	677	1.04

Continued 5.A7

NORTH CENTRAL								
All metropolitan areas	15383497	17148420	16030858	16930179	-1764973	-10.23	-899321	-5.30
Metropolitan areas of:								
3 million or more population	4208411	4883420	4873702	5220548	-675009	-13.81	-346846	-6.63
1 to 3 million	3838723	4532453	4154059	4618030	-693780	-15.30	-463971	-10.04
500,000 to 1 million	2311313	2548996	2292887	2394937	-237683	-9.31	-102050	-4.25
250,000 to 500,000	2131462	2244188	2059506	2063084	-112726	-3.01	-3578	-.16
100,000 to 250,000	2505131	2561445	2316908	2306947	-56314	-2.19	9961	.43
Under 100,000	388457	377918	333796	326633	10539	2.79	7163	2.19
SOUTH								
All metropolitan areas	19215676	18502215	15992091	15647166	714631	3.86	344925	2.20
Metropolitan areas of:								
3 million or more population	0	0	0	0	0	0	0	0
1 to 3 million	5760441	5740136	5593232	5183819	20305	.35	409413	7.90
500,000 to 1 million	5012381	4993649	5913323	3920450	18732	.38	-7127	-.17
250,000 to 500,000	4179244	3833458	3237694	3227549	345786	9.02	10145	.31
100,000 to 250,000	3499430	3261147	2347398	2714502	238283	7.31	-67104	-2.44
Under 100,000	764180	673825	600444	600846	90355	13.41	-402	.-6
WEST								
All metropolitan areas	13129773	11675653	10759171	9794279	1454120	12.48	964892	9.85
Metropolitan areas of:								
3 million or more population	4346159	4250463	4233111	3931047	95596	2.26	302064	7.68
1 to 3 million	3844756	3327388	3109340	2753017	457538	13.50	356873	12.96
500,000 to 1 million	1593526	1950495	1207883	1114485	243031	14.00	93398	8.38
250,000 to 500,000	2018649	1881982	1437072	1806365	386557	23.69	140707	10.85
100,000 to 250,000	1202960	10827	565576	91270	272131	29.26	74406	12.58
Under 100,000	123523	124491	105539	108055	-975	-.77	-2556	-2.35

Note: Metropolitan refers to Standard Metropolitan Statistical Areas (SMSA's), except for New England where New England CountyMetropolitan Areas (NECMA's) are used.
Nonmetropolitan refers to outside SMSA's (NECMA's in New England). Size refers to SMSA/NECMA population in 1970.

TABLE 5.A8.

Central city population change from 1960 to 1970 and from 1970 to 1980, by size of metropolitan area and region, for metropolitan areas as defined in 1974

Region and size	1980 city boundaries		1960 city boundaries		Change, 70-80 (in 1980 city boundaries)		Change 1960-70 in 1960 city boundaries)	
	1980	1970	1970	1960	Number	Percent	Number	Percent
UNITED STATES								
All metrpololitan areas	65588283	66725043	61840932	61482586	-1136760	-1.69	358346	.58
Metropolitan areas of:								
3 million or more population	18174634	19916827	19889757	19915487	-1742193	-8.74	-25730	-.12
1 to 3 million	15849275	16321935	15462257	15252357	-472660	-2.89	209900	1.38
500,000 to 1 million	12041431	12214023	10564522	10665716	-172592	-1.40	-101194	-.94
250,000 to 500,000	10025039	9437777	8418293	8151398	587262	6.22	266895	3.27
100,000 to 250,000	8052894	7510427	6326528	6325810	542467	7.22	718	.1
Under 100,000	1445010	1324056	1179575	1171818	120956	9.16	7757	.66
NORTHEAST								
All metropolitan areas	15715888	17584809	17554838	17889614	-1868921	-18.62	-334776	-1.86
Metropolitan areas of:								
3 million or more population	9619864	10782944	10782944	10763892	-1163080	-10.78	19052	.18
1 to 3 million	1378658	1661732	1661732	1832189	-283074	-17.02	-170457	-9.29
500,000 to 1 million	2865307	3149791	3121006	3210548	-284484	-9.02	-89542	-2.78
250,000 to 500,000	1156062	1275267	1274381	1353709	-119205	-9.34	-79328	-5.85
100,000 to 250,000	632388	649145	648845	664023	-16757	-2.57	-15178	-2.28
under 100,000	63609	65930	65930	65253	-2321	-3.51	677	1.04

Continued 5.A8

NORTH CENTRAL								
All metropolitan areas	15621203	17388971	16250038	17118700	-1767768	-18.16	-868662	-5.04
Metropolitan areas of:								
3 million or more population	4208411	4883420	4873702	5220548	-675009	-13.81	-346846	-6.63
1 to 3 million	4403594	5072354	4667443	5089344	-668760	-13.17	-421903	-3.28
500,000 to 1 million	1906053	2202412	1972634	2120561	-296359	-13.45	-147927	-6.97
250,000 to 500,000	2268535	2359200	2169422	2140155	-90665	-3.83	29267	1.37
100,000 to 250,000	2446153	2493667	2233041	2221457	-47514	-1.90	11584	.52
Under 100,000	388457	377918	333796	326635	10539	2.70	7163	2.19
SOUTH								
All metropolitan areas	20432694	19532080	16876010	16398570	900614	4.41	477840	2.91
Metropolitan areas of:								
3 million or more population	0	0	0	0	0	0	0	0
1 to 3 million	6145582	6133591	5975663	5540087	11991	.20	435576	7.86
500,000 to 1 million	5612138	5441847	4195622	4149925	170291	3.13	45697	1.10
250,000 to 500,000	4380242	4009317	3384834	3307342	370925	9.25	77492	2.34
100,000 to 250,000	3493284	3235366	2685662	2767171	257918	7.97	-81509	-2.94
Under 100,000	801446	711957	6346629	634045	89489	12.57	584	.9
WEST								
All metropolitan areas	13818498	12219183	11159646	10075702	1599315	13.09	1083944	10.74
Metropolitan areas of:								
3 million or more population	4346359	4250463	4233111	3931047	95896	2.26	302064	7.48
1 to 3 million	3921441	3454258	3157419	2790735	467183	13.52	366684	13.14
500,000 to 1 million	1657933	1419973	1275260	1184682	237960	16.76	90578	7.65
250,000 to 500,000	2220200	1793993	1589656	1350192	426207	23.76	239464	17.74
100,000 to 250,000	1481067	1132247	758980	673159	348820	30.81	85821	12.75
under 100,000	191498	168249	145220	145887	23249	13.82	-667	-.43

Note: Metropolitan refers to Standard Metropolitan Statistical Areas (SMSA's), except for New England where New England County Metropolitan Areas (NECMA's) are used.

Nonmetropolitan refers to outside SMSA's (NECMA's in New England). Size refers to SMSA/NECMA population in 1970.

TABLE 5.A9.

Central city population change from 1960 to 1970 and from 1970 to 1980, by size of metropolitan area and region, for metropolitan areas as defined as of January 1, 1980

Region and size	1980 city boundaries		1960 city boundaries		Change, 70-80 (In 1980 city boundaries)		Change, 1960-70 (In 1960 city boundaries)	
	1980	1970	1970	1960	Number	Percent	Number	Percent
UNITED STATES								
All metrpololitan areas	66719447	67709932	62690101	62262770	-990485	-1.45	427331	.69
Metropolitan areas of:								
3 million or more population	18174634	19916827	19889757	19915487	-1742193	-8.74	-25730	-.12
1 to 3 million	15849275	16321935	15462257	15252357	-472660	-2.80	209900	1.38
500,000 to 1 million	12041431	12214023	10564522	10665716	-172592	-1.40	-101194	-.94
250,000 to 500,000	10064792	9477193	8447862	8182585	587599	6.20	265277	3.24
100,000 to 250,000	8433859	7836633	6623448	6587236	597226	7.62	36212	.55
Under 100,000	2155456	1943321	1702255	1659389	212135	10.92	42866	2.58
NORTHEAST								
All metropolitan areas	15715888	17584809	17554838	17889614	-1868921	-10.42	-334776	-1.86
Metropolitan areas of:								
3 million or more population	9619864	10782944	10782944	10763892	-1163080	-10.78	19052	.18
1 to 3 million	1378658	1661732	1661732	1832189	-283074	-17.02	-170457	-9.29
500,000 to 1 million	2865307	3149791	3121006	3210548	-284484	-9.02	-89542	-2.78
250,000 to 500,000	1156062	1275267	1274381	1353709	-119205	-9.34	-79328	-5.85
100,000 to 250,000	632388	649145	648845	664023	-16757	-2.57	-15178	-2.28
under 100,000	63609	65930	65930	65253	-2321	-3.51	677	1.04

Continued 5.A9

NORTH CENTRAL								
All metropolitan areas	16189903	17919606	16727706	17559828	-1729703	-9.64	-832122	-6.73
Metropolitan areas of:								
3 million or more population	4208411	4883420	4873702	5220548	-675009	-13.81	-346846	-6.63
1 to 3 million	4403594	5072354	4667443	5089346	-668760	-13.17	-421903	-3.28
500,000 to 1 million	1906053	2202412	1972634	2120561	-296359	-13.45	-147927	-6.97
250,000 to 500,000	2268535	2359300	2169422	2140155	-90765	-3.83	29267	1.37
100,000 to 250,000	2647270	2685564	2415467	2385544	-38294	-1.43	29923	1.25
Under 100,000	756040	716556	629038	603674	39484	5.56	25364	6.20
SOUTH								
All metropolitan areas	20814490	19851860	17135658	16642396	962630	4.85	493262	2.96
Metropolitan areas of:								
3 million or more population	0	0	0	0	0	0	0	0
1 to 3 million	6145582	6133591	5975663	5540087	11991	.20	435576	7.86
500,000 to 1 million	5612138	5441847	4195622	4149925	170291	3.13	45697	1.10
250,000 to 500,000	4419995	4048733	3414403	3338529	371262	9.17	75874	2.27
100,000 to 250,000	3673134	3369377	2800156	2864510	303757	9.02	-64354	-2.24
Under 100,000	963641	858312	749814	749345	105329	12.27	469	.4
WEST								
All metropolitan areas	13999166	12353657	13271799	10170932	1645509	13.32	3100867	10.82
Metropolitan areas of:								
3 million or more population	4346359	4250463	4233111	3931047	95896	2.26	302064	7.68
1 to 3 million	3921441	3454258	5157419	2790735	467183	15.52	2366684	13.14
500,000 to 1 million	1657933	1419973	1275260	1184682	237960	16.76	90578	7.65
250,000 to 500,000	2220200	1793993	1589556	1350192	426207	23.76	239364	17.74
100,000 to 250,000	1481067	1132247	758980	673159	348820	30.81	85821	12.75
under 100,000	372166	302723	257473	241117	69443	22.94	16356	6.78

Note: Metropolitan refers to Standard Metropolitan Statistical Areas (SMSA's), except for New England where New England County Metropolitan Areas (NECMA's) are used.
Nonmetropolitan refers to outside SMSA's (NECMA's in New England). Size refers to SMSA/NECMA population in 1970.

TABLE 5.A10.

Suburban population change from 1970 to 1980, by size of metropolitan area and region, for metropolitan areas as defined as of January 1,1980.

Region and size	1980 population			1970 population			Balance of SMSA's Change, 1970-80	
	SMSA's/ NECMA's	Central Cities (1980 boundaries)	Balance of SMSA's	SMSA's/ NECMA's	Central cities (1980 boundaries)	Balance of SMSA's	Number	Percent
UNITED STATES								
All metrpololitan areas	165993492	66719447	99274045	150882700	67709932	83,172,768	16,101,277	19.36
Metropolitan areas of:								
3 million or more population	39875200	18174634	21700566	40207454	19916827	20,290,627	1,409,939	6.95
1 to 3 million	50523975	15849275	34674700	45044547	16321935	28,722,612	5,952,088	20.72
500,000 to 1 million	28640172	12041431	16598741	25672133	12214023	13,458,110	3,140,631	23.34
250,000 to 500,000	24882530	10064792	14817738	21287427	94177193	11,810,234	3,007,504	25.47
100,000 to 250,000	18460852	8433859	10026993	15671719	7836633	7,835,086	2,191,907	27.98
Under 100,000	3610763	2155456	1455307	2999420	1943321	1,056,099	399,208	37.80
NORTHEAST								
All metropolitan areas	41715627	15715888	25999739	42480535	17584809	24,895,726	1,104,013	4.43
Metropolitan areas of:								
3 million or more population	17689732	9619864	8069868	18646419	10782944	7,863,475	206,393	2.62
1 to 3 million	9129190	1378658	7750532	9399104	1661732	7,737,372	13,160	0.17
500,000 to 1 million	8501682	2865307	5636375	8397330	3149791	5,247,539	388,836	7.41
250,000 to 500,000	4465922	1156062	3309860	4257525	1275267	2,982,258	327,602	10.99
100,000 to 250,000	1829444	632388	1197056	1688878	649145	1,039,733	157,323	15.13
under 100,000	99657	63609	36048	91279	65930	25,349	10,699	42.21

Continued 5.A10

NORTH CENTRAL								
All metropolitan areas	41166100	16189903	24976197	40126222	17919606	22,206,616	2,769,581	12.47
Metropolitan areas of:								
3 million or more population	11455090	4208411	7246679	11409806	4883420	6,526,386	720,293	11.04
1 to 3 million	12487823	4403594	8084229	12383264	5072354	7,310,910	773,319	10.58
500,000 to 1 million	5299803	1906053	3393750	5186952	2202412	2,984,540	409,210	13.71
250,000 to 500,000	5083362	2268535	2814827	4792383	2359200	2,433,183	381,644	15.69
100,000 to 250,000	5525404	2647270	2878134	5178356	2685864	2,492,492	385,642	15.47
Under 100,000	1314618	756040	558578	1175461	716356	459,105	99,473	21.67
SOUTH								
All metropolitan areas	48697008	20814490	27882518	40087856	19851860	20,235,996	7,646,522	37.79
Metropolitan areas of:								
3 million or more population	0	0	0	0	0	0	0	0
1 to 3 million	17792522	6145582	11646940	14607350	6133591	8,473,759	3,173,181	37.45
500,000 to 1 million	10617526	5612138	5005388	8976844	5441847	3,534,997	1,470,391	41.60
250,000 to 500,000	10629785	4419995	6209790	8650881	4048733	4,602,148	1,607,642	34.93
100,000 to 250,000	8162849	3673134	4489715	6631598	3369377	3,262,221	1,227,494	37.63
Under 100,000	1494326	963641	530685	1221183	858512	362,871	167,814	46.25
WEST								
All metropolitan areas	34414757	13999166	20415591	28188087	12353657	15,834,430	4,581,161	28.93
Metropolitan areas of:								
3 million or more population	10730378	4346359	6384019	10151229	4250463	5,900,766	483,253	8.19
1 to 3 million	11114440	3921441	7192999	8654829	3454258	5,200,571	1,992,428	38.31
500,000 to 1 million	4221161	1657933	2563228	3111007	1419973	1,691,034	872,194	51.58
250,000 to 500,000	4703461	2220200	2483261	3566688	1793993	1,792,645	690,616	38.53
100,000 to 250,000	2943155	1481067	1462088	2172887	1132247	1,040,640	421,448	40.50
Under 100,000	702162	372166	329996	511497	302723	208,774	121,222	58.06

Note: Metropolitan refers to Standard Metropolitan Statistical Areas (SMSA's), except for New England where New England County Metropolitan Areas (NECMA's) are used.
Nonmetropolitan refers to outside SMSA's (NECMA's in New England). Size refers to SMSA/NECMA population in 1970.

TABLE 5.A11.

Suburban population change from 1960 to 1970, by size of metropolitan area and region, for metropolitan areas as defined as of January 1,1980.

Region and size	1970 population			1960 population			Balance of SMSA's Change, 1970-80	
	SMSA's/ NECMA's	Central Cities (1980 boundaries)	Balance of SMSA's	SMSA's/ NECMA's	Central cities (1980 boundaries)	Balance of SMSA's	Number	Percent
UNITED STATES								
All metrpololitan areas	150882700	62490101	88,192,599	128840848	42262770	66578078	21,614,521	32.46
Metropolitan areas of:								
3 million or more population	40207454	19889757	20,317,697	36197354	19915487	16281867	4,035,830	24.79
1 to 3 million	45044547	15462257	29,582,290	36399297	15252357	21146940	8,435,350	39.89
500,000 to 1 million	25672133	10564528	15,107,611	21943511	10665716	11277795	3,829,816	33.96
250,000 to 500,000	21287427	3447362	12,839,565	18199135	8182585	10016550	2,823,015	28.18
100,000 to 250,000	15671719	6623448	9,048,271	13487957	6587236	6900721	2,147,550	31.12
Under 100,000	2999420	1702255	1,297,165	2613594	1659389	954205	342,960	35.94
NORTHEAST								
All metropolitan areas	42480535	17554838	24,925,697	38609277	17889614	20719663	4,206,034	20.30
Metropolitan areas of:								
3 million or more population	18646419	10782944	7,863,475	17339188	10763892	6575296	1,288,179	19.59
1 to 3 million	9399104	1661732	7,737,372	8359837	1832189	6527648	1,209,724	18.53
500,000 to 1 million	8397330	3121006	5,276,324	7497210	3210548	4286662	989,662	23.09
250,000 to 500,000	4257525	1274381	2,983,144	3826064	1353709	2472355	510,789	20.66
100,000 to 250,000	1688878	648845	1,040,033	1500666	664023	836643	203,390	24.31
Under 100,000	91279	65930	25,349	86312	65253	21059	4,290	20.37

Continued 5.A11

NORTH CENTRAL								
All metropolitan areas	40126222	16727706	23,398,516	35472834	17559828	17913006	5,485,510	30.62
Metropolitan areas of:								
3 million or more population	11409806	4873702	6,536,104	10170633	5220548	4950085	1,586,019	32.04
1 to 3 million	12383264	4667443	7,715,821	10867774	5089346	5778428	1,937,393	33.53
500,000 to 1 million	5186952	1972634	3,214,318	4572043	2120561	2451482	762,836	31.12
250,000 to 500,000	4792383	2169422	2,622,961	4272578	2140155	2132423	490,538	23.00
100,000 to 250,000	5178356	2415467	2,762,889	6586199	2385544	2198655	564,234	25.66
Under 100,000	1175461	629038	546,423	1005607	603674	401933	144,490	35.95
SOUTH								
All metropolitan areas	40087856	17135658	22,952,198	32807839	16642396	16165443	6,786,755	41.98
Metropolitan areas of:								
3 million or more population	0	0	0	0	0	0	0	0
1 to 3 million	14607350	5975663	8,631,687	11118659	5540087	5578572	3,053,115	54.73
500,000 to 1 million	8976844	4195622	4,781,222	7508429	4149925	3358504	1,422,718	42.36
250,000 to 500,000	8650881	3414403	5,236,478	7354989	3338529	4016460	1,220,018	30.38
100,000 to 250,000	6631598	2800156	3,831,442	5727568	2864510	2863058	968,384	33.82
Under 100,000	1221183	749814	471,369	1098194	749345	348849	122,520	35.12
WEST								
All metropolitan areas	28188087	11271899	16,916,188	21950898	10170932	11779966	5,136,222	43.60
Metropolitan areas of:								
3 million or more population	10151229	4233111	5,918,118	8687533	3931047	4756486	1,61,632	24.42
1 to 3 million	8654829	3157419	5,497,410	6053027	2790735	3262292	2,235,118	68.51
500,000 to 1 million	3111007	1275260	1,835,747	2365829	1184682	1181147	654,600	55.42
250,000 to 500,000	3586638	1589650	1,996,982	2745504	1350192	1395312	601,670	43.12
100,000 to 250,000	2172887	758980	1,413,907	1675524	673159	1002365	411,542	41.06
Under 100,000	511497	257473	254,024	423481	241117	182364	71,660	39.30

Note: Metropolitan refers to Standard Metropolitan Statistical Areas (SMSA's), except for New England where New England County Metropolitan Areas (NECMA's) are used.

Nonmetropolitan refers to outside SMSA's (NECMA's in New England). Size refers to SMSA/NECMA population in 1970.

SIX

George M. Johnston and A. Allan Schmid

The Impact of Government Policies on Suburban Land Conversion

THEORETICAL MODEL

Two Key concepts form the basis for this analyses; these are economic rent and profit. Economic rent is defined as the return above costs of production which result from a natural limitation in supply. The supply of a particular variety of land is fixed. (An example is land within a given distance of the city centre.) Returns arising from non-natural limitations of supply are termed profits, excess profits, or quasi-rent. Normal profits, on the other hand, include the payments necessary to draw forth the required entrepreneurial and capital resources and are considered costs of production. The implication of economic rent is that, unlike profits, rent cannot be competed away. Factor ownership controls who gets rent. Increasing competition can, however, reduce profit. Inversely, government policies which limit supply can increase profit for at least some of the participants in the land conversion process.

Supply restricting policies could include limiting parcels of land to large sizes, controlling or limiting provision of water, sewer or transportation systems relative to demands, and public tax and pricing policies. Overt private supply restrictions, while potentially important, will not be considered in this article.

The proxy measures to be used for economic rent and profit are land value appreciation and the land site price. Site price includes development costs (clearing land, roads, services, etc.), agricultural opportunity costs and some variation in site size. Ideally, the price paid for land to be converted to urban uses should be used as the basis for calculating land value appreciation. However, data on the price paid for raw land are nearly non-existent, thus price of a residential site (ready for building) has been used as a proxy for raw land value. Variations in site prices across cities in the United States can be explained by agricultural values, lot size and quality, development costs or land value appreciation. If the variation is due to agricultural values, the implication is that agricultural opportunity costs are high and more land is being withheld from the market. If the higher prices are a result of lot size and quality, then larger and better lots are being demanded and purchased. If development costs have increased, then the sources of those increases, whether private or public, could be examined. However, if appreciation has increased, the proxy measure for combined economic rent and profit, then the sources should be isolated and examined. Site price or land value appreciation is calculated as the per cent appreciation over agricultural opportunity costs after development costs and agricultural opportunity cost, adjusted for site size, are deducted. This appreciation is then expressed as a percentage of the farm value.

Birmingham, Alabama, can serve to demonstrate the calculations. In 1969 the site price based on National Association of Home Builders (NAHB) data for Birmingham was $5,451. Development costs are estimated as $2,430 and the calculated agricultural opportunity cost was $82. Development and agricultural opportunity costs are added together ($2,512) and then subtracted from site price leaving a difference of $2,938. Appreciation is then calculated with respect to development costs at 117 per cent and agricultural opportunity costs at 3570 per cent. Table 6.1 summarizes both site price and appreciation for the NAHB data. Another data set from the Federal Housing Administration was also used in the analysis to follow. The NAHB data generally include more expensive homes than the FHA data.

It can be argued, at the general level, that the degree to which particular government policies restrict the supply of land for certain demanded urban uses will affect the price of the land sold and that part of appreciation in land value is attributable to monopoly profits. Zoning, sewer provision and pricing will each be discussed in turn.[1]

Zoning

Zoning in the United States involves the designation of specific land use districts within which various regulations and restrictions apply, such as permitted uses, proportion and size of lot, maximum height and bulk requirements and population density limits. Zoning districts could be classified as residential, business, industrial, agricultural, recreational, unrestricted, etc. The residential classification can be further categorized as single family, multiple family, and apartment building districts. Zoning could be exclusive, allowing one use only, or cummulative zones which allow the previously defined uses in addition to its own designation. Implementation and form of these powers can vary between jurisdictions within a state and within a metropolitan area. Many rural jurisdictions do not have zoning and Houston, Texas, is a major U.S. city presently without zoning.

Zoning has not been considered to be successfully administered to control the speed, direction and final character of the land conversion process (Clawson, 1971). It is argued that the competition for economic rent places great pressure on the development plans of communities. Zoning has not been considered effective in keeping out land uses incompatible with plans of development. Those who compete for the gains from land use other than those permitted will attempt to change the zoning. There are also suburban jurisdictions where low density residential zoning is strongly supported by local residents and public officials (Babcock, 1966).

Minimum lot size requirements can serve as an example of what can be expected from regulations designed to affect the size of lots. Some jurisdictions in a land conversion market might contribute to the withholding of land from the market. This reduces supply and raises prices above costs of production. For example, some communities purposely zone available sites only for large lots, hoping thus to reduce government costs in relation to revenues (Mills and Oates, 1975). The process puts a premium on areas that are open to small lot development or for multiple family housing. If too little land is zoned for small lot development, there could be leap-frogging developments and a leap-frogging pattern of land acquisition. Thus large lot zoning would not only use up more land and at a lower density, but it would also contribute to supply restrictions for other residential construction. This would increase the appreciation on high density zoned land and decrease the overall density of land. The large lots overzoned would be a differentiated product with higher quality (demanded) features which could potentially be sold by the developer to customers at a higher price.

TABLE 6.1

Site price appreciation above agricultural opportunity cost and development costs, NAHB data, 1969 thirty-six cities

	A	B	C	D	E	F	G
	SITE PRICE	AGRICULTURAL OPPORTUNITY COSTS	DEVELOPMENT COSTS	AGRICULTURAL OPPORTUNITY COST + DEVELOPMENT (B+C)	APPRECIATION (A–D)	PERCENT APPRECIATION OVER COSTS (E) –(D) 100	PERCENT APPRECIATION OVER AGRICULTURAL OPPORTUNITY COST (E)–(B) 100
	($)	($)	($)	($)	($)	(%)	(%)
1. Birmingham	5451.	82.	2430.	2512.	2939.	117.	3570.
2. Mobile	4507.	82.	2430.	2512.	1995.	79.	2423.
3. Sacramento	5798.	183.	3960.	4143.	1655.	40.	906.
4. San Francisco	10478.	183.	3960.	4143.	6335.	153.	3468.
5. Denver	5877.	37.	2880.	2917.	2960.	102.	8102.
6. Wilmington	8875.	153.	2610.	2763.	6112.	221.	3982.
7. Tampa	4371.	122.	2610.	2732.	1639.	60.	1340.
8. Atlanta	7281.	98.	2610.	2708.	4573.	169.	4681.
9. Chicago	9847.	181.	3330.	3511.	6336.	180.	3505.
10. Indianapolis	5897.	154.	3330.	3484.	2413.	69.	1564.
11. Louisville	6543.	99.	2430.	2529.	4014	159.	4061.
12. New Orleans	7021.	146.	2160.	2306.	4715.	204.	3226.
13. Baltimore	5931.	188.	2610.	2798.	3133.	112.	1662.
14. Detroit	8172.	115.	3330.	3445.	4724.	137.	4110.
15. Grand Rapids	4500.	115.	3330.	3445.	1055.	31.	917.
16. Minneapolis	7240.	126.	2970.	3096.	4144.	134.	3295.
17. Kansas City	5101.	93.	2970.	3063.	2038.	67.	2199.
18. St. Louis	7027.	93.	2970.	3063.	3964.	129.	4277.
19. Omaha	4918.	113.	2970.	3083.	1835.	60.	1623.
20. Buffalo	5231.	115.	3240.	3355.	1876.	56.	1631.

Continued 6.1

21. Cinnati	7781.	150.	3330.	3480.	4301.	124.	2860.
22. Dayton	8227.	150.	3330.	3480.	4747.	136.	3156.
23. Oklahoma City	5307.	84.	2160.	2244.	3063.	137.	3653.
24. Tulsa	5275.	84.	2160.	2244.	3031.	135.	3615.
25. Portland	5515.	156.	3960.	4116.	1399.	34.	896.
26. Philadelphia	7068.	108.	3240.	3348.	3720.	111.	3429.
27. Pittsburgh	7441.	108.	3240.	3348.	4093.	122.	3773
28. Knoxville	3117.	108.	2430.	2538.	579.	23.	533.
29. Nashville	4384.	108.	2430.	2538.	1846.	73.	1702.
30. Dallas	6410.	75.	2160.	2235.	4175.	187.	5538.
31. Ft. Worth	3546.	75.	2160.	2235.	1311.	59.	1739.
32. Houston	5428.	75.	2160.	2235.	3193.	143.	4235.
33. San Antonio	3757.	75.	2169.	2235.	1522.	68.	2018.
34. Salt Lake City	7034.	72.	2880.	2952.	4082.	138.	5676.
35. Richmond	5663.	127.	2610.	2737.	2926.	107.	2305.
36. Seattle	6274.	114.	3960.	4074.	2200.	54.	1926.

Sources: Site prices from FHA Data for Cities and States (1969).

Agricultural Opportunity Costs calculated as explained in Chapter IV and summarized in Appexdix C.

Development Costs estimates from NAHB sources is explained in Chapter IV.

Given that there is likely to be variation in the attitudes of jurisdictions in the same metropolitan land conversion market, the unfilled demand for a certain land use in one jurisdiction will move to another, less restrictive, jurisdiction which raises the price there. The result of this institutional interdependence is not only to affect the speed and direction of residential location and population growth, but, perhaps, keep the relative price difference between jurisdictions essentially unaltered. The degree of variation in policies followed across jurisdictions should also affect relative prices. If supply restricting policies are widespread, prices should be higher than when such policies are rare.

Therefore, it can be hypothesized that low density zoning will have the following relationship to site price and appreciation. The greater the percentage of low density, residentially zoned land in the land conversion market, the greater will be the appreciation and site price in that market. This hypothesis was examined in the comparative case study to be reviewed later.

Sewer provision and pricing

Sewer provision and pricing could be similarly analyzed. Provision of sewered and zoned land for different uses at supply levels appropriate to demand should result in moderate prices. Over or under provision of sewered and zoned land in proportion to demand can result in similar leap-frog land use patterns but different price structures. Restricted sewer supply should lead to higher prices and over supply should lead to lower prices.

The process could be described as follows: If sewers have been extended to large areas of undeveloped land, developers are likely to buy and construct on large tracts where land is cheaper. The resultant development will be a low gross density and probably a low net density. The rate of development and infilling will depend upon general and relative demand. However, if sewer provision is still further increased because of demands on other areas of the metropolitan area and fringe, complete infilling might never occur. The infilling would also relate to other issues including the zoning by a local jurisdiction. If a suburban jurisdiction is settled with a certain more or less homogeneous group, the zoning may reflect a desire to maintain that homogeneity. This may not be the case where communities on the fringe encourage development. A moderate level of sewer provisions might not have the same result. Supply of sewered lots would be somewhat restricted, therefore the price of a sewered lot is likely to be greater. Demand will determine the price and density. If demand is moderate, prices will not be as great, but density is likely to be lower, though not as low as with over-supply of sewers.

Finally, when much less sewer system is provided than is demanded, the land which is sewered will be highly priced. If the price is too great, developers may find cheaper land much further from the urban area where other alternatives such as privately provided package sewer plants or septic tanks are possible.

The general hypothesis is as follows: the greater the percentage of land in the land conversion market where sewer provision is controlled or restricted, the greater will be the site price and appreciation. However, it is necessary to differentiate between restrictions associated with too much or too little sewer provision. Restricted supply should increase appreciation while over-supply would increase site price because of the sewer component of development cost, but lower the appreciation component of the site price.

Another source of appreciation above agricultural opportunity costs occurs because sewers are provided at prices below costs. A proportion of the value of land is based on the availability of sewers. To the extent that the sewers are limited in supply and made available without or below costs, their value becomes capitalized into the value of the land. For example, sewer service may be provided to new areas at the same price as the central city area even though the cost may be higher. It is the owner of the sewered land who benefits because of the value of the sewer services are capitalized into land values. Therefore, the hypothesis is as follows: The greater the percentage of subsidization of sewer services in a land conversion market, the greater will be the site price and appreciation.

One caution will be mentioned at this point. Local government policy on septic tanks or other sewer alternatives may affect sewer policies. For example, if septic tanks are restricted, it may either increase density in the land conversion market or perhaps extend the boundaries of the land conversion market to areas where septic tanks are allowed. Subsidized provision of sewers might increase density if septic tanks are not a viable alternative. In addition, the over building of sewers combined with subsidization should also relate to any alternative waste disposal by making the use of sewers more attractive.

Property taxes

The final local government policy to be considered is the ad valorum property tax. Property tax affects both the demand for more services and the ability of landowners to withhold land from the market.

From the point of view of the landowner, the property tax can affect the price of land through the present value (holding costs) and reservation price and, therefore, the supply of land at any given time. If the reservation price exceeds the market price, the owner can hold the land for further gains, though prospects may be uncertain. High property taxes can make it unprofitable to invest in land to hold for appreciation. It also should be noted that while a property tax increase can lower prices to lot consumers, it may not necessarily reduce the amount of appreciation above farm value. Since, if the property tax rate increase is general, the price of agricultural land could also be expected to fall. Therefore, the impact of a property tax increase is to reduce the reservation price of land being held for future gains. Lowering tax rates for agricultural land will result in raising present values and reservation prices for fringe land and could be expected to increase landowner gains. The research by Schwartz and Hansen (1975) on preferential taxation supports the analysis that expectations of gains by landowners are greater than the perceived tax benefits of such a policy. Deferred taxation as well as use value taxation also encourage land withholdings.

From the point of view of the property tax effect on housing values, it would be expected that high property taxes lower home values and, therefore, site values. The true value of a home includes site value plus construction costs which is a function of operating costs. Therefore, higher property taxes reduce the derived demand for homes but may decrease the costs of development.

To summarize, high property taxes should increase holding costs of landowners and increase the supply of land for urban uses. The effect on appreciation depends upon the extent to which the high property taxes are applied to agriculture. If there is preferential or deferred taxation for agriculture, while other property taxes increase, then appreciation could become greater.

The unit of analysis of this research is the land conversion market across cities in the United States. This metropolitan market will almost always consist of many local government jurisdictions, interacting with regional and national laws, which adds to both the complexity and richness of the model. Previous research has barely investigated the implications of economic and institutional interdependence within the land conversion market.

MODEL SPECIFICATION

The independent variables used to explain site price and appreciation can be roughly categorized into three groups. The first group consists of general demand variables such as total population, change in population, and mean family income. Many of these variables were used successfully in previous research. The second group of variables is composed of characteristics implicit in the land site such as site size, development cost and agricultural opportunity cost. These variables, as noted, are used in part to calculate an estimate of appreciation from site price data. The third group consists of the instrumental variables related to sewer provision and tax policies. The variables are instrumental in that these variables reflect policies subject to political decisions.

General demand characteristics are introduced into the model through the use of variables for total population, percentage change in population, mean or median family income and a binary variable to represent cities in California since it is such a special market.

Size of the metropolitan population encompasses several aspects of demand. Larger cities cost more to live in and often provide more amenities so prices in general are higher the greater the total population. Moreover, because of the generally larger area or increased congestion, some amenities such as schools, businesses, parks, and cultural activities will be spread further from a given location or site. On the other hand, the dispersal of amenities throughout a large metropolitan area will also disperse demand at the fringe or expand the area considered the fringe. The exact size and implications of this effect on site price or appreciation is unclear given interaction with other variables associated with total population such as income. Per cent change in population can be viewed as both an indication of recent past increases in demand and as a portent for future growth. The greater the percentage increment in population the greater will be the demand and hence price for residential lots. The mean or median family income variable indicates by size the strength of demand or buying power of a region. People with higher incomes are able to pay or bid more for lots with more amenities or locational advantages.

Regional variation in population growth, weather, or demography, could lead to variations in the dependent variables either through demand or development costs associated with weather, input costs, etc. Preliminary statistical analysis indicated the possibility of land market conditions in the State of California varying in size if not characteristically from the rest of the United States. Therefore, limited examination of regional variations was indicated by the use of a binary variable.

The second group of variables concern site characteristics and include development costs, agricultural opportunity costs, and site size.

It is assumed in this research that the supply of urban fringe sites is fixed and price is, therefore, demand determined. Appreciation is a residual affected by the size of development costs. Figure 6.1 demonstrates this assumption. The supply of sites is unaffected by development costs while appreciation is inversely related to development costs. Agricultural opportunity cost should be positively related to site price because of the higher price needed for urban uses in order to meet the offer price of the landowner to cover opportunity costs. If the variable definition has captured any demand characteristics, those characteristics will add to the positive relationship. Over time the size of a lot has decreased as the price of the site has increased.

The instrumental variables include per cent of all homes with public sewer, per cent new homes with public sewer, the property tax proportion of general revenue (per cent), the property tax range and the sewer capital outlay range. (Range refers to difference in values among local governments in the same metropolitan area.)

Percent all homes with public sewer could indicate the cumulative influence and historical policies of local jurisdictions while per cent new homes with public sewers would indicate recent policy. The greater the percentage of either all or new homes with public sewers, the more likely the sewers are being supplied which require homes to be connected to the sewer. Site price and appreciation should be higher. On the other hand, liberal provision of sewer services when there is demand could describe the situation.

While the greater supply of public sewers could lead to scattered residential location as well as under supply, the raw land price might be less with over supply as the increased development costs show up in site price. But under supply also raises prices. Therefore, while either of these variables could indicate past sewer supply policies, the variables are somewhat ambiguous on price and appreciation. However, the role of sewer costs on site improvement might override the supply characteristics and indicate that a larger percent of lots with public sewer would lead to a higher site price.

The property tax proportion of general revenue is an indication of the importance of the property tax vis-a-vis other local government financing methods. The property tax is a less direct way of financing new infrastructure than connection fees or service charges so that the greater the use of the property tax the greater the raw land prices will be. But also note that high property taxes, per se, lower home values and, therefore, site values. Higher property taxes could thereby reduce derived demand for homes but decrease the cost of development.

The range of the average per capita tax can be indicative of two phenomena. First, the range may indicate the disparity between the central city and suburbs. If, as seems likely, the central city has the greatest average per capita property taxes paid, then the flight to suburbs could be indicated. This would indicate that the greater the range the greater the demand, hence, price. The range of the average per capita sewer capital outlay should indicate that, if the central city can be considered to be completely severed, then the greater the range, the greater the current outlay on sewers in the metropolitan fringe. Site price and appreciation should be greater.

A note of further caution is needed to point to some of the interactions between the independent variables. For example, there should be a strong correlation between sewer supply variables and the total population of the metropolitan area. As population becomes greater and generally denser, the need for public sewers becomes greater because of the inability of the land to absorb waste with

Figure 6.1

Development Costs With The Supply of Sites Fixed

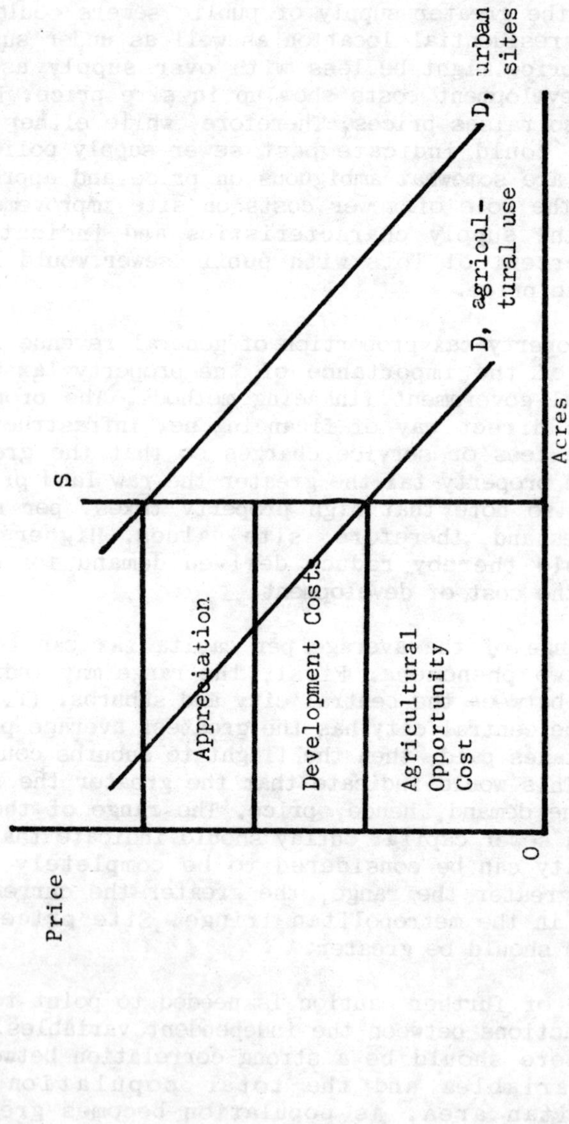

septic tanks or other techniques. Tax variables could be highly correlated with income. As population and income increase, the demand for services also increase, raising taxes. With a greater income range the variation in demand and tastes might also be reflected in the property tax and sewer range variables. To summarize the site price model is as follows:

Site Price = α

		Relationship expected
β_1	Total Population (persons)	+
β_2	Change on Population (percent)	+
β_3	Mean or Median Family Income (dollars)	+
β_4	California Binary	+
β_5	Site Size (square feet)	−
β_6	Development Costs (dollars per site)	−
β_7	Agricultural Opportunity Cost (dollars)	+
β_8	Property Tax Proportion of General Revenue (dollars)	+
β_9	Property Tax Range	+
β_{10}	Sewer Range	+
β_{11}	All or New Family Homes with Public Sewer (percent)	?

where

α = Constant to be estimated

β_1 to β_{11} = Coefficients associated with specified variables

The appreciation model consists of variables β_1, β_2, β_3 and β_9, β_{10}, β_{11}. Site characteristics variables were not used to estimate appreciation because they were used to calculate appreciation. The California binary and the property tax Proportion of General Revenue were not statistically significant in the site price model and were not carried over into the appreciation model.

EMPIRICAL RESULTS

The method used to test the theoretical model consisted of a series of cross-sectional multiple regression equations, pooled cross-sectional and time series equations, and a comparative case study of Lansing, Kalamazoo, and Jackson, Michigan, USA. The regression analysis explored demand variables, site characteristics, and the hypothesized relationship between sewer provision, pricing, and property taxation and the dependent variables. The comparative case study examined the geographical basis and dependent variable definitions of the regression work with more detail.

The comparative case study examined and compared the secondary data used in the econometric models with secondary data available for at least three cities but not available for a large enough sample for statistical or econometric analyses. In addition, region specific reports such as local land use studies combined with interviews with local land use planners and developers provided even greater understanding of the functioning of these land conversion markets. Zoning was explored more thoroughly in the comparative case study while sewers and tax policies received cursory treatment.

The results of both the econometric analysis and the comparative case study are now considered with respect to the zoning, sewer provision and pricing, and property tax hypotheses. The cross-sectional regression tables reported here contain all equations estimated. Not all results are discussed. Equations were estimated sequentially to test relationships with the largest number of cases possible and thereby save degrees of freedom and also to examine issues raised in earlier econometric results. The reader can review the results for the demand and site characteristic variables from these tables.

Zoning

The results of examining normal zoning as well as comments from developers and planners suggested that other factors needed consideration in addition to nominal zoning. The effect of zoning on actual opportunities to build did affect the location decisions of developers. Developers also noted the increased pressures on land use planning when restrictions were considered severe. This behaviour supports the concept of competition, through the political process, for economic rent and profit. Most important, however, was that differences on land values and appreciation between the three cities could be related to a holistic, qualitative, and quantitative measure of zoning variations.

If it were possible to aggregate various characteristics of zoning such as nominal zoning, nominal zoning changes, time and bureaucracy involved in zoning changes, and the uncertainty of the process, then this holistic variable might prove supportive of the hypothesis. But its interpretation would be difficult. The weight of the evidence suggests that zoning restrictions for certain uses, in the aggregate, do affect developer decisions, inter alia, and land value appreciation. Especially significant were developer and planner descriptions of jurisdictional attitudes on zoning and responses by developers in the entire land conversion market. Demand shifts as a result of developer decisions from one jurisdiction to another can lead to higher prices throughout the market. If there are product differentiating effects with respect to large lots, the aggregate price increases could be even larger.

Sewer provisions and pricing

Similar behavioural patterns were seen with sewer provision and pricing. The weight of the research evidence suggests that local government policies regarding both sewer provision and pricing affect the supply of land for certain uses. While the econometric results were mixed, both the percent of all and new homes with public sewer were frequently statistically significant, at greater than the .01 level, in explaining site price or appreciation, especially with the NAHB data. Table 6.2 for NAHB site price data, presents two equations, Regression Three and Regression Four, with percent all homes with public sewer statistically significant with a positive sign at the .007 and .006 level, respectively. Table 6.3 also demonstrates positive results for the NAHB site price regressions while FHA site price regressions were weak, as demonstrated in Tables 6.3 and 6.4. The statistical significant level for all homes with public sewer in the cross-sectional appreciation regressions ranged from a low of .020 to a high of .001 across eight equations, presented in Tables 6.5 and 6.6. In the pooled cross-sectional time series regressions the per cent of new homes sewered was statistically significant in both the site price and appreciation models. The results of the pooled regressions were encouraging and seem to indicate stability of the sewer variable over time.[2]

In addition, comments by planners and developers in the comparative case study supported the behavioural implications, in terms of developer location decisions, of sewer supply policies. Nevertheless, the difficulty in separating other policies from sewer use policies makes interpretation of support for the hypothesis cautious.

Sewer pricing policies were tested by the sewer range in both the cross-sectional analysis and the pooled regression analysis. With the exception of Table 6.5, in which the sewer range was significant at .08 and .07 level in explain-

TABLE 6.2

Site price regressions, NAHB, 1969

Dependent Variable/ Regression Number	Independent Variables: Regression Coefficient, Standard Error in Parenthesis, Significance Level					
Site Price National Association of Home Builders 1969 (dollars)	Total Population 1970 (persons)	Change in Population 1960-1970 (percent)	Median Family Income 1970 (dollars)	Agricultural Opportunity Cost 1969 (dollars)	Development Costs 1969 (dollers)	California Dummy*
Regression One	.0008 (.0001) ≤.0001	3.3755 (4.7419) .478	.5033 (.0959) ≤.0001			
Regression Two	.0009 (.0001) ≤.0001	10.9242 (4.5213) .017		5.1526 (.8330) ≤.0001	.0529 (.2040) .796	-80.4584 (595.3595) .893
Regression Three	.0005 (.0002) .008	-4.6265 (12.7375) .718		8.7160 (1.7627) ≤.0001		
Regression Four	.0003 (.0002) .058		.4089 (.1569) .012	8.0282 (1.6658) ≤.0001		

Continued 6.2

Dependent Variable/ Regression Number				Constant	R^2	R^{-2}	No. of Cases
Site Price National Association of Home Builders 1969 (dollars)	All Homes with Public Sewer 1970 (percent)	Property Tax Range** (1969)	Sewer Range# (1969)				
Regression One				-32.38 (892.51) .971	.42	.40	162
Regression Two				2837. (587.) $\leq$.0001	.46	.44	162
Regression Three	44.3846 (15.6442) .007	2090.8625 (747.7128) .007	-2.5964 (127.697) .984	-1360. (1469.) .359	.57	.52	56
Regression Four	41.5794 (14.4458) .006	2117.0461 (701.0598) .004	-15.6855 (117.5362) .894	-5024. (1969.) .014	.62	.58	56

* Qualitative dummy variable where cities in the State of California were one and all other cities were zero.

** Calculated by subtracting low county average per capita property tax in SMSA from high county average per capita property tax in SMSA and dividing by the overall SMSA average per capita property tax thus resulting in a relative range. Where one county consists of entire SMSA the range is zero.

\# Calculated the same as property tax range but uses the per capita sewer captial outlay high, low and overall averages.

Table 6.3

Site price regressions for thirty-six cities common to NAHB and FHA for 1969

Dependent variable Data source/ Regression number	Independent variables Regression co-efficient, Standard error in Parenthesis, Significance Level					
Market Site Price 1969	Total Population 1970 (persons)	Median Family Income 1970 (dollars)	Mean Family Income 1970 (dollars)	Change in Population 1960-1970 (percent)	Agricultural Opportunity cost 1969 (dollars)	All Homes with Public Sewer 1970 (percent)
NAHB Regression One	.00037 (.00017) .041	.2640 (.1960) .189			7.0689 (2.0144) .001	51.3284 (17.7735) .007
FHA Regression Two	-.0000798 (.0001051) .454	.2194 (.1171) .071			5.1025 (1.2040) ≤.0001	15.7572 (10.6230) .149
NAHB Regression Three	.00030 (.00016) .059		.4621 (.1993) .028		5.9807 (1.9946) .006	43.1096 (17.4170) .019
FHA Regression Four	-.00005653 (.00010638) .599		.1806 (.1289) .172		4.8769 (1.2902) .012	14.6529 (11.2657) .204
NAHB Regression Five	.000213 (.000182) .241		.5671 (.2131) .015	-20.06 (16.30) .228	5.3636 (2.0044) .012	46.99 (17.48) .012
FHA Regression Six	-.00013 (.00011) .254		.2624 (.1395) .070	-14.56 (10.42) .173	4.4510 1.2821 .002	17.75 (11.18) .123

Continued 6.3

Dependent variable Data source/ Regression number Market Site Price 1969	Property Tax * Range 1969	Sewer ** Range 1969	Constant	R^2	R^{-2}
NAHB Regression One	2574.6632 (863.4662) .006	-49.8327 (148.3422) .739	-4407. (2208.) .055	.65	.58
FHA Regression Two	225.0730 (516.0842) .666	-25.0476 (88.6625) .780	-1384. (1320.) .303	.50	.40
NAHB Regression Three	2426.4962 (816.4581) .006	-91.2666 (141.8646) .525	-5228. (1956.) .012	.69	.62
FHA Regression Four	134.1712 (528.1027) .801	-38.6948 (19.7611) .676	-802. (1265.) .531	.48	.37
NAHB Regression Five	2547. (807.) .004		-6027. (2061.) .007	.70	.64
FHA Regression Six	251. (561.65) .631	14	-1437. (1318.) .285		.51.41

* Calculated by subtracting low county average per capita property tax in SMSA from high county average per capita property tax in SMSA and dividing by the overall SMSA average per capita property tax thus resulting in a relative range. Where one county consits of entire SMSA the range is zero.

** Calculated the same as the property tax range but uses the per capita sewer capital outlay high, low, and overall averages.

TABLE 6.4

Site price regressions, FHA, 1969

Dependent Variable/ Regression Number						
Market Site Price, Federal Housing Administration 1969 (dollars)	Total Population 1970 (persons)	Change in Population 1960-1970 (percent)	Mean Family Income 1970 (dollars)	Agricultural Opportunity Cost 1969 (dollars)	Site Size 1969 (square feet)	Property Tax Proportion of General Revenue 1970 (percent)
Regression One	.00017 (.00004) ≤.0001	17.4863 (4.9861) .001	.1263 (.0926) .165	6.8838 (1.2670) ≤.0001	.0270 (.0320) .401	-2.1964 (2.9321) .456
Regression Two	.00014 (.00005) .19	18.8217 (12.0098) .125	.0382 (.1382) .783	6.6977 (1.6424) ≤.0001		
Regression Three	.00014 (.00005) .001	19.6920 (11.4657) .093		6.8578 (1.5206) ≤.0001		
Regression Four	.00011 (.00005) .053	17.4078 (11.8067) .148		7.1571 (1.5028) ≤.0001		

Continued 6.4

Dependent Variable/ Regression Number					Constant	R^2	R^{-2}	No. of Cases
Market Site Price, Federal Housing Administration 1969 (dollars)	New Homes with Public Sewer 1969 (percent)	All Homes with Public Sewer 1969 (percent)	Property Tax Range * 1969	Sewer Range ** 1969				
Regression One	10.0880 (3.9771) .013				-376. (899.) .677	.55	.51	104
Regression Two	5.9518 (5.8896) .318		73.3602 (244.4426) .766	-17.4390 (109.2112) .874	1017. (1190.) .397	.51	.42	50
Regression Three	6.30000 (5.6913) .274		74.5027 (241.7693) .759	-8.6257 (103.3488) .934	1304. (580.) .030	.51	.44	50
Regression Four		15.6648 (12.4014) .213	-3.1865 (244.2632) .990	-16.5633 (103.3439) .873	668. (995.) .488	.51	.44	50

* Calculated by subtracting low county average per capita property tax in SMSA from high county average per capita property tax in SMSA and dividing by the overal SMSA average per capita property tax thus resulting in a relative range. Where one county consists of entire SMSA the range is zero.

** Calculated the same as the property tax range but uses the per capita outlay high, low and overall averages.

TABLE 6.5

Appreciation regressions, NAHB, FHA, 1969

Dependent Variable/ Data Source/ Regression Number	Independent Variables Regtession Coefficient, Standard Error in Parenthesis, Significance Level						Constant	R^2	R^{-2}	No. of Cases
Land Value Appreciation, 1969	Total Population 1970 (persons)	Change Population 1960-1970 (percent)	Mean Family Income 1970 (dollars)	All Homes With Public Sewer 1970 (percent)	Property Tax * Range 1969	Sewer ** Range 1969				
NAHB Regression One	.0006152 (.0001497) ≤.0001	13.34 (5.35) .014	-.04516 (.10840) .678			.051	1980. (1009.)	.13	.11	1o2
NAHB Regression Two	.0001382 (.0001610) .395	2.64 (13.02) .087		48.54 (15.53) .003	1731.67 (748.85) .022	226.94 (130.17) .087	-24.39 (12.06) .049	.39	.33	56
NAHB Regression Three	.00007141 (.00017120) .678		.1329 (.1689) .434	48.93 (15.22) .002	1765.90 (748.85) .022	232.07 (127.13) .074	-37.18 (20.34) .073	.40	.34	56
FHA Regression One	.000002063 (.000000857) .008	.3771 (.0885) ≤.0001	.0009521 (.0012540) .450				1.98 (11.50) .836	.24	.22	104
FHA Regression Two	.000002472 (.000000857) .006	.4272 (.1789) .021		.2163 (.0893) .20	3.8484 (3.7533) .311	-.76175 (1.60650) .638	-7.2617 (1.6065) .638	.32	.24	50
FHA Regression Three	.0000009083 (.0000008541) .291		-.001627 (.001955) .410	.8080 (.1985) ≤.0001	1.8240 (3.7225) .627	-1.0330 (1.6106) .525	-24.67 (19.22) .206	.34	.27	50

* Calculated by subtracting the low county average per capita property tax in SMSA from high county average per capita property tax in SMSA and dividing by the overall SMSA average per capita property tax thus resulting in a relative range. Where one county consists of entire SMSA the range is zero.

** Calculated the same as the property tax range but uses the per capita sewer captial outlay high, low and overall averages.

TABLE 6.6

Appreciation regressions for thirty-six cities common to NABH and FHA, 1969

Dependent Variable/ Data Source/ Regression Number	Independent Variables Regression Coefficient, Standard Error in Parenthesis, Significance Level								
Land Value Appreciation, 1969	Total Population 1970 (persons)	Mean Family Income 1970 (dollars)	All Homes With Public Sewer 1970 (percent)	Change in Population 1960-1970 (percent)	Property Tax Range* 1969	Sewer Range** 1969	Constant	R^2	R^{-2}
NAHB Regression One	.00000016 (.00000021) .462	-.0283 (.2480) .910	66.7646 (22.5632) .006		2714.17 (1073.78) .017	-.5059 (189.6) .998	-3671. (2568.) .163	.37	.27
FHA Regression Two	.00000071 (.0002133) .997	-.1901 (.2443) .443	83.8507 (22.2275) .001		1372.41 (1057.80) .204	-21.0500 (184.1186) .910	-3079. (2530.) .233	.35	.24
NAHB Regression Three	.0002216 (.0002439) .371	-.0868 (.2673) .748	63.59 (23.19) .010	11.18 (21.27) .603	2583. (1080.) .023		-3095. (2758.) .271	.38	.27
FHA Regression Four	.0000318 (.0002411) .896	-.1651 (.2643) .537	83.2854 (22.9342) .001	-5.7272 (21.0351) .787	1417.18 (1068.08) .195		-3333. (2726.) .231	.35	.24

* Calculated by subtracting low county average per capita property tax in SMSA from high county average per capita property tax in SMSA and dividing by the overall SMSA average per capita property tax thus resulting in a relative range. Where county consists of entire SMSA the range is zero.

** Calculated the same as the property tax range but uses the per capita sewer captial outlay high, low and overall averages.

ing appreciation, the sewer range was consistently insignificant. On the other hand, the comparative case study indicated a growing awareness of sewer user charges vis-a-vis location decisions by developers and planners. Combined with sewer provision issues, sewer financing can limit residential growth in some areas and encourage residential growth elsewhere.

Property taxes

Property taxation was tested in the econometric most successfully by the property tax range. This was especially the case with NAHB data as was demonstrated in Tables 6.2 and 6.3 (site price) and Tables 6.5 and 6.6 (appreciation). The property tax range was generally insignificant in the FHA cross-sectional results. Since the pooled regressions used FHA data, it is not surprising that the property tax range continued to be insignificant in the pooled regressions. Developer comments in the comparative case study did not indicate much importance of property tax variations, per se, in location decisions. On the other hand, agricultural opportunity costs in part represent property tax effects on landowners ability to hold land. If the range is large, agricultural land might be taxed closer to use rather than market value, thus increasing the agricultural opportunity cost and the ability to hold land. Agricultural opportunity cost was consistently statistically significant and positive. A comment by one developer substantiated concern over agricultural land taxation and its effects on land availability. Use value taxation, either dejure or defacto, is likely to delay and change the results of land conversion and raise prices and appreciation rather than achieve agricultural land preservation in the long run.

While the interaction between these government policies is complex, the conclusion is that they separately and jointly affect the supply of land and can be a source of appreciation and economic profit associated with land values.

POLICY AND RESEARCH IMPLICATIONS

What policies do individuals or groups support if they want to keep prices and appreciation down? Efforts to lower appreciation will require focusing on all of the governmental jurisdictions in the land conversion market. This research examined the instrumental policies of local governments and their impact on site prices and appreciation. The structure of local governments and its impact on those policies and, hence, site prices and appreciation can be discussed only when the role of the instrumental variables is reasonably clear. Tentative policy implications of zoning, sewer provision, and taxation are presented here with, however, some reference to government structure issues in order to present a range of institutional alternatives and to avoid leaping to conclusions often found in this research area.

As has been noted, zoning policies can increase appreciation which in turn can create further feedback pressures on land use policies such as zoning. Variations in the degree to which supply restricting zoning policies exist will affect both developer and consumer location decisions and, perhaps, speculative activity. The greater the aggregate restrictions relative to demand, the greater the appreciation. For those who would like to lower land values created by this interdependent zoning process, the increased values are a negative pecuniary externality or spillover. The commonly used Tiebout (1956) model assumes no intercommunity spillovers, since people can move to communities offering characteristics they want, without consequences for others. Zoning is one tool for this product differentiation.

If it can be assumed that information about the appreciation effects of restrictive zoning will not change behaviour, given the interests vested in the current structure and competition (or economic rent and profit), then some change in government structure is suggested. Jurisdiction by jurisdiction changes to make zoning less restrictive over the entire land conversion market are unlikely to occur because of the benefits gained by those jurisdictions not changing. Various other land use policy options, whether superseding or coinciding with zoning, must account for jurisdictional interdependence. Chinitz and Cowing (1977) have analyzed the argument that metropolitan government be created to internalize externalities and recognized the geographical difficulties and value conflicts inherent in such policy prescriptions. Institutional changes designed to lower land values and appreciation will affect other preferences; small, homogeneous or high income suburbs, for example.

Other institutional arrangements have been suggested. Transferable development rights, which are designed, in general, to eliminate competition and change the distribution of economic rent and profit by having the winners of the land conversion process compensate the losers by a bargained transaction rather than an administered (zoning) decision. These rights could be exchanged by local government jurisdictions or individuals across the land conversion market. Clawson (1960) suggested several large suburban development districts in a metropolitan area which could have broad planning and infrastructure powers. In the State of California a similar concept, spheres of influence, is used as a basis for a planning device and organization (Local Agency Formation Commissions). This structure has problems interacting with existent governmental jurisdictions which limit their effect (Eells, 1977). The merits of any institutional change should be evaluated on many criteria, recognizing many values, including demand articulation, production economies, as well as prices.

Many of the same issues arise with sewer provision. Tabors et al., (1976) argued that, "the stronger and more centralized the control of the institutions responsible for sewerage planning, the more effective the overall policy is likely to be." (p. 172). Sewer supply relative to demand and timing also need to be considered within the context of the land conversion market but where the authority is placed and who gets included in the decision process will determine the ultimate impact of any change. The impact of a decision by one jurisdiction to limit sewer supply has, perhaps, clearer implications than zoning on other, nearby jurisdictions. With added concern about the appreciation and land value effects, land conversion market jurisdictions could bargain within the context of metropolitan area planning agencies which are becoming more involved in public service supply issues as state and federal involvement increases.

Agricultural taxation issues might also vary within a land conversion market. The empirical results of this research for the property tax range and agricultural opportunity cost support conclusions by Schmid (1968), Schwartz and Hansen (1973), and McMillan (1973) that lower property taxes lead to capitalization of the lower taxes into the value of the farm. Policies which, therefore, tax agricultural land at use rather than market value are likely to lower uncertainty and allow for an increased short run ability to withhold land from the market and, hence, raise appreciation.

The complexity of the land conversion process argues for a complex model. The research indicates that the general directional consequences of the various public policies are as hypothesized; however, the relationships are complex and the results are no doubt affected by other factors and highly idiosyncratic local situations.

NOTES

1. For other perspectives on policy tools, see, Greene, Neeman and Scott (1974), Mills and Oates (1975), Portney (1976), Downing (1974) and Healy and Short (1981).
2. Because of space limitations the pooled regression equations are not reported here. They can be found in Johnston (1980).

REFERENCES

Babcock, Richard F. (1966). **The Zoning Game.** Madison : The University of Wisconsin Press.

Chinitz, Benjamin, and Cowing, Thomas G. (1974). "The Impact of Local Public Service Consolidation on Urban Spatial Structure" in **Local Service Pricing Policies and Their Effect on Urban Spatial Structure.** Downing, Paul B. ed. Vancouver: University of British Columbia Press.

Clawson, Marion. (1960). "Suburban Development Districts." **Journal of The American Institute of Planners.** Vol. XXVI, Number 2. (May).

Clawson, Marion. (1971). **Suburban Land Conversion in the United States: An Economic and Governmental Process.** Baltimore: The Johns Hopkins Press for Resources for the Future, Inc.

Downing, Paul B., ed. (1974). **Local Service Pricing Policies and Their Effect on Urban Spatial Structure.** Vancouver, B.C.: University of British Columbia Press.

Eells, John Martin. (1977). **LAFCO Spheres of Influence: Effective Planning for the Urban Fringe?** Working Paper 77-3. Institute of Governmental Studies: University of California, Berkeley.

Greene, Kenneth V., Neeman, William B., and Scott, Claudia D. (1974). **Fiscal Interactions in a Metropolitan Area.** Lexington, Mass.: Lexington Books.

Healy, Robert G. and Short, James L. (1981). **The Market for Rural Land.** Washington: The Conservation Foundation.

McMillan, Melville. (1973). **Land-Use Control for the Preservation of Open Space on the Rural-Urban Fringe: An Alternative Policy.** Working Paper No. 7. Center for Resource Policy Studies, University of Wisconsin. (December).

Mills, Edwin S. and Oates, Wallace E. (1975). **Fiscal Zoning**

and Land Use Controls. Lexington, Mass.: Lexington Books, D.C. Heath and Company.

Portney, Paul R., ed. (1976). **Economic Issues in Metropolitan Growth.** Baltimore: The Johns Hopkins University Press.

Schmid, A. Allan (1968). **Converting Land from Rural to Urban Uses.** Washington, D.C.: Resources for the Future, Inc.

Schwartz, S.E. and Hansen, D.E. (1975). "Two Methods for Preserving Agricultural Land at the Urban Fringe: Use-Value Assessment and Transferable Development Rights." **Agriculture and Environment**, 2.

Sumichrast, Michael and Frankel, Sara A. (1970). **Profile of the Builder and His Industry.** Washington, D.C.: National Association of Home Builders.

Tabors, Richard D., et. al., (1976). **Land Use and the Pipe.** Lexington, Mass.: Lexington Books, D.C. Heath and Company.

Tiebout, Charles M. (1956). "A Pure Theory of Political Expenditures." **Journal of Political Economy.** vol. 64.

SEVEN

George F. Hepner

Magnitude and Implications of Rapid Residential Development in the Phoenix

Arizona Rural-Urban Fringe

INTRODUCTION

The Phoenix, Arizona rural-urban fringe is experiencing many of the problems inherent to undirected urban expansion. Annexation conflicts, flooding, soil subsidence, escalating costs of remote service purveyance and loss of prime farmland and natural areas are among these problems. Many of the problems and the lack of appropriate institutional response is due to a lack of understanding of the complex nature of the rural to residential land use conversion process (Lee, 1979).

This study is a descriptive analysis of the location and rate of residential land use conversion in a 3548.3 square kilometre (1370 square miles) area surrounding Phoenix for the period 1970-1978 (Figure 7.1). The study area does not include the urbanized area of Phoenix as of 1970 or non-developmental fringe areas, such as the Tonto National Forest or Gila River Indian Reservation. Resultant from these analyses the study suggests a partial basis of explanation of the factors which determine the variations in the spatial pattern of residential conversions in the Phoenix area.

LAND USE CLASSIFICATION

The residential land use conversion data was obtained from corresponding aerial photography for the years 1970 and 1978. The 1970 photography was accessed from the U.S. Department of Agriculture, Agricultural Stabilization and Conservation Service in 1:63360 scale index sheets and

1:7920 enlarged prints. Corresponding 1978 photography was obtained from the Maricopa County Assessors Office in 1:1100 and 1:20,000 formats. Five land use classifications were developed to generalize the multitude of land uses apparent on the photography. These classifications are the culmination of segments of various general land use classification schemes applied to a desert and irrigated agricultural setting in the context of this study (Hyers, 1976; Winikka, 1975).

The level of unit-area resolution of the photographic analysis is 1/16th of a public land survey section or 16.2 hectares (40 acres). The land use occurring on greater than 50 percent of each one sixteenth of a section is considered the use for that area. Any land use conversion of less than 50 per cent within a 16.2 hectare (40 acres) unit is not substantial, especially on the expansive rural-urban fringe of Phoenix. Certain limitations on the information and the analysis are apparent through the use of this procedure. The idle land differentiation is the most difficult. Land that is still functionally oriented toward agricultural use, yet is temporarily "set aside" land in a U.S.D.A. crop stabilization program often appears on the photography as idle. However, most farmers maintain the level contour of both "set aside" land and acreage temporarily rotated out of production. Thus, the noting of sporadic desert vegetation and/or erosional features, and field checking to distinguish idled farm land from farm land only out of production for a short period of time is essential to correct classification.

The differentiation between idle and desert land use is a problem as well, particularly, in areas that supported agriculture previous to 1970. Dropping water tables in these agricultural areas created idle farm land by 1970 which eventually succeeded back to desert land by 1978. The presence of substantial desert vegetation was considered a key indicator to redefining 1970 idle land to 1978 desert land.

The 50 per cent of an ordered 1/16 of a section resolution level tends to underestimate certain land uses. The major example is the strip commercial or the corner commercial use which is surrounded by residential. Most of the time due to meso scale level of resolution the entire 1/16 section would be designated residential. Thus, the other urban land use class is underestimated to a small degree in the analysis. Because the major emphasis of the study is residential land use this is not a great problem, but it is

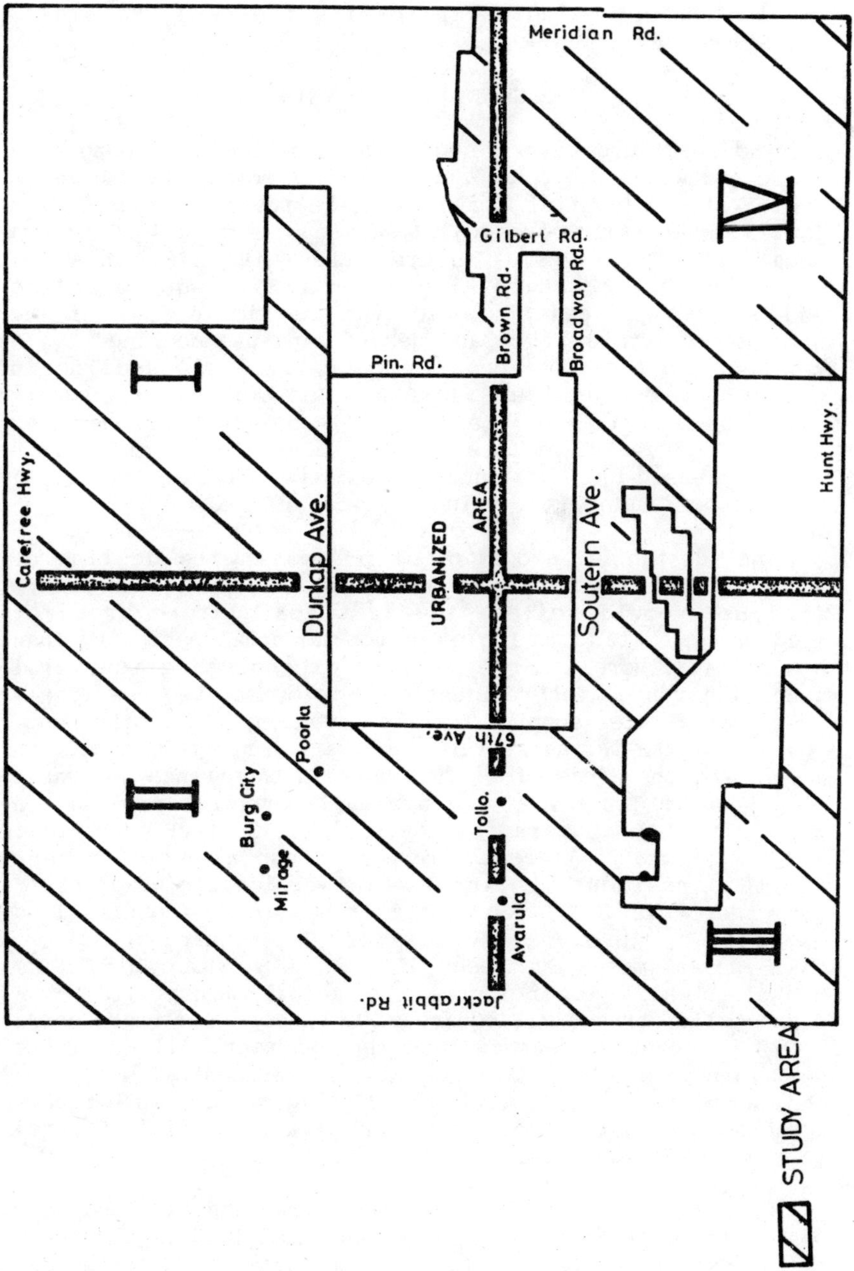

FIG.7.1: Rural-Urban fringe study area by quadrants

one that should be noted in reading the land use classification statistics.

RESULTS AND ANALYSIS

The rural-urban fringe study area is analyzed both as a whole and within a four quadrant framework. As shown in Table 7.1, residential land use in the fringe increased from 166.73 square kilometres (64.4 square miles) in 1970 to 504 square kilometres (194.6 square miles) in 1978. This increase of 337.2 square kilometres (130.2 square miles) equals a 202 per cent increase over the time period. In the same time, agriculture and desert land use declined by 16 per cent and seven per cent respectively. This decline in agricultural use of 226.4 square kilometres (87.4 square miles) is almost twice the decline in desert which amounted to 120.7 square kilometres (46.6 square miles). Other urban uses increased only 8.5 square kilometres (3.3 square miles) or nine per cent on the fringe between 1970 and 1978.

The substantial amount of difference in the decline of agricultural land use on the fringe as opposed to desert land use, could reflect the fact that larger areas of agricultural land are closer to the urban periphery than desert land. More likely, the more expensive agricultural land is favoured for residential development because it already has a water supply, fertile level soil, and other components of the infrastructure necessary for development. The amounts of the areas of various uses in the fringe quadrants are shown in Table 7.2 with a visual portrayal provided in figures 7.1-5. Quadrants I (Figure 7.2), II (Figure 7.3), and IV (Figure 7.5) are the major fringe areas of recent rural to residential land use conversion. In quadrant IV (SE) there was a 236 per cent increase in residential land use with an absolute increase of 126.6 square kilometres (48.9 square miles) between 1970 and 1978. Quadrant I (NE) had a slightly lower increase in actual amount with 102.3 square kilometres (39.5 square miles), but this represented a 272 per cent increase within the quadrant. All quadrants seem to have a substantial increase in residential use. Even though the increase in quadrant III (Figure 7.4) in percentage change is quite large, the land area is minimal compared to the other quadrants.

It appears the primary sources for residential land were desert in quadrant I (NE) and agricultural land in quadrants II (NW) and IV (SE). Idle land in the rural-urban fringe had a substantial increase in the time period in quadrant IV

(SE). This appears to be the area of most pronounced speculative idling of land under development pressure. Water problems, soil salinity increases or any other reasons for idling of the primarily agricultural area were not indicated by supportive analysis.

TABLE 7.1

Change in amounts of land use areas in rural-urban fringe study area

Square kilometres (square miles)

	1970		1978		Amount of change		Percentage change
Residential	166.73	(64.4)	504	(194.6)	+337.3	(130.2)	+202
Other urban	92.72	(35.8)	99.71	(38.5)	+6.99	(3.3)	+9
Agricultural	1420.3	(548.4)	1219.84	(471)	-200.5	(77.4)	-16
Desert	1672.56	(645.8)	1551.86	(599.2)	-120.7	(46.6)	-7
Idle	197.1	(76.1)	200.2	(77.3)	+3.1	(1.2)	+2

Relatively large areas of substantial concentrations of residential development are located within fringe quadrants I (NE), II(NW), and IV (SE). These areas are approximately 10.4 square kilometres (four square miles) or larger of contiguous new residential development. Along the east boundary of quadrant I (NE) is the Fountain Hills area which is relatively remote from the current developed areas of Phoenix and adjacent suburbs. This development seems to have encouraged additional, although less substantial development between Fountain Hills and the northern part of Scottsdale. Analysis indicates that the major factors stimulating development in these areas is the availability of relatively inexpensive, suitable desert land with public services available from Scottsdale, the social prestige of living in or near Scottsdale, and the scenic amenities of this area. Interestingly, multi-lane highway accessibility is limited, thus, appearing to be a lesser consideration in location.

Within quadrant II (NW) three areas of rapid and concentrated rural to residential land use conversion appear to exist. The growth of this area seems directly attributable to the accessibility provided by Interstate 17 which runs north-south through the eastern portion of this quadrant. In 1970 much of this area was desert land under very preliminary development activities, and therefore, classified as idle land in the aerial photographic analysis.

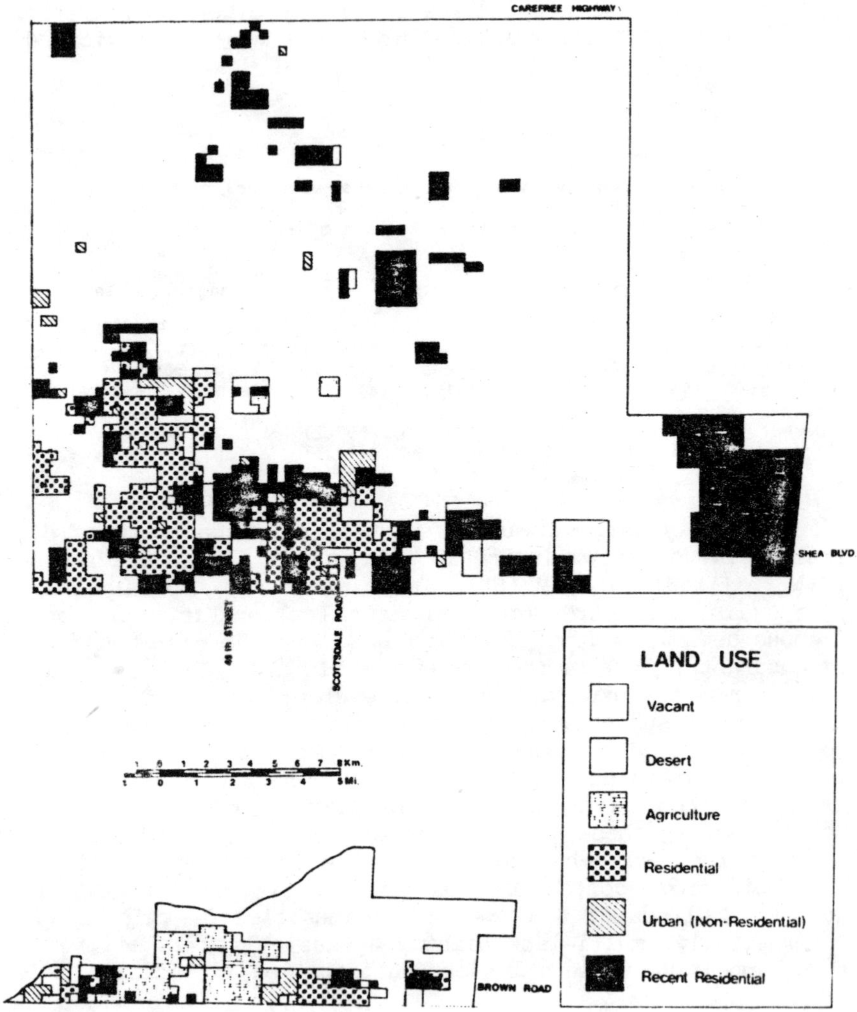

FIG. 7.2: Recent residential growth (1970-1978) and adjacent land uses in quadrant I (NE).

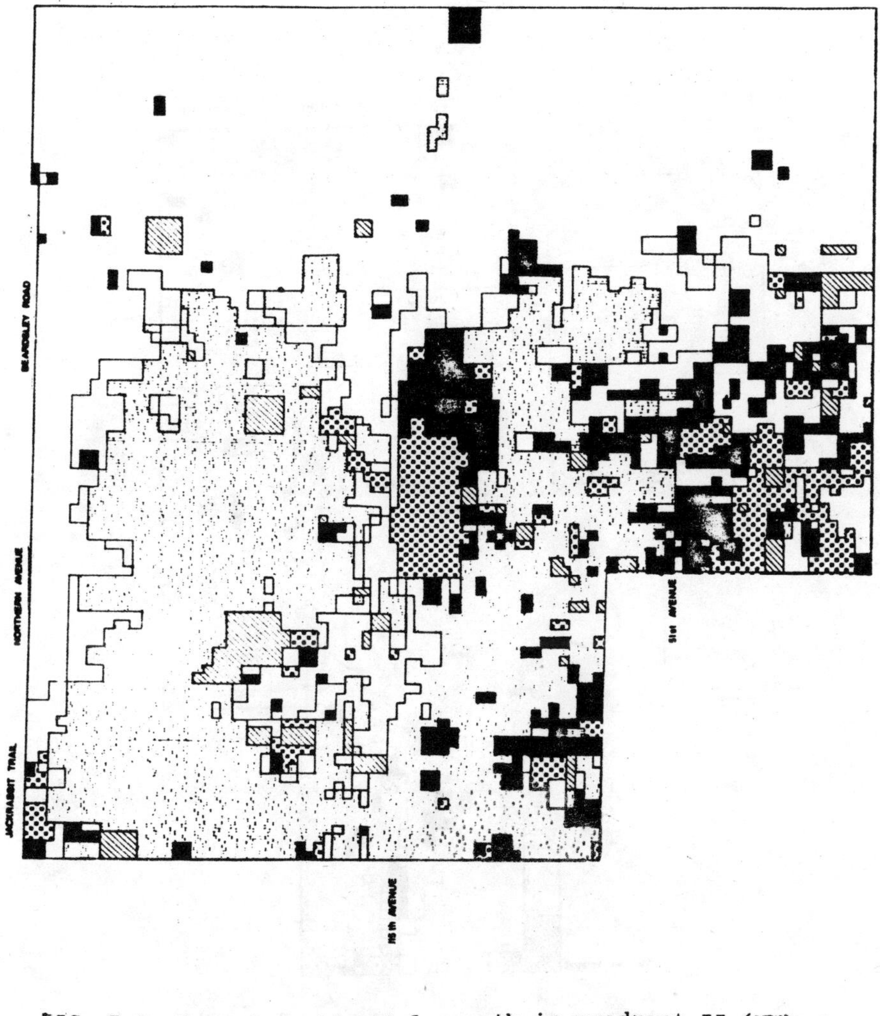

FIG. 7.3: Recent residential growth in quadrant II (NW).

FIG.7.4: Recent residential growth in quadrant III (SW)

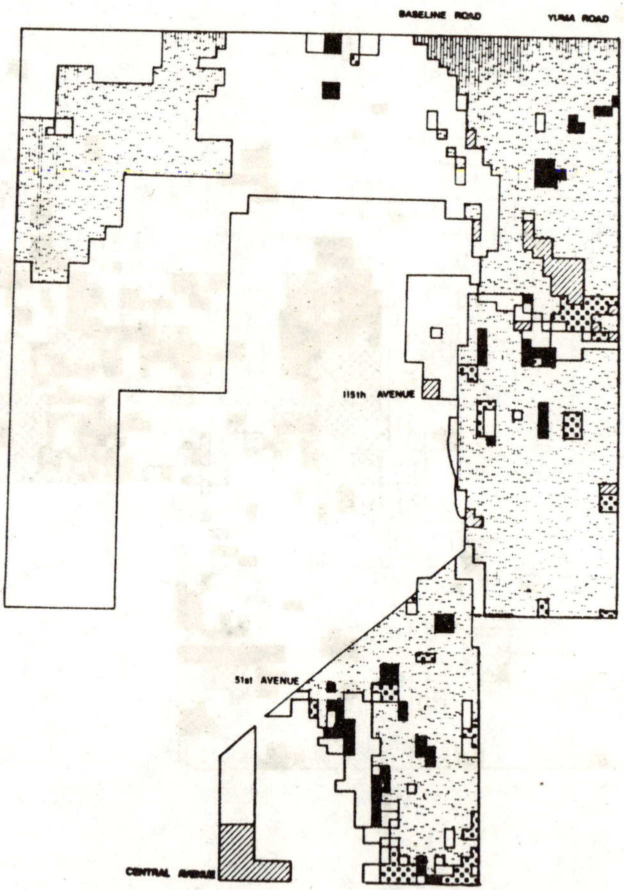

FIG.7.5: Recent residential growth in quadrant IV (SE)

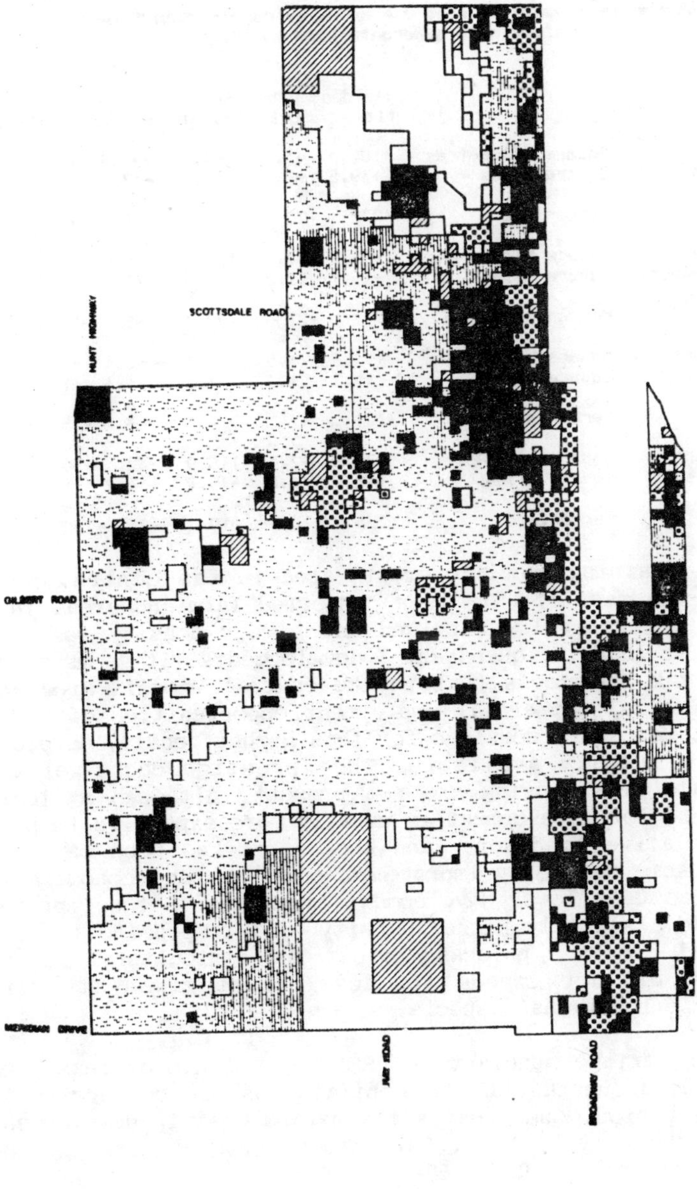

TABLE 7.2

Change in amounts of land use areas by rural-urban fringe study area quadrants 1970 to 1978

		Residen-tial	Other Urban	Agricul-tural	Desert	Idle
Quadrant I (Northeast)	Square kilometres	+102.3	-3.1	-4.4	-95.8	+1.
	Square miles	+39.5	-1.2	-1.7	-37.	+.4
	Percentage	+272	-70	-81	14	+4
Quadrant II (Northwest)	Square kilometres	+93.5	+7.3	-101.8	+25.6	-22.3
	Square miles	+36.1	+2.8	-39.3	+9.9	-8.6
	Percentage	+147	+27	-20	+5	-17
Quadrant III (Southwest)	Square kilometres	+14.8	+.8	+1.3	-8.5	-4.9
	Square miles	+5.7	+.3	+.5	-3.3	-1.9
	Percentage	+121	+7	-.5	-3.	-33
Quadrant IV (Southeast)	Square kilometres	126.6	+2.1	-118.9	-42.	+30.
	Square miles	+48.9	+.8	-45.9	-16.2	+11.6
	Percentage	+236	+4	-19	-25	+130

The remaining specific growth area in the central portion of quadrant Il (NW) is a converted farmland area. This area is generally lower priced and higher density residential units than the quandrant I developments. It seems to be located due to access to both the central Phoenix area and the industrial-commercial employment opportunities of North Phoenix. Necessary services for this higher density development are readily available. The "prestige costs" of the Scottsdale area housing are not present. Although agricultural land for development is usually more expensive to purchase relative to desert land because it has been capitalized to some degree by improvements and has an economically productive use, lower development costs due to the improvements and a slightly higher density will compensate for the increased raw land purchase price. The agricultural use of this area did not impede its development given its very favourable locational aspects.

Within fringe quadrant IV (SE) two definable areas have demonstrated substantial residential land use conversion in the time period. One area is the expanded strip development east of the city of Mesa. This growth appears directly related to the access Route 60-70.

The second area is more related to the suburb of Tempe. It is the southward expansion of the suburb of Tempe. Development in this area is encouraged by the proximity of Interstate 10 which allows access to downtown Phoenix. The location of certain industrial concerns and industrial parks adjacent to Interstate 10 in the southern portion of incorporated Tempe has stimulated growth in this area only a few miles from these industrial areas.

The absence of significant conversion activity in quadrant III (SW) is noteworthy. This predominately agricultural quadrant has not been conducive to development because of barriers of access which include a mountainous area and an Indian reservation. However, the primary factors appear to be related to the perception of this area. It is adjacent to the lower income areas of South and Southwest Phoenix. This situation inhibits development, especially in the Phoenix area, where prestige location is a very marketable housing lure and many builders and buyers came to the Phoenix area to escape the realities of urban poverty and problems.

CONCLUSIONS

Rapid conversion of desert and agricultural land is taking place in the Phoenix area. Between the years 1970 and 1978 approximately 225 square kilometres (87 square miles) of agricultural land and 122 square kilometres (47 square miles) of desert land was converted to urban oriented residential use. Although the conversion process is not being directed by any comprehensive formalized land management mechanism, locational predilections are apparent. While inference from generalized spatial patterns is problematic (Olsson, 1969), several appropriate observations can be made.

Factors of perception of beauty and prestige of a general area are primary in Phoenix fringe residential location, especially for the more expensive market segment. Proximity to access routes, the Phoenix CBD or regional nodes, such as shopping centres and industrial parks is of variable importance in recent conversions. Additional analysis revealed that coincidence of recent development with master plans and capital improvement plans of the various governmental entities is at a level approximating just over 50 per cent. This indicates the necessary services for residential development and zoning protection of the development are being obtained retroactive to the initial location decision.

Agricultural land seems to be preferred for development especially for less expensive higher density developments. While this is "consuming" the prime agricultural land resource of the area, the implications in terms of regional agricultural productivity, net water usage and groundwater recharge are not at all clear.

Given the probable extension of the current regional and national situation, urban growth and corresponding residential development in the rural-urban fringe will continue undiminished in the future. This reality of continued growth per se is not necessarily an unpleasant one for millions of people seeking a favourable quality of life in the Phoenix area. In some respects, this growth is not harmful and may be beneficial to several economic and environmental situations currently existing in the region.

A more important and as yet uncertain aspect of the growth in Phoenix and the rest of the U.S. is whether the quality of life will be maintained given the undirected nature of the current fringe development situation (Ziemetz, 1976; Hart, 1976). The impacts on the quality of life, such as air pollution, soil and flooding problems, and the consumption of agricultural and natural open space, are clearly evident, but the institutional mechanisms to cope with these problems are not apparent at the present time (Council on Environmental Quality, 1978). Coordinated management of capital improvements, services, and perhaps, a marketing response to prestige and amenity factors on the part of public planning agencies could greatly improve the future rural to urban land conversion situation.

REFERENCES

Council on Environmental Quality. 1978. **Environmental Quality.** Ninth Annual Report, Washington D.C.: U.S. Government Printing Office.

Hart, J. F. 1976. Urban Encroachment in Rural Areas. **Geographical Review**, 66: pp. 1-17.

Hyers, A. D. 1976. Land Use, Sediment Characteristics, and Dust Storms. **Evaluation of Highway Dust Hazard Along 1-10 in the Casa Grande-Eloy Region**, M. G. Marcus, ed. Research paper No. 3. Tempe: Center for Environmental Studies, Arizona State University.

Lee, L. 1979. Factors Affecting Land Use Change at the

Urban-Rural Fringe. **Growth and Change,** 4: pp. 25-31.
Olsson, G. 1969. Inference Problems in Locational Analysis. **Behavioral Problems in Geography,** K. Cox and R. Golledge, eds. Studies in Geography 19. Evanston: Department of Geography, Northwestern University.
Winikka, C. 1975. **Arizona Land Use Experiment.** Proceedings of NASA Earth Resources Survey Symposium. Phoenix: N.P.
Ziemetz, K. 1976. **Dynamics of Land Use Change in Fast Growth Areas.** AER325. Washington D.C.: U.S. Department of Agriculture.

EIGHT

Jean Paul Laborie & Jean Frinwis Langumier

The Peripheric Industrialization

An Extension to the Ground Division of Work and to the Social Split

In France, the 1970s have been marked by a slow down in the high urban growth which had started twenty years earlier and by a re-moulding of urban features. Post war urbanization has greatly affected the Capital and the largest towns in the country in a spectacular way. On the ground level, it took on a concentrated and dense form. Between 1946 and 1975, the rate of urbanization went up from 53% to 73% with an increase of over 16 million towns-people during a quarter of a century whereas the national population only increased by 11 million inhabitants. (During the preceding century, from 1846 to 1946, towns had only registered a growth of 14 million towns-people). Between 1954 and 1968, the urban population increased at an average rate of 2% per year (1.9%; 1.8%) which slowed down between 1968 and 1975 (1.1%), although it remained superior to the natural demographic growth rate of the country. During the 1950s and 1960s, the towns of over 100,000 inhabitants developed essentially. Whereas the 1970s benefited mainly to average agglomerations from 50,000 to 200,000 inhabitants. From 1970 onwards, towns-people living in provincial suburbs become more numerous than those of the Parisian suburbs (Table 8.1).

In 1968, 31% of towns-people were then commuters against 33% in 1975. Between these two census years, suburbs spread mainly around eight equilibrium metropolises[1] regrouping 2.5 million inhabitants in 1968, 2.7 million in 1975, that is to say a total increase of 24%. The population of the Parisian suburbs (first and second belts) only progresses by 9% during the same period. But 16% for that of the provincial suburbs, excepting the metropolises already quoted. On the ground level, 1 million housings, most of them collective, were built on about 300 ZUP from 1956 to 1959, with an average density of housings four times superior (100 housings per hectare) to the existing urban network.

TABLE 8.1

Numerical evolution of the population of the Parisian suburb and of the suburbs of provincial towns

	1968		1975	
	Inhabitants per million	%	Inhabitants per million	%
Parisian suburb	5.6	50.9	6.1	48.8
Provincial suburbs*	5.4	49.1	6.4	51.2
Total	11.0	100.0	12.5	100.0

* In the urban units of over 50,000 inhabitants; population calculated according to an inclusive, rough and not very subtle method: the population of the urban unit less the population of the commune-centre.

Peripheric Urbanization and Economic Crisis

The aspect of agglomerations has modified in a new way during the last 10 years; the growth, though weaker, has become more extensive and more diffuse around large and average towns in the country. The peripheric areas, sometimes 30 or 50 kms away from downtown, have been the privileged places of this new phase. Whereas between 1968 and 1975, the total urban units increase by 1.1% a year, the rural communes of the ZPIU develop at a rate of 1.3% a year: they are the setting for the peripheric urbanization phenomenon. In 1975, 5.5 million inhabitants live there. On the contrary, the rural communes, outside the ZPIU, decrease according to a -0.7% rate per year. The peripheric urbanization develops remarkably around big cities but also near average towns, especially in the areas which have mainly benefited by the economic and social boom corresponding to the past phase of high and regular growth. This type of area is the privileged ground for the building of private houses: between 1972 and 1975, over 1/3 of the private houses built in the country has settled there. Between 1965 and 1975, the number of private houses built every year has multiplied by 2 going up from 120,000 to 236,000. Most of them are intended for new property owners and have a size in average superior to that of the flats. This period corresponds to the boom of a new market held by the progression of the middle classes and favourable to private housing.

However, in 1972, the number of private lodgings built becomes stable: about 240,000 per year. Yet, the collapse of the number of collective lodgings built, going down from

310,000 per year to 115,000 per year between 1972 and 1981 increases among the total number of lodgings built. The share of private houses although there is fewer laying down, becomes less important.

In 1979, 280,000 houses have been laid down and 265,000 only in 1980; for the crisis diminishes the solvability of households. This tendency to peripheric urbanization which began earlier in other industrialized countries is not specifically French where what remains original results from the conjunction of this process with the reversal of the macro-economic state of the market. Consequently, the suburban growth of towns increasingly becomes a prospective question concerning especially town and country planning. During a period of growth, some fundamental factors obviously exist which render this suburban extension of cities possible, taking part in the implementation of a consumer society: a perceptible and regular increase in household incomes, bank facilities improving real estate purchases, realizations (by the State and public collectivities) of supplementary public equipments, particularly those intended to allow an increase in people's mobility, etc. A few economic and social indexes account for these evolutions linked to growth. Several points are worth mentioning briefly. Between 1946 and 1972, the value in constant francs of the GNP per inhabitant has almost multiplied by 5. From 1954 to 1975, the number of engineers and technicians has multiplied by 3.5, that of the top executives by 3 and the office clerks and middle managements represent more than 37% of the socio-professional categories of the country against only 19% in 1954. Those "average" stratas have broadly acquired real property and invested in the suburban area these last years. They are generally over represented there. Besides, the average price of a private house has slightly decreased, even when considering the land tax. The evolution of average selling prices of new built housings between 1973 and 1975 in Province shows for example that the private lodgings of the private sector increased less.

Moreover, "most of the individual suburban lodgings benefit by State assistance. Their development appears in this respect as largely induced by the financial help of the State favouring the acquisition of real estate and particularly thanks to the role of premium and loans of the Credit Fancier."[2] On the contrary, we only have to notice that in 1975, only 32% of individual houses laid down in the suburban area do not profit by any public assistance against 49% for all the individual houses in France.

But since 1974, the economic environment of suburban growth has changed a lot: the weakness and irregularity of the progression of the household solvency, inflationary tensions on house prices and mainly on land shares, strong and regular increase of the energy cost, only to quote a few new important data. So that an evolution takes shape from 1975 onwards as for the importance of the incomes of households moving into a suburban area. An index measures the effects of the economic crisis on household solvency: before 1975, 53% of households that had recently moved, had at their disposal less than 60,000 French Francs yearly income (national average); after 1975, the proportion had gone down to 44%. On the other hand, the working expenses linked to the consumption of energy in private houses seem now superior to those of a collective lodging: overheating the house because of its unsufficient isolation[3] and increased domestic equipment: freezers or cars[4] among other things. Finally, the land tax amounted to about 1/3 of the total average cost of a private house in 1979, i.e., about 100,000 francs ; but in 1980, this expense represented about 50% of the purchase price of an average lodging on the national level, against only 10% at the beginning of the century.

The Sesame group from the DATAR tried to estimate the conditions of the duration of the suburban phenomenon in this new economic context. A first set of studies considers the factors of residential demand and offer in those peripheric areas; almost considering them from the residential and sociological aspects mainly, they finally tend to show clearly the dependance of the suburban phenomenon compared to total economic factors: prospects of improvement of the purchasing power of households, the price of land, public loans in favour of the building and purchase of lodgings. It is clear thus particularly difficult to establish a forecasting about an object submitted to so many variable factors and which also depend on the general economic policy of the government. Another method has been adopted which rather stresses the lasting economic springs of the spatial extension of agglomerations from the study of the loosing of activities within enlarged urban regions. The chosen hypothesis of work puts forward that if there exist deep reasons for the operations of regional extensions of productive activities towards suburban areas, even during periods of low growth, the peripheric and extensive development of the agglomerations is a coming phenomenon, the more because the loosing can, in its turn, be partly responsible for changes in residential areas as zones with a residential

TABLE 8.2

	PRIVATE LODGINGS				COLLECTIVE LODGINGS		
	Councilled Houses	Immediate Special Loans	Agreed Real Estate Loans	Free Sector	Immediate Special Loans	Agreed Real Estate Loans	Free Sector
2nd Term 1973	100 1,055	100 1,317	100 1,531	100 1,613	100 1,265	100 1,505	100 1,972
4th Term 1975	158.1 1,669	144.1 1,898	139.3 2,133	139.1 2,244	147.3 1,863	130.2 1,960	143.2 2,824
4th Term 1978	2,090	2,910		3,175	2,210		3,375

Source : INSEE. Index Number : 100 For 1973 And Francs/m2.

vocation only also as specific areas which register in a new ground division of work felt at a local level. Consequently, these territories also represent the germs of new basins for specific jobs more or less autonomous compared with the existing labour market in the initial agglomeration.[5]

A NEW PROCESS OF INDUSTRIALIZATION IN THE SUBURBAN AREAS

The empiric analysis of suburban areas in 7 towns with different economic, social and historical situations (Lyons, Mulhouse, Toulouse, Albi, Carmaux, Castres, Mazamet) brings to light about those three hundred and seventy eight displacements of establishments noticed between 1968 and 1980, some general statements about the present processes of industries towards suburbs. Each loosing area offers its own conditions for the fittings and fixtures of new units of production. The common features between the outskirts of these big cities are not contained in the urban structures and must not be identified as identical processes used on different scales. However, each of these areas is marked by an enduring social division.

An increased economic and social division in the suburban areas

Lyons, Mulhouse, Toulouse, the average towns in Tarn: as many specific cases, as many areas marked by an increased dynamism of social segmentation. A second suburban belt adds to the main suburb of Lyons, especially on the Eastern fringe. The commune of Villeurbanne has been swallowed up during successive evolutions which nowadays make it an area where some activities start and others stop. On the contrary, around Toulouse and in spite of its demographic weight, the loosing of activities remains a recent phenomenon only because of the delay itself registered in the industrialization of this metropolis; centrifugal movements hardly outgrow the limits of the commune-centre but, although they are not very intense, they reveal very obvious tendencies indicating the urban extensions to be. Those peripheric buddings also concern Mulhouse: highly industrialized in a region which, unlike many others, has longer maintained a high growth of industrial production. They can be found again, but at lesser degrees, in average towns of the Tarn department which include new industrial zones in areas in process of rapid differentiation.

In Lyons, the axis of development towards the East is

still receiving activities of production further and further away from the districts of Lyons or Villeurbanne wherefrom they originated. Correlatively, the residential zone of this axis is dominated by a working class population. Whereas, in the North-West area, the suburban houses, peopled with wealthier social classes, extend, whereas industrial parks of rural communes favour more qualified activities of production and of management. The peripheric industrialization of Toulouse together with its Western "Aerospaciale" and electronic and the South-Eastern activities produces as a consequence a geographical distribution of the residential area specific to the different social groups: executives in the South, workmen in the West and the North, employees in the East. The social dynamics proper to both banks of the Garonne are geographically very marked. This evolution can also be noticed around Mulhouse, an average but highly industrialized town.

The splitting of the peripheric area intensifies during a period when the demographic medium-terms estimates attribute more than half the French population to the suburbs. The external growth upsets the organization of the urban area by dissociating the working poles from the lodgings area. Compared with the common place opposition between downtown and outskirts, the town divides into many mini-basins of jobs that draw their cohesiveness from their location in the social division of the peripheric area: the suburban areas in Lyons, Toulouse, Mulhouse, etc., are nothing like homogeneous areas; a basin of suburban employment is replaced by basins of differentiated employments. One is made of a group of communes inhabitated by top executives, the other of communes which gather individual housings for employees or skilled workers, etc. To which extent do the loosings take into account these new conditions? To which extent do the loosings take part in this dynamic?

The loosing : A growth process

The results of the loosings study bring to light four fundamental features of the recent moves of establishments: their tempo, the nature of the concerned activities, the types of institutions concerned and the offers of equipped sites, make us aware of the effects of spatialization of the economic activities upon the terms of peripheric growth.

The loosings movements have not decreased in number after 1974, that is to say during a period of slowed down growth of the industrial production, which strengthens the hypothesis according to which the loosing also expresses the specific economic dynamism of firms and that consequently the analysis of the loosing tendencies requires economic studies on a large scale. The corollary of this established extending loosing of units of production of dynamic firms carries on the processes of peripheric growth provoked by the moving out of some activities. This hypothesis contradicts the results registered in the Ile de France region where the perceptible decrease of the loosing movements after 1974 appeared to be linked mainly to the stoppage of movings of the large firms.

The loosing is everywhere due to small-and medium-size concerns: the 2/3 of the three hundred and seventy eight movements listed affects firms of 10 to 50 wage-earners and only 13% firms of over 100 wage-earners. This fact lessens the contradiction between the conclusion of both studies: in fact, 'it appears that the mobilities of large concerns have become rare, but they were already so outside the Parisian region; on the contrary, the movements of the small-and medium-sized concerns, already numerous, continue.

The small-size of these firms diminishes their demands as for the reception conditions in the suburban areas: their capacity for inserting themselves in areas which gather all sorts of existing advantages cannot be compared with those of large concerns which on the contrary created their environment afterwards. Their rapid answer to the requests of the newly created outskirts or the effects of rejection from their initial surroundings is quicker. Finally, the growing small-and medium-sized firms' mobility adjusts itself better to the production of many peripheric branches, the dimensions of which are reduced to the size of a commune, or a district.

About half the registered moves concern 2 branches of industry: the mechanical and the electric-electronic ones. Once more, this high proportion, just as that of the small- and middle-sized firms within the whole lot of concerns which have displaced their establishments, sends back to the correspondence between internal dynamism and suburban mobility. The mechanical and electric building branches have been among the most performing between 1968 and 1980; consequently, they are better represented among the sampling. Both activities belong to the equipment of industrial groups in which the substitution capital-employment is quick. On the peripheric labour market, the effect of the coming of new, recently built concerns, hence rationalized in addition, cannot be estimated by a simple calculation of job transfers. The loosing does not settle again an already organized market (a few kms away), it recreates it with different contents.

The offer of industrial areas in readiness in urban periphery is a very important factor to provoke and master the loosing movements. These are numerous around Mulhouse precisely because of the important industrial equipment organized. The case of Toulouse is different; little offer and consequently partly nearer loosings or on the contrary, much further ones within the regions or even the country. The industrialists find the equipped zones most suitable as they are less expensive than others with the same outfit. But this does not seem to be the case in the Ile-de-France. This datum could be integrated in the regional diagram of activities in the process of elaboration: a peripheric offer corresponding to the needs, appears to be a good means, a necessary but insufficient condition to maintain the local, most dynamic output potential.

An initial conclusion on the study of the loosing of activities links the movements towards the periphery and the creation of jobs in seventy establishments in which a thorough enquiry has been made: the statement of created or suppressed employments compared to the initial localization, stresses a positive balance of 27%; thus the loosing induces jobs in the periphery of urban areas. Moreover, it is an important element for the consumption of land; it is a process of growth in the towns.

LOOSING AND SOCIO-ECONOMIC MARKING OF URBAN PERIPHERIES

The larger an agglomeration is, the further from the centre do the loosings extend because of the ground saturation, land costs and the capacity of networks required for the increasing activities (movement of goods, information and men), therefore a distribution of the loosings according to concentric, chronologically dated circles.... However, several factors come and modify the common place radio-concentric example.

The geography of the axes of communication aims at determining some axes of progressive drift of establishments that rarely abandon an axis for a new one. Nowadays, establishments wish to dispose of both roads and railways in their new site whereas before, railways were more exclusively looked for. A nearby airport is valorized everywhere (Mulhouse, Lyons, Toulouse). Some establishments go further in order to be able to use greater surfaces or avoid urban regulations concerning the nuisances (the case of activities of transformation of weight materials, of stocking: warehouses, building and public works).

The analyses of the causes of loosing meet with already stated conclusions about the transformation of the land structure of agglomerations: "The town-centre dedicated to contact activities..." the remaining central zones specializing in activities which, from their position in the labour division and from their growth rate, have a strategic function in the structure of the urban ground; the urban periphery rather benefits by the contribution of "commonplace" activities. However, it seems that the relations between the centrifugal residential and economic movements cannot be summed up with the mere description of a radio-concentric example which misses out the deepening social marking of the suburbs.

Loosings and increase of the labour division

A loosing of activities very often corresponds to an increase in the division of labour within the firm or the examined establishment. So, one can say that the more or less important segmentation of the tasks within a unit of production allows a more or less extended choice as for the new peripheric localization. Two linked criteria must be considered: the labour organization and the qualification of the stations of the concerned unit of production. The tasks of production are those that move further from the tertiary tasks of administration, marketing or management and, on the other hand, little qualified. If the functions of production and administration are still part of the unit of production, the latter will tend to remain nearer its original place. The points of stockage or packing also admit a lesser extension to a further loosing.

When considering the moves of some establishments that join together manufacture, stockage, marketing and administration departments, it significantly shows how little the relation between some stages of the division of labour in a firm and some particular sites for the setting up of establishment is. During a first period, the firm answers the demands of a more rational functioning by taking away the manufacturing tasks only. The separation between the new buildings and the old ones in the centre is motivated by some difficulties to abandon the contact potentials offered by the nearby centre. Later, the regrouping of the different services in the new premises imposes itself as something imperative, dictated by the organization of labour in the different establishments. However, in many cases, the tertiary jobs and all the office activities remain on the initial spot.

In fact, the loosing separates the activities according to the complexity of the division of labour: in the country, the division of labour is non-existent; in the town-centre, it is utmost. From the centre to the furthest urban periphery, the industrial establishments first abandon the management, the researches, the administration tasks. Then, if marketing and stockage remain the prerogative of the suburbs and dense centres, the manufacturing jobs occupy little by little a predominant position in the nearby suburbs and are the only ones present at the external limit of the peripheric area.

Loosings and hierarchy of qualifications

The geographical distribution of the establishment emphasizes the localization near the old dense areas of the establishments for specialized small mechanisms: electrical engineering, printing and some other activities that employ a skilled staff. These industries tend not to go far from the centre or rather to remain near their starting points. For sure, such workshops do not settle on large surfaces and can thus hold all the winning cards of a new localization which solves the ground and access problems without cancelling the advantages of an almost central position. A building public works enterprise must not forget that distance implies saving when buying land.

The conclusions drawn from the simple ventilation of localizations of activities are corroborated by analyzing the interviews of some heads of firms - far from the town the difficulty in filling up skilled posts is real, the recruiting of executives works on a rarer and more demanding offer - which are checked by precise observations. In many cases, executives have been renewed within the 2 years following the transfer of establishment. Several times, industrials have manifested their difficulties in recruiting some qualified staff. It seems that, in spite of the state of the labour market, the proximity of downtown seems to enrich the range of qualified jobs. This progressive degradation of qualification can also be noticed concerning the organization of the moves of establishments. The concerns that employ little qualified workers do not appear fearful about the consequences of their transfer on the organization of jobs and the manufacturing. The staff follows or does not; in firms with a high proportion of women, it usually does not follow: each removal increases the number of women looking for jobs on the labour markets in urban centres. In so far as the firm does not require high qualifications, it can assuredly quickly fill up the abandoned posts. On the contrary, when the proportion of qualified staff is high, the transfer takes place in other conditions and the firm tries, as we have noticed for different loosings, to re-localize itself near the area where its manpower live.

These mechanisms partake of a profound logic that would tend to distribute central jobs in the urban periphery according to a gradation of their respective qualification. The size of the units of production renders this ventilation more or less easy and very dependent on the combination of the tasks of production and the administration that take place there.

Loosing and social segmentation of the peripheric urban space

The loosings induce a strengthening of the economic structures of the peripheric areas. These movements partake of the urban dynamism, particularly because they insert themselves in the processes of using social hierarchies in urban areas. The loosing phenomenon is a dynamic phenomenon because it is provoked by ever evolving factors: technological progress, increasing division of social labour, etc. This explains why we can speak of successive belts of loosings together with uninterrupted transfers of activities on these belts with an intensity varying according to the local contexts. The case of the commune of Villeurbanne next to that of Lyons, without being original, is particularly significant in that respect: for about one century, this commune has been successively dominated by primary, secondary activities and tends nowadays to be dominated by tertiary activities: warehouses, but also services companies.

The loosings imply an increase in the technical and social division of work within the unit of production. The choices of the firms tend to favour the advantages of localization and thus reinforce the organization of the radio-concentric example around a centre that contains manifold functions and the highest qualifications. This scheme of distribution of the productive activities would imply the total mobility of the workers or the distribution of their houses in as many successive belts as existing levels of qualification. All the analyses of the growth of the residential suburbs and the periphery insist on the differentiation of the residential areas among which the process of social segregation increases. The firms must take into account this social segmentation of the urban area, because this area is the framework for the mobilization of manpower. During this period of heavy industrialization, large concerns have settled this question with their own policies of building: as for example the Northern coal mines building up their own "corons" or the workmen's dwellings in Lorraine, etc. Nowadays, the problem is not so much one of quantity. The concerns try to find this equilibrium of localization that combines the demands of the division of labour inside the establishment with the potential advantages of peripheric jobs basin.

The massive unfolding of the ready-made clothing workshops towards the fringes of the urbanized areas demonstrates how swiftly the heads of firms have come closer to a basin of employment characterized by a great offer of little qualified, female employment - young girls from an agricultural area, or more often, young women looking for a new job to replace the one that the building of a new residence, very far away from the centre, made them abandon. This example of dependency between mobility of activities and residential mobility seems such dynamic, exaggerated beyond measure mechanisms that industrials consider during their interviews concerning the evolution of the costs of transport. The recent increase in the costs of gathering that would go up from 5% to 10% of the volume of the industrial salaries, would be, according to them, a conclusive factor for the choice of new implantations that would move closer to the areas in which their manpower live. To the question "Before recruiting a new employee, do you take into account his address when you choose him ?" - Most of the heads of firms answer that with "equal ability", they recruit "the one who lives closer to the firm". The increase in the prices of energy could amplify these tendencies observed from their outset.

The areas of work under the rule of their segmentation because of the qualification criterium and the areas of residence under the rule of increased social division, will apparently be, in the future, rather imbricated in specific sorts of areas, making as many new mini-basins of particular employment. This logic of extreme bursting of area will be restrained by the compulsions of the small and average concerns themselves that will not be able to use such a segmentation of posts of labour in the area.

The specific economic future of new peripheric area

Is it thus possible to put forward a few elements liable to enrich a partial futurible of the French urban society? The whole economic context seems less favourable to the pursuit of an intense peripheric growth of the towns, especially concerning its residential component. But these areas must be located again in the wider division of labour that integrates them by assigning them a specific position. The technological innovation often rooted in industrial concerns smaller than before, becomes an indirect factor of geographical mobility for the tasks of management but also of production.

The integration of data processing to the labour process involves for example, a transformation of the factors of localization of the different producing units of a firm. In these conditions, the peripheric areas of agglomerations will be the privileged stand for the new implantations of the most dynamic firms. This consideration is important as it allows us to consider in a new way the future of the peripheric areas.

Nowadays, the recent problems are dominant there; but in the future, these areas might become as important as productive areas centred on new basins of employment, structured by small but very attractive firms and with a performing equipment. This evolution is worth considering now both by the concerned collectivities and the ones arranging them. In a prospective perspective, it would even be a pity to see the loosings of activities amplify and the opportunities of residential loosings decrease in so far as these dynamic, relocalized small and medium-sized concerns may carry along with them the building of lodgings even more perceptible today.

In other words, it is advisable to appreciate well the double nature of these peripheric areas both residential and productive without forgetting their second reality, even if the first one appears nowadays more developed than the second one. A new productive network can settle in these urban fringes, in a diffused way, but re-moulding the actual physionomy of French agglomerations and their environment.

NOTES

1. In urban units of over 50,000 inhabitants; population calculated according to an inclusive, rough and not very subtle method : the population of the urban unit less the population of the commune-center.
2. Rapport Mayoux, Demain l'espace, Paris, 1979-1980. Docum. Francaise.
3. An individual house consumes about 2.5 tons oil equivalent each year against 1.6 tons oil equivalent in an average-sized flat.
4. 45% of the household living in a suburban area use at least 2 cars against an average 13% in France.
5. Refer to the studies on the loosing of industries in Mulhouse, Lyons, Toulouse, Castres, Mazamet: JP LABORIE, L'enjeu peri-urbain. Document 2 : Le desserrement dans les espaces suburbains, Paris, 1981, Documentation Francaise (Travaux et recherches de prospective, 83).

NINE

Anjana Desai and Smita Sen Gupta

Problems of Changing Landuse Pattern in the Urban Fringe

The Case of Ahmedabad

INTRODUCTION

The Objectives of this paper are to understand the process of development of urban fringe and thereby its impact on the changing landuse pattern and finally to analyse the problems that have cropped up along with the growth of urban fringe, exemplified by the case of Ahmedabad.

Until recently, the possibility of decentralisation of population and economic activities remained low in Indian cities. Cities are compact and that has helped residents to save in time and cost on transportation when goods and services are at one place, like the Central Business District (CBD). On the other side, sellers also want to have shops at a central location so that the total number of buyers may not be divided into smaller neighbourhood shopping centres. Moreover, competition of the market makes the price of goods quite reasonable in shops at the city centre. Residents prefer the CBD shops also from the point of view of variety and freshness of perishable goods.

Social reasons are also responsible for such a landuse pattern. Residents have developed a strong sense of attachment for "place" and ancestral property. Residents like to live close to each other at the CBD, so that they can have a social interaction with friends and relatives.

Since last ten to fifteen years or so, the city-limit has started to progress externally. This process of growth of residential suburbs in Indian cities is somewhat different from that of Western Cities. In Western situation, there has been a decline of population at the city-centre and an outmigration of population is responsible for the growth of suburbs. In Indian case, the urban fringe is an outcome of both the outward migration of residents from the city-centre as well as inward migration of residents from other nearby villages or towns. In this spatial process, among the new settlers, relatively richer and younger generation has formed these new suburbs, whereas relatively poorer immigrants have settled in a crowded manner, in the citycore where early settlers, both rich and poor, still continue to live as well. As a result, both the city-centre and the suburbs have grown simultaneously in population. The suburban settlers of the city have a tie with the city as few members still live there in ancestral house. Unlike western situation, the urban fringe of Indian Cities has not developed in infrastructure and suburban residents still maintain strong social and economic ties with the city-centre. This imbalance of structure and process on space has evolved some problems related to landuse pattern in the urban fringe of Indian Cities.

THE STUDY AREA

The city of Ahmedabad

The city of Ahmedabad is going through the same process of suburbanisation as stated earlier. The city of Ahmedabad experienced rapid growth of population, especially after 1960, when Gujarat State was created from Bombay Presidency. Rich merchants started to live in spacious bungalows in the fringe area, while blue collar workers settled down in the city-core in a crowded way in order to minimise cost on rent and transportation.

Suburbanisation in Ahmedabad has not taken place by immigration only. With the economic growth of the city, relatively richer and younger generation have started to move out from the congested and polluted core-city to the urban fringe - seeking spacious place to live in, privacy of life, clean and peaceful environment. A portion of the joint family, both old and young still contiue to live at the city-core which has nearly five hundred "pols" or enclosed, mini-neighbourhoods of social groups by caste, religion or occupation. Residents enjoy social status and have a strong sense of attachment for the "place" as well as for relatives and communities as they are staying there for several generations. As a result, the outmigrated residents still maintain strong ties with the city-core for socio-economic reasons. Since the suburban population is relatively rich, residents can afford to bear the cost of transportation to and from the city-core.

METHODOLOGY AND DATA

In this study, the urban fringe has been decided with the help of an aggregate index, Suburbanisation Index (S.I.), by a combination of variables, with weightage, like distance from CBD, number of housing societies, density of population, number of bus routes, frequency of buses, number of daily commuters. In the fringe area of Ahmedabad, there are several villages which have recently gained a lot of population. Each such suburban area has been given a weighted score (S.I.). The suburbs, which have S.I. score more than 50% have been considered as urban fringe in this study and the rest is considered as rural fringe. Of the total thirty villages, only four are considered here as urban residential fringe; Kali is industrial suburb; rest are rural suburbs having Suburbanisation Index less than 50%. Vejalpur, Vastrapur, Memnagar and Ranip have S.I. more than 50% and are considered as "Urban Fringe" in this study. These villages are also considered to be under Standard Metropolitan Area by Ahmedabad Urban Development Authority (AUDA) in 1981. The data in this study have been collected from respective village Panchayat offices. Field observation and personal interviews have also been helpful in understanding the growth, development and problems of urban fringe in Ahmedabad.

MAJOR FEATURES OF THE CHANGING URBAN FRINGE IN AHMEDABAD

Growth of population

The urban fringe of Ahmedabad has witnessed a phenomenal rate of growth in population during 1971 and 1981 (Provisional). During 1961-1971 (Table 9.1) smaller villages like Vastrapur and Memnagar had a higher growth rate than the larger villages like Ranip or Vejalpur. But during 1971-1981, the rate of growth is much higher in Vejalpur-Vastrapur side, that is located due west of the city, while Ranip, in the northern side, has a relatively lower growth, of population. Memnagar shows a lower growth, as a part of it is already merged in the city itself. In Vejalpur area, Jodhpur is its Falia (a portion) in which the growth of population is rather high. Communication system and accessibility of this area have increased recently. The density in Jodhpur area is mostly seen along the road, while it is low in the interior of the suburbs. Similarly, land-value is higher at the accessible areas compared to that in the interior section.

TABLE 9.1

Growth of population in the urban fringe (1961 - 1981)

Urban Fringe Village	Total Area in km^2	Population 1961	Population 1971 (Provisional)	Population 1981 '61-71'	Growth rate '71-81	Growth rate	Density per km^2 1981
1. Vejalpur	12.35	3,185	7,989	45,759	150.8%	472.8%	3705
2. Vastrapur	4.22	430	1,192	4,922	177.2%	312.9%	1166
3. Memnagar	2.10	735	1,849	6,258	151.6%	238.4%	2980
4. Ranip	5.68	5,256	10,482	35,475	99.4%	238.4%	6246

It is to be noted, that the composition of population varies between the old village-core and that of the new suburbs. The socio-economic background and the life-style of these two groups are remarkably different. In the new urban fringe, a mixed community with higher socio-economic background have settled with modern material possessions, like car, scooter, T.V. radio, refrigerator and electrical gadgets. The majority of residents are engaged in business or services. But in the village-core, the life-style is still in rural fashion, without much modern facilities. There is still relation between caste and occupation (Table 9.2) in the village. With the help of x^2 test, hypothesis can be accepted that there is relationship between caste and occupation in the core village of Jodhpur (a part of the urban fringe of Ahmedabad), at a confidence level of 95%.

TABLE 9.2

Caste and occupation of the core village of Jodhpur (Falia of Vejalpur) 1981

Caste / Occupation	Brahmin	Patel	Thakore	Vania	Gajjar	Jain	Total
Farming	8	69	39	19	7	3	145
Service	30	13	20	7	5	30	105
Total	38	82	59	26	12	33	250

Source: Collected from field work by the Authors

Changing landuse pattern

The growth of population has naturally several impacts on the landuse pattern in general. Firstly, a large proportion of agricultural land has been reduced, due to the increase in population (Table 9.3) and there has been a simultaneous increase in non-agricultural land.

Taking the special case of Jodhpur area of Vejalpur, which has experienced the highest growth of population during 1971-1981, it is found that, the percentage of residential land has increased almost four times (Table 9.4). The correlation coefficient is 0.75, which is significant at a confidence level of .05%. Similarly, the correlation of growth-rate is negative with respect to the percentage of agricultural land in the area.

The growth of population in the urban fringe has thus an associated decrease of agricultural land and an increase in non-agricultural land.

TABLE 9.3

Major landuse of urban fringe (1961-1981) (in percentage)

Village	% of agricultural land		% of agricultural Fellow		%of non-agricultural land	
	1961	1981	1961	1981	1961	1981
1. Vejalpur	62	45	8	10	30	45
2. Vastrapur	42	35	5	5	53	60
3. Memnagar	51	35	14	16	35	49
4. Ranip	52	46	15	12	33	42

Source: Village Panchayat Office

N.B.: Non-agricultural land includes residential units, roads, industries and pastures.

Fallow can be used for agriculture.

Secondly, the non-agricultural land can be further subdivided into major three divisions (a) land for residential use, (b) land which is kept unused (c) land for pasture (Table 9.5). The largest portion of non-agricultural land is used for residential use. Only a portion of it is used for roads. A proportion of land is not used at all for any purpose. This type of non-agricultural land is owned by housing societies. The land is kept vacant even for twenty years in order to fetch a higher price when the demand for it will be at a peak. This can clearly be pointed out from the following table which depicts that, housing societies may have registered in 1960, but houses are not yet built even in 1981. (Table 9.6)

TABLE 9.4

Changing landuse in Jodhpur (1971-1981) (In percentage)

	Type of use	1971	1976	1981
1.	Grain	54.27	43.43	33.19
2.	Vegetable	18.91	17.06	9.50
3.	Residential	7.32	14.32	26.42
4.	Fallow (ag.non-ag.)	10.32	14.63	14.45
5.	Govt. owned	9.62	10.22	19.48
	Total	100.44	99.66	103.04

Source: Village Panchayat Office

TABLE 9.5

Classification of Non-agricultural Land 1981

Village	% of non-ag. and used	% of non-ag. and not used	% of pasture	Total % Non-ag. land
1. Vejalpur	23	6	16	45
2. Vastrapur	44*	12	4	60
3. Memnagar	37	9	3	49
4. Ranip	28	6	8	42

* Nearly 40% of it is owned by I.I.M and Ahmedabad Education Society.

TABLE 9.6

Registered and Built-up Housing Society (1981)

Village	No. of registered Housing Society:1960 onwards	No. of housing society built	No. of Housing Society not built
1. Vejalpur	235	195	40
2. Vastrapur	5	4	1
3. Memnagar	13	10	3
4. Ranip	86	70	16

Source: Village Panchayat Office.

Thirdly, the urban fringe has developed a variety of houses-bungalows, row-houses tenaments and flats. Initially, bungalows were built due to the lower price of land; but recently residents are opting for flats with the rise of price of land, cost of construction and non-availability of space due to pressure of population. Along with private housing complexes, Gujarat Housing Board has also constructed various types of houses, to meet the needs of residents with low, medium and high incomes. The housing complex of the urban fringe area has its own water-tank, sewerage system and electricity. But as these areas do not come under the area of municipality, there is no electricity, sewerage system, garbage removal system outside the housing society. This contrast is immediately visible in the nearby core-village where houses do not have any facility of water, electricity or sewerage system.

Fourthly, the density of population has increased in the urban fringe without much development of infrastructure. This is very much felt by residents in terms of public transportation as they have to depend on the CBD for shopping and social interaction. Very few shops have developed in the urban fringe. Moreover, prices are quite high in these suburban shops. So residents prefer to go to the CBD. Spatial movement has increased due to the growth of the urban fringe. Of-late, crime, mostly burglery, has increased in these suburban houses. There is lack of police and fire protection as these areas are outside the city-limit.

PROBLEMS RELATED TO THE CHANGING LANDUSE PATTERN

A certain number of problems have cropped up with the growth of urban fringe in Ahmedabad. Firstly, the loss of agricultural land in suburbs has increased the cost of vegetables due to the shortage of supply and extra transportation charges for carrying it from a longer distance to the city-centre. Secondly, there has been an increase of non-agricultural land due to the rising pressure of population. Owners of the agricultural land often sell the land at a higher price to a housing society or to a private owner who often leaves the land unused for many years. On one hand, land is not used for any purpose, and on the other hand, the price goes up exorbitantly in the process of land-speculation. Thirdly, population has grown in the urban fringe without much development of the area. The individual society might have developed its own electricity, water-supply and sewerage system. The area as a whole suffers from lack of amenities e.g., shopping centre, recreation facilities, fire and police protection, a network of roads and transportation system, educational and other institutions, electricity, water and sewerage system. Lastly, with the growth of these new settlements, the urban fringe of Ahmedabad has developed a dual character. On one hand, the core-villages in the fringe area has a rural style of life, housing without facilities and residents are often engaged in low-skilled, caste-based, traditional occupation; on the other land, residents, in the new suburbs surrounding the core-villages, have a higher socio-economic background, modern life-style and housing with facilities. This spatial inequality is rather sharp in the urban fringe of Ahmedabad.

CONCLUSIONS

Ahmedabad has started to grow just as other cities of India have grown in the past. It may be difficult to reverse the trend as cities have a strong attraction to the deprived rural population both from economic and non-economic points of view. Under the circumstances, unless the rural areas are developed, not just by infrastructure but also by job-opportunities and recreational facilities suited to residents of a particular region, growth of urban areas cannot be stopped. On the urban side, on the other hand, a comprehensive suburban planning is required for its growing areas. Firstly, unused non-agricultural land should be controlled by regulation by which no land can be left vacant for a long time. Secondly, the urban fringe can be managed by the Urban Authority by providing Government fair price shops, infrastructure in the village core at a low taxation and thereby spatial inequality can be reduced in housing and living conditions. Thirdly, the suburban population have to bear the stress and strain everyday due to inadequate transport and communication system. Provision of public transportation will certainly help residents who maintain socio-economic ties with the city-core. A comprehensive planning is required by managing the unused land, providing infrastructure and improving the living conditions in order to reduce spatial inequality in the urban fringe.

REFERENCES

Desai, Anjana, (1981) "Some Aspects of Environmental Perception in the Core City of Ahmedabad", Research Project funded by the Indian Council of Social Science Research, New Delhi.

Johnson, James H (ed.) (1974) **Suburban Growth**, John Wiley and Sons.

TEN

D.S. Shrivastava

Suburban Development in Central India

A Model for Cities of Madhya Pradesh State*

The Development of suburbs around cities is not a new phenomenon. Even before the beginning of this century settlements with urban characteristics existed away from and adjacent to cities. Beaujeu-Garnier and Chabot (1967:240) note the existence of such settlements much before the introduction of motored and rail transport. Mumford (1938:433) describes the drift to the suburbs as "one of the most conspicuous features of the growth of cities during the past half century".

Mayer and Kohn (1967:531) take note of the rapid expansion of urban population into suburbs of American cities. Among the recent American writers Brown (1981:288) describes the rapid pace of suburbanization since the Second World War: "In 1950, 33% of the United States' population lived in a central city, 23% lived in the remainder of a Standard Metropolitan Area, and 44% was metropolitan. By 1975, the same percentages were 30, 39, and 31". The 1980 preliminary census figures of the United States point to a surge towards suburbs. Of the 56 large metropolitan areas (with over 650,000 population) all but five registered significant increases in suburban population during the last decade (U.S. News and World Report, 1981). Jones (1966:33) rightly sums up the growing importance of suburbs "whereas the suburb was once the appendage to the city, it now often comprises almost the whole city".

* Presented and discussed at the Research Seminar Series, 1982 of the Geography Department, University of Lancaster, England during the tenure of a post-doctoral Bursary awarded to the author by the Royal Geographical Society, London.

The history of suburban development in Britain dates back to the eighteenth century. The industrialization brought into being a large number of settlements which could neither be treated as villages nor were they the market towns. "They were large tracts of brick and mortar which broke across the old division" (Carter, 1972:20). Johnson (1972) in detailed account points out that before the First World War though there was a greatly increased demand in Britain for houses similar to that in the United States, the suburban development, however, could not be so spectacular. The main reason, according to Johnson, was the crippling effect of the War on the building industry. Housing activity during Second World War also came to a halt in both the countries followed by stricter controls in Britain preventing the formless spread of residential building. Land use planning in this country "has tidied up the form of residential expansion and made it more compact" (Johnson, 1972:134).

SUBURBAN STUDIES IN INDIA

Studies of the suburbs have not been made in India on a significant scale. Bibliographic publications of the Indian Science Congress Association: "Fifty years of Science in India - Progress of Geography," upto 1962 and its supplement for 1963-72 do not contain any reference on direct studies of suburbs. One indirect study referred to is of Subrahmanyam (1940) on "Problems of suburban municipality with reference to Saidapet". Another bibliographic compilation, "A Survey of Research in Geography" - Project report of the Indian Council of Social Science Research, documents researches in Geography. Gosal (1972:213) in his editorial comments on urban geography points to the need for concentration of studies on the peripheral areas of cities, for such a study "will help in evolving a rational plan for future growth of urban places". The Census of India (1961) have also prepared a select bibliography containing references on urban geography, of which a few relate to studies of the suburbs in other countries. There are no references for suburban studies on India.

Some other studies on suburbs have appeared during the last two decades. Rajagopalan (1962) has studied suburban ecology of "The Greater Bombay" from sociological point of view. The book mentions urban sprawl and the processes of suburban development in the metropolis. A later study on Geographical aspects of the "Suburbs of Greater Bombay" was made by Deshpande (1973). Sundaram (1977) in his "Urban and

Regional Planning in India" makes a brief mention of suburbs, satellite towns and urban fringes as constituents of a town group. He has identified Indian suburbs with several pockets of peri-urban growth such as industrial estates (industrial suburbs) and dormitary suburbs such as civil lines, refugee colonies, labour and railway colonies.

A number of studies have been made on the rural-urban fringe. Pramila Kumar (1980) has studied agricultural innovations on the fringe of Bhopal. Gopi (1979) has worked on the "Process of Urban Fringe Development" - A model. Some other writers make cursory references to suburbs or to the processes of suburban development. The term "urban fringe", in many instances, has been applied to designate all forms of urban development away from the city-centre. Kurtz and Eicher (1958) with explicit definitions have sorted out the confusion that surrounds the use of terms 'suburb' and 'fringe'. A fringe area, according to the authors lies in the agricultural hinterland, has mixed farm and non-farm dwellings and the workers are engaged in both the rural and urban occupations. A suburb, on the contrary is located in a contiguous area with consistently non-agricultural form of dwellings and with the workers engaged primarily in urban occupations. Breese (1966:69) has made very generalized observations on suburban development in India and comments that housing activities are producing peripheral limitations of foreign suburban patterns with little system in the siting, planning, etc.

SUBURBAN DEVELOPMENT IN CENTRAL INDIA

A study of the suburban aspect of cities in the Central Indian State of Madhya Pradesh has been undertaken because of a gap that exists in the regional urban geography. Several studies though have been made on various other aspects of the discipline, very few attempts, however, have been made on a regional scale to understand the urban.growth away from the densely settled parts of the cities. The present study is rather introductory in nature and is intended to focus researches on various related aspects of the phenomenon.

Suburban development around the large urban centres (Class I cities with 100,000 or more people) has assumed greater importance. With the limited possibilities of development within the central parts, the cities are expanding horizontally in their outer rings. Generalized studies based on observations in each city are likely to point to areas where this development is taking place, factors which contribute to this development, the axis of urban growth, and to possibilities of planned development of suburbs in future.

An unfortunate aspect of the peripheral sprawl of large urban centres in the State is that they are growing in a rather unplanned manner. This free-for-all development takes place largely because of laxity or the absence of control on urban development outside the civic boundaries. When this uncontrolled development proceeds far enough the civic limits of the cities are extended to annex the outer areas. If the areas where suburban development takes place are known in advance and if planning regulations are rigorously enforced, the chaotic conditions in these areas can be prevented.

IDENTIFICATION OF SUBURBS

The problem of evolving a concept for demarcating a city together with its surrounding urban population has been agitating the minds of scholars the world over. Goudswaard (1955) and Gibbs (1966) have written of their concern for the problem. An urban agglomeration is difficult to define in internationally acceptable terms, it "consists of a city and those surrounding communes which contain a part of the urbanized territory that extends beyond the city's limits" (Goudswaard, 1955:35). Gibbs observes that "the administrative boundaries of European cities commonly do not closely coincide with what is urbanized territory from a geographical point of view" (Gibbs, 1966:19).

The Census of India have experimented with several concepts to put the city and the surrounding area together. At the time of 1951 census the 'town-group' concept was introduced but was given up in 1971, for the data of the group comprised of independent towns and became "incomparable from Census to Census as the boundaries of the towns themselves changed and the intermediate areas were left out of account" (Census of India Monograph No. 1, 1971:132). The town-group concept was criticized at the International Geographical Union Symposium on population and the discussion that followed prompted the Census of India to introduce another concept—the Standard Urban Area (SUA). While delimiting the SUA, explains Sundaram (1977:59) the following five considerations were applied :

1. The population trends of the main city were ana-

lysed to assess the magnitude of growth by 1991.
2. Trends of direction and physical constraints on population spread of the principal city were taken note of.
3. Estimates of growth by 1991, of towns and villages outside the municipal limits were made.
4. Inclusion of any other settlement in the SUA on special considerations of interaction with the city.
5. The entire revenue area including all the land around the villages was brought within the SUA.

The demarcation of the SUA is essentially based on field observations of the trends of city-sprawl. Over a decade has passed since the idea was mooted, but unfortunately very little effort seems to have been put by the Census of India and the town and country planning departments to demarcate SUAs for the cities of Madhya Pradesh.

At the time of the 1971 Census another designation the 'urban agglomeration' was used. It consists of an urban centre together with one or more 'out-growth' settlements with urban characteristics outside the statutory limits. The 'out-growth' at the outset appears to be representing suburban areas. In a separate study, based on field observations at several 'out-growths', the author has come to the conclusion that these settlements as such cannot be accepted as representing suburban growth. "The term, therefore, has to be regarded only as a Census of India designation for a settlement outside the statutory limits of an urban centre. It could both be a planned residential colony or a typical village with rather remote possibilities of urban development" (Shrivastava, 1984:107). In spite of the inherent difficulties of this term the data on these settlements cease to be available once they are annexed to the parent centre. At the time of the 1981 Census the out-growths, ranging between 8 and 14 in number, of Indore, Bhopal, Gwalior and Raipur have been merged with the cities because of extensions of civic boundaries.

HYPOTHESIS ON SUBURBAN DEVELOPMENT

The Census data on out-growth, thus are not much of use for a study of the suburban development. The following characteristics, therefore, "were selected with the premise that these would prove to be the indicators which a settlement should possess in order to be termed as a suburb: it should generally be contiguous to the built-up parts of the town, the intervening patches should not be too large, frequent intra-city transport be available, there should be a feeling of correspondence with the townsfolk, the settlement be dependent on the parent centre, etc." (Shrivastava, 1984:107).

In the process of identification of suburbs it was found that the cities with higher decennial growth, higher percentage of workers in manufacturing occupation, with higher literacy rates, etc., were more likely to develop suburbs in their peripheral areas (Table 10.1). The probable suburban localities were selected mainly on the basis of the intensity of transport and the look of the outer localities. Certain physical barriers to a city's expansion also proved to be of help in this selection. The railway lines, a water-body, a hilly tract, a cemetery (grave-yard), etc., often restrict the spread of the city. The peripheral settlement develops only when it becomes possible to overcome these difficulties by constructing a railway fly-over, a bridge, or in the case of hilly tracts, by provision of intra-city transport.

Suburban localities were identified, with the help of civic authorities, Town and Country Planning officials and local geographers. The identification was later confirmed by personal observations and interviews at these localities. It has been possible, thus to list for each surveyed city the causes of suburban development, areas where this development is taking place and the use of the intervening land. Information has been obtained and documented on the prominent features of suburban areas in each city (Table 10.1).

SUBURBAN SURVEYS IN INDUSTRIAL CITIES

Indore, Bhilainagar and Gwalior cities were selected for suburban surveys in centres with the dominance of industrial activity. The cities record more than a third of their workers in factory-type manufacturing (according to 1971 Census). Four localities were visited at Indore while general surveys of extra-urban growth around Bhilainagar and Gwalior cities were made. The decennial growth of Indore city in the period 1961-71 was 37.6 per cent while during the following decade it registered 47.6 per cent increase. Bhilainagar, the only iron and steel manufacturing centre in Madhya Pradesh has witnessed much faster growth. During the decade 1961-71 its growth was 88 per cent while during 1971-81 it has nearly doubled in population. The industrial cities are characterized by low sex-ratios (ranging between 853 and 887) and high literacy rates.

TABLE 10.1

Indicators of suburban development in surveyed cities of Madhya Pradesh

Urban Agglomeration, 1981 Total population	1981: 1. Area km² 2. Density	1981: 1. Sex-Ratio 2. Literacy	Percent Growth 1. 1961-71 2. 1971-81	Outer Census Units: 1. Number % of Total 1971	Outer Census Units: 2. Pop. 1981	1971 % Workers in 1. Manuf. 2. T&C	Intervening Land	Suburban areas: Transport.	Suburban areas: Construction.
1. Indore	113.5	887	42.0	8	Annexed	36.1	Vacant/	Taxi, Bus,	Private/
827,071	7,286	60.6	47.4	3.13	...	23.9	built	Rail	Board
2. Jabalpur	220.8	846	45.7	15	15	24.3	Mostly	Taxi, Bus,	Board/
757,726	3,432	60.7	41.7	10.92	10.83	17.2	built	Rickshaw	Private
3. Bhopal	284.9	866	72.6	20	Annexed	17.3	Mostly	Bus, Taxi	Govt./
672,329	2,360	56.7	74.7	20.86	...	17.1	built		Pvt./Board
4. Gwalior	291.9	859	35.1	13	Annexed	33.5	vacant/	Taxi,	Govt./
559,776	1,918	52.6	37.8	5.26	...	16.8	Reserved	Bus.	Pvt./Board
5. Bhilainagar	104.0	853	102.5	4	8	61.5	Vacant/	Taxi,	Board/
319,428	3,073	55.8	83.2	8.27	25.52	11.7	Reserved	Rickshaw/	Private
6. Raipur	55.0	909	47.4	14	Annexed	16.6	Mostly	Bus, Taxi,	Private/
338,973	6,160	56.6	64.6	15.27	...	26.5	built	Rickshaw	Board
7. Sagar	50.1	860	47.9	5	5	15.8	vacant/	Taxi only	Private/
207,401	4,143	60.5	34.0	5.72	6.94	20.5	built		Board

Notes :

1. Urban agglomerations include the population of areas within civic limits, outside large urban units and of the out-growth settlements. 2. Outer Census settlements do not include military settlements of Jabalpur, Gwalior and Sagar which have been considered as parts of cities. 3. Sex-ratio: Number of males per 1,000 females. 4. Abbreviations: (i) Transport : Taxi- three wheeled two or eight - seater motor vehicles. Rickshaw - three wheeled pedal carriage. Bus - city bus. (ii) Construction: Pvt.- Private, Board-M.P. Housing Board, Govt.-State Govt., (iii) Workers: Manuf.- Manufacturing. T.&C.-Trade and Commerce.

Source:

1. Census of India, 1971, Madhya Pradesh, Series 10, Part II A-General Population Tables.
2. Census of India, 1981, Madhya Pradesh, Series 11, Provisional population Tables.

Indore

Indore with 827,071 persons (1981 Census) is the largest of the fourteen class I cities of Madhya Pradesh State. The city has grown enormously from its initial site around a rail-road junction which now serves as the core of the city. The industrial and commercial composition of the city's working population is largely responsible for its fast growth. A survey by the Town and Country Planning (T & C.P.) department points out that in the year 1974 there were 226 residential colonies in the city which had come up during the last 25 years. In addition there were seventy other localities with slums and other hutments which provided shelter to 100,000 poor people.

Suburban localities

There are several outer areas of Indore which may qualify as suburban. The localities which, however, have been so designated, in consultation with the T. & C.P. officials, local geographers, colonizers, etc., number about a dozen. They include Rajendra Nagar, Rau and Kasturbagram in the south, Manglia and Nandanagar in the north, Manoramaganj, Saketnagar, Kanaria and Dudhia in the east and Laxmi nagar towards the west of the city (Map. 10.1 and 10.2). The places nearer to the city-centre with vacant/earmarked intervening land are the Manikbaah group of residential colonies including Roopram nagar and Khatiwala Tank residential areas. The distant suburban areas include Manglia, Dudhia, Kanaria and Rau which are the former peripheral villages.

INFLUENCE OF TRANSPORT ON SUBURBAN DEVELOPMENT

The city's public transport comprises of a thousand two and eight-seater three-wheeled taxis, 250 horse-drawn carriages (tongas) and a fleet of over a hundred buses. The intra-city train service between Indore and Mhow passes through Rajendra Nagar and Rau suburbs. The distant-suburbs exhibit a considerable impact of the city's rail and bus transport. Rau suburb became an important manufacturing and commercial centre largely due to its location on the Agra-Bombay national highway and due to its rail links. Many other suburbs have developed along the national or state highways.

Congestion in the city was the main cause of the initial dispersal to outer areas while the site attractions along

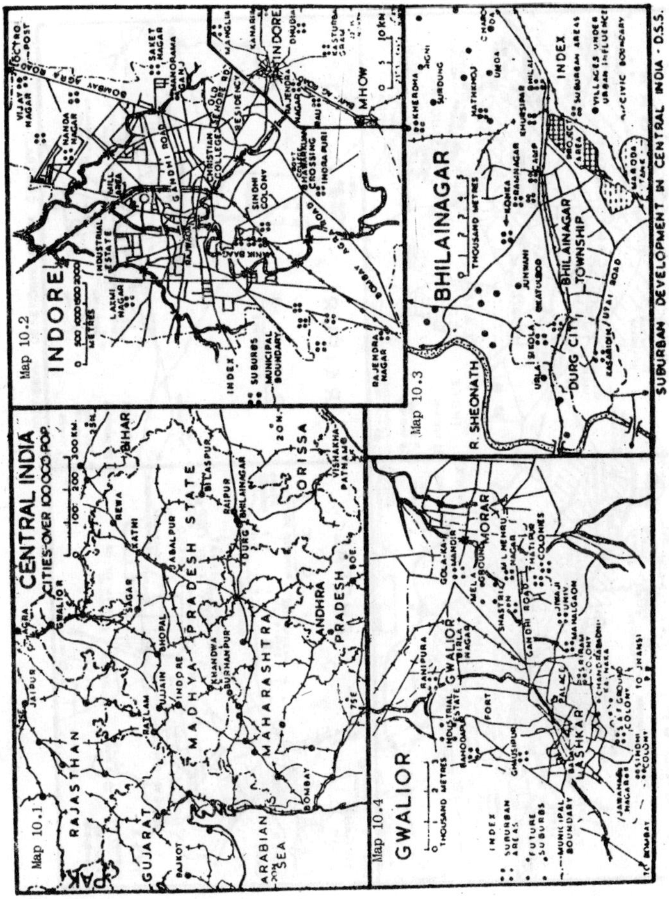
Map 10.1
CENTRAL INDIA
CITIES OVER 100,000 POP.
RAJASTHAN
GUJARAT
MADHYA PRADESH STATE
MAHARASHTRA
ANDHRA PRADESH
ORISSA
BIHAR
ARABIAN SEA
Map 10.2
INDORE
Map 10.3
BHILAINAGAR
R. SHEONATH
DURG CITY
BHILAINAGAR TOWNSHIP
Map 10.4
GWALIOR
LASHKAR
MORAR
SUBURBAN DEVELOPMENT IN CENTRAL INDIA - D.S.S.

MAP 10.2

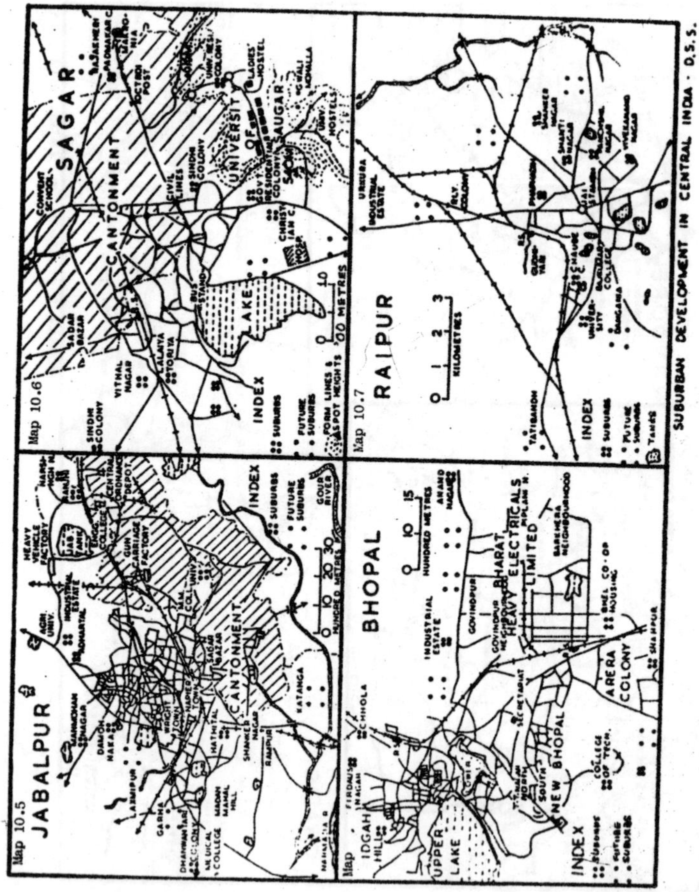
Map 10.5
JABALPUR
CANTONMENT
INDEX
SUBURBS
FUTURE SUBURBS
HUNDRED METRES
Map 10.6
SAGAR
CANTONMENT
LAKE
UNIVERSITY OF SAUGAR
INDEX
SUBURBS
FUTURE SUBURBS
Map 10.7
RAIPUR
KILOMETRES
INDEX
SUBURBS
FUTURE SUBURBS
Map
BHOPAL
UPPER LAKE
BHARAT HEAVY ELECTRICALS LIMITED
NEW BHOPAL
ARERA COLONY
INDEX
SUBURBS
FUTURE SUBURBS
SUBURBAN DEVELOPMENT IN CENTRAL INDIA · D.S.S.

highways have accelerated this process. The location of smaller towns in the vicinity (Mhow at 20 km and Dewas at 37 km) has attracted suburban development in the intervening areas. Availability of cheap and level land and a well organized construction activity are the other factors responsible for suburban development. The M.P. Housing Board, cooperative societies and private builders have constructed residential quarters in almost all directions away from the city-centre, though most of these residential areas, lack shopping and other facilities.

Surveyed localities

Rau

This settlement has gained importance mainly as a haltage point for motor-vehicles because of the civic toll-tax barrier (octori post) on the highway. About one-half of the workers of the settlement is rural business people including rich farmers, a fourth belong to service-class while the others work in the local industrial and commercial establishments. Most service-class people commute to Indore city.

This settlement has a mixed look with the urban form of building along the main road. There are two banks, a telephone exchange, and a higher secondary school. The people however, are dependent on the city for rail and bus terminals, hospitals, higher education, and for shopping in specialized goods. There is a continuous flow of traffic to and from the city.

Rajendra Nagar:

The locality is about six kilometres to the south-west of the city-centre with vacant patches of land in the intervening areas. Construction work began here in the year 1956. The site attractions included cheap and level land near the railway track and the Agra-Bombay national highway. The settlement gets its water, electricity, telephone connections and milk supply through the city.

The locality is a well-planned residential suburb with a total population of about 2,500 persons. About one-half of the workers is employed in the State Government offices in the city while the others work in the city's mills. There is a good number of retired people. The people commute to the city by buses and trains. The people do feel that they live away from the city but at the same time the facilities of commuting make them feel as a part of the life-stream of the parent city.

OTHER SURVEYED SUBURBAN LOCALITIES:

To the south of the city-centre are some other residential areas which can be put into three groups (Map. 10.1 and 10.2). The Khatiwala-tank group of residences has come up near the Sindhi colony at a place which formerly was a shallow tank. The other two residential areas are known as the Manikbaag and Gopalbaag colonies. Site attractions of the area include newly developed land which was available at very low costs, proximity to the national highway and to the palace of the former ruler.

This residential complex is about three kilometres away from city-core. Service and business classes make up for about 90 per cent of the workers. The people depend rather totally on the city. Three-wheeler taxis and tongas are available for transport. The localities present the look of a modern well-planned residential suburb with bungalow-type detached units. Rental values of houses are high. The suburb is rather cut-off from the main stream and the city and the people seem to like this isolation.

Bhilainagar

The 1981 population (319,428) of this industrial city is almost double of that during the last decade. The public sector steel plant and its township are under the administrative control of the Bhilai Steel Plant(BSP) Authority. The BSP township with over 27,000 residential quarters is a well-planned settlement. The area outside the control of the BSP Authority has grown in an unplanned manner, which the T. & C.P. department considers as slum areas. The poorly ventilated houses and huts provide residential accommodation to more than 100,000 people. The slum localities include, among others the Khursipar zone 3, Camp No. 2, and Supela.

The slum development has taken place in an area to the north of the highway. Here are twelve localities which can be termed as suburbs or with suburban tendencies (Map. 10.1 and 10.3). The peripheral villages still retain their rural character, but the areas along the trunk roads have attracted urban housing. The population of the out-growth settlements has increased from 14,430 persons to 81,500 recording a staggering 466 per cent increase during the last decade. To regulate the urban development outside the BSP area and upto the nearby older town of Durg the State Government has constituted a Special Area Development Authority. The M.P. Housing Board and other organized builders have constructed a number of dwelling units for industrial workers at Kohka and Ram nagar.

Industrial estate

Like many other fast-growing urban centres of the State, Bhilainagar also has a separate industrial estate to the north-east of the planned township. The largest single industrial unit of the estate is a cement factory with 1,500 workers. The factory is an ancillary unit which makes use of the slag granule-waste of the steel plant to produce 1.4 million tonnes of cement annually. Other units include industries producing components used in the open-hearths of the steel plant. A heavy industrial complex is proposed to be constructed near Hathkhoj towards the eastern open areas along the highway.

Bhilainagar-Durg linkage

Durg city with 1981 population of 118,572 is only four kilometres away from Bhilainagar. Durg provides accommodation to BSP workers. The development of several planned residential areas and some slum localities has been so fast that the entire city has come to be regarded as a residential satellite of the steel city.

Gwalior

Gwalior city (1981 population 559,776) was the capital of the former Gwalior state. The city still bears the imprint of the past royal regime. The Greater Gwalior encompasses three separate nuclei with the largest centre at Lashkar (Map. 10.1 and 10.4). The other two centres are Morar (cantonment) and the industrial centre of Gwalior.

Suburban areas in the eastern parts of the city are Thatipur and Shastri nagar on the Mahatma Gandhi road and the Mahalgaon residential area towards the South. In the north-eastern direction are Gola-ka-Mandir with vacant intervening land. Ranipura and Jehangirpura localities in the north-west adjoin the industrial area of Birla nagar. Ghausipur and Bahodapur are the fast-developing residential suburbs. Several other localities in the south are also developing into planned residential suburbs. Future suburban development is likely to take place in the Chandra Badni Kanaka area.

Factors responsible for suburban development

The causes of suburban development in Greater Gwalior include the availability of land at lower price in intervening areas of the three nuclei, initiatives of the M.P. Housing Board and other builders and congestion in the city-core where densities reach 750 to 800 persons to a hectare.

Surveyed Localities: Thatipur, Shastri Nagar and Motilal Nehrunagar residential group

This group of residential colonies lies along an important intra-city road, the Mahatma Gandhi (M.G.) Road, which connects Lashkar and Morar centres. The residential area is at a distance of about nine kilometres from the city-centre at Maharaj Bada. Modern housing activity started here in the year 1960 with the construction of houses for the employees of the State Government. The area began to be filled up soon after with residential units constructed by private owners, Government and by the Housing Board.

The people visit the city-centre for employment, higher education and occasionally, for shopping-cum-entertainment. Facilities of shopping and entertainment are available at the nearby Morar township also which is only a kilometre away. Three-wheeler taxis shared by eight passengers are the most frequently available means of intra-urban transport, besides the mini-buses which are available only at peak hours. The residents of the suburban areas use the city's rail and bus terminals for inter-city travel. The settlement has a suburban status. The residents do feel as living away from the city. The houses, both detached and semi-detached, are built at much lower densities compared to the city's congested housing.

SUBURBAN SURVEYS IN CITIES WITH DIVERSIFIED ACTIVITIES

A group of five cities (according to 1971 census) does not display dominance of either manufacturing activity or of any specific service occupation. In fact the number of persons engaged in the 'other services' or in 'trade and commerce' is more than that in manufacturing occupation. The cities with dominance of no specific occupation include Jabalpur, Raipur, Sagar, Bilaspur and Ratlam. Jabalpur records a fairly large number of workers in factory-type manufacturing also but the 'other services' and 'trade and commerce' are equally important with 27 and 17 per cent workers respectively. Jabalpur, therefore can best be considered as a diversified city.

JABALPUR

Jabalpur with 1981 population of 757,726 persons is the second largest city of the State. It has registered 42 per cent growth during the decade 1971-81. The city's literacy rate is high (i.e. 60.7%) while the sex-ratio of 846 is the lowest among the cities of Madhya Pradesh. The occupational pattern (based on 1971 data) presents a diversified character with about a fourth of the total male workers each engaged in factory-type and in service occupations.

Diversity of settlement exists between the open detached houses in the outer areas of the cantonment and the crowded residential localities in the older parts of the city. The city's initial growth centred around Miloniganj and Hanumantal areas which now serve as the commercial core of Jabalpur. The later development of the city occurred south of the railway line in the Garha and cantonment areas. Among the newer residential areas can be included the Wright town, Napier town and the North civil lines. These later settlements are more open and are rather well-planned residential localities. Of equal importance to Jabalpur city are the two defence-production units located in the north-eastern section viz., the Heavy Vehicle Factory and the Khamaria group of ordnance factories.

The outlying areas of the city (with years of first construction) include Dhanwantari (1972), Hathital (1963), Rampur and Shanker Shah nagar (1958), Bargi Irrigation colony and Katanga (1974), Pachpedi and the university campus. On the city's eastern border with the cantonment are Ranjhi and Narsingh nagar suburban settlements (Map. 10.2-1). The other peripheral areas where construction of residential units is taking place, towards the west, include Damoh 'naka' (civic barrier) area, Laxmipur and Garha villages near the medical college. Three other localities have come up recently in the north. They are Adarsh nagar, Anand nagar and Adhartal residential areas.

Surveyed localities

Dhanwantari residential colony

The construction work on this formerly rural land began in the year 1972. The site attractions include proximity to the medical college, extension of city's civic limits and provision of civic amenities together with lower costs of land. The city is growing at a fast rate in this direction along a trunk road.

The residents are employees of the State Government and work in the city or in the nearby medical college. They visit the city for work, shopping-cum-entertainment, and for education. City buses, three-wheeler taxis and pedal rickshaws are available at frequent intervals. The people depend on the city for rail-head and bus terminal. Water is drawn through hand-pumps. There is a small group of shops near the medical college. The locality is a planned settlement, the residents though have a feeling of isolation and insecurity because of it being far away from the dense parts of the city.

Ranjhi

It is a fast-growing residential suburb in the eastern part of the city. During the last fifty years the settlement has grown largely as a result of the demand for residences for the employees of the nearby ordinance factory.

The site attractions include former rural nucleus, vacant land which was available at very low cost, proximity to the Heavy Vehicle and Khamaria factories and to the engineering college. The residential area is rapidly expanding along the main road between the college and Ranjhi settlement. The rural settlements on the eastern periphery of the city have been transformed into urban residential areas. Among the residents the labour and business classes of people are in greater number who work in the nearby factories and business establishments. The people visit the city for shopping in specialized goods, entertainment and for higher education. Public transport is available at reasonable frequencies. The settlement is dependent on the city for inter-city transport terminals and for higher education. Water is drawn from the city's supply system to augment local supplies from tubewells. Rental values of houses are quite high. The people feel like living far away from the city because of the distance.

Rampur residential colony

Situated on the west side of the narrow-gauge rail line

and the Gwarighat road is a residence-cum-office complex of the Madhya Pradesh Electricity Board. It is a hilly site at a distance of five kilometres from city-core. Construction began here in the year 1958. The site-attractions included proximity to the city and availability of land at low costs because of undulation.

RAIPUR

Raipur city with 338,973 persons (in 1981) is the sixth largest in the State. During the past decade the city has witnessed a very high growth —of 64.6 per cent— while during the previous decade the population grew only by 25 per cent. From its initial site at the intersection of inter-city roads, the city has grown in all the directions. The south-western and south-eastern sections along the trunk roads, however, have grown much faster. The six outer localities in the south-west have registered a higher growth. Similarly the areas in the eastern and south-eastern parts of the city also show a larger concentration of population.

Surveyed localities

Shanti Nagar

This locality was the first outer expansion of Raipur city in the eastern direction. The older part of this settlement has congested housing with rather unplanned development. The residential units at the newer section are better-looking and are built at lower density. The residential development has followed a road to a locality farther east.

The site attractions included cheaper land and proximity to the city-centre. The rental values are the highest amongst the suburban areas of Raipur. The people belong mostly to the service-class with only a fourth comprising the labour class who live in hutments. There is a good number of retired people in the locality. The pedal rickshaw is the most widely used means of public transport. People visit the city for work, higher education, and for shopping-cum-entertainment. The settlement depends on the city for rail and bus terminals.

Shanker Nagar

This locality is situated in the north-eastern part of

the city and is about four kilometres away from the city-core. The M. P. Housing Board had taken the lead by building the first group of 500 residential units in the year 1972. Business and service-class people live here almost in equal number. They maintain daily contacts with the city. Pedal rickshaw, taxis and city buses are available for intra-city transport. With modern flat-type dwellings, the settlement is considered among the best suburban areas of Raipur city.

Vivekanand Nagar

Construction work began here in the year 1962. The number of houses is only a hundred where higher-middle class people live. They work in the city. The people feel like living in an exclusive area away from the dense parts of the city while being close to it.

Karbala Talab

Located in the western part of the city along the trunk road to Bhilainagar this residential area is three kilometres away from the citycore. Site attractions included availability of land at lower prices near a road and railway line. The suburb has come to be regarded as a settlement for the economically better-off people. The predominance of a Hindu sub-caste has given a nick name 'Choube colony' to this locality.

State bank colony

This residential area is adjacent to the university campus in the south-western part of the city. Nearby is a large old settlement of Tatibandh. With a total of sixty detached houses built by the employees of the State Bank of India, the locality is about five kilometres away from the city-centre. People depend on the city for all their needs.

Industrial estate

The estate is located in the north, near Urkura village. Factories are located along the railway line. Nearby is a large industrial unit for repair of railway wagons with a work force of 1,500 persons. The five industrial units of the estate with a combined employment capacity of 700 workers are engaged in oil-extraction, welding pin manufacture, etc. Some other smaller units make plastic goods, cosmetics, aluminum utensils, etc. The management of the industrial units is controlled by persons who live in the city. Many skilled labourers also live in the city and commute to their work places. Most other workers are drawn from the adjoining rural areas while some of them live in hutments near their factories.

SAGAR

Sagar Urban Agglomeration with 207,401 persons (1981) has grown by 34 per cent during the last decade. There are no large industrial units in the city. The small scale units comprise mainly of edible oil mills, iron-sheet work, utensil and plastic units. A sizable number of workers is engaged in the manufacturing of 'Bidis' (the poorman's cigar). The city is the headquarters of the district and of the Sagar revenue division. About a fourth of the male workers of the city works in the State Government offices, university, military establishments, banks, schools, etc. Of the five peripheral settlements outside the civic boundary, the university campus is an educational suburb, while the other four places are adjoining villages under urban influence. The population of these out-growths has increased by 62 per cent during the last decade.

Scarcity and high costs of land in the central parts of the city are largely responsible for peripheral urban development. The 'Sindhi' colony along the trunk road, in the east, is the first suburban locality of the city. The entire area near this settlement has been filled up with housing during the last thirty years and is known as civil lines. To the east of this locality is military cantonment which has restricted the spread of civilian housing upto some distances (Map 10.2-2). Suburban development, however, recurs farther east where the civic toll-tax barrier (octori post) on the road to Jabalpur and the villages of Makronia and Rajakheri have acted as nuclei for urban development. The M.P. Housing Board has constructed a large number of residential units near Rajakheri village. During the last decade (1971-81) the population of Rajakheri out-growth has increased by 115 per cent while Makronia village has grown by 53 per cent.

Suburban places in the south-eastern direction include Christian colony and new colony. Towards the west are several suburban localities especially along the trunk roads. A residential suburb, called Vithal nagar is in the Bhagwanganj civic ward. Other suburban places include hill-top settlements of Lalaiya Toriya (red hill top) Macherai and Khusipura. These are old settlements, have crowded houses, narrow roads and are inhabited mostly by the poor people.

Surveyed localities

Civil lines

The area where this locality stands was formerly considered as the periphery of the city. The urban development began along the trunk road at a road-junction where petrol pumps, etc. for inter-city vehicles attracted provision-shops and tea-stalls. The Sindhi colony is located along a bifurcation of the road. Later development followed a large-scale sale of private land. This resulted in an unplanned growth of houses during the fifties and sixties making a part of the civil lines a virtual slum area. Some better-looking dwellings however, have been recently built near the Sindhi colony.

Makronia and padmakar nagar

Urban development of these localities at the extreme eastern periphery of the city can largely be attributed to the location of the civic toll-tax barrier. In order to avoid payment of tax on goods meant for re-export to nearby towns and rural areas, several business houses of the city constructed ware-houses (godowns) outside this road barrier. In due course of time filling-and-service points and a few snack-stalls came up to cater to the needs of people in transit. Intra-city traffic began to increase on this road. Nearby village of Makronia has also come under urban influence. The location of a modern residential complex (Padmakar nagar) near the octroi post perhaps may not have been directly influenced by this civic barrier. The site at a far-off place (about nine kilometres from city-core), however, can only be explained by two factors, i.e., location between two trunk roads and proximity to a developing urban settlement near the octori post.

University campus

The 1981 population (2,095) of the University township of Gour nagar includes the hutment dwellers as well who live on the hill-slopes behind the residential quarters. The suburb is six kilometres from the city-centre. The residents depend entirely on Sagar city for rail and bus terminals, shopping, secondary education, medical facilities, entertainment, etc. The supply of drinking water from the city's pumping station is augmented by wells.

SUBURBAN SURVEYS IN SERVICE-OCCUPATION CITY

Bhopal

Bhopal, the capital city of Madhya Pradesh with 672,329 persons (in 1981), is the third largest city of the State. The predominance of service occupation (with 44 per cent of male workers in 1971) is accounted for by a large number of people who work in the offices of the State Government. Bhopal became the capital of Madhya Pradesh in 1956. This development attracted a Heavy Electrical factory and soon the city's population swelled by over eighty per cent. During the following decade (1961-71) the increase was over sixty per cent, while the preliminary figures for 1981 record an increase of 75 per cent.

During the earlier years the city was ill-equipped to serve as a political centre. The city at that time had a few old palaces of the former ruler besides the closely-built old city. During the last twenty years however, the city has grown at the southern peripheral areas away from and independent of the old city. The eastern area is occupied by the Heavy Electrical factory. In the southern section initially 2,000 residential units were constructed near Malviya nagar locality of old Bhopal. The site is now known as Tatya Tope nagar. During the later years this area has developed into a well-planned settlement with residential quarters for the employees of the State Government. Nearby has come up a prestigious residential complex, known as the Arera colony with bungalow-type dwellings.

Surveyed localities

Idgah hills

This hilly residential area, till a few years ago, was considered an outer area. The development of modern detached residential units began in the late fifties. The most important building activity however, started in the early seventies when groups of houses for bank officials and other private construction work started. The total number of houses of this hill-locality is 1,500. The locality is about four kilometres away from the city-centre at Ibrahimpura. It is separated from the city's built-up tracts by the steep descent of the hill.

The attractions of the area included low-priced house-sites sold by the former ruler's family, scenic beauty and proximity to the city. There are no facilities of shopping or recreation on the hill. Housing is the only asset of the locality which has attracted rich people who like a calm and quiet environment. People feel that they live away from the city.

Arera colony

Located in the southern section of the city this settlement is a planned residential area with predominantly bungalow-type dwellings. One of its sectors however, comprises of eleven hundred flat-type units constructed for the State Government employees. Another sector is being developed by the M.P. Housing Board into detached residential units for people belonging to different income groups. The area occupied by the Arera colony is the only level land available between the centre of New Bhopal and the hills in the south. The locality is nine kilometres from the city-core.

The Arera colony and the other residential areas in the southern parts of Bhopal present a typical example of a new administrative-function city developing near an established centre and ultimately over-shadowing the parent settlement. A wholesale market, cinemas, shopping centres and expansion of the local railway station would, in the near future complete the process of the emergence of a new city. Though some residents feel like living independent of the old city, judging objectively however, one can easily find areas of dependence on the older settlement. The residents of New Bhopal depend on the parent centre for higher education, specialized and competitive shopping, automobile parts and repairs, printing presses, jewellery, building materials and fittings, etc.

Anand Nagar

Located on the eastern margin of the city this settlement was annexed by the municipal corporation in the year 1976. The locality is about eleven kilometres away from the city-core while the distance from the Heavy Electricals township is only one kilometre. The people belong to the labour class and work in the H.E. factory. They visit the city generally on holidays for shopping and entertainment. There are about 8,000 people who live in 2,500 closely-built houses. The settlement has a mixed look. Urban dwellings line the main road while the interior parts of Anand nagar have retained rural character where thatched dwellings are found along the narrow lanes. The locality is a residential suburb of the nearby H.E. factory and provides living accommodation to the poor labourers.

Satellites of Bhopal

Industrial satellite

The township of the Bharat Heavy Electricals Limited (BHEL), which came into existence two decades ago, is an independent new settlement in the eastern part of Bhopal city. The site attractions included vast open land along a trunk road. The factory employs 20,000 workers and produces Rs. 1,400 million worth of heavy electrical equipment annually for home and foreign markets.

The residential quarters of the township are spread in the three neighbourhoods of Piplani, Govindpura and Barkhera (Map 10.2 to 10.4). The neighbourhoods comprise of four sectors each with independent shopping centres. There are labour colonies, two each in the residential sectors, besides several unauthorized hutments around the township. The people depend on the inter-city transport, the higher education, specialized shopping and for entertainment.

This settlement is an independent township and conforms very well to the characteristics outlined by Schnore (1957:121) for satellites which according to him should have a "high degree of independence which stems from their importance as centres of production and employment. The Heavy Electricals factory employs about 85 per cent male workers of the township. The settlement is well laid out with residential quarters, wide roads, shopping centres, hospitals and schools. On the cultural level also the multi-regional and multi-religious society is very well knit. The people feel as living away from the city. This township can best be considered as an industrial satellite which is basically subordinate to Bhopal city while retaining a considerable degree of independence.

Residential satellite of Bairagarh

Situated along the Indore road at a distance of eight kilometres on the western fringe of the city, Bairagarh town has grown into a residential satellite of Bhopal city. The town has grown at a fast rate mainly as a result of the refugee-influx in the year 1947. The population of the town which stood at 16,827 in the year 1961 recorded seventeen per cent growth over the following decade. There has been a significant increase in the town's population during 1971-81 also because of the shifting of several offices of the State Government and also due to the provision of planned residential areas. The township has an independent personality yet there are several areas where the settlement is clearly dependent on the parent city.

GENERAL CHARACTERISTICS OF SUBURBS

The foregoing study of suburban areas points to a variety of reasons for the development of these outer urban forms. Following general aspects emerge with regard to the development of suburbs :

1. Tendencies of suburban development begin to appear when the availability of land at reasonable prices in the city is far exceeded by the demand for it.
2. Suburban development invariably follows trunk roads in the outer areas. The road crossings are special attractions in this regard. Indore city's Bhawar Kuan and old Sehore road crossings provide best examples of such development.
3. Outer areas of the cities have generally registered higher growth during the last two decades but this increase is difficult to measure because separate data for central-city and suburban areas are not available. The data for the 'out-growths', however, are available in some cases where these settlements have not been annexed to the cities over the years. Bhilainagar has recorded 466 per cent growth while Sagar city's five out-growths have recorded 62% and Jabalpur's fifteen such places have grown by 40 per cent during the last decade.
4. Low-lying patches of land, shallow tanks, hilly areas, abandoned graveyards (cemetaries), etc., attract suburban development because of easy availability of land at low costs. Hill-top locations of Sagar University campus and Rampur residential area of Jabalpur provide good examples of such development.
5. In the case of cities with more than one nucleus, the intervening land is filled with suburban areas. Gwalior city is an ideal example where the land between the three nuclei is being filled with suburban development.
6. Suburban areas have largely developed as a result of

large-scale building activity by the co-operative societies, private builders, M. P. Housing Board and by the Government.

7. A distinct feature of suburban development in the State is the influence of refugee settlements. At the time of the partition of the Indian sub-continent in 1947, a large number of Hindu refugees from Sindh (now in Pakistan) came to India. They were provided accommodation throughout the country in separate peripheral localities. In many cities the intervening areas have been filled with residential development.
8. The civic barriers erected for toll-tax collection on the trunk roads, known as octroi posts, have attracted suburban development.

Suburban development model

Several authors have used models to describe generalizations regarding urban development away from the cities. One of the earlier models was introduced by Burgess (1924). "The model is based upon the notion that the development of a city takes place outward from its central area, to form series of concentric zones" (Johnson, 1972:169). Farley (1964:38) and Schnore (1963:84) in their studies of the patterns of suburban growth also support the Burgess model for describing the shifts of the elites to suburban areas. Hoyt (1939:115) is another exponent of this model. Mann (1965:96) has used the structure of a hypothetical city to depict residential areas at the outer rings. Langton (1975) in a study of the residential patterns in pre-industrial cities of seventeenth century Britain has quoted Sjoberg (1960) in explaining the concentration of high-status citizens in the city-core with the lower-classes of the society living outside the city walls. Radford (1979) has drawn a model after Sjoberg for the pre-industrial cities in the United States which depicts the concentration of urban elites in the city-core with a section for domestic servants, while the lower classes and out-castes are shown in the second and third rings respectively.

For the present study a hypothesis on suburban development was evolved and surveys were conducted to identify suburban areas in large urban centres (Class I with 100,000 or more people). Besides personal observations and interviews at suburban localities a set of indicators for cities was also used in formulating the hypothesis. The indicators include urban densities, sex-ratios, literacy, decennial growth and rates of participation of male workers in major occupations. Details regarding use of intervening land and facilities of intra-city transport were found to be of considerable importance in determining suburban status (Table 10.1)

The findings on suburban development can now be stated in the form of a temporal model for cities of the State (Fig. 10.3). The assumptions on which this model is based include the suburban criteria and the general characteristics of suburbs described earlier. The other factors include availability of open land along the axis of city-growth, transport links and former nuclei.

1. **The land** : The urban improvement trusts, the M. P. Housing Board, State Government and other organized bodies have developed large patches of land for residential and industrial uses in peripheral places. Colonizers and individuals have converted even the valuable agricultural land into urban uses.

2. **Axis of city-growth** : Pressure of growth in certain directions away from the city-centre overcomes all the difficulties of land development. Cities generally grow in the direction of the existing industrial, service (including educational) isolated commercial centres. Sindhi refugee colonies which in earlier years were located at the peripheral places now lie in the middle of the choicest residential areas away from the city-core. The examples of such development of residential suburbs are found near civil lines of Sagar, the Khatiwala tank area of Indore and at Jawahar nagar of Gwalior.

3. **Transport links** : The trunk roads and rail lines attract initial suburban development. This is particularly true of road-crossings. Railway stations in the outer reaches generally attract suburban development. The civic toll-tax barriers (octroi posts) on inter-city roads have generally acted as nuclei to which were attracted warehouses (godowns), filling and service stations, light industries, tea-stalls and provision shops. At a later stage residential development has followed taking advantage of regular traffic to these points.

With every extension of civic boundary similar development of suburbs has followed while the area near the former octroi posts develops by its own impetus into a well-knit suburb. The examples of this kind of suburban development are Damoh 'Naka' (civic road barrier) and Garha areas of

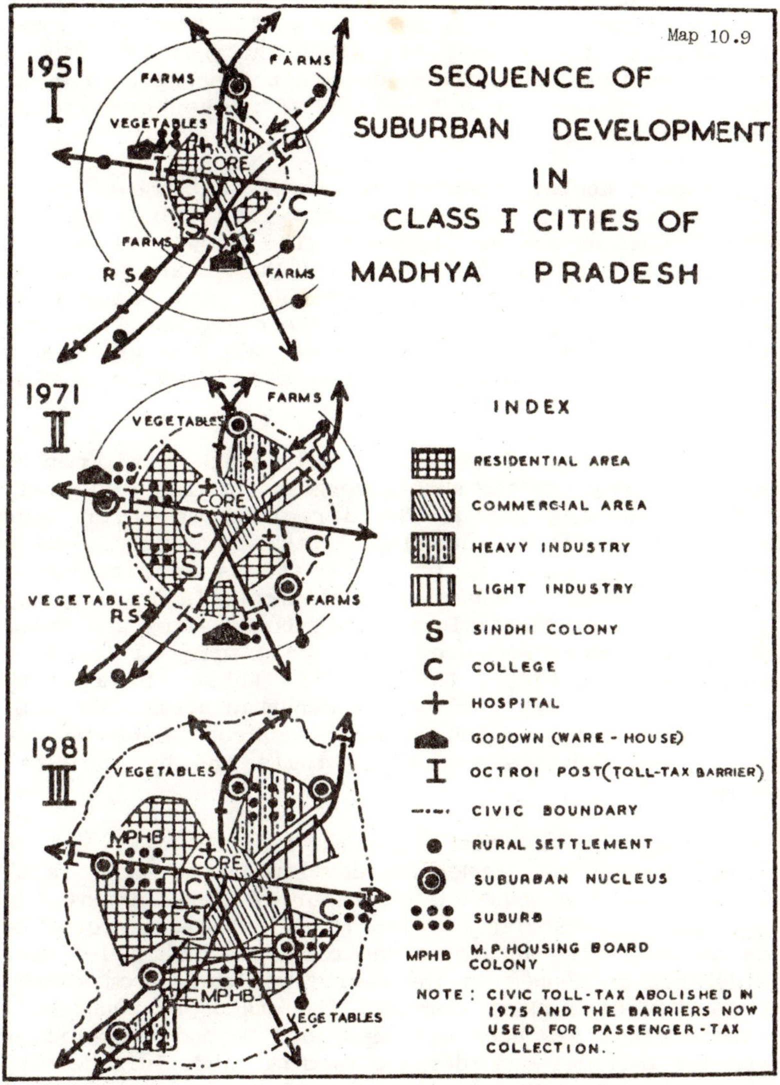

SUBURBAN DEVELOPMENT IN CENTRAL INDIA :
D.S.S.

Jabalpur, Makronia 'Naka' and Diwala 'Naka' of Sagar, Anand nagar to the east of Bhopal, Vijay nagar near the old octroi post in the north and Rau towards the south-west of Indore and Torwa 'Naka' area of Bilaspur city. The State Government has abolished the octroi tax since the year 1975 but the barriers continue to be there and are now being used by the civic authorities for collection of passenger tax from public vehicles.

4. Former nuclei : Peripheral rural settlements in the influence areas of the cities have invariably acted as nuclei for suburban development. The growth around the former villages of Manglia, Khajrana, Dudhia and Rau of Indore, Gulaua and Katanga of Jabalpur, and Ranipur and Bahodapur of Gwalior are some of the examples of suburban development generated by rural nuclei. All the villages in the vicinity of Bhilainagar have witnessed suburban development.

Other features of the model include the development of 'distant-suburbs' by the semi-government bodies especially the M. P. Housing Board. The direction in which these agencies have built residential units shows the trend of suburban push, which in practical terms appears as administrative boost to suburban development. Indore city with 25 per cent of residential units and house-sites and Bhopal (with 21.7%) have received the lion's share of the M. P. Housing board's efforts. Incidentally these are also the centres with the larger number of suburban areas. The urban construction work in the 'nearer-suburbs' however, has largely been done by the individuals and by the State Government.

Shifting of residential land use from the city-core and its replacement by commercial development is shown in the third stage of the sequence of suburban development (Map 10.3). Heavy industries develop in an exclusive sector between the rail line and the trunk road. The industries exert considerable influence on the nearby villages from where a large number of workers commute. The statutory boundary in the third stage has been extended much beyond the built-up tracts and includes considerable farming land. This development signifies the State control on the entire planning area as demarcated by the Town and Country Planning Department. Unfortunately though, this department is not able to alter the former haphazard urban growth in the peripheral areas.

CONCLUSION

Suburbs have developed around all the large urban centres of the State. The Census of India data on urban 'out-growth' relates strictly to centres outside the statutory urban limits and identification of suburbs on this basis alone is likely to overstate the phenomenon. A suburb as understood by this study is any urban development away from the densely settled parts of the city. It may be both within and outside the civic boundary.

The two important distinctions of this development are the 'nearer-suburbs and the 'distant-suburbs'. The nearer-suburbs are characterized by the residences of the employees of State Government and of well-to-do people. The distant-suburbs lie at some distance from the city and have been developed either by the M. P. Housing Board, private colonizers or have grown around a former rural nucleus.

Suburbs play a vital role in the development of cities in the State. It is important that thorough investigations into the processes of this development are made. "Studies of contemporary suburban growth", according to Johnson (1947:2) "may give an insight into the processes likely to operate in the future in the city...". Looking at the chaotic conditions of suburbs in some cities of Madhya Pradesh, it is essential that a strict regulatory control is exercised on all the development in peripheral areas. There are several advantages of control on suburban areas, one of the results, to quote Johnson (1972:150), "is that not much land is likely to lie dormant, unused either for rural or urban purposes, since the areas where building will be allowed are well known for sometimes ahead".

REFERENCES

Beaujeu-Garnier, J. and Chabot, G. (1967):**Urban Geography**, Translated by Beaver, S. and Yglesias, G.M. London : Longmans Green and Co.

Breese, G. (1966) : **Urbanization in newly developing countries.** Englewood cliffs, N.J. : Prentice-Hall, Inc.

Brown, Marilyn, A. (1981) : "A typology of suburbs and its public policy implications". **Urban Geography**, vol. 2, No. 4, pp 288-310.

Burgess, E.W. (1924) : "Concentric theory", Reprinted in Park, R.E., Burgess, E.W., and McKenzie, R.D. (1925) : **The City**, Chicago : University of Chicago Press, Cited in Johnson, J.H. (1972).

Carter, H. (1972) : **The Study of Urban geography.** London : Edward Arnold.

Chatterjee, S.P. (1963 and 1972): (i) **Fifty Years of Science in India** Progress of Geography. (ii) **A decade** (1963-72) **of Science in India Progress of Geography.** Calcutta ; Indian Science Congress Association.

Deshpande, C.D. (1973) : **The Suburbs of Greater Bombay.** Occasional Paper No. 2 Centre for Urban Research, Osmania University, Hyderabad.

Farley, R. (1964) : "Suburban persistence". **Am. Social. Rev.** Vol. 29, pp. 38-47.

Gibbs, J.P., (ed.) (1966) : "Urban units, their nature and boundaries" Introductory note to part I of **Urban research methods**, New Delhi : Affiliated East-West Press.

Gopi, K.N. (1979) : **Process of Urban Fringe development** - A Model. Delhi : Concept Publishing Company.

Gosal, G.S. (1972) : "Urban Geography". In **A Survey of Research in Geography.** A Project Sponsored by the Indian Council of Social Science Research, New Delhi. Bombay : Popular Prakashan.

Goudswaard, G. (1955) : "Some notes on the concepts of 'city' and Agglomeration". **Proceedings of the World population Conference,** 1954. New York : United Nations, 1955, Vol. IV, pp. 685-693. Reprinted in Gibbs, J.P. Editor (1966:31).

Hoyt, H. (1939) : **The structure and growth of residential neighbourhoods in American cities.** Washington: Federal Housing Administration. Citied in Johnson, J.H. (1972:174).

Johnson, J.H. (1972) : **Urban Geography an introductory analysis.** Oxford ; Pergamon Press, Second edition.

Johnson, J.H. (ed.) (1974) : **Suburban growth-geographical processes at the edge of the Western city.** John Wiley and sons.

Jones, E. (1966) : **Towns and cities.** London ; Oxford University Press.

Kumar, Pramila (1980) : **Agricultural Changes in Urban Fringe.** New Delhi : Rajesh Publications.

Kurtz, R. A. and Eicher, J.B. (1958) : "Fringe and suburb - a confusion of concepts". **Soc. Forces.** Vol. 37, pp. 32-7.

Langton, John (1975) : "Residential patterns in pre-industrial cities : Some case studies from seventeenth-century Britain", Vol. 65, pp 1-29. **Trans. Inst. Br. Geogr.**

Mann, P. (1965) : **An approach to urban sociology.** London : Urban Society cited in Johnson, J.H. (1972:175).

Mayer, H.M. and Kohn, C.F., (eds.) (1967): **Readings in Urban**

Geography, Chicago : University of Chicago.

Mumford, L. (1938) : **The culture of cities,** New York : Harcourt, Brace and Company, Inc.

Radford, John P. (1979) : "Testing the model of the pre-industrial city : the case of ante-bellum Charleston, South Carolina", **Trans. Inst. Br. Geogr.,** New Series 4, pp. 392-410.

Rajagopalan, C. (1962) : **The Greater Bombay - A study in suburban ecology.** Bombay : Popular Book Depot.

Schnore, L.F. (1957) : "Satellites and suburbs", **Soc. Forces.** Vol. 36, pp. 121-27.

Schnore, L.F. (1963) : "The Socio-economic status of cities and suburbs", **Am. Social Rev.** Vol. 28, pp. 76-85.

Sjoberg, G. (1960) : **The pre-industrial city : past and present.** Glencoe, Illionois, cited in Radford (1979).

Shrivastava, D.S. (1984) : "Identification of Suburbs in developing regions (with reference to Madhya Pradesh State of India)". **Indian Journal of Marketing Geography** (Gorakhpur), Vol. II, No. 2, pp. 106-115.

Sundaram, K.V. (1977) : **Urban and regional planning in India,** New Delhi, Vikas Publishing House Pvt. Ltd.

REPORTS

Census of India (1961) : A select bibliography on urban studies. New Delhi : Registrar General, India, Ministry of Home Affairs.

Census of India (1971) : **Indian Census in perspective.** Census centenary monograph No. 1.

Census of India (1971) : Madhya Pradesh. Series 10, Part II A. General Population Tables.

Census of India (1981) : Madhya Pradesh, Series II Provisional Population Tables. Paper I of 1981, supplement.

Bhopal Development Plan, 1991 Town and Country Planning Department, Government of Madhya Pradesh.

Indore Development Plan : Town and Country Planning, Dept., Govt. of Madhya Pradesh.

Gwalior Development Plan : Town and Country Planning Department, Govt. of Madhya Pradesh.

Raipur Development Plan : Town and Country Planning Department, Govt. of Madhya Pradesh.

United States, Dept. of Commerce (1981) : "Suburban Surge", U.S. News and World Report.

TABLE 9.4

Changing landuse in Jodhpur (1971-1981) (in percentage)

Type of use	1971	[illegible]	1981
1. Grain	54.27	44.43	33.19
2. Vegetable	18.91	13.06	9.50
3. Residential	7.63	14.52	26.42
4. Fallow (go-cochar)	10.32	14.63	14.47
5. Govt. [illegible]	9.63	10.22	19.48
Total	100.44	99.86	103.06

Source: Village Panchayat Office

TABLE 9.5

Classification of Non-agricultural Land 1981

Village	% of non-agri. land used	% of non-agri. [illegible] not used	% of [illegible] pasture	Total % of Non-ag. land
1. Vejalpur	23	6	16	45
2. Vastrapur	44*	12	4	60
3. Memnagar	37	9	3	49
4. Ranip	28	8	6	42

* Nearly 40% of it is owned by I.I.M. and Ahmedabad Education Society.

TABLE 9.6

Registered and Built-up Housing Society (1981)

Village	No. of registered Housing Society 1960 onwards	No. of housing Society built	No. of Housing Society not built
1. Vejalpur	235	195	40
2. Vastrapur	5	4	1
3. Memnagar	13	10	3
4. Ranip	[illegible]	[illegible]	[illegible]

Source: Village Panchayat Office.

SECTION TWO

RURAL-URBAN CONTINUUM

ELEVEN

Rudiger Voigt

Socio-Economic Change in the Rural-Urban Continuum

INTRODUCTORY REMARKS

The Term rural area' is ambiguous and requires an explanation. Frequently little or no distinction is made between a rural area and an area used for agricultural purposes. This is an error similar to that treating urban and industrial areas alike. Rural and urban areas differ in their population density. Whereas the densely populated areas are defined in German regional development programs and can be identified accordingly; there is no standard description of definition of rural areas. This can very easily lead to misunderstandings. In the following discussion 'rural area' is used as a general category for non-urban regions which, because of a low population density, do not benefit from the advantages of agglomeration in areas of high density (Furst/Vath, 1978). The category includes especially--but not exclusively--rural problem-areas. Not included on the other hand are the fringe areas of high population density. A further differentiation would require an even more detailed analysis which has not yet been made.

STRUCTURAL DISCRIMINATION

The structural discrimination of the rural areas and their population cannot be explained sufficiently by the decreasing growth of the Gross National Product, even though the federal and state governments make this argument to justify existing inequalities. This turns out to be due to the system, insofar as they are the result of land-use policies and the requirements of the process of capital utilization. Of course stagnation or recession increase the difference between developed density populated areas and structurally weak areas. With the decline in the development potential of the rural area (i.e, decreasing growth of population and jobs, less investments capital especially for infrastructure) the possibilities available to the State are reduced. In the 'tax-state' (Steuerstaat: Gold-scheid) public services can be financed only by taxing private production (Grauhan 1978); therefore; declining economic growth regularly leads to reduced services, even if the state tries to compensate by borrowing money in the private sector. The consequences of the continuing structural change in the German economy which leads to an accelerated socio-economic concentration process are felt most intensively in rural areas. This does not mean, however, that in times of economic boom the general discrimination of rural areas is abolished or that the differences between rural areas and densely populated areas are overcome (ROB 1978). Policies pursued by the state in rural areas are most of all designed to neutralize a potential zone of conflict (e.g., "Gruner Plan, tax reductions for farmers, etc.). It is true that development programs have been implemented by the state and the federal governments in recent years which encouraged investments in rural areas (not without consequences on election day). It might be argued therefore, that the need for infrastructure improvements in rural areas has been met to a large extent. Judgements concerning need are really, of course, a socio-political problem and cannot be made exclusively on the basis of economic efficiency. Service delivery in rural areas is still comparatively born in technical infrastructure, higher education facilities, public transport, leisure time infrastructure, etc. The major portion of public spending has been spent for improvements in densely populated areas (e.g., 90% of money provided for large projects in public transport was spent in the nine densely populated regions of West Germany). The reason why this is accepted provided it becomes known or is noticed-lies in the mostly conservative attitudes of the population in rural areas. The events that took place in Wyhl or Gorleben, suggest a slow change in this political lethargy, (e.g., German villages in which farmers have demonstrated against the construction of nuclear power stations). Since the absolute preference for economic growth in densely populated areas benefits these areas directly, state-sponsored economic programs appear to be of limited help in abolishing regional differences. Such state sponsored economic programs, at their best, are able to mitigate within limits the consequences of economic misdevelopment.

REGIONAL CONCENTRATION

Differences in income

Different kinds of disadvantages for rural areas magnify one another (Naschold/Vath, 1968). Most obvious is the connection between differences in income and service delivery. The differences in income between densely populated and rural areas, allow the supposition that the structurally weak areas are about seven to nine years behind. This disadvantage is increased by the lower purchasing power that discourages the rural population from making full use of the public and private services that do exist. On the other hand the higher levels of service delivery for city dwellers, who are provided free or subsidized public services, result in an increased income.

Rationalisation requirements

Since the private providers of essential services react in conformity to the market, there is, in attempt to maximize profits, an obvious concentration of physicians and dentists in densely populated areas. Even substantial subsidies fail to induce physicians and dentists to remain in rural areas (only seven per cent of all physicians work in communities smaller than 2000 inhabitants). Even the state is forced to rationalize when establishing social service institutions, since decisions concerning location are based normally on economic and technical arguments. Hospitals, secondary-schools, homes for the elderly etc., are constructed only, if the population reaches a certain density, which is, of course, to the disadvantages of rural areas. The ever-increasing concentration of such facilities in larger towns is a disadvantage for rural population because of time and travel costs incurred in using these services. The consequences for members of different social groups vary, of course, according to working hours second or even third car in one family, etc.

Unemployment

For employees living in rural areas, further negative factors include a higher unemployment rate, fewer opportunities for career development and continuing education. The higher rate of unemployment in structurally weak areas—almost twice as high as in densely populated areas—is due to the still existing structural change in agriculture and the decline of job opportunities in trade and industry. The potential unemployment in structurally weak rural areas is estimated to be as high as 17% (on estimate made by the Swiss Prognos, Inc.). New and technologically developed employment opportunities are created mostly in densely populated areas. This makes the surrounding territory all the more attractive as working-and living places for young and qualified employees. This means that the increased desire of the rural population to become technically qualified and their success in achieving their goals, results in disadvantage for rural areas. And again, it means an advantage for the densely populated areas offering higher incomes and better career opportunities.

Rural exodus (Wanderungsverluste)

The relative lack of public transport in rural areas (reduction in train service by the German Railway, private bus services, longer regional travelling time, etc.) compared with urban services (see e.g. * * * * 2 of the German transportation finance law) cannot be compensated by the willingness of the rural population to commute, because of the disproportionate increase in costs in terms of health, time and money. The loss of population in rural problem areas over the next decade has been estimated to be closer to a million than to 500,000 people. This rural exodus does not contribute so much to the growth of densely populated areas as it does to the urbanized surroundings of the main cities. The general decrease of population in German affects mostly rural areas, because the labour-drain , consisting mostly of younger people, results in a decreasing propagation energy and a reduction in the traditionally higher 'fertility-rate of rural areas. In addition to a smaller number of qualified employees, one finds an overaged population in rural areas whose relative number is increased by this exodus, and further added too by pensioners moving from densely populated to rural areas.

Deterioration of service delivery

The process of population development in rural areas results in disparities in age structure, family status and socio-cultural structures. The consequence is an enduring disruption of the social structure of rural areas through a lack of homogeneous age groups; pupils and employees spending a large part of their spare time in trains, buses or cars; inadequate participation in club activities, etc. In addition, the decreased density of population means a further expansion of the settlement structure. This increases in prices for delivering of services, the areas supplied by central agencies tend to expand. If the birth rate drops from 18.3 to 11.0, the population necessary for one kindergarten (with two groups of 25 children each) rises from 911 to 1515 inhabitants. In areas with a population density of 20 inhabitants per square kilometre, the radius of the area for pupils of a grammar-school is 18 km. The same is true for the supply of routine goods and services. At the beginning of the 1960s 2,200-3,000 inhabitants were considered enough to set up a business or trade. Today 6,000 and soon 10,000 inhabitants will be needed for the necessary purchasing power.

CRITERION OF 'EQUALITY'

Abstract main objectives

Because of the increasing disadvantages for the rural areas, the German welfare state is attempting to develop a regional economic policy with the help of regional structural policy. While the regional structural policy is oriented toward economic growth by encouraging private investment, the federal regional development program can be seen as a not entirely consistent effort to provide a general model of development for the Federal Republic of Germany. The objectives of this general regional policy remain, however, on a relatively abstract level, which means that there is no controversy concerning main objectives. Government and Opposition agree on the constitutional imperative to preserve the equivalence of living conditions' (Art. 72 GG). This remains an empty phrase so long as the contents of this constitutional postulate are not clearly defined. The common agreement concerning the abstract goal disappears as soon as concrete definitions are suggested.

Definition of contents

Federal and state regional development plans are in agreement that the abstract main objective of equality of living conditions means the delivering of public services and the provision of infrastructural facilities within reasonable distances. It means also the promotion of a comparable social structure in all parts of the Federal Republic. The crucial question, however, is the definition of equivalent and herein lies the source of deep conflict in objectives. Is 'equivalence to be understood as an attempt to make living conditions in rural areas exactly as they are in densely populated areas, or does it simply mean an improvement in the level of services provided in 'under-supplied' regions? Should there be a development toward meeting the needs of population, or should the rural areas serve merely as a reservoir for labour, potential industrial areas (e.g., nuclear power stations), leisure time areas and drinking water?

Passive restoration

Government planning concepts for rural areas have been changed several times since the institutionalization of the regional development policy. Especially critical has been the resulting reduction in public resources from the so-called 'Flachenforderung' (promotion of whole areas or regions) of the 1960s to the so-called 'Schwerpunkt-forderung' (promotion of single focal points) in the 1970s. Although the general promotion of whole areas according to the 'principle of the watering can' was completely insufficient, the transition to the promotion of single projects means a passive restoration of rural areas. This policy is based on the point-axial system, which determines the location of public infrastructural facilities. The goal of this program is first of all an improvement in servicing the population in rural areas. This goal is, however, so flexible that it can be used for concentrating as well as for deconcentrating purposes.

According to the concept of promoting single projects, the gains achieved by centralization in the development of forced points must be paid by losses of centralization in the surrounding areas. This applies especially in times of reduced economic growth. The local shops lose their economic basis if a central shopping centre is built. A centrally located school means the closing of many little local schools. A hierarchical system of focal points in a step-like system of centralization prevents the further social development of the surrounding towns and leads to their complete devitalization. The lack of certain crucial advantages in the somewhat smaller focal points hinders the development of an independent economic development and does not create a focus of economic growth with positive consequences for the surrounding areas.

Area functional division of labour

The consequence of the failure of this concept is a gradual re-orientation in the regional development policy (Raumordnugspolitik) from the promotion of single focal point to a functional concept. This places the old demand for equality of living conditions in opposition to the demand for an increased division of labour by function and area (Beirat fur Raumordnung, 1976). According to this concept, the delivering of goods and services should be offered in those areas which are best suited for these purposes. In this functional division of labour between densely populated and rural areas, certain functions are defined for rural areas according to their characteristics and development. Recreation, water supply and certain environmental-ecological functions are the main tasks of rural areas. According to this concept, land use policy in rural areas should become at least the "instrument of compensatory politics for the unsolved disparities in densely populated areas" (Funk/Haubermann/Will, 1976). The federal government still insists (at least verbally) that all regions are to be developed as multi functional areas with equivalent living conditions (German Bundestag 1977). Since the concept of a functional division of labour by area is facing political opposition in these affected areas, one can expect that the established concept of balanced functional areas will gain importance.

CONCENTRATION AT THE EXPENSE OF RURAL AREAS

Outdated strategies of promotion

The concept of the traditional strategy of promotion for which the common task[1] "improvement of the regional economic structure" is characteristic, is designed to overcome production price, disadvantages in rural industrial areas vis-a-vis the densely populated areas by subsidizing capital investments. This effort extends only to a limited extent the autonomous decision-making of private business. This strategy is more static than dynamic, because it does not take into account the differing requirements of areas with varying structure levels of development. Concentrating on the promotion of infrastructure improvements benefits especially traditional branches of industry with limited prospects for growth. Even if it should be possible to encourage the settlement in rural areas of industries with a potential for economic growth, these are not included in the promotion policy. In later phases of economic development the so called household oriented infrastructure, the provision of the so called 'human capital' and the access to scientific, political and technological information becomes more and more important.

Functional underdevelopment

The traditional strategy of promotion has not led to improved development opportunities in the focal points, nor has it provided the accompanying impulses for economic growth in structure. Instead, it has encouraged the formation of branch enterprises which employ largely unskilled workers and as a result are especially susceptible to crisis. Concentrated in these problem areas are mostly small, very often family-operated-enterprises, subcontractors, suppliers etc., which have to reduce or even close production according to the market situation. To the extent that the decreasing rates of economic growth lead to reduction in the general growth of standardized production, no new enterprises will be founded in rural areas. This brings about the functional underdevelopment (Ewers, Wettmann, 1978) of rural areas, namely their lack of qualified labour, information and essential functions of enterprise, combined with a lack of knowledge in management techniques. As a consequence this means that this traditional strategy of promotion has no stable foundation.

Large scale concentration

The strong dependence on exports in the Federal Republic and the resulting competitive struggle for the world markets enforce the trend mentioned above. Not only the cycle of national economic growth, but most of all market fluctuations in the world economy, changes in the international division of labour, and the rapid growth of multinational enterprises influence directly the development chances of structurally weak areas. The most obvious sign of these changes is a tendency towards large scale concentration in Western European industrial states (Ewers, Wettmann, 1978). This can be seen especially in the high technology and capital-intensive areas of the economy. Given the sharp competition between the Federal Republic and other European countries and among densely populated areas within the Federal Republic, the signs of environmental deterioration and other kinds of overload are given less serious attention than the economic advantages of agglomeration, especially because of the disproportionate share of the rising costs of agglomeration which are paid by the state (e.g., public transport).

Economically insecure industrial plants

Multinational industrial concerns locate their European headquarters almost exclusively in selected developed areas as close as possible to political decision-making centres which can influence the distributation of economically relevant public funds. The increasing combinations of large concerns with small and medium enterprises in rural areas lead normally to a transfer of the essential headquarters functions to the metropolitan centres. Only labour-intensive production plants are likely to remain in rural areas. The problem is, that these 'lenghthened work benches' are those production plants that are especially jeopardized by closings. The relatively low wages, costs for land and environmental protection expenses in rural areas are no longer sufficient advantages when compared to the competition with foreign countries where low wages are paid. In the age of technology-oriented concentration the advantages of large agglomerations become increasingly important, e.g., proximity to information sources, banks and transportation centres. Especially in times of stagnation the stronger concerns concentrate their investments in densely populated areas. These investments are to an increasing extent 'job eliminating rationalizations rather than 'job creating'. In view of the continuing structural changes in the German economy, the objective of a well balanced development of all areas of the Federal Republic seems to be an utopian hope.

STRATEGIES TO ACHIEVE CONSENSUS

Latent conflict of objectives

Due to the high degree of abstraction in the main objectives, there is an appearance of a common consensus in the various regional development policies, although there are latent conflicts behind this facade which might come to the fore at any time. Such a conflict could arise, for example, if the population of a structurally weak area is not satisfied with the degree of service delivery that has been planned for this area by the regional economic policy and falls under the framework of the concept of promoting single focal points (Schwerpunktforderung). Furthermore, an intensified regional struggle for public funds can be observed since it has been established that no region can expect to experience population growth. In order to increase the legitimacy of regional policies, more exact criteria for measuring quality of living standards, in the sense of economic development opportunities, than those now available (e.g., GNP) will be required. For some time regional development policy (Raumordnugspolitik) has been oriented toward using social indicators which serve in the analysis of the existing situation and the development opportunities of a certain area. These social indicators are used also to provide more concrete and quantifiable data about the intended objective: the establishment of priorities for control purposes.

Securing objectivity via social indicators

The main contribution of the social indicators for regional development policy (Raumordnungspolitik) has been in the quantification of regional objectives which define future regional minimum standards. This requires that these minimum standards are correspondingly low, and/or that they apply to larger and larger areas. The main task in the measurement of differences in rural structures and development as well as the delivering of services and facilities. Of courses the indicators used in the continuing observation of areas measure only, the input side, that is, they cover the level of service delivery and facilities as well as feasible limits, not the regional living conditions. The result of these measurements provide nevertheless the framework for the decisions concerning the goals of regional policy. Although social indicators do not give any information about the chances of implementing regional development policy as against economic policy, their use has had a significant influence on the definition of the abstract goal of creating equivalent living conditions.'

Determination of existing disparities

German regional development policy is based on the measurement of disparities in the areas of business activities and infrastructure, its evaluation requires an extension of the indicators to include housing patterns, social structure and environmental conditions. Of course the procurement of comparable data for the different rural areas remains an unsolved problem. The analysis of disparities is supposed to be based on functional required units of varying size of population density. The purpose of this refinement is to avoid the appearance of balance in the calculation of an average for areas with lower and higher levels of service delivery. While this result can be assessed positively, the changes in the basis of the analysis lead to a retention of existing disparities between areas of different density in one region and thus to a permanent discrimination of rural areas. It is probable that the establishment of seemingly objective regional minimum standards will in fact promote consensus-building in the affected population as well as between the federal government, the states (Lander) and the communities, and among economically strong and weak states (Lander).

PROBLEMS OF ENFORCING REGIONAL DEVELOPMENT

Vertical distributions of competence

The achievement of a consensus between states (Lander) and municipalities is very important for the federal government, because federal regional development instruments have not been given the necessary authority to enforce the government's objectives. For this, the federal government always depends on other policy areas (economic, traffic, federal economic policy etc.) and on other political levels, which are responsible for most federal administration, (i.e., states and communities). In the political system of the Federal Republic there are not only relatively autonomous areas for decision-making by state (Land) and municipal governments, but also for the various federal and state (Land) planning agencies which are in competition with each other and with other agencies. Enforcement opportunities of the federal government are improved, however, by the orientation of the states and municipalities toward interregional and inter-municipal competition, thus preventing a front of solidarity. Most of all the densely populated areas fear that a policy of developing structurally weak areas will affect adversely their own economic strength. A combination of regional development policy objectives and medium-term financial planning as demanded by the (former) CDU/CSU opposition in the German parliament (Bundestag) might possibly clarify the conflicting goals of various bureaucratic actors and levels demonstrate the dominance of economic policy. It would not, however, chance the 'toothless' power to enforce regional development policy of the federal government. The discrimination against rural areas can be overcome only in the unlikely event that a radical shift were to take place in the founding of rural areas.

Minimizing of obligations

Characteristic for the insufficient enforcement instruments of federal regional development policy is a lack of correspondence between policy-formation and implementation responsibilities. Whereas federal land-use policies are the responsibility of the federal minister for building (Bundesbauminister) and the executive office of the minister-presidents (Lander-governors) or relevant ministries in the states, the competence for the regional structural policy is a matter of the federal or ministries of state (Lander-Wirtschaftsminister) economies. If considered as an "accumulation of villages and farms", however, the rural areas are the responsibility traditionally of the minister of agriculture. It is therefore difficult to avoid contradictory conceptions and planning. Constant compromising, normally at the cost of the development opportunities of rural areas, are typical political practice; in the meantime there are no political decisions about regional development (Raumordung) (Naschold, 1978). This can be seen in the example of the village renewal program for future investments for which the federal minister of agriculture is responsible. This program was intended to improve the agrarian structure in the villages in isolation from all the other and more urgent problems of rural areas. The consequence of growing problems of enforcement becomes obvious in the increasingly non-obligatory nature of regional development planning (Scharpf/Schnabel, 1978). This is expressed in the transition from law to a mere program and in the mixture of contradictory conceptions, for example, in the federal regional development program.

Socio-political counterforce

A negative factor for enforcement opportunities in regional development policies lies not only in the lack of clear responsibility for specific areas but above all in a lack of an interested and organized lobby. Regional development policy therefore stands a small chance of becoming a political issue. At this point one could point to the concept of'an alternative regional policy' suggested by Naschold (1978). Since there is an ever increasing number of needy areas, Naschold believes that it is possible to form an effective socio-political counterforce by activating this political and economic potential. With the help of this counterforce the dominance of the power-complex of industrial and financial monopolies and oligopolies could be restricted and perhaps even reduced. The heterogeneous structure of the needy areas and their constituent parts is, of course, a serious problem in activating them as a pressure group. This problem probably can be overcome only under conditions of long term stagnation. Naschold sees indications for such a mobilization in citizen-initiatives, regional voting behaviour, ecological "green" parties and also in the attitudes of official political representatives of rural areas. Without the active support of the trade unions this socio-political counterforce hardly has a slim chance of succeeding. Whether the traditional orientation of the unions towards the urban working class can be changed in favour of rural areas, as Naschold seems to assume, is highly questionable.

NOTES

For suggestive discussions I have to thank my American colleague, Arthur B. Gunlicks, Ph.D., Professor of Political Science at the University of Richmond, Virginia.

1. 'Common task' is the translation of the German word 'Gemeinschaftsaufgabe', according to the German constitution at the reform of 1969. These common tasks are described as assignments for which federal and state (Lander) governments are equally responsible.

REFERENCES

Ewers, Hans-Jurgen and Reinhart W. Wettmann, Innovationsorientierte Regionalpolitik - Uberlegungen zu einem regionalstrukturellen Politik- und Forschungsprogramm. **Informationen zur Raument-wicklung** 1978, pp. 467.

Flore, Carl, Regionale Wirtschaftspolitik unter veranderten Rahmenbedingungen. **Informationen zur Raumentwicklung** 1976, pp. 775.

Furst, Dietrich and Joachim Jens Hesse, **Landesplanung. Dusseldorf**: Werner Verlag. 1981.

Funk, Albrecht and Hartmut Haeussermann and Hans-Dieter WILL, "Staatsapparat und Regionalpolitik", pp. 281 in Rolf Ebbinghausen (ed.) **Burgerlicher Staat und politische Legitimation.** Frankfurt/ Main: Suhrkamp. 1976.

Gatzweiler, Peter and Ludwig Rung, Regionale Disparitaten im Bundesgebiet. Erste Ergebnisse der Laufenden Raumbeobachtung. **Informationen zur Raumentwicklung**, 1978, pp. 669.

Goldscheid, Rudolf and Joseph A. Schumpeter, Beitrage zur **politischen Okonomie der Staatsfinanzen** (R. Hickel ed.). Frankfurt/Main: Suhrkamp. 1976.

Hesse, Joachim Jens (ed.), Politikverflechtung im Foderativen Staat. Studien zum Planungs- und Finanzierungsverbund zwischen Bund, **Landern und Gemeinden.** Baden-Baden: Nomos. 1978.

Naschold, Frieder, Alternative Raumpolitik. **Ein Beitrag zur Verbesserung der Arbeits- und Lebensverhaltnisse.**

Kronberg: Athenaeum. 1978.
Scharpf, Fritz W. and Fritz Schnabel, Durchsetzungsprobleme der Raumordnung im offentlichen Sektor. **Informationen zur Raumentwicklung** 1978, pp. 29.
Vaeth, Werner, Raumplanung. Probleme der raumlichen Entwicklung und Raumordnungspolitik in der Bundesrepublik. Konigstein: Hain. 1980.
Voigt, Ruediger, "Aktionsbedingungen politischer Teilhabe im laendlichen Raum" in Regine Roemheld and Heinz Zielinski (eds.) **Kommune im Aufbruch.** Frankfurt/Main and Bern: Peter Lang. 1983.

TWELVE

Frank L. Sweetser

Community Size and the Urban-Rural Continuum

Australia and the United States

It has not recently been fashionable among social ecologists interested in residential areas to consider the effects of city size on neighbourhood and community characteristics. In large part this is due to a dominating concern with internal differentiation in large metropolitan communities accompanied by an almost total neglect of the neighbourhoods of smaller cities. Because of this bias, the "profound and far-reaching effect" of differences in community size on urban neighbourhoods is the "most impressive substantive finding" of a recent analysis of the entire universe of Australian urban residential areas.[1] The study compared five factorial dimensions and 73 single variables across four urban community size classes - from very large to large, medium-sized and small cities - and found that a majority of the indicators varied monotonically, with regular, and sometimes large increases and decreases from size class to size class. This finding raised the question as to whether such continuous variation extended also into rural areas; in short to the problem of the validity of the concept of an urban-rural continuum.

Prevailing wisdom suggested that the continuum was, perhaps, "real, but relatively unimportant", and that it cannot "be regarded as unidimensional".[2] Exploration of the issue on the Australian data was accomplished by adding the universe of rural neighbourhoods as a fifth size-type class to the four urban categories. Differences from very large, large and medium-sized cities to small cities and rural communities were indeed often continuous; if anything, the urban-rural contrasts tended to be stronger than inter-city size differences. Accordingly, a general theoretical conclusion was formulated:

> The hypothesis of a unitary urban-rural continuum of neighbourhood variation in urban industrial societies must be rejected in favour of the view that city size and the urban-rural contrast exert differential linear effects on neighborhood characteristics.
> (Sweetser, op. cit., p.178)

This formulation rejects Dewey's contention that the continuum is unimportant, and accepts the Duncan and Reiss view that it is not unidimensional. But it also goes further to argue that the process of urbanization as reflected in community size and urban-rural neighbourhood differentiation produces similar "forms and meanings" attributable to "the prevailing historic, economic, social and cultural conditions" of the more developed urban industrial societies.[3]

It is the purpose of this paper to report an initial test of the proposition that the two modes of differentiation are indeed similar in separate urban industrial societies by comparing available data from Australia in 1971 and for the United States for 1950.

TERMS OF THE COMPARISON

Duncan and Reiss, in their classic study of Social Characteristics of Urban and Rural communities, 1950 reordered the abundant data of the U.S. 1950 Census according to community size and type into eleven classes, from very large urbanized areas through smaller urbanized areas, and a range of independent cities and smaller places to the rural nonfarm and farm categories. While, as has been noted, they reject the idea that the rural-urban (or urban-rural) continuum is unidimensional, they nevertheless show that many individual variables do indeed vary continuously or almost continuously across their size-type categories. The more striking of these are described in a "Quick summary of findings"; some 25 variables are picked out for emphasis in figures 3-6 (op. cit., pp. 32-40). Twelve of these variables were replicated, or could be approximately matched, by twelve of the forty-one variables that were especially relevant in describing differential city size and urban-rural linear effects in the Australian study.[4] The twelve pairs of matched variables are displayed in Table 12.1. They include specifications on age-sex structure, marital status, ethnicity, migration, education, employment and occupation, thus providing a broad selection of data fairly representative of the indicators usually examined by social ecologists. Moreover, they are rather closely replicated in the two nations, being either virtually identical as with the per cent of women married, or differing only in petty detail, as in the pairing of a selected nationality group for Australia with the totality of the foreign born in the United States. Even the poorest match, linking median school years in the U.S. with the proportion of Australians who are vocationally qualified or studying, appears on its face to provide indicators of the same general educational phenomenon.

Three additional aspects of the comparison require mention. First, means compared are derived from component 'census tracts' for Australia and from component communities for the United States. This is an entirely negligible difference for present purposes, since tract means for a community would normally be very nearly equal to community measures. Second, comparing 1950 and 1971 data for two nations might appear to introduce confounding diachronic variation into what is basically a synchronic comparison. In fact, the addition of the temporal to the spatial separation of the two societies is viewed as an advantage; similarity across both time and space would appear to be stronger evidence of persisting parallel structure than would similarity across space alone. Third, it was impossible to disaggregate the five Australian size-type classes to match the eleven categories used by Duncan and Reiss, so the latter had to be collapsed to match the Australian. Since the two censuses employed very similar concepts, this is reasonably straightforward. For large communities, American urbanized areas and Australian urban centres conceptually identify agglomerations including both central cities and their suburbs. And for smaller communities, Australian urban centres are like American places. In each instance, data are accumulated for populations of fairly compact settlements, defined on the basis of their geographic rather than their political characteristics. Moreover, numerical cutting points in the two studies could be matched to produce five American size-type categories very similar to the Australian, as shown in Table 12.2.

DATA

The essential data of the study are presented in Table 12.3, where means for the five community size-type categories are deployed across the page in pairs for the United States and Australia.[5] The sixth column contains na-

TABLE 12.1

Matched variables
United States and Australia

United States, 1950	Australia, 1971
fertility ratio	fertility ratio
(children under 5 per 1000 women 20-44)	(children under 5 per 1000 women 15-44)
% male, total population (transformed from sex ratio)	% male, age 20-64
% male, age 65 and over (transformed from sex ratio)	% male, age 65 and over
% women married	% women married
% of white pop. native born	% of total population Australian born
% of white population foreign born	% of total population born in South East Europe
% of 1949-1950 in-migrants from farms	% of residents in-migrant from rural areas 1966-1971
median school years completed by persons age 25 and over	% age 16+ vocationally qualified or studying (transformed from NOT qual. or study)
% of labour force unemployed	%of labour force unemployed
% women in labour force	% women in labour force
% employed males in clerical occupations*	% employed males in clerical occupations
% employed women in clerical occupations*	% employed women in clerical occupations

* These variables were included to match "white collar" employment as nearly as possible. The Duncan and Reiss "white collar" variable was not replicated in the Australian study, but the two clerical variables were available for both countries.

tional means, and the last column, which is the basis for the ordering of the table, is the Index of urban-rural effect, a statistic developed for the present analysis. This measure is the difference between medium-sized and rural communities expressed as a per cent of the difference between very large cities and rural communities. The rationale is that differences between cities of 10,000 to 100,000 population ('medium-sized') and rural communities may properly be associated with an urban-rural effect on neighbourhood and community characteristics. Conversely, differences between cities of 1,000,000 or more population ('very large cities') and medium-sized cities are properly associated with a city size effect. An inverse index of city size effect - equal to]100-Idx(U-R)[- is thus utilized below in the discussion of findings.[6]

TABLE 12.2

**Five community size-type categories
United States and Australia**

Analytical Category	Australian Definition	U.S. Definition
Very Large City	urban centre with 1,000,000,+ pop.	urbanized area with 1,000,000,+ pop.
Large City	urban centre with 100,000-999,999 population	urbanized area with under 1,000,000 population*
Medium-Sized City	urban centre with 10,000-99,999 population	place outside UA with 10,000+ population*
Small city	urban centre with 1,000-9,999 population**	place with 1,000-9,999 population
Rural community	rural villages and other rural area	place under 1000 pop, rural nonfarm and rural farm population

* For the U.S., the large city category includes a few urbanized areas with50,000 to 100,000 popultion. Conversely, the medium-sized city category has few places larger then 50,000.

** A negligible scattering of settlements with under 1,000 population are designated "urban".

CONTINUA IN THE UNITED STATES AND AUSTRALIA

Gradients

Row-by-row inspection of the mean values of variables for community size-types in Table 12.3 will reveal that all but one of the twenty-four tend to increase or decrease more or less regularly from very large to rural communities, and do so in parallel for the United States and Australia.[7] Moreover, thirteen variables, seven Australian, and six

American are monotonic in their progressive rise or fall. The degree of cross-national similarity was measured by correlating the paired variables, with these results:

TABLE 12.3

Urban-rural gradients
United States (1950) and Australia (1971)

Variables	Nation	Very Lg. City	Lg. City	Med-Size City	Sml. City	Rural Com.	Total	Urban-Rural Effect (Index = %) *
		Community Size Class						
% male: tot pop	US	48.5	48.4	48.3	48.3	51.6	49.4	100
age 20-64	AUS	50.2	50.1	49.9	51.8	54.1	51.3	100
Educ: median s. yrs.	US	10.5	10.7	10.5	9.8	8.7	9.9	100
% qual or stdy	AUS	27.0	27.9	23.4	18.8	14.6	22.8	71
% Women married	US	63.0	64.0	63.5	65.4	70.7	66.0	94
	AUS	62.8	65.1	66.5	69.5	75.0	67.5	70
% male age 65+ Nt Wht	US	40.4	41.9	42.2	43.8	52.7	45.7	85
total	AUS	39.1	41.3	44.3	47.5	53.0	44.5	63
% of migs. from farms	US	2.9	7.7	13.9	20.9	58.4	24.8	80
% pop rural in-migs.	AUS	.8	1.8	3.6	5.6	8.8	3.8	65
Fertility ratio **	US	453	506	524	584	733	576	75
	AUS	402	415	477	541	602	478	63
% fgn. born white	US	13.9	6.4	4.8	3.9	2.9	6.7	17
% SE Eur. born	AUS	9.8	5.6	2.1	1.9	1.7	5.2	5
% native born: white	US	75.7	82.9	86.2	88.0	85.4	82.8	0
total	AUS	73.7	77.2	87.6	90.6	92.1	82.3	25
% unemployed	US	5.4	4.5	4.7	4.8	3.5	4.5	63
	AUS	1.5	1.9	2.2	1.9	1.5	1.7	50
% male clerks	US	9.8	8.6	6.9	5.4	2.7	6.5	59
	AUS	10.6	10.8	6.6	4.8	2.3	7.5	52
% women in Lab Force	US	33.6	34.0	33.2	29.3	18.9	28.4	97
	AUS	47.0	40.8	34.7	33.4	32.1	39.2	17
% women clerks	US	35.0	30.7	24.8	20.9	14.0	24.7	51
	AUS	46.4	48.2	44.3	38.2	26.9	40.8	89

* "Urban-rural effect" is the percent of change from very large cities to rural communities attributable to the difference between medium-sized cities and rural areas.

** Base is no. of women 20-44 for the U.S.; 15-44 for Australia

Sources: U.S. data - Hatt and Reiss (1956), Tables 3,6,8,9,23,26,29,32,33, Fig. II & accompanying text; Australian data - Sweetser (1982), Appendix Table D.

variable	r	variable	r
% male, total	.89	% foreign born	.97
education	.80	% native born	.86
% women married	.95	% unemployed	.16
% male, 65+	.92	% male clerks	.97
rural migrants	.96	% women in L.F.	.64
fertility ratio	.95	% women clerks	.92

All the correlations are positive, ten of twelve are at 80 or above, and the mean coefficient is +.83, even when the discrepant very low r for unemployment is included in the calculation. One could scarcely ask for a closer general correspondence of indicators from different countries. Clearly, the marked variation among these indicators associated with changes in city size and urban-rural location tends to be very similar in Australia and the United States.

The urban-rural and city size effects

A glance down the last column of Table 12.3 will show that indexes of urban-rural effect exhibit values of the same order of magnitude for ten of the twelve cross-national comparisons. Values are relatively high at 63 to 100 for the first six variable pairs; relatively low at 0 to 25 (implying high indexes of city size effect at 75 to 100) for the next two; and intermediate in value at 50 to 63 for the next two. Only for the last two pairs of variables are there wide differences between index values for the two countries: there is a gap of 80 points for women in the labour force, and one of 38 points for women clerks. Patterns of urban-rural and city size influence are thus shown to be very similar in the United States and Australia for four-fifths of the variables studied, with six showing a definite preponderence of urban-rural effect, and two an equally definite weighting of city size effect, while two more display a balance of urban-rural and city size influence.

Figures 12.1-4 have been prepared to accentuate the bearing of the data of Table 12.3 on this major conclusion. All four figures distinguish the urban-rural from the city size effect graphically, indicating the relative amount of influence that may be attributed to each for each variable. The six pairs of variables listed first in Table 12.3 and illustrating a dominant urban-rural effect are shown in Figure 12.1. these include two measures of sex composition, education, women married, rural migrants and the fertility ratio.

Figure 12.2 contains the two pairs of variables measuring native and foreign birth, both of which display a massive city size effect for both countries. Differences in ethnic proportions are large among larger cities, but virtually non-existant among small cities and rural communities, on average. Pronounced city size effects were much more prominent in the Australian study, accounting for almost half of the significant gradients discovered. Even allowing for possible bias in the variable matching procedure, this suggests that the passage of time and increasing urbanization may have tended to mute urban-rural effects in favour of city size effects on neighbourhood and community characteristics. This notion finds some additional support in Table 12.3. Indexes of urban-rural effects are larger than for Australia in nine comparisons, equal in one, and lower in two. This could mean that the urban-rural effect was stronger - and the city size effect weaker - in the United States of 1950 than in the more highly urbanized Australia of 1971. Although speculative on the present data, this seems a credible hypothesis which merits systematic testing.

Figure 12.3 displays two variables for which the effects of city size and urban-rural differences are relatively balanced, with both indexes close to 50. There is a rather steady diminution of percents of employed men in clerical occupations in both countries as one moves from very large to large, to medium-sized, to small cities and on to rural communities. The unemployment variable shows a like pattern for the United States; but as previously noted, city size and urban rural effects are equal and opposite for Australia.

Finally, in Figure 12.4, relative city size and urban-rural effects of two measures of feminine economic activity are presented. U.S. 1950 percents of women in the labour force are not only generally lower than in the Australia of 1971, but they also display a very strong urban-rural effect, with an index of 97. This is due to the near-identity of mean percents for the three large community size classes at 33.6, 34.0, and 33.2 (Table 12.3), and their sharp diminution to 29.3 and 18.9 in small cities and rural communities. For Australia, however, the index of city size effect is 83 (inferred from Table 12.3 and Figure 12.4), and although the trend of mean values is downward from very large cities to rural communities, all the action occurs in the first three steps from 47.0 percent working women in the

FIGURE 12.1 DOMINANT URBAN-RURAL GRADIENTS

United States and Australia

```
---------------------------------------------------------------------
                          | city size effect   | URBAN-RURAL EFFECT |
Variable Pair      Nation |        =.....      |       =******      |
                          0........25........50........75........100
                          100******75********50********25**********0
--------------------------|-----------------------------------------|
                   US     |*****************************************|
% male, tot, adult        |                                         |
                   AUS    |*****************************************|
--------------------------|-----------------------------------------|
                   US     |*****************************************|
Education                 |                                         |
                   AUS    |............*****************************|
--------------------------|-----------------------------------------|
                   US     |..***************************************|
Women married             |                                         |
                   AUS    |............*****************************|
--------------------------|-----------------------------------------|
                   US     |.....************************************|
% male age 65+            |                                         |
                   AUS    |...............**************************|
--------------------------|-----------------------------------------|
                   US     |........*********************************|
Rural migrants            |                                         |
                   AUS    |..............***************************|
--------------------------|-----------------------------------------|
                   US     |..........*******************************|
Fertility ratio           |                                         |
                   AUS    |...............**************************|
---------------------------------------------------------------------
```

FIGURE 12.2 DOMINANT CITY SIZE GRADIENTS

United States and Australia

```
---------------------------------------------------------------------
                          | city size effect   | URBAN-RURAL EFFECT |
Variable Pair      Nation |        =.....      |       =******      |
                          0........25........50........75........100
                          100******75********50********25**********0
--------------------------|-----------------------------------------|
                   US     |..................................*******|
Foreign born              |                                         |
                   AUS    |.......................................**|
--------------------------|-----------------------------------------|
                   US     |.........................................|
Native born               |                                         |
                   AUS    |...............................**********|
---------------------------------------------------------------------
```

FIGURE 12.3 BALANCED SIZE-TYPE GRADIENTS

United States and Australia

```
------------------------------------------------------------------------------
                             | city size effect    | URBAN-RURAL EFFECT   |
Variable Pair         Nation |       =.....        |       =******        |
                             0........25........50........75........100
                             100******75********50********25*********0
-----------------------------|----------------------------------------|
                   US        |...............*************************|
Unemployed                   |                                        |
                   AUS       |....................********************|
-----------------------------|----------------------------------------|
                   US        |.................***********************|
Male Clerks                  |                                        |
                   AUS       |...................*********************|
------------------------------------------------------------------------------
```

FIGURE 12.4 CONTRASTING SIZE-TYPE GRADIENTS

United States and Australia

```
------------------------------------------------------------------------------
                             | city size effect    | URBAN-RURAL EFFECT   |
Variable Pair         Nation |       =.....        |       =******        |
                             0........25........50........75........100
                             100******75********50********25*********0
-----------------------------|----------------------------------------|
                   US        |.***************************************|
Women in Lab Force           |                                        |
                   AUS       |.................................*******|
-----------------------------|----------------------------------------|
                   US        |....................********************|
Women clerks                 |                                        |
                   AUS       |....************************************|
------------------------------------------------------------------------------
```

very large cities to 40.8 per cent in large cities and 34.7 per cent in medium-sized cities. At that point the gradient abruptly flattens and small city and rural community means, at 33.4 and 32.1 per cent respectively, are little different from the mean of medium-sized cities.

The other pair of variables in Figure 12.4, percents of working women in clerical occupations, have a very regular downward gradient for the United States with the two effect indexes nearly equal at 51 (rural-urban) and 49 (city size). But for Australia, the urban-rural effect dominates (index=89), and there are very small differences among the three larger city sizes, followed by a sharp drop to lower means in small cities and especially in rural communities.

Absolute variable values

There is one more - somewhat surprising - evidence of Australian-American similarity in Table 12.3; in spite of temporal and spatial separation, absolute values of half the pairs of more closely comparable variables are remarkably like.[8] Ratios of U.S. to Australian national means are as follows :

variable	ratio	variable	ratio
% male, total	.96	fertility ratio	1.21
% women married	.98	% foreign born	1.29
% male, 65+	1.03	% unemployed	2.65
% native born	1.01	% women in L.F.	.72
% male clerks	.87	% women clerks	.61

The virtual identity of national means for two measures of sex composition, proportions of women married, and nativity (all of which fall within four percentage points across the two countries) suggest that the Australia of 1971 and the United States of 1950 were remarkably alike in these basic aspects of demographic structure. Even the proportion of men in clerical occupations, for which the cross-national difference is only 13 percentage points, is fairly similar. For the fertility ratio and the per cent foreign born, at the head of the second column above, the indicated 20 or 30 percent higher values for the United States is partly artifactual: for both variables, the Australian means would have been larger - and the U.S./Australian ratios therefore smaller - had the exact American formula been used for the Australian data.[9] These two pairs of variables would therefore also appear to be rather similar for the two nations.

The sharp divergence of the percent unemployed, with the United States mean two-and-two-thirds of the Australian, may be at least partly explained by the temporal difference, since the U.S. was still in the throes of the post-World War II recession when the census was taken in April of 1950. Probably the traditionally lower rates of unemployment characteristic of the Australian economy in the 1950s and 1960s also contribute to the contrast.

The substantially lower proportions of women in the labour force in the United States of 1950 than in the Australia of 1971 is primarily a consequence of the broad movement of women into the labour force throughout the urban industrial world in the decades after World War II, which had only started in 1950, but was well developed by 1971. Smaller proportions of women in clerical occupations in the U.S. (the national mean is only 61 percent of the Australian) probably also reflect aspects of the femininization of the labour force and a somewhat greater persistence of traditional women's roles in Australia.

PATTERNS OF URBAN-RURAL AND CITY SIZE CONTINUA

The preceding discussion demonstrates for the United States and Australia generally very close similarities in the patterning of differences of a dozen social indicators along the continuum from very large through large, medium-sized and small cities to rural communities. As predicted, both urban-rural and city size effects are clearly evident in the data, and they are manifested in almost identical ways for most variables in both nations. The proposition that two modes of linear differentiation, one relating to city size, and one to the urban-rural contrast, explain many of the differing characteristics of neighbourhoods and communities in urban industrial societies is strongly supported by these findings.

NOTES

1. Frank L. Sweetser, **Urban Residential Areas in Australia**, Canberra: The Australian National University Press (forthcoming, 1982).
2. Richard Dewey, "The Rural-Urban Continuum: Real but Relatively Unimportant", **American Journal of Sociology**, 56, no. 1 (1960), pp. 65 ff; Otis D. Duncan and Albert J. Reiss, Jr., **Social Characteristics of Urban**

and Rural Communities, 1950, New York: John Wiley & Sons, 1956.

3. The quotes are from Oscar Lewis, "Urbanization without a breakdown: A Case Study:. **The Scientific Monthly,** 75 (July 1952).
4. These 41 variables revealed "significant gradients"; that is, two or more successive significant differences across the five community size-type classes from very large cities to rural communities. Cf. Sweetser, **op. cit.,** pp. 155,6.
5. The values for the U.S. variables are weighted means, with the distribution of total U.S. population in 1950 providing the weights.
6. Computation of the index of urban-rural effect was accomplished algebraically. This required adjustments of three extremes falling a few points above 100 or below zero to the 0 to 100 scale. In one instance, % unemployed in Australia, there was no difference between the very large city and the rural means, and the index could not be evaluated because it called for a division by 0. However, city size and urban rural differences for this variable were equal (though in opposite directions), justifying the assignment of a value of 50 (percent) to each index.
7. The exception is the unemployment variable for Australia, which increases from very large to medium-sized cities, but decreases from medium-sized cities to rural communities. The variable thus displays two opposite gradients (both significant): one attributable to an urban size effect, and one to a an urban-rural effect.
8. Variables measuring educational attainment and in-migration from rural areas, although providing indicators of the same phenomena in the two countries, are incommensurate.
9. The Australian formula for the fertility ratio included females age 15-19 in the denominator; excluding them as in the American formula would decrease the denominator, making the computed fertility ratio larger. For the percent foreign born, the Australian numerator - and the computed percentage - would have been larger had all foreign born been included as in the American measure.

SECTION THREE

DELINEATION OF UMLAND IN INDIA

THIRTEEN

Ram Swaroop Dixit

Glimpses of the Umland of a Metropolis

The Case of Kanpur

UMLAND

The Term 'umland' is no longer a new jargon in the literature of urban geography. 'city hinterland has been an active field of research for some time past and hinter-land studies have been made in different parts of the world' (Dikshit and Sawant, 1968, p.2). Apart from the work on city region and hinterland done by planners and economists in India and abroad, the geographers have also substantially contributed to the delineation of the umlands of various urban centres. However, only a few scholars have gone deep to unfold the controversy of genesis of the term 'umland'. Further, hardly any Indian geographer has endeavoured to present a systematic treatment of such studies. Here, an attempt has been made to answer a few questions, viz., what is the real origin of the term 'umland'? How far are the city and its umland the two facets of the one and the same organic whole? What empirical and quantitative approaches have been introduced as parameters to delimit an umland? To what extent have the geographers contributed to such studies in India?

Concept of Umland

Origin and meaning

The genesis and use of the term 'umland' provides an interesting study. Credit goes to Allix (1914), a French Professor, who traced the term 'umland' in a German-French Dictionary. He used it to express his concept of 'economic domain', an interior city as distinct from the hinterland of a port (Allix, 1922). Dodge (1932), and Whittlesey (1937) adopted it in the same sense in their studies. For Whittlesey, umland meant "immediately tributary area extending 30 or 40 miles around a city." Vancleef (1941) included in the umland those communities that work locally within the political limits of the primary centre and its hinterland. Gilbert (1951) views that the origin of the word 'umland' must have been related to the Swedish word 'omland' which has the same connotation. The French word 'Banlieue' (Garnier et al., 1967) also has the same meaning although it is less clear as compared to the term 'umland'. In later studies, the term has been used by several urban geographers and many synonyms have also been put forth. However, most of the geographers have opted for the term 'umland' and hold it to be of the German origin.

Among the Indian geographers, Singh (1955) defined the term 'umland' in his pioneer study on Banaras 'as the area in which the region and city are socio-culturally, economically, and politically interrelated.' Stamp (1961) followed this explanation in his glossary of geographical terms. Several Indian scholars, in the later studies, have used the term in the same sense. Dikshit and Sawant (1968) have used the term 'hinterland' for an inland centre like Poona and have remarked that such a region is defined on the basis of nexus of relationship where the building force of the region expresses itself in the circulation of goods, movement of people, flow of ideas, and a considerable degree of interdependence between the core and the periphery. Dutta (1963) in his study of 'Umland of Jamshedpur' has leaned towards Vancleef.

In fact, whatever the terms have been used they all mean that the 'umland' is a tributary area immediately around the city and functionally (economically, socio-culturally, and politically) integrated with it. In terms of regional taxonomy, it is a functional/nodal region.

City-umland relations

Jefferson (1931) was the first to emphasize the role of umland in the growth of a town. 'Cities do not grow of themselves but it is the countryside which sets them to do tasks which must be performed by them' (Jefferson, 1931, p. 453). The definition and delimitation of umland, as aptly remarked by Stamp (1961, p.167) becomes actually a matter of definite practical importance in commerce and industry. The natural conditions of the umland, the character of its people and their ways of life contribute greatly to the fashioning of the city' (Spelt, 1970, p.270). City does not bloom and exist by itself or in isolation. 'Urban centres do not live for themselves and by themselves but they grow out of their umlands and serve them. They epitomise the regional culture and act as the central and co-ordinating institutions through the services they render' (Singh, 1965, pp. 70-71).

The role of umland has considerably increased in the present age of industrialization/urbanization. Besides, supplying foodgrains to the city dwellers and absorbing the new-comers who no longer wish to settle exclusively in the city proper, it provides the city dwellers several opportunities to relax themselves from congested and noisy conditions of the city itself which generally lack in open space. The prosperity of town depends upon the prosperity of the umland. Smailes (1967, p. 129) has also observed and remarked that the towns are not only in the country but they are of it. Town and the country area are mutually interdependent-economically and socially. In the past the production functions of town and country were distinct, the people resided where they worked. Now because of the separation of the place of work and the place of residence, the commuters' stream has become a hallmark. City depends upon its umland for its labour force. Growth and development of a city and its umland are interrelated. For the balanced regional development, city and its umland should be taken as an integrated unit. Municipal boundaries are not the appropriate limits of town-planning. 'If modern town planners want to measure up the task they will have to plan for both city and its umland as one unit' (Spelt, 1970). Thus, the study of umland has become an imperative need for the town and country planners. In the formulation of masterplans for cities, the analysis of the setting, problems, and prospects are always to be worked out in the perspective of city's umland. Hans Carol has emphasized that the town and umland are only two different aspects of one and the same coherent whole. The relationship between city and its umland is so intimate that one puts imprints on the other. Writing on these relations, Kolars and Nystuen (1974, p.56) have aptly remarked, 'the journey to work may be nothing more than a housewife's walking from the bed room to the kitchen in the morning.'

The umland serves the city and the city serves the umland in myriad ways. They weave a closely knit matrix of centripetal and centrifugal forces, inbound and outbound flows of goods, services and ideas. Thus, between city and umland, there is an intrinsic relation. This aspect does demand a serious consideration by the town and country planers who are engaged in formulating prospective regional plans.

Umland delimitation: Parameters

(i) Empirical Approach: In defining the extent of the umland of a city the overriding parameters are the essential services and functions of urban centres. The cities act as administrative headquarters of political divisions and centres of social, cultural and religious organizations. As regards prime economic functions, cities act as centres of employment, as collecting and marketing centres for the produce of their umlands and as distributing points for goods from outside. The natural barriers play a negative role and the human factors a 'positive' one in delimiting the umland of a city. In fact, during the sent age of scientific and technological developments the town-country relationships are dynamic ones due to changing patterns of resource utilization. Consequently, the umland also tends to be flexible.

Dickinson (1930, 1934) in delimiting the regions of various cities applied a number of parameters such as wholesaling, retailing, newspaper circulation and so on. Park and New Comb (1933) adopted newspaper circulation for delimiting the social and economic regions of a city. Harris (1941) included as many as twelve services rendered by city e.g., retail trade, wholesale grocery trade, wholesale drug sale, radio broadcasting, newspaper circulation, religious influence, telephone links, oil distribution, bakery distribution and a few other services. On the basis of these services a generalized boundary of Salt Lake City region was drawn. Touminen (1949) demarcated the umland of Turku taking up the parameters such as traffic flow of school children, shop keepers and patients. Green (1950) worked out the urban hinterlands of various towns in England and Wales on the basis of bus service. He also suggested different types of hinterlands such as commercial, industrial, professional and administrative, and observed that various hinterlands could not exactly coincide. For obtaining an average boundary he feared that the average boundary might not always be a mean boundary. He, therefore, suggested to use the criterion of transport facilities provided and used in the region. Schultze (1951) delimited the sphere of influence of at least forty urban centres employing various urban functions as the parameters. Brush (1953) also made a similar attempt while discussing the urban influence of towns of south-western Wisconsin. Bracey's (1954) attempt for delimiting the service area of Somerset was also based on bus service. Green (1955) in delimiting the umlands of New York City and Boston considered seven indicators, viz., transportation, commuters, communication, agriculture, recreation, manufacturing, and finance. He also analysed the parameters employed by Dickinson and those by the National Resource Committee. Green worked out a composite boundary, the median boundary or middle boundary of the umland. Similarly, Spelt (1958), Ellefeson (1962), Whitelaw (1962), Scott (1964), and Efrat (1964) have delimited the umlands of a couple of towns by adopting various urban functions and services. Vivian Huguette, Blanche Mouteux, Claire Berthe, and Jean Coppolian also made valuable contributions, (Garnier and Chabot, 1967, p. 426). Smailes (1967) advocated social (education, health, entertainment, and cultural), and economic (daily and weekly newspaper circulation, pull of labour force, wholesale and retail sales, and transportation) functions for delimiting such regions. L. Fisher, K. Hock and Eicher adopted the Thunian concentric circles around the centre of the city for delimiting the zone of a city's influence.

Following the tradition of the European and American geographers, the Indian geographers worked out the umlands of various towns, Singh (1955) delimited the umland of Banaras by employing six parameters, viz., vegetable supply, milk supply, newspaper circulation, bus service, agricultural commodity supply, and the administrative links. In later studies, the Indian scholars, however, added a few more parameters such as educational service, health service, police, bank, cinema, retail sales, drug sales, livestocks, fish, rickshaw, bicycle, and bullock cart zones. The other note-worthy attempts made in this direction are: Singh (1956), Vasanta (1957), Tiwari (1958), Singh (1961), Reddy (1961), Nath (1962), Mukherjee (1962), Janaki (1962), Gopalkrishan (1963), Dutta (1963), Dwivedi (1964), Singh R.L. (1964), Singh, M. (1964), Alam (1965), Chatterjee (1965), Saxena (1966), Dikshit and Sawant (1968), Mathur (1968), Mahadeva and Jaishanker (1969), Gopalkrishan and Agarwala (1970), Singh, H.H. (1972), Singh (1972), and Misra (1975).

Many small towns in India do not publish even a single daily newspaper. This criterion, therefore, cannot be applied in all the cases. The commuting, education up to intermediate level, rickshaw, bicycle, retail sales, cinema, banks, vegetable and milk supply zones although assume compact shapes but such umlands are too small. On the other hand, bus service zone provides an irregular shape over a vast region. The services rendered by drug sales, hospitals, police, and administration provide by and large a medium size umland. Most of the geographers view that the umlands delimited on the basis of empirical studies present vague boundaries because the umlands of nearby cities generally interpenetrate therefore precise delimitation is a difficult task. Generally, the boundaries are defined by superimposing the unifunctional zones and making minor adjustments with administrative boundaries. It is noteworthy that the various functional zones of a city are not co-terminus as well as the urban influences exhibit a characteristic gradient. Consequently, according to the degree of influence of the central city, the surrounding region may be graded into primary, secondary and even tertiary umlands. Thus a hierarchical organization exists in the cobweb system of umlands of a city.

ii. Quantitative or theoretical Approach: Recently, mathematical models have been fairly used in explaining the structure of urban areas and problems of urban development. The gravity and potential models have been employed in solving problems, viz., market analysis for shopping centre location, population and migration forecasting, traffic flow analysis, and allocation of land for residence, business, industrial and other uses. Carrothers (1956) made a successful attempt to present the historical development and use of mathematical formulations in human sciences.

Sir Issac Newton formulated his laws of gravitation in 1687. Carey (1958) introduced the gravity concept in social sciences. Ravenstein (1885) and Young (1924) incorporated similar ideas in laws of migration of population. Reilly (1929, 1931) used the gravity model in delineating the trade areas between competing towns on the basis of his empirical observations. His formula is as follows:

$$\frac{Ba}{Bb} = \frac{(Pa}{(Pb} \ \frac{Db^2)}{Da^2)} \quad \ldots \ \ldots \ \ldots \qquad (1)$$

Where

Ba = the proportion of the retail business from an intermediate town attracted by city A,

Bb = the proportion of the retail business from an intermediate town attracted by city B,

Pa = the population of city A,
Pb = the population of city B,
Da = the distance from the intermediate town to city A, and
Db = the distance from the intermediate town to city B.

Converse (1948, 1949) modified Reilly's formula to calculate the approximate point between two competing cities where the trading influence of each was equal. As a consequence, a city's retail trading area could be delineated by simply calculating and connecting the breaking-points between it and each of the competing cities in the region (Huff, 1964). The breaking-point formula derived by Converse (1949) is:

$$Db \quad \frac{Dab}{1 + \sqrt{\frac{Ma}{Mb}}} \qquad \ldots \quad \ldots \quad \ldots \quad (2)$$

Where
Db = the breaking point between city A and city B (in distance units from B),
Dab = the distance separating city A from city B,
Ma = the size of city A, and
Mb = the size of city B.

Some Indian geographers (Singh, 1960; Rao, 1964; Dutta, 1966, Mahadeva and Jaishankar, 1969; Singh H.H. 1972; Misra, 1975) have adopted mathematical formulations for delimiting the spheres of influence of urban centres. Rao (1964) used his model for designing a map for locational analysis of towns of Mysore state. Dutta (1966) formulated an index for measuring the average radius of consumer catchment areas of markets. In their study on Mysore city, Mahadeva and Jaishankar (1969) suggested a modified form of Newton's law as the following construct:

$$Ii = \frac{Pi \quad \alpha\beta r}{dij \quad xy} \qquad \ldots \quad \ldots \quad \ldots \quad (3)$$

Where

Ii = the propensity index of town i,
Pi = the population of town i,

$\alpha \beta r$ = the weights on population,
dij = the distance between town i and town j, and
xy = the weights on distance.

Singh H.H. (1972) used a vague expression to delimit the umland of Kanpur. Misra (1975) in his study on Allahabad makes use of two forms of gravity models. While delimiting the umland of Allahabad he adopts the interaction model, for delimiting the umlands of the small towns he uses the breaking-point equation. (Nagia (1976) has made an attempt to delimit the Delhi Metropolitan Region on the basis of both the characteristics of some formal and functional indicators.

An overview of the above discussion reveals that the Indian geographers, following their colleagues abroad, have made attempts for delineating the umlands of some Indian cities, mostly on empirical observations. However, a few attempts have been made for testing the empirical boundaries by quantitative techniques. The author feels that the only meaningful empirical boundaries are those which can be tested and verified by mathematical formulations and field work (Dixit, 1979, pp. 27-39).

THE UMLAND OF KANPUR

Of late, Kanpur has acquired the distinction of being one of the metropolitan cities of India. It has certainly been the industrial metropolis of Uttar Pradesh. Trade and commerce have further accelerated its growth and development (Dixit, 1977, p. 77). As regards the Umland of Kanpur, the author has tried to answer two very pertinent questions viz., what attempts have been made in the direction of the delimitation of the Umland of Kanpur? What is the rational and reasonable Umland of Kanpur at present? Thus the theory of the concept has been applied herewith to resolve the problem of the delimitation of the Umland of the Metropolis, Kanpur (Dixit, 1979, pp. 39-66).

Previous approaches

Several attempts have been made for the delineation of the region/umland of Kanpur. Of these, the work done by the Planning Commission (1965, pp. 39-40) merits the first attention. The planning commission listed the Kanpur-Lucknow region comprising Kanpur, Lucknow, and Unnao districts for metropolitan development. For agricultural development it listed Kanpur, Etawah, and Farrukhabad under the south-western Uttar Pradesh, Plain. From the point of view of industrial development and urban growth, Nath (1966, pp. 29-31) listed Kanpur and Lucknow in one region. Sharma and Norman (1966, p. 1), while delimiting Kanpur region in terms of dispersion of industries and population, conceptualized an integrated and comprehensive economic and social development of Kanpur oriented region. An attempt to delimit the Kanpur region was made also by the Town and Country Planning Department (pp. 478-504) of Uttar Pradesh. The objective behind the study was to prepare a masterplan for the metropolitan region of Kanpur. To measure the extent of the region, the department employed the empirical parameters such as: vegetable, milk and foodgrains supplies to Kanpur, and newspaper circulation, medical service, and bus service outflowing from the Metropolis. The study led to the delimitation of the umland of Kanpur comprising Bilhaur, Bhognipur, Akbarpur, Ghatampur, and Kanpur tahsils of Kanpur district; Bindki and Fatehpur tahsils of Fatehpur district; Purwa and Unnao tahsils of Unnao district; Auraiya tahsil of Etawah; and Kannauj tahsil of Farrukhabad district.

Tripathi (1966, pp. 14-15) included thirty tahsils in the secondary as against ten tahsils in the primary region. Desai (1969, p. xvii) referred to the extent of the Kanpur region as delineated by the Research Cell of the Indian Institute of Technology, Kanpur (1967) constituted for the purpose, extending for 250 kms in east-west and 160 kms in north-south direction. It consisted of the districts of Kanpur, Farrukhabad, Etawah, Jalaun, Hamirpur, Fathepur (excluding Khaga tahsil), Banda (excluding Mau, and Karwi tahsils), and a narrow stretch of land lying to the south of Unnao and Hardoi road of Hardoi district. Bose (1969, p. 132), from the point of view of policy formulation noted that the exclusion of Lucknow and inclusion of the three backward Bundelkhand districts of Uttar Pradesh i.e., Banda, Hamirpur, and Jalaun in the umland of Kanpur was not helpful for its integrated socio-economic development. Rajgopalan (1969, p. 141) holds that the region is within a parallelogram formed by connecting the surrounding four cities of Agra, Jhansi, Allahabad, and Lucknow. It measures on an average, 241 kms from east to west and 161 kms from north to south, Thomas (1969, p. 311) conceptualized the Kanpur region comprising the eight districts of Banda (excluding Mau and Karwi tahsils), Etawah, Jalaun, Hamirpur, Fatehpur (excluding Khaga tahsil), Farrukhabad, Kanpur and Unnao.

Agarwala's studies (1967, pp. 10-12; 1969, pp. 7-35) related to the economic-agricultural aspects of the metropolitan region of Kanpur accept the limits laid down by the International Seminar held at the Indian Institute of Technology, Kanpur in 1967.

Singh, H.H. (1972, pp. 122-132), While delimiting the umland of Kanpur, considered as many as seven indices, such as: bus service, medical service, educational service, commuting labour, vegetable supply, milk supply, and newspaper circulation. Thus, the delimited primary umland extends for 155 kms in length and 90 kms in width. The secondary umland extends for about 360 kms in length and 170 kms in width. The boundary of the secondary umland runs so as to leave Lucknow about 20 kms to north east, Rai-Bareli about 10 kms to east, Allahabad about 70 kms to south east, Kasganj about 8 kms to north, and Shahjáhanpur about 15 kms. This boundary goes beyond Panna (M.P.) for about 15 kms, Bhind (M.P.) about 5 kms and Shikohabad about 10 kms. Thus, it embraces far distant places and the places which are closer to other big cities, viz., Panna, Chattarpur etc. Singh also claims that the umland, thus delimited, was verified statistically. But, in fact, his findings seem to be somewhat erroneous as the primary and the secondary umlands are too small and too big in size respectively.

Delimitation and typology

Dixit (1977, pp. 77-92) made an attempt to resolve the problem on the basis of meaningful and measurable empirical parameters which have been further tested by quantitative techniques.

In this connection, the following inflows and outflows of goods and services are of great use and, therefore, these are employed as parameters to measure the extent of the empirical umland of Kanpur (Table 13.1)

(i) Inflows—IF/1 Milk Supply Zone: The metropolitan city of Kanpur depends upon its umland for the supply of milk to its inhabitants. The Kanpur Gaushala Samiti, the Government Agricultural College Dairy, the Military Dairy, the Kanpur Milk Board, and milk sheds of milkmen, the 'gwalas' and 'ghosis', distribute milk to the city. The Co-operative dairy, private dairies, and individual milkmen collect milk from various places in the surrounding area of Kanpur with the help of various agencies.

The milkmen bring over 1,25,000 liters of milk daily

from all directions of Kanpur by bicycles. On Kalpi Road: Akbarpur, Bara, Rania, Bhauti, and Munidpur; on Bela Bithoor Road: Ganasarpur, Gambhirpur, Bikunthapur, and Dalipnagar; on Kannauj Road: Bilhaur, Uttaripurwa, Chaubeypur, Shivarajpur, and Mandhana; on Fatehpur Road: Sirsaul, Maholi, Narwal, Prempur, Tikra, and Bansar; on Unnao Road: Shuklaganj, Magarwara, Safipur, Achalganj, Makhi, Karori, and Ugu; on Hamirpur Road: Kathara, Shambhua, Bidhnu, Patara, and Bhingawan are the important milk supplying centres. The bulk of milk supply amounting to 1,25,000 liters daily is brought by those who bring milk on trains from Araul, Unnao, Bindiki Road, Bhimsen, and other stations on the Central, the North-Eastern, and the Northern railway upto 50 kms or about two hour-time-distance (from Kanpur). Thus, about 3,00,000 liters of milk is brought to the Metropolitan city daily which meets about 82% of the city's demand for milk.

TABLE 13.1

Inflow and outflow of goods and services

	Inflow/outflow of goods and services	Metropolis of Kanpur
(A)	Milk Supply	A. IF/1
(B)	Vegetable Supply	B. IF/2
(C)	Labour Supply	C. IF/3
(D)	Foodgrain Supply	D. IF/4
(E)	Medical-Health Service	A. OF/1
(F)	Educational Service	B. OF/2
(G)	Newspaper Circulation	C. OF/3
(H)	Bus Service	E. IF/5 / D. OF/4

Various co-operative societies, more particularly the one which is located in Niralanagar, collect milk through their agencies or branches at various centres on different roads radiating from Kanpur particularly Fatehpur Road, Kannauj Road, Kalpi Road, and Hamirpur Road. The Milk Board collects about 12,000 liters of milk daily through its forty collecting centres. Across the Ganga, the influence is limited due to the physical barrier i.e., the river Ganga and in addition to this the proximity of Lucknow also inversely affects the supplies to Kanpur from the Ganga Par area.

The zone, thus, extends for about 110 kms north-west to south-east and about 55 km north-east to south-west (Fig. 13.1).

F

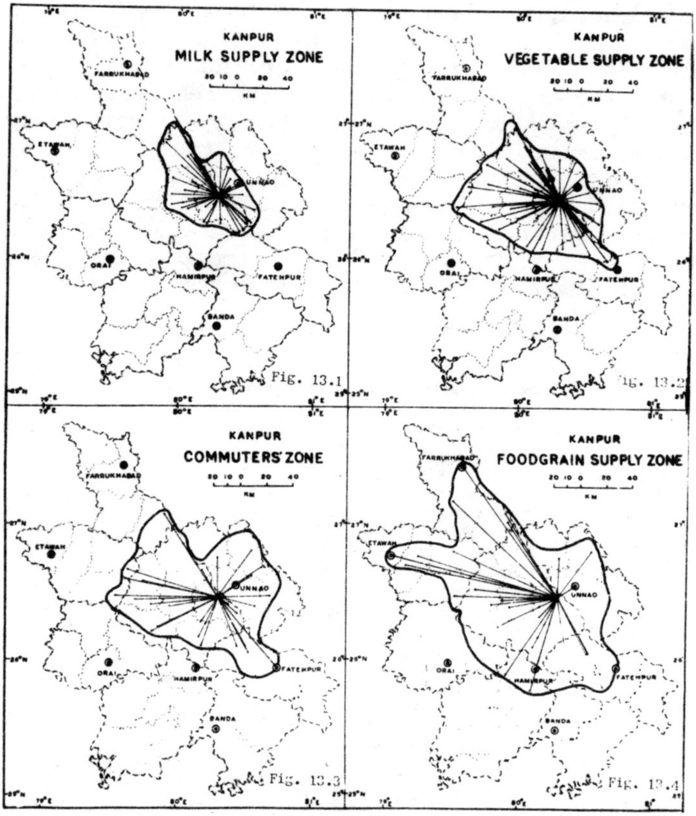

Fig. 13.1 Fig. 13.2 Fig. 13.3 Fig. 13.4

IF/2 Vegetable Supply Zone: Vegetables to the city are supplied by a vast area surrounding the Metropolitan city. The city is a wholesale market for vegetables and fruits. Big vegetable markets ('subji mandies') are located in Badshahinaka, Nawabganj, and Sisamau. Among others, mention may be made of Jhuhiki Chauki on Hamirpur Road, Ghasiari Mandi on Canal Road, Aryanagar, Gwaltoli, Parade, Dwarikapuri, Gumti No. 5, Hariharnath Shastrinagar, Kalyanpur, Govindnagar, Jajmau, Rawatpur, Chakeri, Kidwainagar, and Armapur Estate, Bullock carts, bicycles, rickshaws, horse-driven carts - 'tongas' and 'ekkas' and trucks are used to transport vegetables to the city. Vegetables are supplied by all the tahsils of Kanpur district and the neighbouring tahsils like Bindki, Fatehpur, Kannauj, Auraiya, Unnao and Purwa. Sometimes far off towns also supply vegetables to the city. Several rivers like Pandu, Arind, Non and Sengur flow in the surrounding plains consisting of 'kachhars' and 'katries' which grow vegetables and fruits even during the dry months of the year. Availability of sandy silt and sandy loam soils as well as good transportation facilities have largely helped the production of vegetables in the city region.

All types of green vegetables including cabbage, cauliflower, ladies-finger, brinjal, green-peas, tomato, green leaves, and salads as well as durable vegetables such as jack-fruit, onion and potato, etc., are grown in the surrounding areas of Kanpur. The Ganga-Pandu lowland track has specialized in fresh vegetable production. The vegetable collecting centres have developed on all the roads radiating from the city. Main centres are Bindki Road, Mahrajpur, Uttaripurwa, Shivarajpur, Chaubepur, Kannauj, Magarwara, Sachendi and Bindhnu.

The zone, thus, extends for about 140 kms north-west to south-east and about 70 kms north-east to south-west (Fig. 13.2).

IF/3 Commuters' Zone: The term 'Labour-shed' is commonly applied to that area from which a city draws commuting labourers. So far, not much study has been made of this concept but labour-sheds are beginning to receive increasing attention from urban analysts (Alexander, 1963, p. 556). Kanpur is the only industrial metropolis of Uttar Pradesh. Commerce and manufacturing are the fundamental characteristics of this metropolitan city. Various industries of national level such as Chemical (e.g. I.E.L.), Iron and Steel (e.g. Singh Engineering Works), Cotton Textiles (Elgin

Mills), Woollen (Lal-Imli), Vanaspati (Ganesh Mills), Jute (J.K. Mills), Defence (ordnance Factory and Small Arms Factory) and many others are located in Kanpur. Although labour force comes from the states of Bihar, Madhya Pradesh, and Rajasthan but commuting labourers come from the surrounding districts, i.e., Unnao, Farrukhabad, Etawah, Jalaun, Hamirpur, Banda, Rai-Bareli, and Fatehpur only.

The commuters' zone extends for about 130 kms north-west to south-east and 70 kms north-east to south-west (Fig.13.3)

IF/4 Foodgrain Supply Zone: The city depends upon its umland for its foodgrains and raw materials such as wheat, gram, 'Jowar', 'bajra', barley, peas, cotton, oil seeds and sugar cane etc. The noteworthy granary of collectorganj draws agricultural produce from a vast region. Apart from the wholesale grain market of Collectorganj many new grain markets have come up in the city. Govindnagar, Gwaltoli, and Deputy-ka-Parao are worth mentioning. The city of Kanpur is surrounded by riverine plain, rich in alluvial soil with very high fertility, and enough facilities for irrigation resulting into large agricultural yield in respect of both quantity and quality. Transportation facilities are sufficiently available. Various means of transport: bullock carts, trucks and railways are employed for transporting foodgrains to Kanpur. Consequently, one-third part of Rai-Bareli; one-half of Banda; two-thirds of Fatehpur; in addition to the districts of Kanpur, Unnao, Farrukhabad, Etawah, Jalaun and Hamirpur send foodgrains to Kanpur. Several grain-markets have come up as collecting centres in different parts of the umland. Chhibramau and Gursahaiganj in Farrukhabad; Pukharayan, Ghatampur and Rura in Kanpur; Kalpi in Jalaun; and Bindki in Fatehpur are of great significance. The centres of secondary importance are: Rasdhan, Narwal, Rajpur, Sachendi, and Akbarpur of Kanpur; Phaphun, Bharathana, Bidhuna, and Auraiya of Etawah; Kaimganj, Kannauj, and Taligram of Farrukhabad; Khajuha and Jahanabad of Fatehpur; and Safipur and Bangarmau of Unnao districts.

The intensive foodgrain supply zone, thus, extends for about 160 kms north-west to south-east and about 90 kms north-east to south-west (Fig. 13.4).

ii. Outflows Of/1 Medical/health Service Zone: Kanpur attracted patients from far distant places but due to the pull factor of the medical colleges at Jhansi, Agra, Allahabad, and Lucknow the sphere of influence of the city has shrunk although the number of patients pushed to Kanpur has increased (due to considerable increase in population of the Umland) in spite of the fact that there is a dearth of facilities available to all patients in Kanpur. A large number of Mahapalika dispensaries serve the local population. A large number of people are attracted by various medical centres and institutes providing specialised treatment such as the Murari Lal Chest Institute , the J.K. Institute of Cancer and Radiology, the Laxmipat Singhania Institute of Cardiology, the Kamlapat Singhania Institute of Medicine, and the Dwarika Nath Bagla Infectious Disease Hospital. These centres attract the patients from far off places but percentage of such patients is very low.

The centres attracting a considerably large number of patients from the surrounding areas are the Lala Lajpat Rai Hospital (serving most of the patients from the districts of Farrukhabad, Etawah, and Jalaun; and Akbarpur, Derapur and Bilhaur Tahsils of Kanpur district); and the Ursala Horseman Memorial Hospital (serving most of the patients from southern part of Unnao, south-west Rai-Bareli, western Fatehpur; and northern parts of Banda and Hamirpur districts). Apart from the above two centres there are other important hospitals extending medical services to the surrounding districts. The Ganesh Shanker Vidyarthi Medical College, the Dufferin Hospital, the Kamlapat Memorial Hospital, the upper India Sugar Exchange Maternity Hospital, the Catherine Hospital, the McRobert Hospital, the Mariampur Hospital, and the Chacha Nehru Children Hospital are worth mentioning units.

Of all the patients drawn by these hospitals and medical institutes etc., 40% belong to Kanpur, 55% to surrounding districts and only 5% belong to far distant places. The patients from far distant places come to Kanpur for treatment because their relatives are settled in the city.

The reasonably compact medical/health service zone of the metropolitan city of Kanpur extends for about 200 kms north-west to south-east and 100 kms north-east to south-west (Fig. 13.5).

OF/2 Educational Service Zone: In recent past, Kanpur had a vast area under the jurisdiction of the Kanpur University. But with the opening of other state universities its area has shrunk. On the other hand, formerly the students were not attracted from far distant places due to the pull factor of the Agra, Lucknow and Allahabad universities, but now due to several professional institutions and research

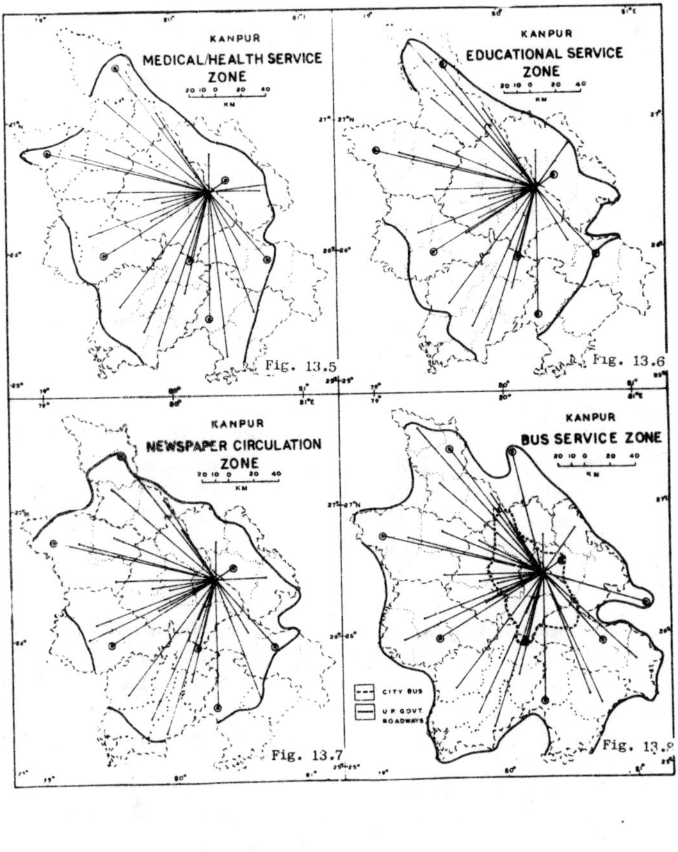

Fig. 13.5 Fig. 13.6 Fig. 13.7 Fig. 13.8

centres (i.e. the Indian Institute of Technology, the Ganesh Shanker Vidyarthi Medical College, the Chandra Shekhar Azad University of Agriculture and Technology, the Harcourt Butler Technological Institute, the National Sugar Research Institute, the Government Textile Institute, the Government Leather Institute, and the Government Polytechnic Institutes etc.) far distant students are also attracted by the city. The percentage of the students from various far distant places is, of course, very small.

On the academic side, there are about 90 high schools and intermediate colleges and 15 degree and post-graducte colleges located in the city imparting education to the students numbering about 9% of the population of the city. The B.N.S.D. Intermediate College and the D.A.V. Post-graduate College are the biggest colleges at their level of education in the state. Among the students, 43% of them are from the locality its 53% come from rural areas of Kanpur and its surrounding districts, and only 4% from far distant places.

The educational service zone of Kanpur is of two types: One which includes the districts under the jurisdiction of the Kanpur University such as Kanpur, Farrukhabad, Mainpuri, Etawah, Sitapur, Hardoi, Kheri, Rai-Bareli and Fatehpur; and the other which includes the places pushing students to the colleges and other institutions of the city. The reasonably compact umland of the second order consists of the districts of Kanpur, Fatehpur, Jalaun, Unnao, Hamirpur, Banda, Jhansi, Etawah, Farrukhabad and Hardoi. This umland extends for about 200 kms north-west to south-east and 150 kms north-east to south-west (Fig. 13.6)

OF/3 Newspaper Circulation Zone: Among the communication services performed by the city, newspaper service stands above all with regard to sphere of city's influence. This index has been considered as a very important criterion in the European and the American countries. The circulation area of local newspapers claims a special importance as a measure and index for a regional set-up. This is the medium through which leadership of the city in the umland is developed. It is a socio-cultural, and economic (by way of advertising in the newspaper) link which unites the region. It spreads the effects of the metropolitan city over a large area. Kanpur publishes nearly a dozen daily newspapers in addition to a few weeklies. Two Urdu dailies and the important Hindi dailies are: Siyasat Jadid, Paigam, Dainik Jagran, Aaj, Vishwamitra, Ganesh, Vir Bharat, Satya Sanwad, Deshmeet, Dainik Gatha, Dainik Lagam, Jai Bharat and Dishera. As regards English dailies, Kanpur had to face hard competition with Lucknow and Delhi therefore it stopped English daily newspapers. However, the most important English Daily has been the 'Daily Action'. The 'Dainik Jagran' which ranks first among the 'dailies' sends not less than twelve hundred copies daily to each of the districts: Farrukhabad, Etawah, Jalaun, Hamirpur, Banda, Fatehpur, Rai-Bareli, Unnao and Lucknow. The 'Dainik Jagran' claims to publish 54,000 copies daily of which about 20,000 copies are circulated in the Umland. The 'Aaj' claims to publish 20,000 copies most of which are circulated locally. The 'Siyasat's claim is only for 12,000 copies. Although Lucknow receives two thousand copies of the 'Dainik Jagran' everyday but there is no reason to include Lucknow in the Umland as Lucknow itself sends its Hindi, English and Urdu dailies to Kanpur even more than twice the number of the 'Dainik Jagran'. The 'Dainik Jagran' also sends its copies to other towns of the state but the number is small.

Thus, the compact newspaper zone of the Metropolitan city extends for about 250 kms north-west to south-east and about 150 kms north-east to south-west (Fig. 13.7).

iii. Inflow and Outflow: Interflow - IF-5/OF-4-Bus Service Zone: Kanpur plays a very important role as the biggest traffic centre in Uttar Pradesh. The deluxe express, and ordinary buses are run and maintained by the state government in addition to the 'mofussil' buses which are run by private organizations very efficiently keeping up schedule-time. Kanpur is well connected with other towns of the state by regular bus services. The city has both the 'City Bus Service' and the 'U.P. Govt. Roadways Bus Service'.

The city buses, run by the Juhi and the Fazalganj depots, ply as long as Jahanabad, Hamirpur, Bindki Road, Bindki, Akbarpur and Araul. Each of the above places is linked with Kanpur having at least two 'to and from' bus services (daily). The influence of city buses is a very important index measuring the extent of umland of a town like Kanpur. Over a dozen city buses ply to and from Kanpur-Bithoor, and Kanpur-Bilhaur daily. The city buses also ply to far off places but their frequency is not so high.

The Roadways Bus Service has a considerably large region under its influence. The Chunniganj and the Collectorganj bus depots run buses to far distant places also, such as Ballia, Deoria, Haldwani, Delhi, Agra, Jhansi, Mirzapur, Mathura, Khajuraho, Varanasi, Basti, Gorakhpur, Azamgarh,

Aligarh, and Sagar etc. But their frequency is less as compared to those for Farrukhabad, Mainpuri, Mahoba, Banda, Allahabad, Faizabad, Sitapur and Hardoi. Not less than four buses ply to and from every hour of the day. Such centres are Hamirpur, Orai, Jalaun, Etawah, Kannauj, Fatehpur, Rai-Bareli, and Sultanpur. The Kanpur-Lucknow route has a frequency as high as 124 buses to and from daily (The U.P. Govt. Roadways had started night bus service long back and is maintaining the same at present too.)

The reasonably compact 'Roadways Bus Service' Zone, thus, extends for about 350 kms north-west to south-east and about 200 kms north-east to south-west (Fig. 13.8).

The city has different sets of umlands on the basis of the variety of functions it performs. The various umlands of a city do not coincide, rather each of them is a single factor region (Dikshit and Sawant, 1968, p.4). So also Singh (1961, p. 38) holds the view that the umland of a metropolitan city may consist essentially of a series of areas rather than one continuous geographical region.

On the basis of the preceding discussion various types of umlands of Kanpur have been identified (Fig. 13.9; Tab.2)

TABLE 13.2

Typology of umlands of Kanpur

Umland	Farthest Length	Extent in km Width
U.P. Govt. Roadways Bus Service Zone	350	200
Newspaper Circulation Zone	250	150
Educational Service Zone	200	150
Medical/Health Service Zone	200	100
Foodgrain Supply Zone	160	90
Vegetable Supply Zone	140	70
Commuters' Zone	130	70
Milk Supply Zone	110	60
City Bus Service Zone	120	60

The necessity of defining a composite umland has been felt over a long time. Dixit (1977, p. 85) has made an attempt in this direction also. Various radii diverging from Kanpur were drawn at 15° interval on the super-imposed map of nine functional zones. Thus 24 radii, cutting all the nine boundaries of the functional zones, were drawn on the map. The median value of each radial-cut was found out and the points thus located were joined serially. The region, thus emerged, is the median umland synthesizing the various umlands of Kanpur.

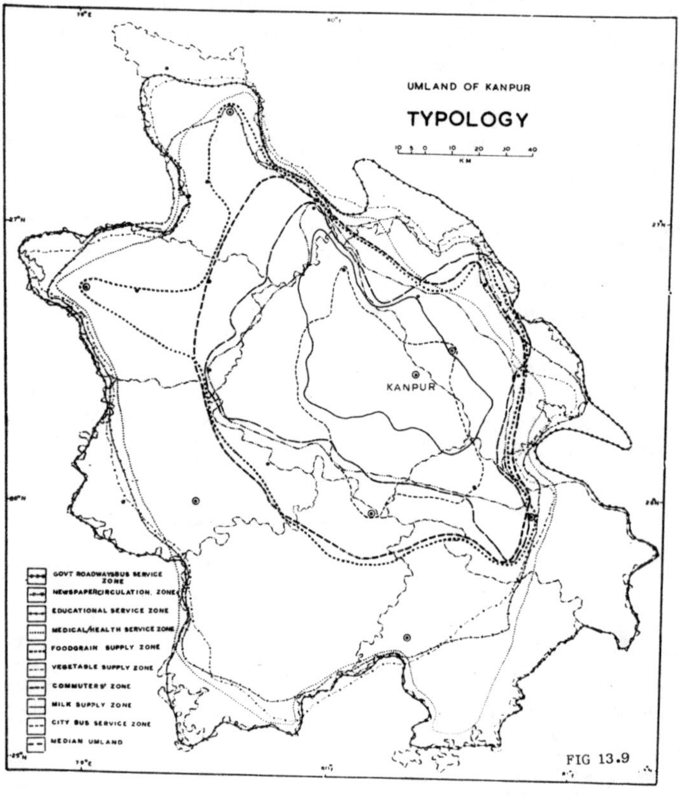
UMLAND OF KANPUR
TYPOLOGY
KM
KANPUR
GOVT ROADWAYSBUS SERVICE ZONE
NEWSPAPERCIRCULATION ZONE
EDUCATIONAL SERVICE ZONE
MEDICAL/HEALTH SERVICE ZONE
FOODGRAIN SUPPLY ZONE
VEGETABLE SUPPLY ZONE
COMMUTERS' ZONE
MILK SUPPLY ZONE
CITY BUS SERVICE ZONE
MEDIAN UMLAND

FIG 13.9

Hierarchy of umlands

After the study of delimitation and typology of the umlands of Kanpur it seems proper to develop a hierarchy of the umlands on the basis of the sum total of intensity of interflows of ideas, goods and services. Every metropolis has a cob-web of umlands from its core to the outer limits. Kanpur is not an exception to this general rule. On the basis of the intensity of 'flows' the following hierarchy has been observed.

i. First Order Umland- It consists of two high intensity zones:

a. Inner Primary Zone: This zone includes Unnao tahsil of Unnao district; Kanpur tahsil, Akbarpur tahsil and Chaubepur Kalan block of Bilhaur tahsil of Kanpur district. The zone more or less conforms to the City Bus Service Zone, Milk and Vegetable Supply Zones, and Commuters' Zone of Kanpur.

b. Outer Primary Zone:- This zone comprises the remaining parts of Kanpur district, Hamirpur tahsil of Hamirpur district, Kalpi tahsil of Jalaun district, Kannauj tahsil of Farrukhabad district, Bindki tahsil of Fatehpur district, and Nawabganj block of Hasanganj tahsil of Unnao district. The zone roughly conforms to the considerably high frequency U.P. Govt. Roadways Bus Service Zone.

ii. Second Order Umland:- This zone consists of Etawah district; Banda, Baberu and Naraini tahsils of Banda district; and rest of the parts of Farrukhabad, Jalaun, Hamirpur, Fatehpur and Unnao districts. Broadly speaking, the zone conforms to the newspaper Circulation, Medical/Health Service, Educational Service and moderately high frequency Roadways Bus Service Zones.. This is the secondary umland.

iii. Third Order Umland:- This zone includes the peripheral areas which also fall under the direct urban influence of any other big city in the surrounding area of Kanpur (e.g. Agra, Allahabad etc.) but in one way or the other they are also linked with Kanpur. Such areas are parts of Etah, Mainpuri, Hardoi, Lucknow, Rai-Bareli, Banda (eastern area), Jhansi, and Bhind (M.P.) districts. This may be called as the tertiary umland of Kanpur.

UMLAND OF KANPUR
HIERARCHY
10 5 0 10 20 30 40
KM
IV HOURS
III HOURS
II HOURS
III HOURS
II HOURS
II HOURS
I HOUR
KANPUR
2 HOURS
3 HOURS
50 KM
III HOURS
4 HOURS
100 KM
IV HOURS
INNER PRIMARY UMLAND
OUTER PRIMARY UMLAND
SECONDARY UMLAND
ISOCHRONES
RADIAL DISTANCE

Fig. 13.10

Figure 13.10, showing radial distances and the isochronic picture of the Umland of Kanpur, indicates that any place in the inner primary zone is not more than 60 kms (from Kanpur) which can be covered by bus within 90 minutes. The outer primary zone is within a radius of 100 kms which does not take more than two and a half hours travel-time for Kanpur. The secondary umland is not beyond 170 kms/five hours of bus journey from Kanpur while the tertiary umland lies beyond these limits.

For all practical purposes the tertiary umland may be neglected and the 'Secondary' may be treated as the real Umland of Kanpur. The Umland, thus derived, justifies that it is closely integrated with the Metropolis of Kanpur. The influence of the Metropolis has been neither over-estimated nor under-estimated to make the Umland unduly too big or too small.

Testing

At this stage it is worthwhile to test the empirical approach by some suitable quantitative techniques. To meet this objective, two well known methods have been employed here: the 'breaking-point-formula' and the 'index of urban influence' of the gravity models as follows :

i. Influence of city B in terms of distance units

$$Db = \frac{Dab}{1 + \sqrt{\frac{Pa}{Pb}}}$$

????

Where Db = the breaking point between city A and City B (in kilometres from B).

Dab = the distance separating city A from City B,

Pa = the population of city A, and

Pb = the population of city B.

(ii) Index of urban influence

$$Iij = \frac{Pi\ Pj}{Dij}$$

Where Iij = the index of influence,

i,j = two cities,

Pi,Pj = the population of two cities respectively, and

Dij = the distance between the two cities.

The first model has been applied to delimit the gravitational pull of Kanpur with reference to Allahabad, Lucknow, Jhansi and Aligarh. The distances have been taken from the Railway Time Tables (N.E.R., N.R., C.R.). For ascertaining the size of the various cities, data, regarding total population; population engaged in trade and commerce; population engaged in industry; and total working population have been taken from the District Census Handbooks (1971). The comparative results of the computations have been shown in Table 13.3. However, the final results of the table are based on the 'total working population' criterion which seems to be more rational. It is clear from Table 13.3 that districts of Kanpur, Unnao, Farrukhabad, Etawah, Fatehpur, Jalaun, Hamirpur, and western two-thirds part of Banda fall under the gravitational pull of Kanpur.

TABLE 13.3

Results of the computation on the first model

Distance from Kanpur (km)	Gravitational pull of Kanpur (km) on the basis of					Distance from Kanpur (Km) (km)	Whether not within Kanpur influence
	Total Population	Popu. in Trade & Commerce	Popu. in Industry	Popu. in Trade Com., & Industry	Total Working Popu.		
Allahabad (192)	117.48	120.36	130.22	125.10	118.29	Khaga (110)	Yes
						Chitrakut dham (213)	No
Lucknow (73)	40.58	42.10	45.60	43.70	41.98	Luck-Unn. distt:boun. (42)	Within beyond Yes/No
Jhansi (220)	157.80	168.20	175.27	170.50	161.70	Mahoba(150)	Yes
						Orai (106)	Yes
						Month 9165)	No
Aligarh (309)	213.18	218.17	218.85	217.20	218.50	Farrukhabad (140)	Yes
						Kannauj (170)	Yes
						Etawah (139)	Yes
						Kasganj (248)	No

The second model has been employed to measure the urban influence of Kanpur with reference to other important cities in the surrounding area of Kanpur. The distances have been taken from the Railway Time Tables (N.E.R., N.R., C.R.) and/or the U.P. Govt. Roadways Time Tables. The data regarding total working population of various cities have been taken from the District Census Handbooks (1971). The results of the computation have been shown in Table 13.4. It is interesting to note that its final conclusion is similar to the one derived from Table 13.3.

TABLE 13.4

Results of the computation on the second model

Distance from Kanpur (km)		Distance in between (km)		Influence of Kanpur in kilometres on the basis of total working population	Whether or not within the sphere of Kanpur's influence
Etawah	(139)	Agra-Etawah	(113)	160.72	Yes
Kaimganj	(170)	Aligarh-Kaimganj	(135)	244.61	Yes
Etah	(224)	Aligarh - Etah	(70)	170.98	No
Charkhari	(170)	Jhansi-Chakheri	(140)	233.14	Yes
Mauranipur	(206)	Jhansi - Mau	(65)	164.84	No
Fatehpur	(76)	Allahabad-Fatehpur	(116)	152.85	Yes
Hardoi	(126)	Lucknow-Hardoi	(102)	98.35	No
Unnao	(18)	Lucknow-Unnao	(55)	65.16	Yes
Chitrakut	(213)	Allahabad-Chitrakut	(135)	153.82	No
Mahoba	(150)	Jhansi-Mahoba	(138)	276.31	Yes
Atarra	(176)	Allahabad-Atarra	(172)	206.46	Yes
Rai-Bareli	(120)	Lucknow-Rai-Bareli	(77)	106.11	No
Shikohabad	(194)	Agra-Shikohabad	(57)	98.00	No
Garautha	(166)	Jhansi-Garautha	(78)	106.99	No
Jalaun	(132)	Jhansi-Jalaun	(138)	183.72	Yes

It is remarkable to note that the empirical findings regarding the secondary umland of Kanpur are substantiated by the quantitative findings. After making minor adjustment with the administrative boundaries, the Umland of Kanpur Metropolis, therefore, comprises the districts of Kanpur, Unnao, Farrukhabad, Etawah, Fatehpur, Jalaun, Hamirpur, and Banda (excepting Karwi and Mau Tahsils).

GEOGRAPHY OF THE UMLAND OF KANPUR

The pattern of life and economy of people of any region is the product of the interaction of its physical and cultural milieu. Here, an attempt has been made to present an analysis of the geographical landscape of the Umland of Kanpur (Dixit, 1979, pp. 67-109).

Historical background

The historical perspectives of the Umland of the Metropolis of Kanpur unfolds two important spatial facets :

i. One part of the Umland, lying to the north of the

Sind (a tributary of the Yamuna) and the Yamuna presents an amalgam of pre-historic to present culture. Because of its vicinity to the capital of the country, it has enjoyed relatively greater stability, of course, with interruption from time to time during shorter transitions induced due to the change over of the dynasties. The Aryan-Vedic culture flourished in the Ganga-Yamuna Plain. This area is a part of the region occupied by man during remote ancient period. This has been a part of Madhya-desha or the 'middle country' (the core of the Aryavarta) of the epics, the Mahabharata, the Ramayana, and the Puranas. Unnao and Bithoor were the ancient hermitages of Maharishi Valmiki. Farrukhabad was a part of Panchala state during the epic-age when Kampil was an important city. Kannauj was the capital of Harsha Vardhan during the seventh century, King Jaichand ruled Kannauj during the twelfth century. This area has been 'Hindostan' of the Muslim historians. Farrukhabad was named after Farrukhsiyar during the eighteenth century. In fact, this is a part of the heart of the country, typically Indian and securely Indian (Ali, 1966, p. 134). This has been a part of the region of which 'nature and the historico-political values have been intriguing, challenging, and rewarding to the rulers of India' (Singh and verma, 1971, p. 126), as well as it attracted trade channels to pass through the northern and southern parts of the country. The British rulers assessed the strategic value of this region and took steps for developing the agricultural economy of this area by inducing irrigational, transportational, and other facilities. 'This resulted in the rise and revival of cities and the rapid progress of Kanpur from a small trade depot to a large industrial giant' (Singh and Verma, 1971, p. 129).

ii. The other part of the Umland lying south of the Sind and the Yamuna presents its various traditions, inscriptions, and other records which show that the original settlers of the region were the Gonds. Although parts of this sub-region have also played an important role as being the area of stay and work of Rishis like Parashar (Parasan-Jalaun), Valmiki (Babina-Jalaun), Kronch (Konch-Jalaun), Ved Vyas and Kapaldeo (Kalpi-Jalaun), and Vamdeo (Banda). The earliest information about the region dates back to the sixth century B.C. During this time this area formed parts of 'Chedi Janapada'. With the passage of time, the rulers have been Nandas, Mauryas, Shungas, Gurjar-Pritiharas, and Chandel Rajputs, etc. Rasin (Naraini-Banda) and Banda have been the capitals of the Chandels and of Nawab Ali Bahadur. Kalinjar (Banda) is still an important religious and historical place. The Bundelas appeared on the scene during the fifteenth century. They settled at mau, Kalinjar, Kalpi in the beginning and at other places afterwards. Although some of the Bundela chiefs have been with the Moghul rulers but others harassed them with the strategy of guerilla warfare in the rugged country of the Betwa ravines with which they were fully familiar. This area has been politically unstable upto the end of the eighteenth century. Later, British rulers made efforts for the stabilization of economy by constructing some canals.

Physical landscape

Spatial relations

i. Location:- The Umland of Kanpur comprises parts of the Ganga-Yamuna Doab and the Bundelkhand region of Uttar Pradesh. It stretches from 24° 52'N latitude to 27° 43' N latitude and 78° 45' E longitude to 81° 20' E longitude. Lucknow, the capital town of the state, is only 31 km from a point on the north eastern boundary of the Umland. The Umland is surrounded by Karwi tahsil of Banda district and Allahabad and Rai-Bareli districts in east; Lucknow district in north-east; Hardoi, Shahjahanpur, Budaun, Etah and Mainpuri districts in north; Bhind district of M.P. and Agra and Jhansi districts in west; and Chhatarpur, Panna, and Satna districts of M.P. in south (Fig. 13.11).

ii. Size:- The areal coverage of the Umland is 39,924 km^2. It is 13.74% of the area of Uttar Pradesh and 1.24% of the area of the Indian Republic. The major axis, 370 kms assumed by the Umland, is in the north-west to south-east direction while the north-east to south-west direction, the axis is 220 kms.

The administrative set up of the Umland consists of one district i.e., Unnao of the Lucknow division; four districts i.e., Farrukhabad, Etawah, Kanpur and Fatehpur of the Allahabad division; and three districts, namely, Jalaun, Hamirpur and Banda (only western part) of the Jhansi division of Uttar Pradesh. Thus, in the Umland there are 8 districts (Banda, of course, not whole) and 33 tahsils (only 3 tahsils of Banda fall in the Umland). There are 83 development blocks in the Umland.

iii. Shape:- Haggett and Chorley (1969, p. 70) have compiled a list showing alternative ratios for comparison of shape of closed figures. The results, derived after computations on various models for the present case, depict somewhat an elongated pattern. Such a conclusion has been derived by Singh (1972, p. 132) also.

However, the visual observation suggests an octagonal shape, although a number of irregularities do exist due to the impact of the means of transportation lines and natural barriers. It is also somewhat similar to a star. According to the Central Place Theory the ideal trade area of a centre is ought to be hexagonal. Since the ideal condition rarely exists, the shape of the Umland of Kanpur is, therefore, not hexagonal.

Relief

The Umland has two distinct physiographic units (Fig. 13.12). The Ganga Plain, a large alluvial plain lying north of the Sind-Yamuna line, and the Bundelkhand area lying south of the above mentioned line. The districts of Unnao, Farrukhabad, Etawah, Kanpur and Fatehpur form parts of the Ganga Plain while the remaining part of the Umland is included in the Bundelkhand.

i. Ganga Plain:- The ganga Plain is characterized by monotony in relief due to absence of topographic prominence. Of course, there is preponderance of local steps, the whole sub-region is below 150 m excepting Kaimganj tahsil and the western margins of Etawah tahsil. The doab area, i.e., between the Ganga and the Yamuna shows the 'bhangar' lands which sometimes rise even more than 30 m above the adjoining flood plains (Ullah, 1963). Numerous streams run almost parallel to their master streams.

On the basis of the micro-level topographic features, this sub-region can be differentiated into two units: the 'Khadar' and the 'Bhangar'. These lower order units are recognized in the form of the flood plain and the interfluvial lands respectively.

ii. Bundelkhand:- The keynote of the Bundelkhand physiognomy is its 'senile topography' (Spate, 1954, p. 433). The region is dominated by subdued topography that tends to convert into a perfect level plain towards north. Parts of Orai, and Rath tahsils and the tahsils of Konch, Charkhari, and Mahoba are all above 150 m. The eastern part of Naraini tahsil is composed of Vindhyan series. This series assumes an altitude over 300 m at Kalinjar. In some areas it has an altitude over 375 m also. Escarpments are common near the main streams i.e., Betwa, Dhasan, and Ken

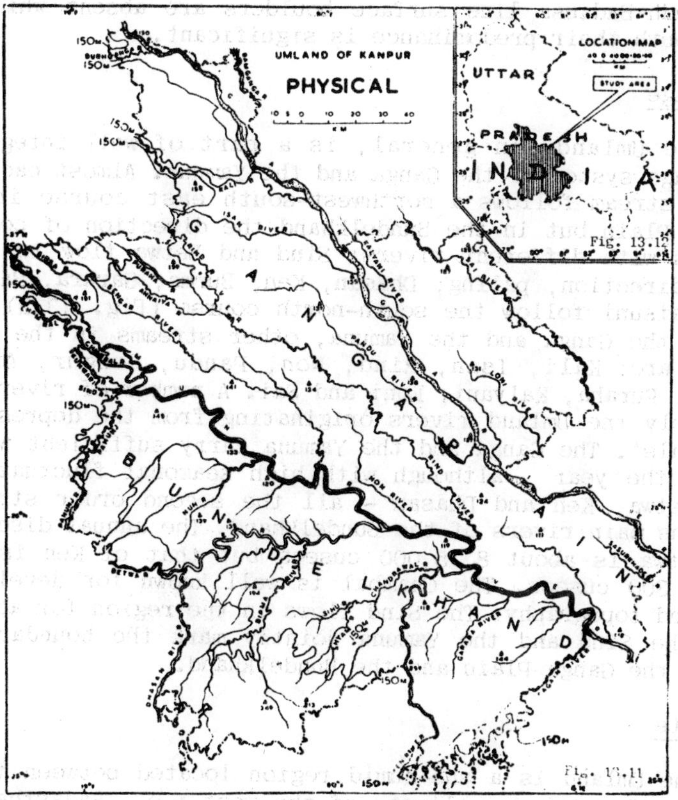
UMLAND OF KANPUR
PHYSICAL
KM
LOCATION MAP
STUDY AREA
UTTAR
PRADESH
INDIA
Fig. 13.12
GANGA PLAIN
BUNDELKHAND
150m

Fig. 13.11

and their tributaries. The Yamuna is well known for its ravines. The Bundelkhand Plain spreads over the northern halves of the districts of Jalaun, Hamirpur, and Banda. It is composed of soft and unconsolidated material deposited by the rivers. This part is below 150 m. To the north of Rath-Mataundh-Badausa line surface boulders are absent while in the south their predominance is significant.

Drainage

The Umland, in general, is a part of well integrated drainage system of the Ganga and the Yamuna. Almost each and every stream follows a northwest-south east course in the Ganga Plain but in the Bundelkhand the direction of courses varies with different rivers: Sind and Betwa flow in west-east direction, paling, Dhasan, Ken, Burma, Garara, Baghain and Paisuni follow the south-north course (Fig. 13.2). Besides the Ganga and the Yamuna, other streams in the Ganga plain are: Kali, Isan, Rind, Non, Pandu, Sengur, Arind, Bagar, Puraha, Kalyani, Loni and Sai. A number of rivers are entirely the Umland rivers originating from the depressions or 'tals'. The Ganga and the Yamuna carry sufficient waters round the year , although with high seasonal fluctuations. The Betwa, Ken and Dhasan - all the second order streams, are the main rivers of the Bundelkhand. The annual discharge of Betwa is about 8,15,000 cusecs but that of Ken is only about 800 cusecs. The Chambal is well known for developing badland topography. The Sind flows in the region for about 8 km. The Sind and the Yamuna jointly mark the boundary between the Ganga Plain and the Bundelkhand.

Climate

The Umland is a sub-humid region located between tropical continental dry climate of the west i.e., Rajasthan and humid middle Ganga Plain of the east. It, therefore, naturally partakes the characteristics of the two regions. With relatively higher amount of winter rain, the Umland distinguishes itself from the eastern region; and relatively higher amount of summer rain, it distinguishes from the west. The micro-level diversities are, no doubt, observed due to the nature of terrain in the Ganga Plain and the Bundelkhand area.

The average weather conditions resulting from combined effects of various factors lead to the recognition of four clear cut seasons: the hot summer, the wet summer, the pre-winter transition, and the winter. The temperature starts rising gradually from February and increases rapidly during May/June when the maximum temperature exceeds 40°C. Some times it is modified by humid easterlies. The mean seasonal temperatures in summer varies from 26°C to 32°C, but actual temperatures are much higher. The scorching effect of the '100' (the hot and dry westerlies) is because of the lower relative humidity (30-40%). The pre-monsoon (March-May) showers are rarely seen if ever not more than 5 cm. The temperature in May-June sometimes rises to 45°C. Nights are also hot and the temperature seldom goes below 15°C.

With the advent of rainy season in the later half of June the regional temperatures fall abruptly by 5.5°C giving a sense of general relief. The mean seasonal temperatures during rainy season are between 20-25°C with relative humidity varying from 70-80%. The weather conditions during July and August are, therefore, muggy and sultry. July and August (each 300 mm) are usually the rainiest months followed by September (155 mm). The 85% of the precipitation occurs within a short span of only three months, but the monthly rainfall is highly variable and capricious. The amount of annual as well as seasonal rainfall decreases from east to west as well as from north to south. The agricultural operations depend upon the onset, withdrawal, breaks, and nature of the monsoonal rain.

October and November are the transitional months. During this period, the relative humidity is comparatively low and weather conditions are generally unsuitable. Gradually, the weather crystalizes into a pleasant one as the winter conditions set in. Generally, the weather is dry but when western depressions bring rain it becomes very chilly and the temperatures are considerably lowered. The winter rains are beneficial for the 'rabi' crops.

The mean annual precipitation varies between 750 mm in the west to about 1,250 mm in the east. The incidence of double maxima (Jan-Feb and July-Aug.), though not comparable in magnitude is an important feature of precipitation. Wind velocity varies from season to season and is minimum in winter while maximum during summer. The highest, lowest, and mean maximum temperatures in January and May during the year 1976-77 were recorded as 44.8°C, 1.5°C, 23°C, and 42.6°C at Orai; 44.2°C, 3.2°C, 23.4°C, and 42.3°C, at Fatehpur; 46.4°C, 5.1°C, 23.7°C, and 43.0°C at Banda respectively. The normal and actual rainfall of the above three stations during 1976-77 was recorded to be 1.029 mm, 1.187mm; 870 mm; 895 mm and 980 mm, and 1,005 mm.

Soils

In view of the variety of soils the study region has two distinct units i.e., the Ganga Plain, and the Bundelkhand.

The Ganga Plain carries the alluvial soils. On the basis of the topographic variations they can be classified into two groups: the 'Khadar' soils, and the 'Bhangar' soils. The 'Khadar' soils are spread over the flood plains. These soils, therefore, lack in organic matter such as phosphorous and have sandy to loamy texture. These are known to have immature profiles with regard to texture, concretion, and proportion of salts etc. These are neutral to alkaline in reaction (pH-6-8). Because of floods and siltation these are renewed every time and, therefore, have very high fertility. The 'bhangar' soils are wide-spread and predominate in inter-fluvial zones. They lack salts, calcium. and other solubles with neutral to highly acidic reaction. They have mature profiles, and assume a variety of colours. Their texture varies from loamy to sandy-loam near the Ganga while from sandy to sandy-loam near the Yamuna.

The Bundelkhand soils have relatively mature profiles and have three well marked varieties: the upland or rocky soils, the lowland or black-red-yellow soils, and the riverine or tari-kachhar-rankar soils. The first variety predominates in Banda district near the Vindhyan Range having clay loam to sandy loam. The second type is spread over a large plain area of the Bundelkhand. The 'mar', moisture retentive calcareous, and black frequently includes 'kankars' and is suitable for wheat, and gram cultivation. The 'kabar' is a sub-variety of 'mar' only. It is a highly diffused soil. Red soils are associated with sand stones. The red, yellow, brown, grey, and chocolate colours of the soils are the results of varying proportions of iron, black soil, and distance from the exposed gneissic surface. 'Pandua', receptive to irrigation, is a fertile soil. The third variety varies from coarse sand to fine clays. It is found near the streams. While the 'tari' spreads over the adjoining areas of the channels, the shelving banks have a cover of 'kachhar', both of these soils are fertile. The higher flood plains where the calcium nodules are exposed along the sloping surfaces due to continuous erosion contain 'rankar' an unsuitable soil for agriculture.

Minerals

There is a scarcity of minerals in the Umland. The Ganga Plain has hardly any minerals. Only the Bundelkhand is known for some minerals. Banda and Hamirpur are rich in building stones like granites and sandstones. The distant transportation of these stones is discouraged by their heavy weight. These minerals are, therefore, locally used. Agates of great beauty and variety are common in the river-bed of Ken, known as Banda-stone. Majhagawan has special significance as it produces diamond also. Gaurahri is famous for soft stone of which various utensils/articles of household necessities are manufactured. China clay is commonly used in Banda for making potteries and toys. Besides, the fine sand of both the Ganga and the Yamuna, and the coarse sand of the Betwa are well known as building materials.

Cultural Landscape

Demographic characteristics

The Kanpur Urban Agglomeration has a population of 1,275,242 (1971) and the Umland of Kanpur (i.e. the region excluding the Kanpur Urban Agglomeration) has a population of 10,101,454. Thus, the total population of the entire region is 11,376,696. The arithmetic density of population in the Umland is 253 persons per km^2. Owing to the larger area and a higher density (which, of course, is due to the interaction of favourable physical setting and an organized cultural set-up) the absolute population in the Ganga Plain is very high (8,764,512 including the K.U.A.) against 2,612,184 in the Bundelkhand. Singh and Verma (1971, p.137) have remarked on the demographic features of the Ganga Plain that 'the large population and its spatial distribution, density, and occupational structure reveal that here man has been not only the creator of cultural landscape but also a basic constituent of the ecosystem of the region'. The 'bhangar' and the 'khadar' soils have undoubtedly influenced the growth and density of population. During the earlier decades of the 20th century the relationship between population and agriculture was more pronounced. Later on, rapidly improving health/sanitation conditions and urbanization have greatly influenced the demographic characteristics.

i. Growth of Population:- There has been an overall growth of 22.77% in the population of the Umland during the decade 1961-71 while the U.P. average was only 19.79%. Thus, it is evident that the growth rate of population in the study area has been higher than that in the state itself. However, the growth rates of population in various districts vary greatly: Unnao (20.9%), Farrukhabad (20.2%), Etawah (22.4%), Kanpur (25.8%), Fatehpur (19.1%), Jalaun (22.6%), Hamirpur (24.38%), and Banda (23.9%). The highest rate has been in the district of Kanpur. Hamirpur and Banda districts also recorded the growth rate above the average rate of the Umland. Fatehpur, however, showed the minimum growth rate. The districtwise growth of population from 1901 to 1971 is clearly demonstrated by Fig. 13.13.

Table 13.5 shows the intercensal growth of population (%) in various districts of the Umland. It is evident from the table that each and every district of the Ganga Plain had decreased its population during the 1901-1911, while the Bundelkhand districts had gained the same. During the decade 1911-1921 Kanpur and Jalaun added to their population numbers (although Jalaun's addition was only a nominal one). Rest of the districts recorded a decrease in their population numbers. During 1931-1971 there has been a consistent increase in the population of each and every district. However, the highest increase in each and every district was recorded during 1961-71. The growth of population in the Ganga Plain, the Bundelkhand, and the Umland is shown by Fig. 13.15.

TABLE 13.5

Intercensal growth of population (%)

Years / Districts	1911	1921	1931	1941	1951	1961	1971
Unnao	-6 73	-10.80	+4.46	+12.14	+11.20	+14.98	+20.90
Farrukhabad	-2.77	-4.82	+4.50	+8.80	+14.34	+18.54	+20.20
Etawah	-5.79	-3.50	+1.70	+18.40	+9.90	+21.79	+22.40
Kanpur	-9.26	+0.56	+5.54	+28.38	+24.65	+22.76	+25.80
Fatehpur	-1.38	-3.63	+5.58	+17.15	+12.65	+18.04	+19.10
Jalaun	+1.68	+(Negli)	+4.85	+14.02	+7.39	+19.80	+22.60
Hamirpur	+2.00	-4.21	+6.71	+13.79	+2.67	+19.57	+24.38
Banda	+4.20	-6.57	+6.31	+15.51	+6.76	+20.69	+23.90
G P	-5.68	-4.10	+4.43	+17.83	+15.84	+19.71	+22.45
B	-2.77	-4.05	+6.06	+14.50	+5.57	+20.06	+23.72
R	-4.54	-4.08	+4.89	+16.98	+13.06	+19.80	+22.77

Source: District Census Handbooks 1961, 1971 and the computations done by the author.

ii. Population Projections:- The State Government Reports on the 5th Five Year Plan of various districts incorporated the population projections from 1971 to 1979 as well as for the years 1981, 1984 and 1989. However, the information about Banda district could not be given due to

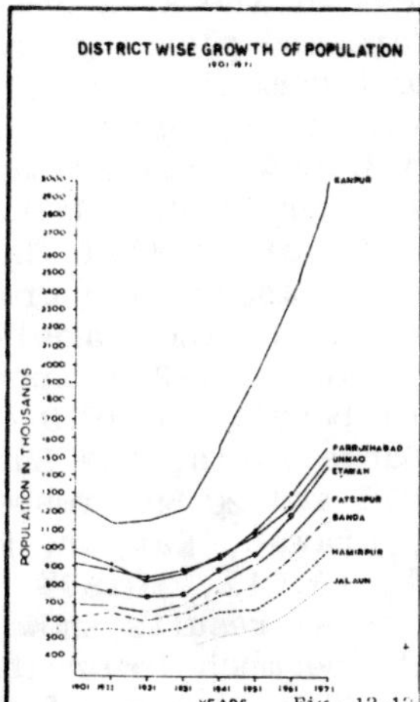

Fig. 13.13

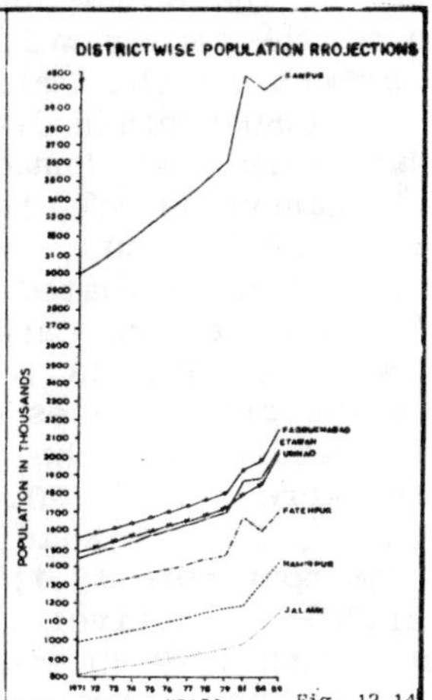

Fig. 13.14

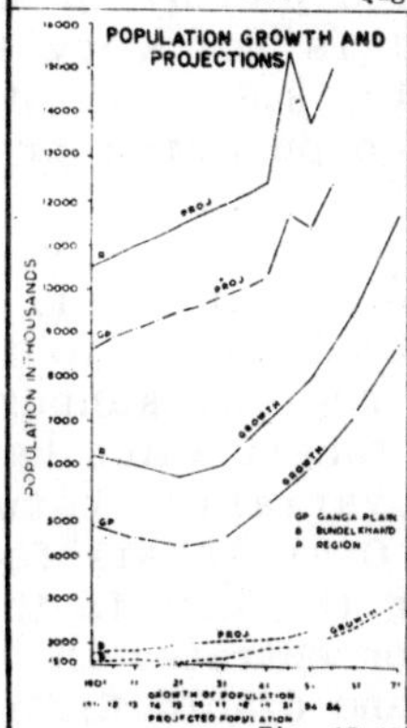

Fig. 13.15

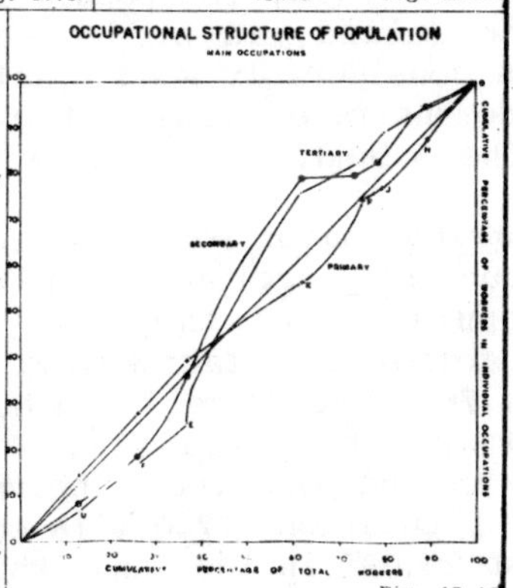

Fig. 13.16

non-availability of the complete list. With due emphasis on the family welfare and planning programmes, the rate of growth of population in successive decades has been reduced in the projections. The growth rate in 1979 shows only 17.48% increase over 1971 population of the Ganga Plain while two districts of the Bundelkhand show an increase of 18.32% because of the backwardness of the area and less implementation of the family welfare and planning programmes. The rate of growth in the Umland comes to be 17.6%. The projections for 1989 contain district-wise growth of population over that of 1971 as: Unnao 37.06%, Farrukhabad 38.47%, Etawah 40.81%, Kanpur 49.24%, Fatehpur 33.33%, Jalaun 41.20% and Hamirpur 44.73%. Thus, it is clear that the highest growth rate has been estimated for Kanpur. The growth percentage in the cases of the Ganga Plain, the Bundelkhand and the Umland were 41.55, 43.14, and 41.82 respectively. However, when the growth rates of population 1979 - 89 were computed, the results for the Ganga Plain, the Bundelkhand and the Umland were 20.51%, 20.97% and 20.59% respectively. Those for Unnao, Farrukhabad, Etawah, Kanpur, Fatehpur, Jalaun, and Hamirpur were 18.11%, 19.71%, 19.87%, 24.23%, 20.08% and 21.70% respectively. These results show that the growth rates during 1979-89 would be much lower than those during 1961-71. Thus, the population picture of the years ahead of the Umland, as projected is not very alarming rather it is considerably good (Table 13.6). Fig. 13.14 and Fig. 13.15 demonstrate clearly the population projection aspects of the Umland.

iii. Distribution of Population:- Kanpur tahsil, including the Kanpur Urban Agglomeration, contributes to 13.48% of the total population of the study region. Kanpur tahsil ranks first followed by farrukhabad tahsil which has a percentage of 4.76 only. There is much variation between the Bundelkhand and the Ganga Plain. Orai tahsil feeds only 1.41% of the Umland population, being the last in the array. Of the total population, 77.04% is concentrated in the Ganga Plain against 22.96% in the Bundelkhand (Table 13.7).

iv. Density of Population:- The arithmetic density of population of the study area is 253 persons per km^2, which is less than that of Uttar Pradesh (300). There is much variation among the densities of various tahsils of the Umland. It is evident that physiography, variety of soil, life and economy of the people have largely influenced the density in the study area. Each of the five districts of the ganga Plain has a density higher than the state average: Unnao, 323; Farrukhabad, 357; Etawah, 334; Kanpur, 490; and

TABLE 13.6

Population projections (,000)

Areal Units & Years	Unnao	Farru-khabad	Etawah	Kan-pur	Fateh-pur	Jalaun	Hamir-pur	GP	B	R
1971	1,484	1,558	1,448	2,997	1,279	813	968	8,764	1,801	10,565
1972	1,510	1,584	1,478	3,055	1,29[illegible]	829	1,008	8,925	1,837	10,762
1973	1,538	1,612	1,505	3,128	1,320	849	1,030	9,103	1,879	10,982
1974	1,556	1,641	1,535	3,198	1,340	862	1,052	9,280	1,914	11,194
1975	1,597	1,673	1,568	3,279	1,367	881	1,075	9,484	1,956	11,440
1976	1,627	1,704	1,600	3,354	1,391	899	1,100	9,676	1,999	11,675
1977	1,655	1,732	1,631	3,433	1,414	916	1,123	9,865	2,038	11,904
1978	1,687	1,766	1,664	3,514	1,438	935	1,147	10,069	2,082	12,151
1979	1,722	1,801	1,701	3,604	1,466	956	1,175	10,294	2,123	12,425
1980	1,795	1,934	1,872	4,496	1,673	982	1,190	11,770	2,172	15,346
1984	1,850	1,990	1,886	4,066	1,603	1,061	1,312	11,389	2,373	13,762
1989	2,034	2,156	2,039	4,473	1,704	1,048	1,143	12,406	2,378	14,984

Source: Fifth Five Year Plan - District Plans (1974-75 to 1978-79) and Regional Perspective of Industrial and Urban Growth (Desai, 1969).

Fatehpur, 306. However, seven tahsils of the Ganga Plain have their density below the state average but higher than the average for the Umland. All the twelve tahsils of the Bundelkhand have their densities much below the Umland average owing to the physiography, fertility of soil, and economic backwardness of the area. The exceptionally high density, 1455 persons per table 13.7 km^2, is a noteworthy feature of the tahsil of Kanpur. This, obviously, is due to the huge concentration of population in the Metropolis of Kanpur. Farrukhabad (426) stands second while Bhognipur (276) ranks last in the Ganga Plain. On the other hand, Jalaun with only a density of 216 persons per km^2 stands first in the Bundelkhand while Charkhari (124) ranks last. The average density of the Ganga Plain (318) is higher than that of the state, but the density of the Bundelkhand (160) is much below. The variation between the densities of the Ganga Plain and the Bundelkhand is, therefore, very large (Table 13.7). The dispersion aspects of total as well as of rural density of population have been shown at the tahsil level by fig. 13.17 and fig. 13.18.

v. Occupational Structure:- the percentages of working population in various districts are : Unnao, 30.29; farrukhabad, 29.43; Etawah, 27.30; Kanpur, 29.38; Fatehpur, 33.52; Jalaun 28.71; Hamirpur, 32.71; and Banda, 34.04. These values can be compared with that of the state which is 32.2. Agrarian society predominates the whole economic scene of the study area. Unnao district (72.3%) has the highest percentage of its workers engaged in cultivation followed by Farrukhabad (68.7%), Etawah (67.9%), Fatehpur (59.1%), Kanpur (37.9%), Jalaun (60.3%), Banda (56.1%), and Hamirpur (51.7%). Such a percentage for the state is 56. Thus, all of the districts except Kanpur and Hamirpur have the percentages above that of the state. Although the percentage of workers engaged in agriculture is low in Kanpur as people are engaged in secondary and tertiary activities there, but the reason behind the low percentage in Hamirpur is quite different. It is actually because Hamirpur district, economically, is very poor and therefore, very large percentage of population is engaged in the agricultural pursuits. The second highest percentage of workers is to be found in 'agricultural labour' (only excepting the Kanpur district). The workers in all the other occupations are only a few (excepting, of course, the Kanpur district). The analysis of the working population in the primary, secondary, and the tertiary occupations has been demonstrated through Table 13.8 and the graphical representation i.e., the Lorenz Curve (Fig. 13.16).

TABLE 13.7

Population distribution and density (1971)

Tahsils	Population	% of the Umland	Rank on %	Density	Rank on Density
Unnao	347,321	3.05	11	332	6
Safipur	340,408	2.98	14	317	8
Purwa	435,325	3.82	4	307	10
Hasanganj	361,339	3.17	9	307	11
Farrukhabad	531,316	4.76	2	426	2
Kaimganj	298,381	2.61	19	315	9
Chhibramau	380,621	3.34	7	351	4
Kannauj	346,612	3.04	12	334	5
Etawah	413,356	3.63	5	359	3
Bharthana	342,341	3.00	13	305	12
Bidhuna	331,078	2.90	15	298	15
Auraiya	360,927	3.16	10	325	7
Kanpur	1,525,835	13.48	1	1,455	1
Bilhaur	304,084	2.67	18	290	18
Derapur	305,428	2.68	17	285	19
Akbarpur	278,161	2.44	23	291	17
Bhognipur	271,162	2.38	24	276	21
Ghatampur	311,562	2.73	16	282	20
Fatehpur	505,070	4.43	3	304	13
Bindki	397,182	3.48	6	292	16
Khaga	375,994	3.29	8	300	14
Jalaun	289,722	2.54	20	216	22
Orai	154,776	1.41	33	164	27
Kalpi	177,380	1.55	31	139	29
Konch	191,612	1.67	29	181	23
Hamirpur	164,417	1.49	32	151	28
Maudhaha	219,589	1.92	27	139	30
Charkhari	182,706	1.59	30	124	33
Mahoba	197,601	1.73	28	136	31
Rath	223,902	1.96	26	134	32
Banda	285,767	2.50	21	174	26
Baberu	279,320	2.45	22	176	24
Naraini	245,392	2.15	25	176	25
G P	8,764,512	77.04		318	
B	2,612,184	22.96		160	
R	11,376,696	100.00		253	

TABLE 13.8

Cumulative percentage of workers

Districts	Total Workers	Primary Occupation	Secondary Occupation	Tertiary Occupation
Unnao	13.0	14.5	8.5	6.5
Farrukhabad	26.0	28.0	19.0	17.0
Etawah	37.0	39.5	26.5	26.0
Kanpur	62.0	56.0	79.0	76.0
Fatehpur	74.0	69.5	85.5	82.5
Jalaun	80.0	77.0	89.5	89.0
Hamirpur	89.0	87.0	94.5	94.0
Banda	100.0	100.0	100.0	100.0
Region	100.0	100.0	100.0	100.0

vi Sex Ratio:- The ratio of females per 1,000 males in Uttar Pradesh is 879. All the districts of the Umland excepting Unnao (889), and Fatehpur (900) have the sex ratio below the state average. Kanpur district (812) has the lowest because of the fact that a large number of males engaged in the secondary and the tertiary activities cannot bring their families either due to their low income or because of scarcity of houses in the city.

Settlements

i. Rural Settlements:- There are 11,773 villages in the Umland out of which 10,703 are inhabited villages while 1,070 are uninhabited. The ratio between these two types stands to be the same as that of the state. Kanpur district has the largest number of villages (2,063) against Hamirpur district which has the minimum (1,151) in the Umland. The number of inhabited villages in the above two districts respectively is 1898 and 930, again being the maximum and the minimum in the Umland. There are 597; 8,136; and 8,733 villages uninhabited, inhabited and overall total in the Ganga Plain while only 473; 2,567; and 3,040 respectively in the Bundelkhand. The largest number of uninhabited villages is found in Hamirpur (221) on the other hand Etawah district accounts for the minimum (78). Fig. 13.19 gives detailed information about the distribution of villages based on population size in various tahsils of the Umland.

The area-wise stratification of villages in various districts reveals that Banda has the largest number (52) of the largest size villages (about 5,000 acres). Hamirpur district ranks second (40) and Jalaun third (11). Each of the other districts has a number below 10. Unfertile soils, rugged terrain, and relatively scanty rainfall are responsible for the concentration of big villages in the Bundelkhand. On the other hand, highly fertile soil, uniform surface configuration and economic development are the factors responsible for small number of big size villages in the Ganga Plain. There are only 6 villages in Jalaun, 6 in Hamirpur and 15 in Banda having the size of 50 acres or less. Fatehpur (129), however, tops the list of such villages in the Umland. The areal size of most of the villages in the study area varies from 100 to 2,000 acres.

As regards the distance of the villages from their nearest town, most of the villages fall in the 6 to 50 km class. In case of the number of villages within 5 km from the nearest town, Etawah district, with 120 villages, ranks

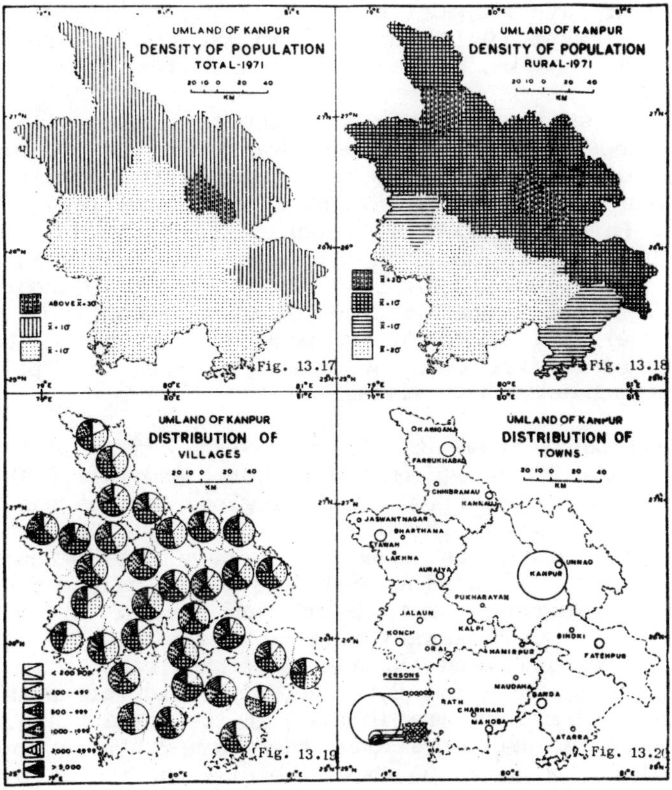

Fig. 13.17 Fig. 13.18 Fig. 13.19 Fig. 13.20

first while Unnao lags far behind having a number of only 26, as there is only one town, i.e., Unnao in the district. Hamirpur district (92) ranks second in this order. In Kanpur district, besides the Kanpur Urban Agglomeration, there is only one more town i.e., Pukharayan. The districts of Unnao and Kanpur have respectively, the largest (1175) and the second largest (941) number of villages which are located between 26 - 50 km. distance from the nearest town.

In the study area, 85.57% of the total population lives in villages. There are not much variations as regards percentage of rural population in various districts except that of Kanpur which has only 57.15% of its total population as rural. In the districts of Unnao, Farrukhabad, Etawah, Fatehpur, Jalaun, Hamirpur, and Banda the percentages are 97.43, 89.13, 90.25, 96.63, 86.22, 90.08, and 91.86 respectively. In the Ganga Plain 80.55% of its population and in the Bundelkhand 88.25% of its population is rural. It is a crystal clear fact that the Umland is rural unsurprisingly as India also lives in villages.

ii. Urban Settlements:- There are only two class I towns i.e., Kanpur Urban Agglomeration (KUA), and Farrukhabad Urban Agglomeration (FUA) in the region. Besides the Kanpur Urban Agglomeration the district of Kanpur has one more town, i.e., Pukharayan. Unnao is the only town in Unnao district. In the remaining districts all tahsil headquarters (excepting Bidhuna, Khaga, Baberu, and Naraini) are towns of varying classes. Jaswantnagar (Etawah tahsil), Atarra (Naraini tahsil) and Lakhana (Bharthana tahsil) add three more towns to the list. Both the Kanpur and Farrukhabad urban agglomerations are located in the Ganga Plain. Apart from these two agglomerations, there are 23 more towns in the Umland. Fig. 13.20 shows the distribution of towns in the study area.

From the perspective of functional character, the Kanpur Urban Agglomeration performs a variety of specialised functions. Three of its eight constituents are purely service towns while other three specialize in transport functions. One town performs industry-cum-services and another one services-cum-industry functions. Among the other towns of the Umland, two perform only service functions, eight operate primary-cum-other functions and the rest render services and operate commercial functions.

Kanpur, the youngest among the 'KAVAL' towns of Uttar Pradesh, is the only industrial town in the Umland.

Originally, it was a military base of the Britishers and was located at the border line dividing the then British frontier from the Province of Avadh and the territory of the Moghul Kings of Delhi (Singh, 1959, pp. 1-11). Lord Clive selected Kanpur because of its strategic position as the best station in the Nawab of Avadh dominion to canton the brigade lent to him subject to a subsidy for the protection of the frontier (Forest, 1977, p. 237). Now, it is the only industrial metropolis of Uttar Pradesh and is also one of the most important industrial centres of the country. It has a population of 1,275,242 (1971). Farrukhabad is the second largest town (110,835). All of the other towns have population below one lakh. The two smallest towns are Lakhana (5,320), and Pukharayan (7,089).

Kanpur district, undoubtedly, stands first as 42.85% of its population is urban. Unnao district (2.57%) ranks last. Fatehpur district has 3.37% of its population as urban. All of the rest districts have about ten per cent of their population as urban. The percentages of the urban population in the Ganga Plain, Bundelkhand, and the Umland are 19.45, 11.75, and 14.33 respectively.

Agricultural economy

Agriculture dominates the regional economy. More than 75% of the total population is directly dependent on agricultural operations. The percentage of the area of the cultivable land in various districts of the Umland varies from 76 to 93. The real cultivated area in the Ganga Plain (68.05%) is little bit higher than that in the Bundelkhand (67.49%). The actual cultivated land in the study area is 67.80% of its geographical area.

i. Number and Size of Holdings:- There is a significant variation in the number of holdings from district to district. Jalaun, and Hamirpur districts have smaller number of holdings than other districts as the area/size of holdings in these districts is larger which itself is due to the physiographic and the geographic characteristics. Each of Jalaun and Hamirpur districts has holdings below two lakhs while each of Fatehpur, Etawah, and Banda has 2 to 3 lakhs of holdings. The remaining three districts fall beyond the above class.

The average size of holdings in Farrukhabad district is only between .5 to 1 hec. while that in the cases of Unnao, Etawah, Kanpur and Fatehpur is between 1 to 1.5 hec. but in all of the three districts of Bundelkhand it is between 2 to 3 hec.

ii. Land Utilization:- The largest net sown area is found in Banda district (497,000 hec.) while Hamirpur district (488,000 hec.) stands next. Fatehpur district stands last in the array with only 291,000 hectares of land as net sown. The Ganga Plain and the Bundelkhand account for 1,613,000 hectares and 1,331,000 hectares respectively. Thus, the overall net sown area in the Umland is 2,944,000 hectares.

iii. Cropping Pattern - 'Rabi' and 'kharif' are the two important/primary crops while 'zaid' is a secondary one in the Umland (Table 13.9). 'Rabi' ranks first as regards its area, production and value. The cereals-wheat and barley; pulses-gram, peas and masur; and commercial crops-mustard, and rapeseed are grown in the season of 'rabi' crop. The 'kharif' includes rice, 'jowar', 'bajra', and maize among the cereals; and 'mung', 'urad', 'arhar', and 'month' among the pulses. Important commercial crops grown in the Umland are sugarcane, potato, tobacco, groundnut and soyabean. The area and the production of various crops reveal that wheat is the first ranking cereal crop of the region followed by rice.

TABLE 13.9

Area under various crops (000 hecs.)

Crop District	'Rabi'	'Kharif'	'Zaid'
Unnao	187	210	1.0
Farrukhabad	210	197	5.0
Etawah	203	170	1.0
Kanpur	285	222	3.7
Fatehpur	187	164	1.4
Jalaun	286	70	0.19
Hamirpur	343	164	0.27
Banda	328	233	-
G P	1,072	963	12.1
B	957	467	0.46
R	2,029	1,430	12.56

Source: Fifth Five Year Plan : District Annual Plan 1977-78 of all the respective districts.

Table 13.10 clearly shows that from the standpoint of crop significance, wheat and rice predominate the Ganga

Plain while gram and wheat have their firs say in the Bundelkhand.

TABLE 13.10

Crop significance

Districts	Crops
Unnao	Wheat, Rice, Gram
Farrukhabad	Wheat, Maize
Etawah	Wheat, Rice, 'Bajra',Gram
Kanpur	Wheat, Gram, Rice
Fatehpur	Gram, Rice, Barley, Wheat
Jalaun	Gram, Wheat
Hamirpur	Gram, Wheat, 'Jowar'
Banda	Gram, Wheat, Rice, 'Jowar'

As regards pulses, 'arhar' is the first ranking crop followed by gram, while important commercial crops, as regards both their production and area, are mustard, rapeseed, potato, and sugarcane.

In various districts of the Umland the yield of wheat per hectare varies from 1,122 kg. to 1,435 kg. In Etawah district it is the highest (1,435 kg.) followed by Banda (1,329 kg.). Jalaun district accounts for 1,122 kg. only. The highest yield of rice has been recorded in Unnao district (1,125 kg.) followed by Kanpur (1,098 kg.). The minimum yield of rice has been noted in Hamirpur (538 kg.) only. The yield of gram is highest in Etawah (1,190 kg.) followed by Kanpur (1,147 kg.) while Banda district (743 kg.) ranks last in the list.

(iv) Irrigation: - Only 36.54% of the net area sown in the Umland is under irrigation. The conditions are worst in the Bundelkhand as only one-fifth (20.06%) of the net sown area is irrigated. However, the Ganga Plain accounts for half (50.09%) of its net sown area as irrigated. In Etawah district irrigation facilities are available to 64.5% of its net sown area followed by Farrukhabad (54.5%). In the Umland, Banda district suffers from insufficient facilities of irrigation which are available to only 15.34% of its net sown area. Further, the conditions are worst in case of the total sown area as only 31.96% in the Umland, 46.47% in the Ganga Plain, and 11.33% in the Bundelkhand is under irrigation.

The total irrigated area in the Umland, the Ganga Plain, and the Bundelkhand is 1,113,980, 950,500 and 163,480 hectares respectively. In this case, Kanpur district stands first. In the Umland, in the Ganga Plain, and in the Bundelkhand 749,000, 712,000, and 37,000 hectares of 'rabi' crops respectively are irrigated. The irrigated 'kharif' land is 278,000; 226,500; and 51,500 hectares in the above regions respectively. Only 10,470 hectares of 'zaid' land avails the irrigation facilities in the study area.

Industrial economy

All the districts of the Umland excepting, of course, Kanpur have been declared by the State Government as industrially backward districts. At the same time it is important to mention that Kanpur city is the only industrial metropolis of Uttar Pradesh. The percentage of industrial workers in the Umland of Kanpur (i.e., excepting the KUA) is almost negligible. The large scale industries are located in the Metropolis of Kanpur while the house hold/small scale/village/cottage industries are located in the Umland. Several industries of the national level such as chemical, iron and steel, cotton textiles, woollen, vegetable oil and jute etc., are located in the 'regional capital'. Moreover, mention may be made of some industries of the Umland which are gaining importance these days. Unnao is noted for copper, chemical, cardboard, tanneries, agricultural equipments and engineering industries; Farrukhabad for dyeing and printing of cloth, sandalwood oil, perfumes, rolling mills, and agricultural equipments; Etawah for spinning and weaving, handloom cloth, rice, 'dal', edible oils, wooden furniture, 'Ayurvedic' medicines, plastic, and agricultural equipments; Fatehpur for rice, 'dal', edible oils, steel pipe, ball bearings, and agricultural equipments; Jalaun for hand-made paper, 'dal', edible oils, wooden furniture, soap, 'Ayurvedic' medicines, and agricultural equipments; and Banda for 'bidis', carpets, rice, 'dal', edible oils, wooden furniture and agricultural equipments.

Transport

'Though the present system of the regional transport comprising roads, railways, and airways is the product of the last 100 years, some crude and rather unbridged roads, cart tracks, and river routes have been anciently instrumental in the process of regional land occupance and resource uses' (Singh and verma, 1971, p. 175). The Grand Trunk Road and the Ganga system of rivers connected the region with the different parts of the country since long. The spatial development of transport network varies in its density. While the overall road and railway net is adequate in the Ganga Plain, the nature of terrain along with its cumulative effects on economy has relatively hindered the development of means of transportation in the Bundelkhand.

TABLE 13.11

Road network

District	Length	Maintained by			Under construction by			New Construction proposed
		PWD. Deptt	Other	Total	PWD.	Other Deptt	Total	
Unnao	kms.	551	65	616	160	-	160	287
	%	14.5	33	15.5	8	-	7.4	12.4
Farrukha- 290		km.	455	66	521	314	8	322
bad	%	12	33	13	15	31	15.00	13
Etawah	km.	249	19	268	67	7	74	219
	%	6.5	9.00	6.7	3.07 27	3.4	10	
Kanpur	km.	637	17	654	255	9	264	774
	%	17	19	16.4	12	34	12.3	32
Fatehpur	km.	406	10	416	271	2	273	243
	%	11	5	10.4	13	8	12.9	10.6
Jalaun	km.	363	22	383	258	-	258	135
	%	10	11	0.9	12.00	-	12.3	6
Hamirpur	km.	559	-	559	337	-	337	305
	%	15	-	14.2	16	-	15.7	12.00
Banda	km.	547	-	547	449	-	449	78
	%	14	-	13.9	21	-	21	4
GP	km.	2298	177	2475	1067	26	1093	1813
	%	61	89	62	51	100	51	78
B	km.	1469	22	1491	1044	-	1044	518
	%	39	11	38	49	-	49	22
R	km.	3767	199	3966	2111	26	2137	2331
	%	100	100	100	100	100	100	100

Source : Sixth Five Plan - P.W.D. of the respective districts (April 1977).

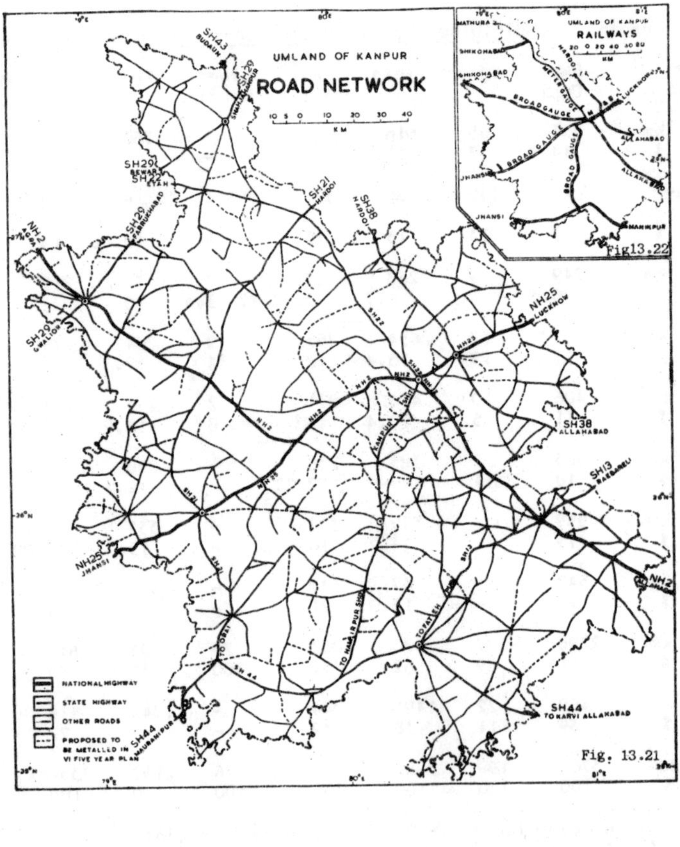

Fig13.22

Fig. 13.21

i. Road Network:- The National Highways traverse the whole Umland from both the directions i.e., north west-south east (N.H.2) and north east-south west (N.H. 25). The N.H. 2 enters the Umland from Etawah tahsil and through Etawah, Auriya, Bhognipur, Pukharayan, Kanpur and Sarsaul it runs to Allahabad. The N.H. 25 enters the Umland from Konch tahsil and through Orai, Kalpi, Bhognipur, Pukhrayan, Kanpur and Unnao it runs to Lucknow. There are eight state highways in the Umland. The places through which these SHs run are: SH-13, from Banda to Rai-Bareli via Fatehpur; SH-17: from Mahoba to Kanpur via Hamirpur; SH-21: from Panwari in Charkhari tahsil to Hardoi via Rath, Orai, Jalaun, Auraiya, and Kannauj; SH-29: via Etawah, Farrukhabad to Shahjahanpur; SH-43: from Farrukhabad to Budaun; SH-22: via Chhibramau, Kannauj to Kanpur; SH-38: via Safipur, Unnao to Allahabad; and SH-44: via Panwari, Mahoba, Banda, and Atarra to Allahabad.

TABLE 13-12

Railways

Districts	Length	Broad Guage	Meter Guage	Total
Unnao	Km	150	40	190
	%	16	17.5	16
Farrukhabad	Km	27	118	145
	%	3	52.5	12
Etawah	Km	96	-	96
	%	10	-	8
Kanpur	Km	304	69	373
	%	32	30	32
Fatehpur	Km	88	-	88
	%	9	-	8
Jalaun	Km	90	-	90
	%	9.5	-	7.5
Hamirpur	Km	130	-	130
	%	14.5	-	11.5
Banda	Km	60	-	60
	%	6	-	5
G P	Km	665	227	892
	%	70	100	76
B	Km	280	-	280
	%	30	-	24
R	Km	945	227	1,172
	%	100	100	100

Source: Fifth Five Year Plan: District Annual Plan, 1976-77 of all the respective districts.

Besides, the Umland has a good net of district roads (Table 13.11). The Umland has a net of roads of 3,966 kms of which those maintained by the Public Works Department are 3,767 kms and the other departments maintain 199 kms; besides, 2,137 kms of roads are under construction. It has been proposed that 2,331 kms of new roads should be constructed in the Umland in the Sixth Five Year Plan. The Bundelkhand is relatively less developed as only 39% of the Umland roads maintained by the P.W.D. and 11% of the Umland road maintained by the other departments serve this area. Thus, the Ganga Plain enjoys a better position. However, there is a good sign that 49% of all the Umland roads under construction by the PWD are in the Bundelkhand (Sixth Five Year Plan, P.W.D.).

ii. Railways:- The railway net is considerably good in the Ganga Plain but poor in the Bundelkhand (Fig. 13.22). The Central Railway (broad gauge), the Northern Railway (broad gauge) and the North-Eastern Railway (meter gauge) serve the people of the Umland. Kanpur and Lucknow are linked by both the broad gauge and meter gauge railway lines. In the Umland, the meter gauge line enters from Kaimganj tahsil and runs to Lucknow via Farrukhabad, Kannauj, Kanpur and Unnao. A small link of meter gauge branch line exists also in between Kalyanpur and Bithoor. Rest of the lines are broad gauge lines. Kanpur district has an excellent net of railway lines followed by Unnao district. All the three districts of the Bundelkhand are very poor in terms of the railway network. On the whole there are 1,172 km (945 km broad gauge and 227 km meter gauge) of railway lines in the Umland. Out of this, 76% falls in the Ganga Plain itself (Table 13.12).

REFERENCES

Agarwala, A.N. 1967 : **Agricultural profile of a metropolitan region**, Allahabad, Agro-Economic Research centre, pp. 10-12.

------ 1969 : **Economic of metropolitan region**, Allahabad, Agro-Economic research Centre, pp. 7-35.

Alam, S.M. 1965 : **Hyderabad and Secunderabad twin cities - a study in urban geography**, Bombay, Allied Publishers, pp. 36-53.

Alexander, J.W. 1963 : **Economic geography**, Wisconsin, Prentice-Hall, p. 556.

Ali, S.M. 1966 : **The geography of Puranas**, New Delhi, Peoples Publishing House, pp. 134, 176.

Allix, A. 1914 : **La foire de concelin**, Annales de University De Grenoble, 26, pp. 359-94.

-------1922 : The Geography of Fairs : illustrated by old world examples, **Geographic Review**, 12, pp. 532-48.

Bose, A. 1969 : Delimitation of Kanpur Region and Urban Growth, in Desai, P.B. et al., (eds.) **Regional Perspective of Industrial and Urban Growth - The case of Kanpur**, Bombay, Macmillan, p. 132.

Bracey, H.C. 1954 : Towns as Rural Service Centres - an index of centrality with special reference to Somerset, Transactions and papers - **Institute of British Geographers**, 19. pp. 95-105.

Brush, J.E. 1953 : The Hierarchy of Central Places in South western Wisconsin, **Geographical Review**, 43, pp. 380-402.

Carey, H.C. 1958 : **Principles of Social Science**, Philadelphia, Lippin cott.

Carothers, G.A.P. 1956 : An Historical Review of the Gravity and Potential Concepts in Human Interaction, **Jour. of American Institute of Planners**, 22, Spring, pp. 94-102, reprinted in Ambrose, p. (ed.) **Analytical Human Geogrpahy**, London, Longmans, pp. 226-42.

Chatterjee, A.B. 1965 : Hinterland of a symbolic city, Howrah - a case study, **Geographical Review of India**, 27, pp. 55-71.

Converse, P.D. 1948 : Consumer buying habits in selected south central Illinois, Univ. of Illinois, **Bureau of Economic and Business Research**, Research studies, 6.

-------1949: Laws of Retail Gravitation, **Jour. of Marketing**, 14, 3, II, pp. 379-84.

Desai, P.B. et al. (eds.) 1969 : **Regional perspective of industrial and urban growth** - the case of Kanpur, Bombay, Macmillan, p. XVII.

Dickinson, R.E. 1930 : The regional functions and zones of influence of Leeds and Bradford, Geography.

-------1934 : The metropolitan regions of the U.S.A., **Geographical Review**, 24, pp. 278-81.

Dikshit, K.R. and Sawant, S.B. 1968 : Hinterlad as a Region, its types, hierarchy, demarcation, and characteristics, illustrated in the case study of the hinterland of Poona, **The National Geographical Jour. of India**, 14, I, pp. 2, 4.

Dixit, R.S. 1977 : On the Delimitation of the Umland of a Metropolis - Kanpur : a case study, **National Geographer**, 12, I, June, pp. 77-92.

-------1979 : **Market Centres and their Spatial Development in the Umland of Kanpur**, D. Phil. Thesis, Unpublished, Allahabad Univ. Geog. Deptt.

Dodge, S.D. 1932 : Bureau and the Princeton Community, **An-**

nals of the Association of American geographers, 22, pp. 159-209.

Dutta, A.K. 1963 : Umland of Jamshedpur, **Geographical Review** of India, 26, pp. 84-98.

------1966 : Daily Shopping in Howrah, **The National Geographical Jour. of India**, XII, p. 3.

Dwivedi, R.L. 1964 : Delimiting the Umland of Allahabad, **Indian Geographical Jour.**, 39, pp. 123-39.

Efrat, E. 1964 : The Hinterland of the city of Jerusalem and its economic Significance, **Economic Geography**, 40, III, pp. 254-60.

Eilafeson, R.A. 1962 : City and Hinterland Relationship in India', in Roy Turner (ed.) **India's Urban Future**, Bombay, Oxford.

Forrest, G.W. 1977 : **Cities of India**, New Delhi, Metropolitan Book Co., p. 237.

Garnier, J.B. and Chabot, G. 1967 : **Urban Geography**, London, Longmans, p. 426.

Gilbert, E.W. 1951 : Urban Hinterlands, **Geographical Review**, 117, p. 365.

Gopalkrishan, 1964 : Spatial Analysis and Vegetable Supply to a Planned City: Chandigarh, **The National Geographical Jour. of India**, **16**, pp. 1-15.

Gopalkrishan and Agarwal, S.K. 1970 : Umland of, a Planned City: Chandigarh, **The National Geographical Jour. of India**, 16, I, March, pp. 31-36.

Green, F.H.W. 1950 : Urban Hinterlands in England and Wales: an Analysis of Bus Service, **Geographical Jour.**, 116, pp. 64-81.

Green, H.L. 1955 : Hinterland Boundaries of New York City and Boston in Southern New England, **Economic Geography**, 31, pp. 283-300.

Haggett, p. and Charley, R.J. 1969 : **Network Analysis in human geography**, London, Edwin Arnold, pp. 70-72.

Harris, C.D. 1941 : Location of Salt Lake City, **Economic Geography**, pp. 204-12.

Huff, D.L. 1964 : Defining and Estimating a Trading Area, Jour. of Marketing, 28, pp. 34-38 in Ambrose, P. (ed.) **Analytical Human Geography**, London, Longmans, pp. 161-71.

Janaki, V.A. 1962 : Tributary Area of Baroda, **Jour. of M.S. Univ. of Baroda**, 11, 11, Science, pp. 81-99.

Jefferson, M. 1931 : The Distribution of World's city folks - a Study in Comparative Civilization, **Geographical Review**, 21, p. 453.

Kolars, J.F. and Nystuem, J.D. 1974 : **The Study of Locations, Culture, and environment**, New York, McGraw Hill.

Mahadeva, P.D. and Jaishankar, D.C. 1969 : Concept of City

Region: an approach with a case study, **Indian Geographical Jour.**, 49, pp. 15-26.

Mathur, S.P. 1968 : Regional Analysis of Umland of Dehra Dun, **Geographical Knowledge**, 1, pp. 39-48.

Misra, H.N. 1975 : **Urban Centres in the Umland of Allahabad: a Study in Urban Geography**, D. Phill. Thesis, Unpublished, Allahabad Univ. Geography Department.

Mukherjee, A.B. 1962 : The Umland of Modinagar, **The National Geographical Jour. of India**, 8, pp. 250-69.

Nangia, S. 1976: **Delhi Metropolitan Region: a Study in Settlement Georgraphy**, New Delhi, K.B. Publications.

Nath, V. 1962 : The Concept of Umland and its Delimitation, **The Deccan Geographer**, 1, p. 34.

------1966 : **Planning for Urban Growth**, New Delhi, pp. 29-31.

Park, R.E. and New Comb, C. 1933 : **Newspaper Circulation and Metropolitan Regions in Mackenzie's Metropolitan Community**, pp. 98-110.

Planning Commission 1965 : Research Development Regions and Divisions in India, New Delhi, Govt. of India pp. 39-40.

Rajagopalan, C. 1969 : The Nature and Characteristics of urbanization in Kanpur region, in Desai, P.B. et. al., (eds.) **Regional Perspective of Industrial and Urban Growth: The case of Kanpur**, Bombay Macmillian, p. 141.

Rao, V.L.S.P. 1964 : Towns of Mysore State, p. 31.

Reddy, S.N. 1961 : Vegetable Markets and Regional Relationships of HYderabad City, **Geographical Review of India**, 23, pp. 81-99.

Reilly, W.J. 1929 : Methods for the Study of Retail Relationships, Univ. of Texas, **Bureau of Business Research**, Res. Monograph, 4, Univ. of Texas Bulletin pp. 29-94.

-------1931 :The Law of Retail Gravitation, New York.

Saxena, N.P. 1966 : Diurnal Population Mobility within the Service Area of Meerut City. U.P., **The Geographer**, 13, pp. 75-82.

Schultze, J.H. 1951 : Zur Anwendbar Keitder, Theorie der Zentralan Orte, Petter manns, Mitteilungen.

Scott, P. 1964 : The Hierarchy of Central Places in Tasmania, Australian Geographer.

Sharma, K.N., and Norman, R.T. 1966 : Introduction, Research Unit Bulletin No.2 Kanpur, **Indian Institute of Technology**, p. 1.

Singh, H.H. 1972 : **Kanpur - a study in Urban Geography, Varanasi**, Indrasini Devi, pp. 119-32.

Singh, L. 1956 : The Umland of Agra based on Bus Service, **The National Geographical Jour. of India**, 22, pp. 141-53.

Singh, L.R. 1965 : **The Tarai Region of U.P. - a Study in Human Geography**, Allahabad, Ram Narain Lal Beni Prasad, pp. 70-71.

Singh, M. 1964 : Urban Field of Meerut, **The Deccan Geographer**, 2, pp. 85-99.

Singh, R.L. 1955 : **Banaras: a Study in Urban Geography**, Varanasi, Nandkishore, pp. 116-35.

--------1964 : **Bangalore : An Urban Survey**, Varanasi, Tara Publications, pp. 82-94.

--------1972 : The Concept of Umland with reference to Indian Cities : a Trend Report, in ICSSSR's **A Survey of Research in Geography**, Bombay, Popular Prakashan, pp. 226-31.

Singh, U. 1959 : The origin and growth of Kanpur, **The National Geographical Journal of India**, 5,1, March, pp. 1-11.

--------1960 : Cultural zones of Allahabad, **The National Geographical Jour. of India**, 6, pp. 95-104.

-------1961 : Umland of Allahabad, **The National Geographical Jour. of India**, 7, I, pp. 37-51.

--------1966 : Changes in Built-up Area of Kaval Towns, **The National Geographical Jour. of India**, 12, IV, p. 22.

Singh, U. and Verma, R.V. 1971 : Upper Ganga Plain, in Singh, R.L.(ed.) **India - A Regional Geography, Varanasi**, The National Geographical Society of India, pp. 125-82.

Smailes, A.E. 1967 : The Geography of Towns, London, Hutchinson, pp. 129.

Spelt, J. 1958 : Towns and Umlands, Economic Geography, 34, p. 362, in Putnam, G. (ed.) **A Geography of Urban Places**, Toronto, Methuen, pp. 270-76.

Spate, O.H.K. 1954 : **India and Pakistan**, London, Methuen, p. 433.

Stamp, L.D. 1961 : **Applied Geography**, Bungay, Suffolk, Pelican, p. 167.

Thomas, W. 1969 : Planning the Growth of Kanpur Region, in Desai P.B. et al., (eds.) **Regional Perspective of Industrial and Urban Growth - The Case of Kanpur**, Bombay, Macmillan, p. 311.

Tiwari, A.R. 1958 : The Urban Regions of Agra, **The Agra Uni. Jour. of Research**, 6. 101-14.

Town and Country Planning Department : Master Plan of Kanpur, Unpublished, Lucknow, U.P. Govt., pp. 478-504.

-------- : Master Plan of Lucknow, Unpublished, Lucknow, U.P. Govt., pp. 19-28.

Tripathi, V.B. 1966 : **Delimitation of Kanpur Region**, Research Unit Bulletin No. 2, **Kanpur**, Indian Institute of Technology, pp. 14-15.

Ullah, R. 1968 : **The Growth and Distribution of Population** in Relation to Agricultural Resources in the Upper Ganga Yamuna Doab (1901-51), Ph.D. Thesis, Unpublished, Aligarh Muslim Univ. Geog. Deptt.

Vancleef, E. 1941 : Hinterland and Umland, **Geographical Review**, 31, pp. 308-11.

Vasanta, A. 1957 : A method of delimiting areas of urban concentrate, **Indian Geographical Jour.** 32.

Whitelaw, J.S. 1962 : **The measurement of urban influence in Waikato**, Newzealand Geographer.

Whittlesey, D. 1937 : Kano: A Sudanese Metropolis, **Geographical Review**, 27, pp. 177-99.

Young, E.C. 1924 : The Measurement of Farm Population, **Station Bulletin**, 426.

Government Reports -

District Gazetteers, Allahabad, Govt. Press :-

Drake Brockman, D.L. 1909 : Jalaun, Vol. XXV.

-----1909 : Hamirpur, Vol. XXII

-----1909 : Banda, Vol. XXI.

-----1911 : Etawah, Vol. XI.

Neave, E.R. 1911 : Farrukhabad, Vol. IX.

Nevill, H.R. 1903 : Unnao, Vol. XXXVIII.

-----1906 : Fatehpur, Vol. XX.

-----1909 : Kanpur, Vol. XIX.

Census 1961 : District Census Handbook, Uttar Pradesh, of the abovementioned eight districts.

-----1971 : District Census Handbook, Uttar Pradesh, X A and B, of the abovementioned eight districts.

-----1965 : Techno - economic Survey of Uttar Pradesh, New Delhi, National Council of Applied Economic Research.

-----1973 : Agricultural Atlas of Uttar Pradesh, Pantnagar, G.B. Pantnagar University of Technology and Agriculture, Tables - 25.

-----1974 : Agricultural Census of Uttar Pradesh, Lucknow, Board of Revenue, Uttar Pradesh, pp. 47-52.

-----1974-75 to 1978-79 : Fifth Five Year plan, Lucknow. Government of Uttar Pradesh, of the following districts Unnao, Farrukhabad, Etawah, Kanpur, Fatehpur, Jalaun, Hamirpur, and Banda.

-----1977-78 : Fifth five year district plan - annual plan, Lucknow, Government of Uttar Pradesh, of the abovementioned eight districts.

-----1975-1976 : Statistical abstract of Uttar Pradesh, Lucknow, Government of Uttar Pradesh - State Planning Institute, Bulletin No. 126.

----1977 : Sixth Five Year Plan - proposals and list of existing roads and roads under construction, Lucknow, Government of Uttar Pradesh, Public Works Department, of the abovementioned eight districts.

----1977 : Statistical Diary, Lucknow, Government of Uttar Pradesh State Planning Institute.

----1978 : Basic Statistics of Development Blocks, U.P. (1974-75), Lucknow, Government of Uttar Pradesh, State Planning Institute, pp. 19-90.

FOURTEEN

Dashrath S. Pal

Functional Classification of the Service Centres of the Umland of Kanpur Metropolis

INTRODUCTION

Before we begin to discuss with the various functional characteristics of the Service Centres, it would be worthwhile to highlight on their definitive explanation and to differentiate them from the Central Places and Growth Centres. As per general definition the growth centre is an urban core being capable of promoting growth through government intervention.[1] It is a logical extension of a service centre on the continuum of settlements based on functional characteristics.[2] The Central places are the locations which provide functions and services to their tributary areas. They are generally located at the centre of the minimum aggregate travel distance.[3] Service Centre is the focal point for its surrounding area, which is functioning as the service centre.[4]

But in India, in most of the cases there are found some common characteristics, in all these three types of centres (Central places, growth centres and service centres) in terms of the existence of some central functions therein, through which they serve their respective tributary region. Generally, such centres enjoy the entity of their Central Location. In most of the cases, in India due to the unplanned economy the service and growth impulses are running together. Therefore, in the present study the term 'Service Centre' has been used commonly.

The study area

The study area 'the Umland of Kanpur' situated around

the Kanpur Metropolis in Uttar Pradesh State of India (Fig. 14.1). The Umland boundary has been decided through an empirical method.[5] It extends from 25° 15' N to 27° 45' N Latitudes and from 79° 30' E to 81° 15' E Longitudes sprawling over an area of about 39,158.7 Sq. kilometres Physically the region is riverine plain bisected by major rivers the Ganga, the Yamuna and their tributaries. It enjoys the conditions of the tropical climate. Agriculture is the backbone of the economy of the region. Out of the total 10,860 settlements consisting 27 urban centres (1971 census) only 56 settlements have been identified as service centres with the help of the criteria of the presence of some central functions in the settlements.

Methodology

The method to classify the service centres in the present study is based on the Nalson's standard deviation method with some modifications. For the sake of convenience the nine categories of the workers (As per 1971 Census classification) have been arranged in seven groups. These groups are (i) Primary activities, (ii) House hold industries, (iii) Manufacturing, (iv) Construction, (v) Trade and Commerce, (vi) Transport and (vii) Other services.

Further, on the basis of seven groups of working population the functional specialization Index (FSI) for all the 56 service centres has been worked out. The degree of functional specialization has been measured through the mean of the functional specialization index (Table 14.1) and the standard deviation (SD) from the mean for each functional group of the service centres. The various levels of functional specialization are thus based upon the addition of SD value with the mean value of each group of working population. The required data has been taken from the D.C.H. 1971.

FUNCTIONAL CLASSIFICATION AND SPECIALIZATION OF SERVICE CENTRES

The study reveals that most of the service centres, with few exceptions, are multi-functional in nature. In general, it is observed that the large size centres seem to be specialized in more than one function (Table 14.1). The other worth observing point is that the major share is marked to be in the service centres of the small size group of population. This fact, thus, explains that the functional specialization index (FSI) of primary activities decreases with the increase in the size of service centres.

LOCATION OF STUDY AREA

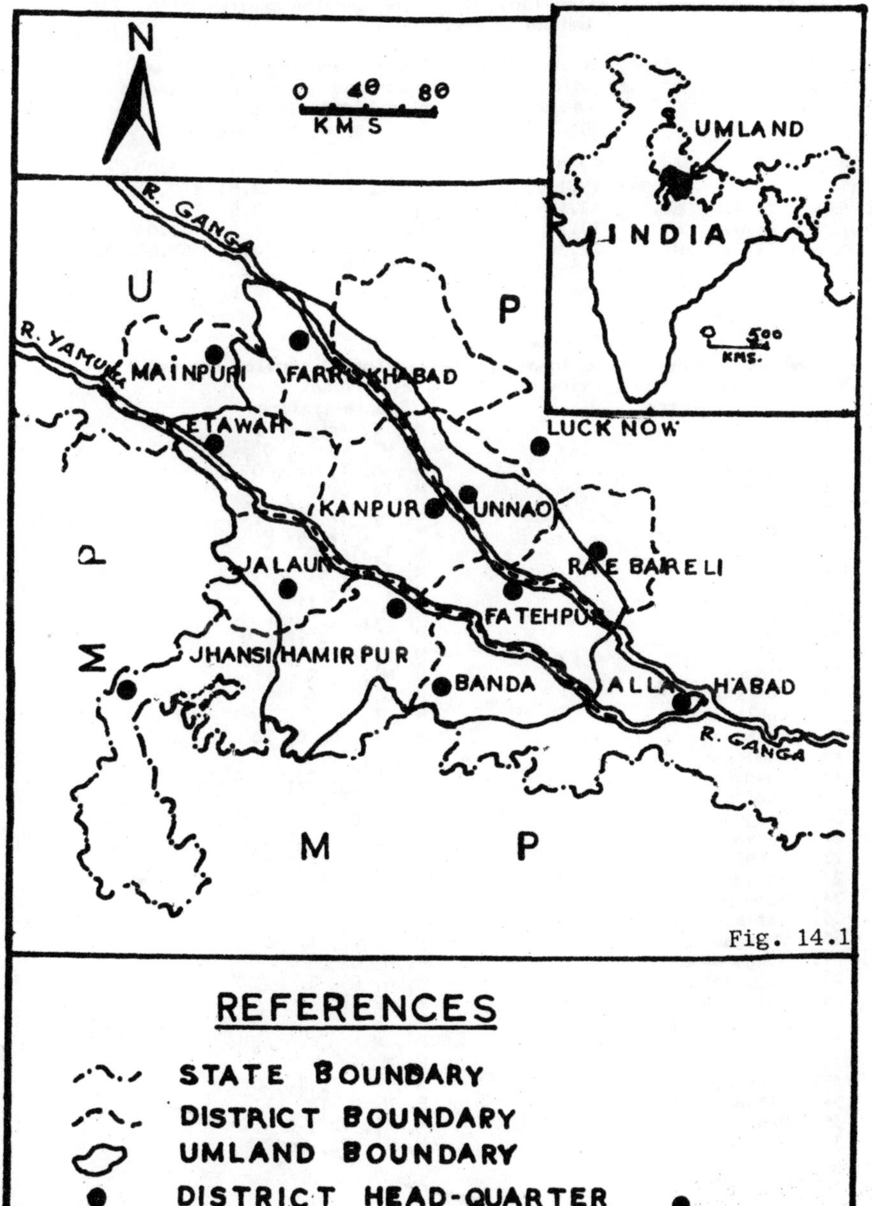

Fig. 14.1

Table 14.1

Funcational specialization Index (FSI) for service centres of umland of Kanpur

Degree of Speciali-zation	Primary Activity	House-hold Indus-try	Manu-factu-ring	Cons-truc-tion	Trade and Comm-erce	Trans port & Commu-nication	Other Service
1.MEAN	40.0	7.0	8.5	2.0	17.5	3.0	22.0
(S.D.)	(22.50)	(5.10)	(7.00)	(1.50)	(7.50)	(2.5)	(10.0)
2.MEAN + 1S.D.	62.5	12.10	15.5	3.5	25.0	5.5	32.0
3.MEAN + 2S.D.	85.0	17.20	22.5	5.0	32.5	8.0	42.0
4.MEAN + 3S.D.	107.5	22.30	29.5	6.5	40.0	10.5	52.0

Table 14.2

The Umland of Kanpur Functional specialization of service centres

S.N.	Name of the service centre	Functional Specialization
1.	Kanpur	M^3, T, Tc^2, O
2.	Farrukhabad	H, M^2, T, Tc, O^1, C
3.	Etawah	H^1, M, T, Tc^1, O^1, C
4.	Fatehpur	M, Tc, O, C
5.	Banda	M, C, T^2, Tc^2, O^2
6.	Oral	M, C^2, T^2, Tc, O^1
7.	Unnao	M, T, Tc, O^2, C
8.	Kannauj	M, T, O, H, C
9.	Auralya	M, T^1, Tc^1, O
10.	Rath	H, M, Tc, O^1
11.	Kalpi	M^1, C^1, T, Tc^2, O^1
12.	Jalaun	M, C, T, Tc^1, O
13.	Bindki	H, M^1, T, O
14.	Charkhari	P, C, O
15.	Chhibramau	M^1, T, O
16.	Kalmganj	M^1, T^1, O, C, Tc
17.	Hamirpur	C^1, T, Tc, O^2
18.	Maudaha	H, T, Tc, O, C
19.	Bharthana	M^1, C, T^2, O^1
20.	Bilgram	P, M, C
21.	Purva	P, T, H, C, Tc
22.	Sandi	M, C, T, Tc^2, H
23.	Jaswant Nagar	H^3, T^1, Tc, O
24.	Sumerpur	P, H, C
25.	Safipur	P, C^2
26.	Bhongaon	H. M, C^2, T, Tc
27.	Bangaramau	P, H, C
28.	Kulpahar	P, H, C
29.	Ghatampur	M^1, C, Tc
30.	Mohammadabad	P^1, H
31.	Baberu	P^1, M
32.	Akbarpur	P, H, Tc
33.	Gursahganj	H^2, M^2, T, TC, C
34.	Bilhaur	P, H, C, Tc
35.	Bewar	M, T^1, Tc^1, O
36.	Pukhrayan	H, T^1, Tc, O, C

lated with their population size. It is found that the centres registering above 15,000 population are specialized in case of manufacturing activities.

Construction specialized centres

There are 27 centres having specialization in construction activities. Out of these centres Bhongaon records a high level of population engaged in construction (with M + 2 SD) while Orai, Kalpi and Hamirpur experience a moderately high share (M + 1 SD). Overall assessment explains about the fact that this function of construction is more common (Fig. 14.3C) in the centres located in Trans-Yamuna region.

Trade and commerce centres

There are 30 centres (Table 14.3) having specialization in this function. The centres observed various levels of specialization as Bharthana (M + 2 SD) in the first level, about 11 centres in the second level (M + 1 SD) and remaining 18 centres in the lowest category of specialization. Such centres are distributed (Fig. 14.3G) more in number in the doab region of the umland, specially in the Etawah and Farrukhabad districts.

Transport and Communication Centres

There are 28 centres accounting for 50 per cent of the total service centres having specialization in the activities of transport and communication. The four centres namely Kalpi, Banda, Kanpur and Sandi register the highest degree of specialization (M + 2 SD). Out of the remaining centres 5 are specialized upto medium level (M + 1 SD) and the rest experience the lowest degree of specialization (Table 14.2). Such centres are distributed (Fig. 14.4F) in all the parts of the umland more or less with a uniform pattern.

Centres specialized in other services

There are only 27 service centres that may be stated to have the activities of miscellaneous services. The analysis of the levels of specialization reveals that there are only two centres of Hamirpur and Unnao characterized with a highest level (M + 2 SD) of specialization, 7 centres with medium level (M + 1 SD) and the remaining 18 centres fall under the score of lowest degree of specialization (Fig. 14.4H).

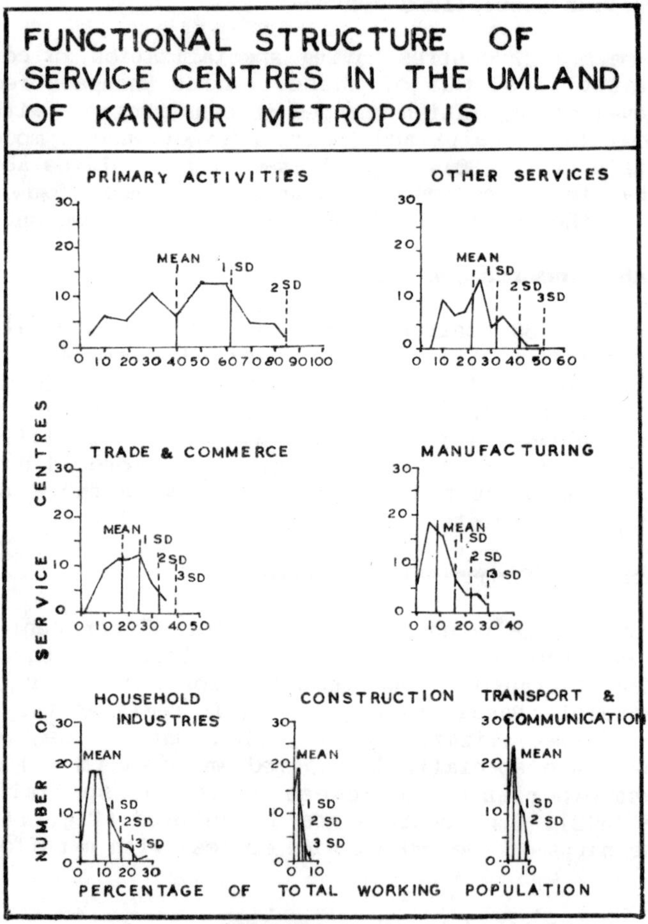
FUNCTIONAL STRUCTURE OF SERVICE CENTRES IN THE UMLAND OF KANPUR METROPOLIS
PRIMARY ACTIVITIES
OTHER SERVICES
TRADE & COMMERCE
MANUFACTURING
HOUSEHOLD INDUSTRIES
CONSTRUCTION
TRANSPORT & COMMUNICATION
MEAN
1 SD
2 SD
3 SD
NUMBER OF SERVICE CENTRES
PERCENTAGE OF TOTAL WORKING POPULATION

Fig. 14.2

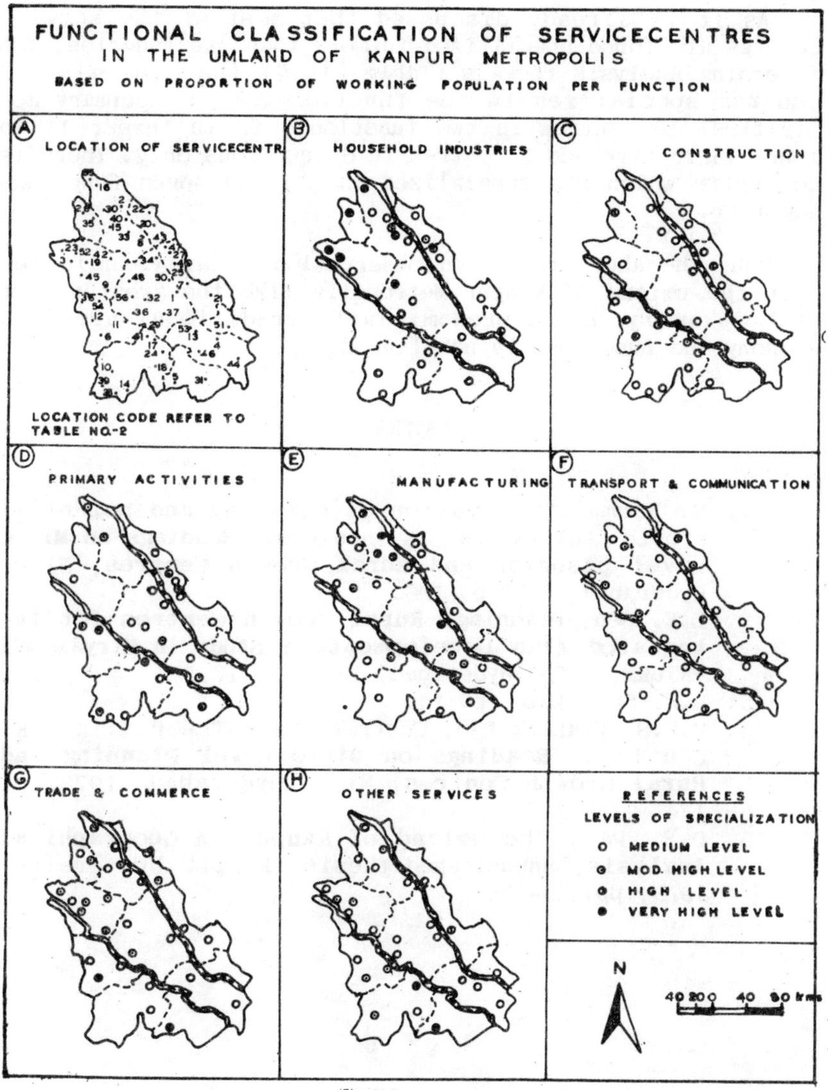
FUNCTIONAL CLASSIFICATION OF SERVICECENTRES
IN THE UMLAND OF KANPUR METROPOLIS
BASED ON PROPORTION OF WORKING POPULATION PER FUNCTION
A LOCATION OF SERVICECENTR
LOCATION CODE REFER TO TABLE NO-2
B HOUSEHOLD INDUSTRIES
C CONSTRUCTION
D PRIMARY ACTIVITIES
E MANUFACTURING
F TRANSPORT & COMMUNICATION
G TRADE & COMMERCE
H OTHER SERVICES
REFERENCES
LEVELS OF SPECIALIZATION
MEDIUM LEVEL
MOD. HIGH LEVEL
HIGH LEVEL
VERY HIGH LEVEL
N
40 20 0 40 80 kms

Fig. 14.3

FUNCTIONAL COMPOSITION OF SERVICE CENTRES

As it is already discussed that most of the service centres are found specialized in more than one function. The foregoing analysis reveals (Table -14.2) that there are 7 centres specialized in one function i.e., in primary activities. 10 centres in two functions, 13 in three, 11 in four, 13 in five and 2 centres in 6 functions only. There is no centre which has specialized in all the seven functions together.

Thus the above mentioned observation clearly indicates that the umland of Kanpur Metropolis like the greater part of the country, has a predominantly traditional agrarian economy and functionally unbalanced.

NOTES

1. S. Wanmali, 'Location of existing and potential growth centres, in L.K. Sen (ed.) **Readings on Micro Level planning and Rural Growth Centres,** NICD, Hyderabad, 1972 p. 196.
2. **L.K. Sen, Planning, Rural Growth Centres for Integrated Area Development. A Study in Miryalguda Taluka,** NICD, Hyderabad, 1971, p. 17.
3. L.K. Sen, Ibid, p. 14.
4. V.L.S. Prakara Rao, Central Place Theory 'in L.K. Sen (ed.) **Readings on Micro Level Planning and Rural Growth Centres**, NICD, Hyderabad, 1972, p. 174.
5. D.S. Pal, **The umland of Kanpur: A Geographical Analysis,** unpublished thesis, Kanpur University, 1979, pp. 33-53.

FIFTEEN

M.L. Soni

Functional Classification of Service Centres in the Umland of Lucknow

INTRODUCTION

The analysis of the functions of service-centres is undoubtedly very important aspect of regional central place studies. Their relative importance is invariably reflected in the quality of functions performed by them. In this endeavour the geographers and other students of central place studies have classified the service-centres according to their dominant functions. Such works have their usefulness as a reference tool. With the help of the results of such type of studies we can plan and propose developmental works for the betterment of the region keeping in view the desired goals. Service-centres are the economic, social and cultural foci of the countryside. Service-centres[1] have a special role to play in the present national context. The Government has laid special emphasis for the development of these centres.

The author being closely associated with the Umland of Lucknow[2] has obviously selected this region for the study. It constitutes the heart of Uttar Pradesh comprising the districts of Lucknow, Barabanki and Sitapur and parts of Kheri, Bahraich, Gonda, Faizabad, Sultanpur, Rae Bareli, Unnao and Hardoi districts. It extends over an area of 38,198 square kilometres. The total population of the region in 1971 was about 12.88 million, i.e., about 14% of the total population of Uttar Pradesh. According to the 1971 census, only 28 settlements of the region come under the category of urban centres. But the field study and several other empirical works reveal that many settlements irrespective of the census-definition of their urban character, perform important services to their countryside. Keeping the fact in view, eightysix service-centres[3] have been selected.

Further, all these service-centres have been grouped into sixtyseven service-centres and service-centre-groups.[4]

As a matter of fact all these service-centres vary from a hamlet to the biggest urban agglomeration. Of these nine are district headquarters and sixteen are tahsil headquarters. Some are market centres of varying size and many others are production centres. The average decennial growth of population (1961-1971) in these centres was about 27 per cent.

In order to study the functional structure of the selected service-centres and service-centre-groups, the data for the non- agricultural working population for 1971 census were compiled for the different occupational groups and using Nelson's method[5] the averages and the Standard Deviations were calculated for certain[6] functional groups (Table 15.2). The individual service-centres were then put to test using this table. The functional significance derived, therefrom, were compiled in another table. It clearly hows the functional importance of different centres in 197

The application of Nelson's method and the resultant functional categories show that out of the 67 service-centre-groups, 16 are mono-functional, 23 are bi-functional, 23 are tri-functional and 5 are multi-functional.

Mono-functional centres

Mono-functional character of these centres does not exhibit that they lack in other functions. But none of the other functions exceed the regional average. All these centres are either industrial or other service centres. Eight centres are household industrial centres among which Rampur Bhawanipur Group (Barabanki) tops the list for which small scale handloom industries deserve the credit. Khamaria Pandit (Kheri) is on the top of the list of other than household industrial centres as Aira Sugar Mill is situated here. Dabha Semar (Faizabad) comes highest in other services group as it is the headquarters of Masodha Vikaskhand. Most of the mono-functional centres are small-size settlements except Laharpur (20,205), Rudauli (18,933) and Zaidpur (13,554). A lower number of people employed in a single activity out of small total population very well create a higher percentage and consequently higher in SD computation.

TABLE 15.1

Population of service-centres/groups in 1971 in the umland of Lucknow

Sl. No.	Service-Centre/ Group	Population
1	Hardoi Group	51,432
	Hardoi	46,639
	Nanakganj Grant	2,402
	Anang Behta	1,132
	Dhir Mohalla	1,259
2	Sandila	22,365
3	Pachhiyaon	4,034
4	Maurawan	8,269
5	Purwa	11,912
6	Nihalgarh	3,026
7	Musafirkhana	3,433
8	Maholi	3,748
9	Machhrehta	2,891
10	Nimsar-Misrikh	6,832
11	Sarai Pitthu Group	5,306
	Sarai Pitthu	2,156
	Jahangirabad	1,625
	Husainganj	1,525
12	Sitapur Group	67,990
	Sitapur	66,715
	Deeppur	1,275
13	Laharpur	20,205
14	Khairabad	17,335
15	Biswan	19,336
16	Sidhauli	4,601
17	Paintepur	5,711
18	Mahmudabad	11,651
19	Malihabad	9,438
20	Chinhat	2,794
21	Lucknow Group	8,32,527
	Lucknow Urban Agglomeration	8,13,982
	Qila Muhammadnagar	2,533
	Bahera	2,761
	Sarsawan	3,342
	Ibrahimpur	2,270
	Kharika	5,021
	Bhadruk	2,618
22	Goshaiganj	4,950
23	Amethi	6,568
24	Sisendi	3,195
25	Salehnagar	1,559
26	Tilokpur	3,349
27	Saadatganj	4,116
28	Fatehpur	12,601
29	Dewa	5,198
30	Barabanki Group	47,415
	Barabanki Urban Agglomeration	43,172
	Shahabpur	4,243
31	Jahangirabad	4,194
32	Masauli	6,293
33	Zaidpur	13,554
34	Rudauli	18,933
35	Rampur Bhawanipur Group	6,907
	Rampur Bhawanipur	5,740
	Chaukhandi	1,167
36	Haidargarh	3,812
37	Ganeshpur	1,461
38	Bachhrawan	5,482
39	Mahrajganj	2,880
40	Rae Bareli	38,765
41	Jais	12,638
42	Sheogarh	1,015
43	Khamaria Pandi	2,074
44	Oel	6,155
45	Lakhimpur	43,752
46	Kheri	12,006
47	Maigalganj	2,257
48	Gola Gokarannath	21,677
49	Palia Kalan	9,771
50	Balrampur	36,191
51	Utraula	12,637
52	Khargupur Imilia	4,252
53	Dhaneypur	4,826
54	Gonda Group	53,927
	Gonda	52,662
	Dalpur Hazari	1,265
55	Colonelganj	11,743
56	Nawabganj	7,284
57	Mihinpurwa	4,443
58	Maina Bargaon	2,418
59	Kewalpur	3,843
60	Nanpara	18,732
61	Bamhaura Group	3,361
	Bamhaura	2,105
	Alinagar	1,256
62	Bahraich Group	75,350
	Bahraich	73,871
	Chhaoni Sarkar	1,479
63	Chakia	1,661
64	Kaisarganj	1,036
65	Gilaula	1,364
66	Dabha Semar	1,047
67	Faizabad Group	1,12,170
	Faizabad Urban Agglomeration	1,09,806
	Khojanpur	1,311
	Paharganj	1,053

TABLE 15.2

Average and standard deviations for the non-agricultural functional groups of service-centres in the umland of Lucknow - (1971)

	Household Industry	Other than Household Industry	Trade & Commerce	Transport & Communication	Others
Average	17.9	11.7	25.1	5.1	30.9
Standard Deviation	18.5	10.0	12.2	3.9	18.7
1 SD	36.4	21.7	37.3	9.0	49.6
2 SD	54.9	31.7	62.4	12.9	68.3
3 SD	73.4	41.7	74.6	16.8	87.0

Bi-functional centres

Out of the 23 bi-functional centres only five are tahsil headquarters. Maximum number of these centres range between 2,000 to 5,000 population except Sandils (22,365). Most of them are production-cum-commercial centres. Six centres (Sandila, Pachhiyaon, Khairabad, Biswan, Salehnagar and Nawabganj) have other than household activity as first-ranking function, three centres (Nihalgarh, Machhrehta and Amethi) have household industrial activity as first-ranking-function. As regards the spatial distribution of these production centres, only Nawabganj (Gonda) and Nihalgarh (Sultanpur) are located in the eastern half of the region. Ten centres have trade and commerce as first-ranking function including important regional market centres like Goshaiganj (Lucknow), Mahrajganj (Rae Bareli), Maigalganj (Kheri) and Colonelganj (Gonda). Kaisarganj (Bahraich) is the only bi-functional centre which has other services as first-ranking function.

Tri-functional centres

Twentythree centres including five district headquarters, seven tahsil headquarters and five vikaskhand headquarters are tri-functional. About two-third service-centres (15) are in 2,000-20,000 population group. Both the cities of the region (Lucknow & Faizabad-cum-Ayodhya) are in this category. Other services rank first in eight centres (Maholi, Barabanki, Bachhrawan, Rae Bareli, Oel, Balrampur, Utraula and Kewalpur) and stand second in six centres (Musafirkhana, Malihabad, Lucknow, Palia Kalan, Gonda and Faizabad). Most of them are performing some or other type of administrative functions. Six centres have trade and com-

TABLE 15.3

Functional classification of the service-centres in the umland of Lucknow

ABBREVIATIONS USED

Household Industries	Hh
Other than Household Industries	M
Trade & Commerce	C
Transport & Communication	T
Other Services	P

The figures 1, 2 and 3 alongwith the abbreviations show plus one, plus two or plus three S.D. (Standard Deviation) above the average. The plain abbreviations indicate that the service-centre is an average one with respect to the particular function.

Sl. No.	Name of the Centre	Functional Classification
Hardoi District		
1	Hardoi Group	T^1 P C M
2	Sandila	M T
Unnao District		
3	Pachhiyaon	M C
4	Maurawan	P^1
5	Purwa	C M T
Sultanpur District		
6	Nihalgarh	Hh^1 C
7	Musafirkhana	C^1 P Hh
Sitapur District		
8	Maholi	P Hh M
9	Macchrehta	Hh^1 C
10	Nimsar-Misrikh	P^1
11	Sarai Pitthu Group	M^1 Hh T
12	Sitapur Group	T^1 P C M
13	Laharpur	Hh
14	Khirabad	M T
15	Biswan	M T
16	Sidhauli	C^1 T^1 Hh
17	Paintepur	Hh
18	Mahmudabad	C M T
Lucknow District		
19	Malihabad	T^2 P C
20	Chinhat	C Hh T
21	Lucknow Group	T^2 P M
22	Goshaiganj	C^2 Hh
23	Amethi	Hh C
24	Sisendi	P^2
25	Salehnagar	M^1 T^1
26	Tilokpur	Hh^1

27	Saadatganj	Hh^3
28	Fatehpur	Hh^1
29	Dewa	T^1 Hh
30	Barabanki Group	P^1 M T
31	Jahangirabad	T^2 P^1
32	Masauli	Hh^1
33	Zaidpur	Hh^1
34	Rudauli	M
35	Rampur Bhawanipur Group	Hh^3
36	Haidargarh	C^1 Hh
37	Ganeshpur	C^1 M

Rae Bareli District

38	Bachhrawan	P C T
39	Mahrajganj	C^1 T
40	Rae Bareli	P M T
41	Jais	C M
42	Sheogarh	T^1 P C Hh

Kheri District

43	Khamaria Pandit	M^3
44	Oel	P Hh M
45	Lakhimpur	T^1 P C M
46	Kheri	T^1 M
47	Maigalganj	C^1 M
48	Gola Gokarannath	M^2 C T
49	Palia Kalan	C^1 P T

Gonda District

50	Balrampur	P M T
51	Utraula	P C M
52	Khargupur Imilia	Hh^1 C T
53	Dhaneypur	M^1 C Hh
54	Gonda Group	T^3 P M
55	Colonelganj	C M
56	Nawabganj	M^1 C

Bahraich District

57	Mihinpurwa	C^1 Hh
58	Maina Bargaon	C^1 M
59	Kewalpur	P C T
60	Nanpara	
61	Bamhaura Group	p^{2-}
62	Bahraich Group	P C M T
63	Chakia	P^3
64	Kaisarganj	P^1 M
65	Gilaula	C^1 P

Faizabad District

66	Dabha Semar	P^3
67	Faizabad Group	T^1 P M

merce as first-ranking function. The centres of trade and commerce being widespread exhibit that commercial function is fairly distributed all over the region. Household industrial function ranks first only in Khargupur Imilia (Gonda) which is situated in the tarai region and possesses small scale industries based on forest-products.

Multi-functional centres

Hardoi Group, Sitapur Group, Sheogarh, Lakhimpur and Bahraich group perform more than three functions which have a percentage of employed population more than regional averages. Except Sheogarh, a small service-centre (Population - 1,015), all are district headquarters of a population more than 40,000 each. Remarkably all these four district headquarters have similar functional structure.

To summarize the spatial distribution of service-centres in the Umland of Lucknow, it can be said that most of the multi-functional centres are located in the northern half of the region (Hardoi, Sitapur, Lakhimpur and Baharaich). Only one multifunctional centre, Sheorgarh (Rae Bareli) is in the southern half of the region. Sheogarh having a little over one thousand population possesses a multi-functional character due to fruitful above average (regional) percentage. There is no positive correlation between quantity and quality. Some of the most significant activities which give a city its specific importance are sometimes carried out by a very small number of people.[7]

About a two-third of tri-functional centres are located in the western half of the region. A concentration of mono-functional centres is noticed in Barabanki district and a tri-channel pattern of service-centres with a foci in Barabanki district is being observed.

Northern half of the Umland of Lucknow has experienced a lesser degree of urbanization hence district headquarters have to perform more and more functions. A sparse network of service-centres encouraged the diversified nature in the centres. Gonda district has five tri-functional, two bi-functional and no mono-functional centres. Kheri district has only one mono-functional centre (Khamaria Pandit) out of seven service-centres.

NOTES

1. Eightysix service-centres with 1,000 or above

population and dominantly non-agricultural, have been selected and grouped into 67 service-centres and service-centre-groups.

2. Several geographers have delimited the Umland of Lucknow in their urban studies. The author, too, has delimited the sphere of influence of the city by a recent study of the service areas of different functions by the town.
3. The author has selected eightysix settlements as service-centres, which fullfil the following modified conditions:-(a) The population of the settlement should be above 1,000. (b) The population of the settlement should be dominantly non-agricultural, i.e., it should employ less than 50% of its working population in agricultural activities. (c) The settlement should have at least a weekly market. (d) The settlement should have some public utility services like Vikaskhand or Police Station or a Post Office or a Public Health Centre.
4. During field-survey it was observed that some settlements are not performing non-agricultural functions within their administrative boundaries yet their population is dominantly non-agricultural. Actually these are commuting centres to their nearby bigger service-centres and consequently joined with the bigger centres and termed as service-centre-groups.
5. Nelson, H.J., A Service Classification of American Cities, Economic Geography, xxxi, 1955, pp. 189-210.
6. The region has no mining activities of any importance as its general economy is agrarian and construction activities are also very negligible, hence omitted.
7. Bergel, E.E., Urban Sociology, New York, 1955, p.148.

Index